PHILOSOPHY   Made Simple

Richard H. Popkin, PhD, and
Avrum Stroll, PhD

Advisory editor
A. V. Kelly, MA(Oxon)

Made Simple Books
HEINEMANN : London

© 1981 William Heinemann Ltd.

Made and printed in Great Britain
by Butler & Tanner Ltd., Frome and London,
for the publishers William Heinemann Ltd.,
10 Upper Grosvenor Street,
London W1X 9PA

First edition April 1969
Reprinted June 1972
Reprinted July 1973
Reprinted February 1975
Reprinted February 1977
Reprinted January 1979
Reprinted January 1981

SBN 434 98452 3

PHILOSOPHY   Made Simple

The Made Simple series
has been created
especially for self-education
but can equally well
be used as
an aid to group study.
However complex the subject,
the reader is taken
step by step,
clearly and methodically
through the course. Each volume
has been prepared by
experts,
taking account of
modern educational requirements,
to ensure the most
effective way of
acquiring knowledge.

In the same series

Accounting
Acting and Stagecraft
Additional Mathematics
Administration in Business
Advertising
Anthropology
Applied Economics
Applied Mathematics
Applied Mechanics
Art Appreciation
Art of Speaking
Art of Writing
Biology
Book-keeping
British Constitution
Business and Administrative Organisation
Business Economics
Business Statistics and Accounting
Calculus
Chemistry
Childcare
Commerce
Company Administration
Company Law
Computer Programming
Computers and Microprocessors
Cookery
Cost and Management Accounting
Data Processing
Dressmaking
Economic History
Economic and Social Geography
Economics
Effective Communication
Electricity
Electronic Computers
Electronics
English
English Literature

Export
Financial Management
French
Geology
German
Housing, Tenancy and Planning Law
Human Anatomy
Italian
Journalism
Latin
Law
Management
Marketing
Mathematics
Modern Biology
Modern Electronics
Modern European History
New Mathematics
Office Practice
Organic Chemistry
Philosophy
Photography
Physical Geography
Physics
Psychiatry
Psychology
Rapid Reading
Retailing
Russian
Salesmanship
Secretarial Practice
Social Services
Soft Furnishing
Spanish
Statistics
Transport and Distribution
Twentieth-Century British History
Typing
Woodwork

Foreword

'Let no one when young delay to study philosophy, nor when he is old grow weary of his study. For no one can come too early or too late to secure the health of his soul.' These words were written by the Greek philosopher, Epicurus, over two thousand years ago at a time of great social and political upheaval. Although we might express the sentiment differently, it remains substantially true for us today when social change is equally rapid. It is important at all times for men to examine their presuppositions, to question their beliefs—in short, to think for themselves. It is particularly important to think for oneself at times of rapid change, for then tradition, custom and habit will not suffice when dealing with new problems and new situations. At such times, if men do not think for themselves, someone else must think for them.

When a man thinks for himself, he has become a philosopher, but such a man has much to gain from a formal study of philosophy. It can provide him with techniques that will help him achieve coherence and rigour in his thinking; it can bring him knowledge of the thoughts of great philosophers of the past, so that he can measure his own views against them; and it can make him aware of those questions which cannot be answered by rational methods. Without this kind of basis, his own thinking will not take him very far.

The problem for most people, however, is how to get started. Plato said, 'the first stage of every task is the most important', and while this is true of any study, it is especially true of philosophy. Unless one can quickly come to recognize the significance of the questions philosophers have wrestled with and the answers they have offered, one can easily miss the whole point and see philosophy as no more than a pleasant academic pastime. For this reason—in order to get beginners off to a good start—we have tried in this book to show the relevance of philosophy to human development.

Philosophy is possibly the most difficult of studies to 'make simple', and, as the need for simplicity has been our priority throughout, we have had to cut many corners. We have been selective in the problems chosen for discussion and we have had to create artificial barriers by dividing philosophy into 'branches'. This has, unavoidably, led to some repetition of problems and theories as we have looked at them from different points of view. However, we hope the experienced philosopher will forgive our use of these devices if we have achieved the purpose of providing a foundation course on which the reader can build, either by following the suggested reading offered, or by guided studies under a tutor.

Philosophy Made Simple is for both the interested layman and the student coming to a formal study of the subject for the first time.

Primarily, we have had in mind students entering university to read philosophy, particularly those whose philosophy is ancillary to their main course of studies—students of Education, for example, and of Sociology. We also feel that, with guidance from teachers, this book will play a useful part in the increasing number of Sixth Form courses in philosophy, and in all liberal studies courses that venture into this field.

A. V. KELLY

Table of Contents

WHAT IS PHILOSOPHY?

Philosophy is generally regarded as perhaps the most abstruse and abstract of all subjects, far removed from the affairs of ordinary life. But although many people think of it as being remote from normal interests and beyond comprehension, nearly all of us have some philosophical views, whether we are aware of them or not. It is curious that although most people are vague about what philosophy is, the term appears frequently in their conversation.

Popular Usages. The word 'philosophy' is derived from the Greek term meaning 'love of wisdom'; but in current popular usage many different ideas are involved in the ways we employ the term. Sometimes we mean by 'philosophy' an attitude towards certain activites, as when one says 'I disapprove of your philosophy of doing business' or I am voting for him because I favour his philosophy of government.' Again, we talk about being 'philosophical' when we mean taking a long-range, detached view of certain immediate problems. When one is disappointed, we suggest to him that he ought to be more 'philo-sophical', as when one misses a train. Here we mean to say that he should not be over-concerned with the events of the moment, but should try instead to place these in perspective. In still another sense we think of philosophy as an evaluation or interpretation of what is important or meaningful in life. This usage may be indicated by the story of two men who were drinking beer together. One of them held his glass to the light, scrutinized it thoughtfully, and then observed, 'Life is like a glass of beer.'

His companion looked up at the glass, turned to his friend, and asked, 'Why is life like a glass of beer?'

'How should I know,' he answered, 'I'm not a philosopher.'

Popular Conceptions. By and large, in spite of the many different ways we may use the words 'philosophy' and 'philosophical' in ordinary speech, we tend to think of philosophy as some extremely complex intellectual activity. We often imagine the philosopher (as in Rodin's statue of the Thinker) as one who sits, pondering questions of the ultimate significance of human life while the rest of us have only the time or the energy to live it. Occasionally, when our newspapers or magazines publish a story about the important philosophers of our time, such as Bertrand Russell or Albert Schweitzer, the impression is given that they have devoted themselves to contemplation of the problems of the world in a most abstract manner and have arrived at views or theories that may sound splendid, but can hardly be of much practical value.

While this picture has been created of the philosopher and what he is trying to do, there is also another image. This is that the philosopher is one who is ultimately responsible for the general outlook and the ideals of certain societies and cultures. Thinkers such as Karl Marx and Friedrich Engels, we are told, are the ones who have created the point of view of the Communist party; while others, such as Thomas Jefferson, John Locke and John Stuart Mill have developed the theories which prevail in democratic societies.

The Philosophical Enterprise. Regardless of these various conceptions of the role of the philosopher, and regardless of how remote we may think his activities are from our immediate concerns, the philosopher has been engaged in considering problems that are of importance to all of us, either directly or indirectly. Through careful critical examination, he has tried to evaluate the information and beliefs we have about the universe at large, and the world of human affairs. From this investigation, the philosopher has attempted to work out some general, systematic, coherent and consistent picture of all that we know and think.

This sort of understanding has provided an outlook or framework in which the ordinary person can place his own—possibly more limited—conception of the world and human affairs. It has provided as well a focus through which we can see our own roles and activities, and determine if they have any significance. Through such an examination and evaluation, we may all be better able to assess our ideals and aspirations, as well as understand better why we accept these, and possibly whether we ought to.

From the very beginnings of philosophy in ancient Greece, over two and a half millennia ago, it has been the conviction of the serious thinkers who have engaged in this pursuit, that it is necessary to scrutinize the views that we accept about our world and ourselves to see if they are rationally defensible. We have all acquired much information and many opinions about the natural and human universe. But few of us have ever considered whether these are reliable or important. We are usually willing to accept without question reported scientific discoveries, certain traditional beliefs, and various views based upon our personal experiences. The philosopher, however, insists upon subjecting all this to intensive critical examination in order to discover if these views and beliefs are based upon adequate evidence, and if a reasonable person may be justified in adhering to them.

The Socratic Contention. Socrates, at his trial in 399 B.C., maintained that the reason he philosophized was that 'the unexamined life was not worth living'. He found that nearly all of his contemporaries spent their lives pursuing various goals, such as fame, riches, pleasure, without ever asking themselves whether these are important. Unless they raised such a question, and seriously sought the answer, they would never be able to know if they were doing the right thing. Their entire lives might be wasted pursuing useless or even dangerous goals.

All of us have some general outlook about the kind of world we think we live in, the sort of things that are worthwhile in such a world, and so on. Most of us, like Socrates' contemporaries, have never bothered to examine our views to discover their foundations, whether we have adequate or acceptable reasons for believing what we do, or whether the totality of our views has any general consistency or coherence. Hence, most of us, in one sense, have some kind of a 'philosophy', but we have not done any philosophizing to see if it is justified.

The philosopher, following Socrates' contention, insists upon bringing to light what our implicit beliefs are, what assumptions we make about our world, ourselves, our values. He insists that these can only be accepted by reasonable and intelligent men if they can meet certain tests set up by the logical mind. Rather than merely possessing an unorganized mass of opinions, the philosopher feels that these must be inspected, scrutinized and organized into a meaningful and coherent system of views.

What Does a Philosopher Do? One may be tempted to observe at this point that these initial comments give some slight idea, perhaps, of what philosophy deals with, but that they are too vague to make clear what it is all about. Why can't one just give a straightforward definition of the subject, and then proceed, so that one can see clearly at the outset what a philosopher is trying to do?

The difficulty is that philosophy can be better explained by doing it than by trying to describe it. It is in part a way of dealing with questions, as well as an attempt to resolve certain problems which have been the traditional interest of the persons who have called themselves, or have been called, 'philosophers'. As we shall see throughout this book, one of the subjects that philosophers have never been able to agree upon is what philosophy consists in.

Varieties of Philosophy. The people who have engaged seriously in philosophizing have had varying aims. Some have been religious leaders, like Saint Augustine, and have tried to explain and justify certain religious points of view. Some have been scientists, like René Descartes, who have attempted to interpret the meaning and importance of various scientific discoveries and theories. Others, like John Locke and Karl Marx, have philosophized in order to effect certain changes in the political organization of society. Many have been interested in justifying or promulgating some set of ideas which they thought might aid mankind. Others have had no such grandiose purpose, but merely wished to understand certain features of the world in which they lived, and certain beliefs that people held.

Who Are Philosophers? The occupations of philosophers have been as varied as their aims. Some have been teachers, often university professors giving courses in philosophy, as in the instance of St. Thomas Aquinas in the Middle Ages, teaching at the University of Paris, or John Dewey in the twentieth century, lecturing at Columbia University. Others have been leaders of religious movements, often taking an active part in the affairs of their organizations, like St. Augustine, who was Bishop of Hippo at the decline of the Roman Empire, or George Berkeley, who was the Bishop of Cloyne in Ireland in the eighteenth century. Many philosophers have had ordinary occupations, like Baruch Spinoza, who was a lens-grinder by profession. John Locke was a medical doctor; John Stuart Mill was a writer for magazines, and briefly a Member of Parliament. A good many of the most prominent philosophers have been scientists or mathematicians. Some have had careers which kept them far removed from the excitement and crises of everyday life; others were continually occupied in the most active pursuits.

Regardless of their aims, or their occupations, philosophers have, by and large, shared a common conviction that thoughtful examination and analysis of our views, and our evidence for them, is important and worthwhile. A philosopher thinks about certain matters in certain ways. He wants to find out what various basic ideas or concepts that we have mean, what we base our knowledge on, what standards should be employed in arriving at sound judgments, what beliefs we ought to adhere to, and the like. By reflecting upon such questions, he feels that he can achieve more significant comprehension of the universe, natural and human.

Recently one of the authors of this book began his lectures in a course entitled 'Introduction to Philosophy'. He tried to give the class some idea of what sort of material they would be considering throughout the course by raising a question that Plato had asked twenty-three hundred years ago: 'What is justice?' To suggest what this question might mean, he raised related problems, among them: 'How do we distinguish just acts from unjust ones?' 'How do we tell what we ought to do, or what is right?' 'Is justice based only on legal conventions, or are there other, more basic standards?' After the lecture, a student remarked to the professor that many questions had now been asked and he wondered if the answers would be forthcoming in the near future. The teacher told him that they would consider some *possible* answers in the course, but he could not guarantee that they would be the *right* answers. The student answered, 'That's all right, so long as we get answers—just so that we don't have to think.'

The philosopher does not want *any* answers, and is unwilling to accept them merely because they purport to be answers. The student might be willing enough to live 'the unexamined life', but the philosopher wants to find the right answers, those that a rational man can feel are warranted after most thoughtful consideration. The fact that some answers have been offered, or even that some have been accepted by almost everybody in a given society, does not suffice for the philosopher. Even that one might feel that certain answers are the right ones is not an adequate basis for relying upon them. Rather, the philosopher insists, one must know, be completely certain, that these answers are the true ones, before a rational man can adopt them as his own. Otherwise, the best that we may be able to accomplish by philosophical examination is only to realize the inadequacy of all answers that have been thus far presented.

The student, like so many people in all ages, was willing to sell his 'birthright' rather than undertake the effort required to philosophize. He was abdicating his proper function as a rational human being in order not to have to be bothered with the problem of finding some justification for what he believed, with discovering some consistent and coherent system for his views. But the philosopher claims that fundamentally the questions which he considers are too important to be answered in any quick and lazy fashion. It would be far better to have no answers than unexamined answers or, worse, answers that might be wrong.

Two Examples. In order to make clearer what the philosopher is seeking and what he does, let us consider briefly two examples from the earliest history of philosophy, which indicate the sort of situations that have given rise to intellectual consideration of various fundamental beliefs. The first instance is that of the first Greek philosophers, who lived in the sixth century B.C., in one of the Greek colonies in Asia Minor, the part which is now Turkey.

The Greek Philosophers. From the little we know of this era it seems that the vast majority of the populace was willing to accept a mythological explanation of events, an explanation like those we find in the works of Homer. Natural occurrences were accounted for in terms of the activities of gods or spirits who inhabited the natural world. The wars, jealousies and rivalries among the gods, and their relations with men and women, were taken to account for the events of the visible world.

The thinkers who began the philosophical quest were those who found that when they scrutinized these accepted beliefs they were seen to be inadequate. Different societies had different legends and mythologies. Most of these either conflicted with the others or with themselves. The explanations were always based upon insufficient evidence, and could never adequately account for all the information people had acquired about the world. The philosophers, to the dismay of their contemporaries, challenged the believers in mythology to prove their views, or to find a better theory, one that would satisfy reasonable people. Out of this rejection of traditionally accepted beliefs, and the search for more plausible or more defensible theories, came the attempts of thoughtful men to explain the natural world in some consistent and rational fashion.

Book of Job. Similarly, in the Bible, in the *Book of Job*, we are given a picture of the beginning of the philosophical quest. Job is portrayed as living in a world in which people accept the view that the universe is governed by a just and good God who rewards the just and punishes the wicked, and that this system of divine retribution works out immediately in everyone's lifetime. Job, we are told, 'was perfect and upright, and one that feared God, and eschewed evil', and yet he was punished.

Job and his 'comforters' discussed this apparent conflict between the accepted belief in God's goodness and justice and what was happening before their very eyes—i.e., the torments of Job. The 'comforters' refused to examine their view with critical eyes, and instead denied the facts. They attempted to convince Job that he must have been a wicked man, otherwise he could not be in his predicament. Job, on the other hand, saw that the accepted system of belief could not be adequate to account for what we do in fact know about the world, namely, that the wicked flourish and the just suffer in this supposedly divinely-governed cosmos.

The *Book of Job* reveals the defects of the traditionally-held view about the nature of the world. Because of these, a different, and more rationally defensible, theory has to be sought. Several possible ones are examined in the course of the Book, and finally the only remaining solution is that man is unable by means of reason, to discover any satisfactory answer. Rather than rest content with inconsistent theories, or unjustifiable ones, the philosophical writer of the *Book of Job* could only pose a question. The people who lived 'the unexamined life' tried their best to avoid facing the problem. But the philosopher, because of his need for intellectually satisfactory beliefs, had to examine it. Even if he could not find a better theory than the traditional one, at least he would not accept a view that he knew was inadequate.

In these examples—both instances from the beginnings of philosophical activities in ancient times—we can discern some of the drive that sets the philosophical quest in motion. There are always people who are ready to accept almost any view. But there are others who are troubled by what appear to be inconsistencies in these views, or are troubled because they do not see why these views ought to be accepted, or why they are true. These philosophers begin to raise questions and seek solutions. How they do this, and what they have accomplished, is the subject-matter of philosophy.

Conclusion. If one asks, what is the point of all this searching for some consistent and coherent system of beliefs, of demanding rationally satisfactory explanations, possibly a kind of answer is contained in a story about a recent catastrophe. According to the newspaper accounts, a Georgia bootlegger ran out of liquor with which to supply his clients. There was a great demand, and to satisfy this, he concocted a brew out of some anti-freeze and other ingredients. The results were disastrous—some thirty people died from drinking the beverage. When the bootlegger was arrested, he was asked if he had anything to say about what had happened as a result of his nefarious activities. 'Well,' he commented, 'it makes a man think.'

Philosophy, in a less dangerous way, also makes a man think—think about the basic foundations of his outlook, his knowledge, his beliefs. It makes one inquire into the reasons for what one accepts and does, and into the importance of one's ideas and ideals, in the hope that one's final convictions, whether they remain the same, or whether they change as a result of this examination, will at least be rationally held ones.

Whether this desired consequence is actually superior to declining to examine one's life, is a philosophical question, and one that can better be decided after reading this book. One may well decide, after seeing what philosophy is, and what philosophers have done, that it is all a waste of time. On the other hand, one may find that the consideration of problems in the various branches of philosophy—logic, ethics, theory of knowledge, metaphysics, and so on—provides solutions to the most urgent questions. Any conclusion that the reader comes to, we hope, will be based upon a thoughtful consideration of the material that is to follow, and hence will be the result of the reader's own philosophizing.

We repeat: the best way to discover what philosophy is, is by studying it, and by philosophizing.

CHAPTER I

ETHICS

The Definition of 'Ethics'. As with so many words in common use, the term 'ethics' has a number of different meanings. In one of its most frequent uses, it refers to **a code or set of principles by which men live.** Thus, we speak of 'medical ethics' and mean by this phrase the code which regulates and guides the behaviour of doctors in their dealings with each other and with their patients. Or again, when we speak of 'Christian ethics' we are referring to the principles which prescribe the behaviour of those who are Christians, such as the rules for conduct which are found in the Ten Commandments.

Philosophers, however, do not only employ the word in this sense when they speak of 'ethics'. They also mean by it **a theoretical study,** very much as the physicist means by 'physics' a theoretical study. But whereas the physicist studies certain natural phenomena, such as moving bodies and their laws, the objects which are studied in ethics are theories. These theories, sometimes called 'ethical theories', deal with such questions as 'How ought men to behave?' 'What is the good life for man?' and so on. An example of an ethical theory studied in the branch of philosophy called 'ethics' is **Hedonism.** This is an ancient theory which contends that the good life is ultimately one of pleasure.

Philosophers study such theories as Hedonism not merely because these doctrines have important consequences for living and for understanding human nature, but also because many ethical doctrines which appear plausible at a first glance, such as Hedonism, are found upon careful examination to suffer from certain defects. For example, does it not make sense to speak of 'bad pleasures', i.e., of the things which may give us momentary pleasure, such as drinking alcohol, but which may result in a life of subsequent pain and travail? If this is so, then how can the good life be identical with a life of pleasure, since there are pleasures which are bad? But if it is not pleasure which constitutes the good life, then what does? Part of the motivation for studying ethics lies in the attempts by philosophers to construct satisfactory answers to questions like those we have mentioned above. In what follows, we will consider some of the famous classical and modern ethical theories to see how they answer such questions. We will examine their advantages and their defects, and by so doing, we will engage in the philosophical study we have designated as 'ethics'.

Ethics Originates in Everyday Life. It would be a mistake to regard ethics as a purely 'academic' study, having no intimate connections with the daily lives of men. Every man who is reflective and who is troubled by certain situations in his daily life is a philosopher of ethics to that extent. Suppose a man believes that he should not take a

1

human life, and suppose he also believes that he has an obligation to defend his country against foreign enemies. What should he do when his country is at war? If he refuses to fight for his country, then he reneges on his belief that he has an obligation to do so. On the other hand, if he does fight for it, in the course of doing so he may take human life. What should he do in the circumstances? How can he decide? Reflections of this sort which engage the attentions of ordinary men are the raw material of which ethical theories are made. The difference between the reflections of the ordinary man and the reflections of the philosopher is that the latter are frequently more systematic, although not always so, and are usually more general. The ordinary man may merely be trying to solve a particular problem and may try to do this by deciding on a particular course of action in the relevant circumstances. The philosopher tries to **generalize;** he does not only ask: what is the right course of action for this man in these circumstances? but rather: what is the good life for all men? What is the goal for which all men should strive? Is it the accumulation of pleasure? Is it happiness? Is it identical with doing one's duty? Like the ordinary man, the philosopher begins his consideration of ethics by reflecting about common situations, but he goes beyond these to discussions of a more general sort. It is this sort of abstract speculation which constitutes 'ethical theory' as we shall employ the term.

Classification of Ethical Theories. There are many ways of classifying ethical theories. All of these different classifications are important because they help not only to organize the various types of doctrines into groupings which make them simpler to understand but also because they help direct our attention to certain features which make the theories distinctive. The simplest and most obvious classification is an historical one. We can divide theories into those which are 'classical' and those which are 'modern'. Roughly speaking, a theory will be classical if it does one of two things, or both: if it attempts to answer the question: 'What is the good life for man?'; and if it attempts to answer the question: 'How should men act?' We shall discuss the characteristics of modern theories later in this chapter.

CLASSICAL THEORIES

PLATONISM

Most classical theories do not carefully distinguish between these two questions. It is generally assumed in such theories that if we know what the good life is we will naturally act in such a way as to try to achieve it. This is the basis of the first famous classical theory we will consider: Platonism. Although the philosopher PLATO did not put forth philosophical views under his own name (his writings are mainly in the form of conversations called 'Dialogues', between Socrates and other Greek philosophers of the fifth century B.C.), nevertheless certain views are often attributed to Plato as being his own. Although there is some controversy about whether Plato or Socrates held the position that if a man knows what the good life is, he will not act immorally, in what follows we shall speak as if this is Plato's own view. According to this position, **evil is due to lack of knowledge.** If a man can discover what is right, Plato believes he will never act wickedly. But the problem is to discover what is right, or as Plato called it, **'the good'.** How can this be done when men differ so greatly in their opinions about the good life?

Plato's answer is that **finding the nature of the good life is an intellectual task very similar to the discovery of mathematical truths.** Just as the latter cannot be discovered by untrained people, so the former cannot be either. In order to discover what the good life is men must first acquire certain kinds of knowledge. Such knowledge can be arrived at only if these men are carefully schooled in various disciplines, such as mathematics, philosophy, and so on. Only when they have been through the long period of intellectual training that Plato suggested, would they have the capacity to know the nature of the good life.

It is important for an understanding of Plato to make a distinction at this point. Plato did not maintain that one must have knowledge in order to lead the good life. He maintained only the weaker doctrine that *if one did have* knowledge he would lead the good life. Even without the possession of knowledge it is possible for some men to lead the good life, but they will do so haphazardly or blindly. It is only if we have knowledge that we can be assured of leading such an existence. And this is why, in his suggested programme for training men to lead good lives, Plato believed that they must be instructed in two different ways. They must develop, on the one hand, **virtuous habits of behaviour,** and on the other, they must develop their **mental powers** through the study of such disciplines as mathematics and philosophy.

Both of these types of instruction are necessary. To begin with, some men may not have the intellectual capacity to acquire knowledge; these men will not be able to understand what the 'good life' is, just as some men do not have the intellectual power to apprehend high mathematics. But if they **imitate and are guided** by those people who have knowledge of the good, and who accordingly act virtuously, they, too, will act virtuously even though they do not understand the essential nature of the good life. On the basis of this sort of reasoning, Plato went on to advocate the necessity of censorship in what he called an 'ideal society'—the society which is portrayed in his famous book, *The Republic.* Plato felt that it was necessary to prevent young people from being exposed to certain sorts of experiences if they were to develop virtuous habits and thus lead the good life. Secondly, it is necessary for some especially gifted men to develop their mental powers and consequently to undergo rigorous intellectual training which will do more for them than to develop virtuous habits. This is so because these exceptional men must finally be the rulers of the ideal society. In such a society, the rulers, having developed their intellectual capacities, would also have acquired knowledge, and having acquired knowledge they would understand the nature of the good life. This would guarantee their acting rightly or morally, and hence would ensure their being good rulers. For, as we have seen, it was Plato's belief that if a man could acquire knowledge, in particular knowledge of what was good, then he would never act evilly.

A second basic element in Plato's philosophy is what contemporary scholars term his **absolutism.** According to Plato, there is fundamentally **one and only one** good life for all men to lead. This is because goodness is something which is not dependent upon men's inclinations, desires, wishes, or upon their opinions. Goodness in this respect resembles the mathematical truth that two plus two equal four. This is a truth which is absolute; it exists whether any man likes such a fact or not, or even whether he knows mathematics or not. It is not dependent upon men's opinions about the nature of mathematics or the world. Likewise, **goodness exists independently of men and remains to be discovered if men can be properly trained.**

This can be put in another way. Plato is arguing for the **objectivity** of moral principles as opposed to all philosophies which contend that morality is merely a 'matter of opinion' or 'preference'. Plato's view can be roughly summarized as saying that a certain course of action is right or wrong absolutely and independently of anyone's opinion, just as the statement, 'This is a typewriter,' is either right or wrong independently of anybody's opinion. Thus, the Germans who murdered 6,000,000 Jews in gas chambers were *absolutely* wrong in their behaviour; it was not that we, with differing ethical standards, merely *thought* them to be wrong—but more than that, we were *right* in so thinking, for they were *wrong*. It is an absolutely objective moral law that 'Thou Shalt Not Commit Murder', and the Nazis violated this law.

Platonism has had a tremendous impact upon religious philosophy, for most theologians have assumed that moral laws such as 'Thou Shalt Not Steal', or 'Thou Shalt Not Commit Murder' are **absolute and objective** in the Platonic sense. The development of Plato's philosophy which is known as Neo-Platonism was the nearest Greek philosophy came to itself becoming religion and had a direct influence on the development of Christian theology. But it should be pointed out that although Platonism and most theologies agree in contending that moral standards are objective, there is a fundamental difference between them which should not be overlooked. Plato himself believed that **moral standards were superior even to God;** goodness is anterior to God, and God is good if and only if he acts in accordance with such a standard. This is quite distinct from the traditional Judaeo-Christian view, for example, that God creates goodness. This point will be examined more fully in Chapter IV.

CRITICISM OF PLATONISM

As we have seen, Platonism as a moral philosophy rests upon two basic assumptions. One is the assumption that if a man has knowledge of the good life, he will never act immorally. The other is that there is one and only one good life for all men; just as there is no moral alternative to the command: 'Thou Shalt Not Steal'. Let us now examine criticisms of these basic assumptions, beginning with the belief that if a man has knowledge of the good he will never act immorally.

Most philosophers who criticize Plato have interpreted this thesis as expressing a **psychological judgment about how men will act under certain conditions.** The conditions are that if men have a certain kind of knowledge, they will behave in a certain way. Let us see if Plato's view is true. Suppose I intend to embezzle money from a bank where I work. Suppose it is pointed out to me that stealing is wrong. Now I may not agree with this assertion. I may think, and even argue, that stealing is right. If so, ordinary men would consider me deficient in moral knowledge, since stealing is in fact wrong. It is much as if I had argued that two plus two equal five. In holding such a view, I am simply mistaken. If I proceed to steal money from the bank, it is plausible to say that I have acted immorally because of a deficiency in knowledge. And this is indeed what Plato would say about me— that I simply do not understand what is meant by the 'right way of life'. In so far as Platonism can be applied to this case, it seems in accord with common-sense views of morality. On the other hand, interpreted as a psychological account of how men behave *in every case*, the theory seems to have grave defects. For some men may well understand that stealing is wrong; but they may still persist in stealing. Plato would say of such men that they really do not understand what is meant by 'stealing' since no man willingly will do what he knows to be wrong. But if we talk to such people and if they give the usual signs of understanding what it means to steal, and further, if they admit it to be morally wrong but still persist in doing it, it appears as if Plato's account must be rejected, since it seems that some men will act evilly while knowing what the right course of action is. This was the view of human nature taken by Aristotle.

But Plato's account is much more subtle than the above discussion would indicate. What makes it attractive is that it attempts to supply a general solution to a common type of difficulty which arises in daily life. Men often find themselves in situations where they do not know how to behave because they do not know what the right course of action would be in those circumstances. Is it right to defend my country if this means killing someone, or is it right never to kill anyone? What Plato suggests is that if we had more information, if we had been more carefully trained, we could discover the answer. We would know what the right course of action would be in those circumstances and thus our perplexity would be relieved. The situation seems analogous to many problems which a doctor faces. Should he operate now or wait until tomorrow? Should he administer this drug or not? These are problems which would be hopelessly bewildering to the average man since he does not have the training and hence the knowledge to solve them. But to a trained person, the difficulty disappears. Plato's point is that moral difficulties in many cases are theoretically solvable by the acquisition of further knowledge—and this is a point of view which cannot be lightly dismissed.

The major objection to it, however, is this. Moral conundrums do not seem to be, in the final analysis, analogous to scientific questions. When all the relevant facts have been gathered in a scientific issue, we can in principle always decide the issue. But this is not so in a moral situation. We may know all the relevant facts in a given situation. We may know, for instance, that the effect of dropping an atomic bomb on a certain area will be to kill 100,000 people, to make that area uninhabitable for one century, and, on the other hand, we may also know that if we drop the bomb, a currently disastrous war will be shortened by years. But our perplexity still exists. Should we or should we not drop the bomb? It must be conceded that sometimes the acquisition of further information about a situation will solve difficulties we have about acting in that situation, but it must also be recognized that this is not always so, and if not, Platonism cannot be accepted without considerable qualification. Moral knowledge is not analogous to scientific or mathematical knowledge and Plato's mistake was to think that it is.

A further criticism that arises from this is that, since Plato regards morality as being a matter of knowledge, a prerequisite of moral behaviour is the intellectual ability necessary to apprehend the abstract truths of morality, so that he seems to exclude the possibility of fully moral behaviour for all but a few intellectually gifted men. It is not sufficient to say that those of us who have not this ability can live good lives by allowing ourselves to be ruled or advised by those who have, since to behave morally presupposes that one has responsibility for one's actions. An action is not truly moral—or immoral for that matter—unless it is the result of the free choice of the individual performing it. To make this choice the individual needs the kind of moral understanding that Plato says is possible only for a few. Again we shall find Aristotle showing a clearer awareness of this basic feature of moral behaviour than Plato.

The second basic assumption of Platonism is that there is one and only one right course of action for all men—we have called this his 'absolutism'. Since we shall discuss this problem in more detail when we come to modern ethics, we shall not consider it directly here. However, even in ancient times this view was tellingly criticized, again by Plato's greatest pupil, the philosopher ARISTOTLE. Let us turn, then, to Aristotle's moral philosophy in order to see how it differs from Platonism, and in particular how it rejects the Platonic tenets that there is one and only one right course of action in a given moral situation, that good behaviour is possible without moral understanding and that a knowledge of the good will necessarily lead to virtuous behaviour.

ARISTOTLE: THE DOCTRINE OF THE MEAN

It was characteristic of Greek philosophy to be highly speculative. This trait is exhibited most strikingly in **metaphysics, where many Greek philosophers attempted to discover the true nature of the world by the use of reason alone.** It is found less commonly in the ethical writings of the Greeks, but even here it is a noticeable feature of their philosophizing. Such philosophers as Heraclitus, Plato and the Stoics **derived their ethical views in part from certain metaphysical positions they held.** The Stoics, for example, believed that **all behaviour is rigidly determined by natural laws.** This led them into puzzles about whether a man can behave **freely, for if not, no man can be held**

morally responsible for what he does. In general, such speculation is of a non-scientific sort: it does not patiently try to collect facts and then derive conclusions from them; rather it tries to *deduce* facts about the nature of the world and the nature of man by the use of reason alone. Aristotle is, of course, one of the great metaphysicians in this sense; but curiously enough in his ethical writings he departs from this tradition and adopts a **scientific or empirical approach to ethical problems.** Instead of trying to discover the nature of the good life for all men by reflection alone, he examined the behaviour and talk of various people in everyday life. He noticed that plain men regard some people as leading what they call 'good lives' and others as leading what they call 'bad lives'.

He noticed further that the various lives which men of common sense consider to be 'good' all contain one common characteristic: **happiness.** And similarly, the lives which ordinary people regard as being bad lives all have in common the characteristic of being unhappy. Therefore in answer to the question 'What is the good life for man?' Aristotle's answer can be stated in one sentence: **'It is a life of happiness.'**

But this answer is in a way too simple. We still would like to know, beyond this, what the common man means when he says the good life is a 'happy' one. Does he suggest that it is a life of pleasure, of success, of fame, or what? Exactly what does the word 'happiness' mean? Unfortunately, the plain man is unable to help us if we ask him what he means by 'happiness'. Either he is inarticulate, or he gives different and contradictory answers. Aristotle's work in ethics is a philosophical attempt to supply the answer: he tries to explain more clearly than the ordinary man can what moral words like 'happiness' mean. The *Nicomachean Ethics*, which is the title of Aristotle's chief work on ethics, can thus be regarded as one of the earliest essays in what is now called 'analytical philosophy'. Aristotle in this work was trying to analyse or explain the use of certain moral terms which occur in everyday speech in a clearer way than the average man could do, even though the plain man could use these words quite properly in everyday speech.

In the *Nicomachean Ethics*, Aristotle gives a definition of the word 'happiness' which has since become famous. 'Happiness,' he says, 'is an activity of the soul in accord with perfect virtue.' Unfortunately, this definition may not be much clearer to the reader than the original question 'What is happiness?' since it is couched in obscure terminology. In fact, it has been a source of puzzlement to philosophers for centuries, and various interpretations of it have been offered. A plausible interpretation, although not the only one, is this: Aristotle is stressing the fact that happiness is not something which is static, but is an **activity.** What does he mean by saying it is not 'static'? Men tend to think that happiness is something we arrive at—a certain fixed goal which awaits us if we behave in certain ways. Those who hold this view tend to think of happiness as an object of a certain sort; just as London is an object we can arrive at by driving southward steadily along the M.1. Once we finish our tour through life's daily activities, so to speak, then we will have arrived at this goal called 'happiness'.

But this is precisely what Aristotle is *denying*. Happiness is *not* a goal in this sense. Rather, it is something which *accompanies* certain activities, instead of being the *goal* of these activities. Happiness, as a characteristic of men's lives, is something like persistence. A man who engages in a course of conduct persistently does not arrive at a goal called 'persistence'. Instead it is **a way of doing things;** for instance, of refusing to be defeated by circumstances. Happiness is like this: it is **a way of engaging in the various activities of life,** such as eating, making love, working and so on. If one engages in these activities in a certain way, then we can declare him to be happy. For instance, if he enjoys eating, intellectual pursuits, friendship, and so on, and is not frequently downcast, depressed, anxious—then he is a happy man. This roughly is what Aristotle means by saying that happiness is an activity—but it should be stressed that these brief remarks are to be regarded as a preliminary aid to the reader rather than an exhaustive account of the doctrine.

As we have mentioned already, classical ethical theories attempt to answer two questions: 'What is the good life for man?' and 'How ought men to behave?' Aristotle is a classical moralist in both senses. In answer to the first question, his reply is: **'The good life for man is a life of happiness.'** The answer to the second question is equally direct: **'Men ought to behave so as to achieve happiness.'** But again, this answer seems vague. If we ask: 'More specifically, how should we behave in order to achieve happiness?' Aristotle's answer is to be found in the well-known formula called **'The Doctrine of the Mean',** or sometimes popularly referred to as the **'Golden Mean'.** We shall now turn to a discussion of the Doctrine of the Mean, and in this way we will show how Aristotle's moral philosophy differs from that of Plato.

Being happy, according to Aristotle, is like being well-fed. How much food should a man eat in order to be well-fed? Aristotle's contention is that there is no general answer to this question in the sense of fixing a specific amount, like two pounds of meat per day. It depends on the size of the man, what sort of work he does, whether he is ill or well, and so on. A man who works at digging ditches will need more food, in general, than a man who sits at a desk; and a large man will, in general, need more food than a small one. Now the proper amount for anyone to eat can be ascertained only by trial and error: if we eat a certain amount of food and still feel hungry, we should eat more; if we eat the same amount and feel uncomfortable, then we should eat less. The correct amount is a 'mean' between eating too much and too little. It is important here not to interpret the word 'mean' as being synonymous with 'average'. Suppose that one pound of food per day is too little, and that two pounds is too much. Does this suggest that the average amount (i.e., one and one-half pounds) is the correct amount? Aristotle's answer is that it may or may not be—but in general, one cannot say that the correct amount is exactly one and one-half pounds; all one can say is that it is an amount *somewhere* between one pound and two pounds; and this is what he intends by the word 'mean'. We should eat an amount of food which is more than one pound and less than two; but the exact amount can be ascertained only after we eat various portions and see how we feel.

So with happiness. **The proper way for man to behave in the moral sphere is in accordance with the mean.** For example, in order to be **happy, he must be courageous, liberal, proud, witty, modest, and so on.** But all of these 'virtues', as Aristotle designates them, are virtues of **moderation:** courage is the mean between cowardice and rashness; liberality between prodigality and frugality; pride between vanity and humility, and so forth. Aristotle's philosophy of the 'golden mean' can be condensed as follows: **In order to achieve happiness, men must act moderately, they must act so as to be striving for the mean between two extremes.** If they do this, then they will be happy. But the mean will vary from man to man: some men can be more courageous than others, and some less; and each will be proper for that man. Plato, it will be remembered, contended that 'goodness' is an absolute characteristic. Either a man is 'good' or he is not— there is one and only one proper way for him to behave in a given set of circumstances. But this is precisely what Aristotle is disputing: there are *many* 'good' lives—in fact there may be as many as there are differences between men. All of these have in common the fact that if men behave in accordance with the mean they will achieve happiness: but there may be many ways of so behaving, thus many ways of being happy.

The important consequences of this doctrine for ethics are **that there are various correct ways of living for different men. What is good for one person may not be good for another. And, further, one cannot tell prior to actual experimentation, by the use of reason alone, which is the correct way of living for him. This can be ascertained only by experimentation and by trial and error.** We can summarize these two points by saying that Aristotle is both a **relativist** and an **empiricist** in ethics.

Aristotle shows a similar disagreement with Plato over the question of whether a man is really acting morally if he acts without a full understanding of the situation. He makes an important distinction between actions which are done 'willingly' and those done 'not unwillingly', pointing out that we do not praise or blame someone if we believe that he did not understand what he was doing. Moral behaviour in the full sense requires moral understanding but all men can hope to achieve this, since what is involved is not a purely intellectual appreciation of absolute moral truths but the kind of practical wisdom and awareness of the need for moderation that we have just described.

Furthermore, Aristotle does not agree with Plato that a knowledge of the good will necessarily lead to virtuous behaviour. He shows a more realistic view of human nature by introducing into his discussion of ethics the notion of moral weakness or lack of self-control. He tells us, much as St. Paul was to tell us later, that the evil that we would not, that we do, and the good we would, we do not. A knowledge of what we ought to do is not sufficient without the kind of self-discipline necessary to ensure that we do it. For we can be too easily led astray by the pleasures of other forms of behaviour. We must, therefore, receive a sound training in good habits when we are young, so that when we come to understand what the 'golden mean' is for us we will also have the self-control to follow it.

Aristotle is one of the first great philosophers of common sense in dealing with ethical matters. Unlike Plato, who lays down rigid requirements for all men to follow, regardless of their inclinations, desires, temperaments, stations in life, and so on, Aristotle is much less narrow. And this can be seen in his **doctrine of pleasure.** Aristotle rejects the view that pleasure is entirely bad. His view is that no man can be happy without a certain amount of pleasure in his life; this is expressed in his famous epigram, **'No man can be happy on the rack'.**

In spite of its common-sense outlook, however, the Aristotelian view of ethics is **not** without its difficulties and we will consider some of these now.

CRITICISM OF ARISTOTLE

Although at first glance it seems plausible to hold that men always ought to follow the middle course between certain kinds of activities, there seem to be situations in which this advice will not do. For example, there is no middle course between keeping a promise and not keeping one. We tend to feel that any man who keeps a promise is moral in so far as he does it, and immoral in so far as he breaks it (unless there are certain other overriding factors). But the main point is that in such a case there is no middle ground between the two: either one keeps a promise or one does not. The same applies to telling the truth: either one does or does not tell the truth and once again the doctrine of the mean cannot be applied to such cases. Such virtues as keeping promises or telling the truth seem to be better analysable by the Platonic view: they seem to be *absolute* virtues, and are *not relative* to various men and situations as are virtues like courage (which is the mean between rashness and cowardice).

A second, and perhaps more important, criticism of the Aristotelian doctrine is this: **Aristotle is primarily proposing a philosophy of moderation.** His view is that happiness will result from moderate behaviour. This is true, of course, in some cases; but there are hosts of cases where only 'immoderate' behaviour is *proper* behaviour. A man who is temperamentally passionate and romantic may find that 'moderate' behaviour does not suit him. He cannot be happy if he is forced to control himelf in all situations of life. For people of this temperament the Aristotelian ethic is not an appealing one; and the rise of Romanticism in philosophy can be regarded in this way as a criticism of the Aristotelian way of life.

HEDONISM: THE PHILOSOPHY OF EPICURUS

As we have indicated, Plato maintained that the good life is in no way connected with pleasure. Aristotle moderated this doctrine. Although denying that the good life was *identical* with a life of pleasure he admitted that **'pleasure must be in some way an ingredient**

of happiness'. EPICURUS disagreed with both of them. Epicurus was the exponent of a type of philosophy which has persisted down to the present time. He held a view which is sometimes called 'Hedonism', **the doctrine that pleasure is the sole good.** The influence of his philosophy can be judged from the fact that the English language still contains the word 'epicure', which is based upon the view of Epicurus. As with so many words, however, the connotations of the word 'epicure' as it is now employed do not represent accurately the sort of philosophy which was held by Epicurus himself. An 'epicurean' is now depicted as a *gourmet*, as a person whose main delight consists in the enjoyment of exotic or fastidiously prepared food and rare wines. As a matter of fact, Epicurus himself suffered for years from stomach trouble and was never an 'epicure' in the modern sense. He ate frugally, allegedly drank only water, and, in general, lived in a highly abstemious fashion. (His letters contained such sentences as the following: 'I am thrilled with pleasure in the body when I live on bread and water, and I spit on luxurious pleasures, not for their own sake, but because of the inconveniences that follow them'.)

The ethical philosophy of Epicurus consists mainly of advice for living moderately but pleasurably. He considered pleasure to be *the* good, but he also realized that **if a person pursues pleasure too arduously, pain will follow.** If a man drinks too much he will suffer headaches and stomach pains the next day. The proper way to proceed in life is to **live pleasantly without suffering from any of the undesirable effects of such living.**

In fact, Epicurus' philosophy may be regarded as containing instructions which are designed not only to enable one to acquire pleasure but also to enable one to avoid pain. If one engages in a life of pleasure which leads to pain then such a life would be regarded as a bad one by Epicurus. Since some pleasures are obviously accompanied by pain, Epicurus distinguished between those pleasures which are accompanied by pain and those which are not, and regarded only the latter as good. He called the former **'dynamic'** pleasures and the latter **'passive'** pleasures. Sexual love, for example, is bad because it is accompanied by fatigue, remorse and depression. Other 'dynamic' pleasures are gluttony, fame, drinking and marriage. All of these are bad because they are accompanied by pain: gluttony will lead to indigestion, fame may be accompanied by all sorts of distress, drinking will lead to headaches, disease, and so forth. The result is that Epicurus advocated (and himself led) a life which we would now consider highly ascetic. This is because he seemed to believe that **it is better to avoid pain than to seek pleasure if it will produce pain.** Friendship, on the other hand, is a 'passive pleasure'. It is not accompanied by pain and hence is permitted and, indeed, encouraged by him.

Hedonism, as a philosophical doctrine, has two forms. We can call the first form **'Psychological Hedonism'**, and the second type **'Ethical Hedonism'. Psychological Hedonism is the doctrine that in fact men do pursue pleasure, and only pleasure, in their lives. All activities, according to this theory, are directed toward the acquisition of pleasure and the**

avoidance of pain. EUDOXUS, who was a famous Greek mathematician and an earlier contemporary of Aristotle, is supposed to have held such a view. Aristotle says of him:

> Now Eudoxus thought pleasure to be the chief good because he saw all, rational and irrational alike, aiming at it: and he argued that, since in all what was the object of choice must be good and what most so the best, the fact of all being drawn to the same thing proved this thing to be the best for all: 'For each,' he said, 'finds what is good for itself just as it does its proper nourishment, and so that which is good for all, and the object of the aim of all, is their chief good.'

Epicurus is generally interpreted as being a Psychological Hedonist in this sense. He apparently believed that all men were motivated in their daily lives to attempt to acquire pleasure: did not men strive for riches, for fame, for sensual delights because the attainment of these produced pleasure?

Epicurus is also an Ethical Hedonist (with certain important qualifications). **Ethical Hedonism is the view that men not only in fact seek pleasure, but further that they ought to do so since pleasure alone is good.** It is obvious that Psychological Hedonism does not entail Ethical Hedonism. One might hold either doctrine without necessarily holding the other. For example, one might believe that men are motivated to seek pleasure, and one also might believe that they ought *not* to do so. In fact, this is roughly what Epicurus held, as we have seen. His view was that even if men are motivated to acquire pleasure, certain pleasures are bad and ought to be avoided. On the other hand, he held that some pleasures, such as friendship, conversation about philosophy and so on, are such as ought to be cultivated; and the good life consists in acquiring pleasures of this sort. He can consequently be interpreted as holding a modified form of Ethical Hedonism, as well as adhering to the psychological version of the theory.

CRITICISM OF HEDONISM

Hedonism is a complex moral philosophy, consisting of at least two parts, one of them a psychological theory, the other an ethical theory. The psychological account is supposedly a true description of how men are motivated to action in conducting their daily lives. According to this account every conscious action is motivated by the search for pleasure. Whether a man is a hermit, or whether he seeks fame, in either case—if we are to accept Psychological Hedonism— he is motivated to act as he does because he is striving for pleasure. Ethical Hedonism, on the other hand, goes beyond the psychological account: it contends that men *ought* to seek pleasure, for ultimately this is the only thing worth having for itself.

Both aspects of Hedonism seem plausible not only to the unsophisticated reader, but even to professional thinkers. Let us show in somewhat more detail why this is so, considering Psychological Hedonism first. What the theory attempts to do is **to provide a single explan-**

ation for every possible type of conscious or voluntary action men engage in. It is a source of satisfaction to all thinkers to find the most general explanation for a group of phenomena, especially if this explanation turns out to be a very simple one. And Psychological Hedonism tries to provide an explanation of this sort. Consider any kind of conscious behaviour—why do men do it? The answer is always the same—they are seeking pleasure. At this point, we can mention a famous philosophical distinction which can be used to support Psychological Hedonism. The distinction has various names, one of the most common of which is the 'means-ends' distinction. The point of the distinction is this: some things may not be worth having in themselves, but are worth having because they enable us to achieve certain goals. On the other hand, other things may be worth having in themselves. They are, as philosophers say, 'intrinsically valuable'. We value them not because they enable us to achieve something else, but for their own sakes. Exercise, for instance, may not be worth doing in its own right, but it has value in that, by doing it, we will become healthy, which *is* valuable in itself. In terms of the above distinction, exercise is valuable as a 'means' while health is valuable as an 'end'. Now the position of the Psychological Hedonist is that the ultimate end towards which all activity is directed is pleasure; such things as fame, riches, success are all means to these ends. Thus, all conscious human behaviour can be explained by saying that men are motivated *ultimately* or *basically* by pleasure—it is the end for which all men strive. Put this way, Psychological Hedonism has been a theory which has attracted both philosophers and plain men, and it has accordingly had a great influence throughout the history of Western thought.

However, in so far as this part of Hedonism is interpreted as a purely scientific account of men's conscious behaviour it does not withstand present-day scientific scrutiny. Psychologists agree that men are *sometimes* motivated by the search for pleasure, but they go on to point out that such is not always the case. For although some men may begin by trying to acquire riches as a means to pleasure, after a time they may come to regard wealth as an end in itself. In psychological language, they become 'fixated' upon the acquisition of wealth and disregard the use to which it may be put for acquiring pleasure. (Such men are commonly called 'misers'.) Psychologists point out that these men may be so strongly motivated by the attempt to acquire money that they may disregard or even reject the pursuit of pleasure as being of any value to them if it interferes with the acquisition of money. We are all familiar with newspaper accounts of men and women who are found living in squalid conditions even though they may possess a fortune hidden in the mattress. The acquisition of money, not pleasure, becomes an end for them—and for this reason, psychologists tell us that Psychological Hedonism cannot be accepted as an accurate picture of *all* conscious human motivation. And this is merely one instance of such exceptions.

Unfortunately, Psychological Hedonism is not simply a scientific theory, and it cannot be refuted merely by an appeal to the latest scientific findings. This can be seen when we consider the sort of reply the Psychological Hedonist will make to the objection we have just considered. He will claim that the miser *actually* gains pleasure by hoarding money. The miser is merely giving up the usual means for acquiring pleasure, such as living in a decent home, eating well and so on. All he has done, the Hedonist argues, is to limit the means for acquiring pleasure to the collecting of money. Money has not become an end in itself for him—rather it has become the sole means for achieving pleasure; but pleasure is still the end for which he strives.

At this stage, the theory has been removed from the area where any scientific finding can possibly confirm or refute it. It has now become a philosophical, rather than a scientific, problem, for no collection of facts can be gathered which would resolve the problem. But when Psychological Hedonism is interpreted in this way, it can still be attacked on philosophical grounds. **For when any theory cannot be refuted by facts, then it loses its explanatory force.** It becomes true **'by definition' but no longer refers to the world in the way in which genuine scientific theories do,** since its truth or falsity no longer depends upon the *facts*. When this happens, the theory may be rejected on the ground that it has lost its power to provide us with a satisfactory explanation of the facts it started out to explain. It has now defined 'pleasure' as 'what men desire', so that in asserting that all men are motivated by a desire for pleasure, it is asserting no more than the tautology that all men are motivated by a desire for what they desire. It has become irrefutable by becoming trivial—i.e., it is not worth refuting.

Ethical Hedonism, as contrasted with Psychological Hedonism, can be divided into two parts, which may be regarded as answers to the questions: 'What is the good life for man?' and 'How *ought* men to behave?' The answers, according to the Ethical Hedonist, are that the good life for man consists of a life of pleasure, and that one *ought* to act so as to acquire pleasure. Let us now examine objections to these replies.

We have already pointed out that even Epicurus, the founder of Hedonism, recognized that some pleasures may be accompanied by pain, or that they may produce pain. For example, smoking opium may give us pleasure, but it will produce physical and mental deterioration if persisted in. It thus appears that some pleasures are bad, and if so we cannot contend simply that the good life is *identical* with a life of pleasure. Epicurus attempted to avoid this difficulty by finding pleasures that do not produce painful consequences, and argued that such pleasures constitute the good life. But this approach will not do, since even friendship, which he regards as a passive pleasure, may sometimes be accompanied by tribulation. For example, if a friend dies, one may suffer intensely from sadness at his death.

A second way of defending the view that pleasure is good is to hold that pleasure itself is never bad—even the pleasure one gets from smoking opium. It is only the painful consequences themselves which are bad. For example, if a drug could be devised which would eliminate the painful consequences of smoking opium—who would deny that the pleasure one got from it was good?

This defence is logically unassailable, but it has practical difficulties which make it dubious that Ethical Hedonism can offer acceptable guidance for one's conduct in daily life. For we cannot, as a matter of fact, always separate the painful consequences of a course of action from the pleasurable ones. If we smoke opium, we may be given pleasure, to be sure, but we will also suffer pain as a result of doing so. To advise one, as Ethical Hedonists do, to seek pleasure is in effect frequently equivalent to advising one to seek pain as well, since the two sometimes cannot be disassociated. Ethical Hedonism, consequently, must sometimes advise one not to pursue pleasures when those pleasures are followed by pain, and thus its practical effect seems incompatible with the theory.

Finally, let us consider the doctrine that men ought to behave so as to acquire pleasure. This view likewise seems plausible at first glance, but further reflection shows that it violates our common-sense beliefs about how we ought to behave. Consider the following case: a soldier is put on guard duty at an important post. He is forced to walk back and forth, and this is monotonous for him. It is a hot night. It would be more pleasant not to remain at his post but to leave for a bar where he can have a cool drink. Most men would say that if he deserted his post for this reason, then he would be acting wrongly. If he says that he acted as he ought to have done because he was seeking pleasure, this defence would be laughed out of court. The plain man feels that sometimes one ought to act so as to acquire pleasure, but not always. Sometimes one has certain obligations which he must fulfil and in these cases he ought to behave so as to fulfil them even if in doing so he does not acquire pleasure. If Ethical Hedonism is interpreted as a systematic theory about how men ought to behave in society, the objection we have just cited shows that it cannot be regarded as an adequate account of such behaviour.

Hedonism, even though theoretically attractive, can thus be seen to violate our ordinary feelings about what constitutes moral behaviour. Do we not object on moral grounds to the 'playboy'? The objection is not merely that he seeks superficial pleasures, such as those of the table, the grape and so on; but more fundamentally, that pleasure is not the sole object which men should strive for. The plain man is, with regard to pleasure, more an Aristotelian than an Epicurean. He feels that sometimes pleasure is a worthwhile object, and in fact that no life can be happy without some pleasure in it; but he finds the doctrine that pleasure is the *only* worthwhile goal, objectionable—and rejects it as containing advice that he cannot in fact follow.

CYNICISM

We have spoken of Platonism, Aristotelianism and Epicureanism as if they were ethical philosophies which were devised by their authors in isolation from the social conditions of the time. For many purposes, this sort of abstraction is useful; but at the same time, it should be stressed that moral philosophies to a great extent *are* products of their times. If one does not recognize this fact, it may be impossible for him to account for the widespread appeal which such theories have had for so many people. Great philosophies, especially moral

B

philosophies, may be regarded as saying more clearly and usually more strikingly what many common people only vaguely realize. This is especially true of **Cynicism** and **Stoicism** whose attraction for so many cannot be fully appreciated apart from some knowledge of the social conditions from which they developed. To some extent, this is even true of Hedonism. **When men suffer great catastrophies, they may grasp at pleasure as providing some comfort and security in a collapsing world. Hedonism is a philosophy which justifies their behaviour,** and under such conditions they will be attracted to it. In this regard, **Hedonism may be considered a philosophy which arises out of despair.**

Cynicism and Stoicism resemble Hedonism in being, generally speaking, philosophies of consolation. But instead of suggesting that the acquisition of pleasure is the proper goal of life, they offer different advice. Let us turn to these doctrines now in order to see why they arose when they did, and what sorts of answers they give to such persistent questions as 'What is the good life for man?' and 'How should men act?'

There are various ways in which men can deal with adversity. They can succumb to it, fight it, escape from it, accept it and so on. For each of these types of behaviour there is a corresponding ethical theory which justifies it. **Quietism,** for example, is an Oriental ethical philosophy which advises men to accept and succumb to adversity, Hedonism can be looked at as a way of escaping from it, and **Utilitarianism** as a way of combating it. **All ethical theories arise because men are dissatisfied either with their personal lives or with the world in which they live.** If a man is content with his lot and with the situation in which the world finds itself, he will not in general seek to change it. What would be the point of trying to do so? But when he is dissatisfied, he will attempt to alter the circumstances in which he finds himself—as we have said, he may fight these circumstances or try to escape from them. Likewise, philosophers do not develop theories about how one *ought* to behave unless they are discontented with the way people do in fact behave: they offer these theories as advice for altering the situation as they see it.

This is particularly true of Cynicism. It can be regarded as prescribing behaviour for those whose lives became intolerable owing to the collapse of the world about them or for reasons of personal despair. This collapse in part began with the decline of the Greek city state (note the frequent wars between Sparta and Athens, or Sparta and Thebes, with the incredible loss of life and destruction that they entailed) and is considerably accelerated by the turmoil that was attendant upon the collapse of the Alexandrian Empire. When social institutions of this magnitude break down, men are naturally led to consider how they may achieve *personal* salvation—and Cynicism offers one answer to this question. **It holds that all the fruits of civilization are worthless—government, private property, marriage, religion, slavery (in the Greek social order), luxury, and all artificial pleasures of the senses. If salvation is to be found it is to be found in a rejection of society and in a return to the simple life—to a life of ascetic living.**

The early Cynics, such as DIOGENES, practised frugal and even miserable living to such an extent that they were likened to animals in their mode of life. In fact, the word 'Cynic' comes from the Greek word 'kunos', which means 'dog-like' (we find a cognate of it in the English word 'canine'). Diogenes, for example, is supposed to have lived in a large tub, and rejected all refinements—of dress, food, personal cleanliness and so on. There is a famous story told about him and Alexander, then the greatest potentate in the world. Alexander came to visit Diogenes, and asked him if there was anything he could do for him to relieve him of the miserable conditions in whch he existed. Diogenes is supposed to have replied: 'Yes, you can stand out of my light and let me see the sun.'

The Cynics believed that the world was fundamentally evil; in order to live properly a man must withdraw from participation in it. But at the same time, even if a man lives a private life, such a life may be devoted to acquiring the usual goods of the world—such as money, a house, fine clothes and so on. And all of these things are precarious, too—for **if we trust our happiness to the possession of them, we may find ourselves again betrayed.** Consequently, all externals, whether private or public, must be dispensed with. **If a man is to find salvation in the world he must find it within himself**—this is what virtue consists in. The Cynics thus advocated a rejection of the goods of the world, and in this way tried to show men that by ignoring such externals they would be emancipated from fear. (We will indicate later that a much more sophisticated version of this theory is to be found in the philosophy of Spinoza and considerable elements of it occur in Stoicism.)

It is interesting to speculate upon how the word 'cynical' acquired its modern meaning. The rejection of external goods includes the rejection of other people, so that a complete indifference and lack of feeling for others resulted. Furthermore, although the early Cynics such as Diogenes and ANTISTHENES lived moral and upright lives of extreme frugality in accordance with the precepts we have mentioned above, later followers used the doctrine for personal advantage. They borrowed money and food from friends, and then applied the doctrine of 'indifference' when it came time to repay these debts. People gradually came to feel that the doctrine was being applied insincerely and callously—and out of such feelings the word 'cynic' developed its modern meaning.

It can be seen that Cynicism is primarily a doctrine which is **antisocial.** It does not attempt to describe how men can be happy as social beings, but instead tries to propose ways for achieving individual salvation. In this way, **it contributed considerably to the philosophical undermining of social standards, arguing that only individual virtue was of fundamental importance.** This outlook considerably abetted the moral chaos into which the ancient world fell after the collapse of the Alexandrian Empire.

Not only is Cynicism anti-social, but it is also one of the forerunners of **asceticism.** By rejecting the claim that worldly possessions are of value, it was one of the precursors of the sort of asceticism which we find so brilliantly pictured in Anatole France's novel *Thais*, where men are depicted as living solitary, miserable lives in the Egyptian desert—

lying on hard ground at night, fasting for days at a time and in general subjecting themselves to physical and mental torture.

Cynicism as a philosophy has not only had great influence upon plain men, but it was a considerable factor in the development of early Christian philosophy. The monk, in a way, can be pictured as a man who follows the advice of the cynic: he lives a simple, frugal, cloistered life, shunning the world's goods—such as marriage, the accumulation of private property, and fame—and all this so that he may develop his character as an individual and cast aside the world for an unencumbered devotion to God. The general effect of Cynicism is thus other-worldliness, and this is why it has played so great a role in influencing the way of life advocated by **pietistic** religions such as Christianity.

STOICISM

It is fair to describe **Stoicism as the most influential ethical doctrine of the ancient Western world before Christianity.** It swept over Greece after the fall of Alexander, and dominated Roman thought until it was superseded by Christianity. But unlike Hedonism and Cynicism, which remained more or less unchanged from the time of their inception, Stoicism was a doctrine which went through a number of radical developments in its long history. It began as a development of Cynicism, and ended as a form of Platonic idealism. Most of the changes which took place, however, were in the metaphysical views of the Stoics, and in their logic. Their ethical views remained relatively stable, and consequently in this section, since we are concerned with ethics, we can ignore the minor variations which took place in Stoic moral theory and treat the doctrine as if it had persisted unaltered.

The founder of Stoicism was named ZENO (not to be confused with Zeno of Elea, the originator of the famous logical paradoxes). Zeno is supposed to have lectured in the third century B.C. from a porch, and Stoicism gets its name from this fact, since 'stoa' is the Greek word meaning 'porch'.

Like the Cynics, the Stoics were tremendously depressed by the collapse of the Greek city states and the Alexandrian Empire. They felt that no hope for social reconstruction was possible. Consequently, **their philosophy consists of advice to individual men for attaining personal salvation in a crumbling world.** Although Stoicism, as we shall see, is a fairly complex moral theory, its basic tenet for achieving personal salvation is very like that of the Cynics and can be stated in one sentence: **Learn to be indifferent to external influences!**

EPICTETUS, who began life as a Roman slave, and who rose to be an official in the Roman government, was one of the most famous and influential of the Stoics. In his famous discourse on 'Progress or Improvement', he tells us why a man must learn to cultivate a philosophy of indifference:

> Where then is progress? If any of you, withdrawing himself from the externals, turns to his own will to exercise it and to im-

prove it by labour, so as to make it conformable to nature, elevated, free, unrestrained, unimpeded, faithful, modest; and if he has learned that he who desires or avoids the things which are not in his power can neither be faithful nor free, but of necessity he must change with them and be tossed about with them as in a tempest, and of necessity must subject himself to others who have the power to procure or prevent what he desires or would avoid; finally, when he rises in the morning, if he observes and keeps these rules, bathes as a man of fidelity, eats as a modest man; in like manner, if in every matter that occurs he works out his chief principles as the runner does with reference to running, and the trainer of the voice with reference to the voice—this is the man who truly makes progress, and this is the man who has not travelled in vain. But if he has strained his efforts to the practice of reading books, and labours only at this, and has travelled for this, I tell him to return home immediately, and not to neglect his affairs there; for this for which he has travelled is nothing. But the other thing is something, to study how a man can rid his life of lamentation and groaning, and saying, Woe to me.

As can be inferred from the above quotation, the Stoics believed that **good or evil depends upon oneself.** Other men have power over external matters that affect you—they can put you in prison and torture you, or they can make a slave of you: but none the less **if a man can be indifferent to these events, others will not in a significant sense have power over him.** Epictetus expressed this by saying that **virtue resides in the will—that only the will is good or bad.** If a man has a good will (and he can have one by remaining indifferent to external happenings), his essential character cannot be destroyed by the external events in his life. When a man is indifferent to such happenings **he is a free man.** He is no longer bound by adherence to events outside of himself. **By practising indifference he becomes independent of the world** —and thus, even though the world may be in chaos, this will not prevent him from achieving personal salvation.

The ethical views of the Stoics cannot be fully understood apart from their metaphysics. They believed in **predestination, i.e., that all happenings in the world are fixed by God according to some preconceived plan.** Nothing happens fortuitously. Virtue consists in a will which is in agreement with the happenings of nature. In less complicated terminology, **a man is virtuous if he can learn to accept what happens and if he can understand that all this is part of a divine arrangement which he is powerless to alter.** Consequently, he can avoid frustration, heartbreak and despair in trying to alter the course of events if he understands that prior to making any such attempt these events have been *ordained* to take place. A man becomes *free* when he understands this; it is only the man who struggles to change things who is *not* free. By practising an indifference to events one puts himself in a frame of mind such that the events cannot affect his fundamental character— and when he does so, he is being virtuous. In particular, the **Stoics felt it was important to free oneself from desires and passions.**

Stoicism differs from Cynicism in a fundamental respect. The Cynics felt that they were powerless to prevent the collapse of the world in which they lived and hence they renounced it. They lived like 'dogs'. But the Stoics argued that this sort of renunciation was unnecessary. One does not have to renounce the material things of the world; he can live a life of pleasure or of material success, **provided that he does not become trapped by these things. He must remain indifferent to them,** so that if he should lose material possessions his feeling towards them will not change. It is only in so far as he is affected by these things that he is not free; but if he can remain unaffected in the sense indicated, there is no reason why he should not continue to enjoy them.

The main effect of Stoicism was to place the responsibility for becoming a good or bad man directly upon the individual himself, rather than upon society. If an individual can cultivate a frame of mind which makes him indifferent to the usual goods of the world, then he will be virtuous; and nothing that happens to him can alter his essential character.

CRITICISM OF STOICISM

There are three major difficulties in Stoicism: (1) a logical difficulty involving the notions of **freedom** and **predestination;** (2) the difficulty that the doctrine of **indifference** has consequences which seem paradoxical to common sense; and (3) the difficulty that Stoicism appeals to men only in **unusual circumstances,** and hence cannot be accepted as a *universal* ethic. We will consider each of these, turning to the logical difficulty first.

The Stoics held that *every* event which occurs, whether it is the falling of a meteor or whether it is one's thinking about having dinner tonight, is predestined to occur according to a divine plan. If this doctrine is accepted, then it becomes impossible to alter any of the circumstances in which we find ourselves. If these events were *destined* to occur, then there is nothing we can do about it. In a very significant sense, we are powerless to alter our lives. This can be put by saying that we are not 'free' but instead we are chained to our destinies in accordance with the divine plan. **But this outlook is inconsistent with the Stoic view that a man can alter his character.** According to the latter, a man can learn to change his frame of mind in such a way that he will become indifferent to things that he formerly prized. In holding this position, the Stoics were implying that a man is free to alter his character; that he can change some of the natural events in the world, namely those that go into making up his will. It thus appears there is a fundamental inconsistency at the basis of Stoic theory: man is *both* free and not free. It can be seen that if we accept the latter of these alternatives (i.e., that man is not free) it is pointless to tell him to change his character. If his character is rigidly determined by natural laws, then how can he change it? On the other hand, if man is free to alter his character, then the thesis that all events are predetermined by some master plan must be false.

This dilemma, which is sometimes called **The Problem of Freedom of the Will,** is one of the most persistent and troublesome of philosophical problems. It has not only appeared in Stoic philosophy, but it also occurs in religious philosophy, as well as in modern psychology. For example, to take up the last case, modern psychologists have sometimes contended that our environment and past experience cause us to be the sort of people we are. Thus, if I murder somebody, the view is that I have done so because of events in my past life. Given these events, plus a certain physical and mental constitution, it was impossible for me not to murder the person I did murder. In short, my behaviour was completely determined by factors over which I had no control; hence I was not free. But if I was not free, then how can I be punished by the law? For the law assumes that I have control over my actions. There is no point in punishing a meteorite which kills somebody, since we believe the meteorite had no control over its path. But we do believe that some criminals *do* have control over their actions and when we punish them it is because we hold them responsible for what they do. Thus, it seems as if the findings of modern psychology are inconsistent with the existence of criminal law. As we have tried to indicate, this difficulty occurs at the basis of Stoic philosophy, and the Stoics were never able to solve it.

(Modern philosophical techniques have enabled us to see that this perplexity is in part 'linguistic', that a solution to it involves clarifying the notions of 'freedom', 'compulsion', and 'causal determinism'. For further discussion of the subject, the reader is advised to refer to a collection of philosophical essays called *Readings in Ethical Theory*, edited by Wilfred Sellers and John Hospers.)

Another major difficulty in Stoicism stems from the doctrine of indifference. Men of common sense do not believe it is right to cultivate indifference to the exclusion of all other 'virtues'. If a friend dies, it would appear callous to most men to suggest that indifference is the proper way to react to such an event. Moreover, it seems to follow from Stoic theory that acts which would normally be regarded as immoral are right if performed indifferently. Murder committed from a sense of indifference would seem to be proper if we follow out the implications of Stoic theory—and such a moral outlook is obviously inconsistent with our usual ethical beliefs.

Finally, Stoicism gives plausible advice for living only when one is living under very special circumstances. If one knows beforehand that he may be tortured for military secrets by the enemy in time of war, it makes sense to try to develop an attitude which will enable him to withstand the torture. The philosophy of indifference may be helpful in such a situation; by trying not to think about the pain which is being inflicted upon him, he may be able to avoid giving in to it. Or again, it is frequently the case that men brood over events which are not really important in their lives. Suppose a man's car is accidentally scratched and the paint is ruined—this may cause him extreme mental distress. Stoic philosophy may be helpful here in contributing to his equanimity. Stoicism suggests that it is stultifying to be easily upset by events which are not basic to the conduct of one's life; by practising a certain indifference to the minor distractions which occur in everyday life one may avoid considerable unhappiness. But apart from these sorts of circumstances, it would seem to most men that to practise consistently a doctrine of indifference would be to rob life of many of the things which make it most enjoyable: love, friendship, achievement and so on. For this reason, Stoicism loses its appeal when the external circumstances in which people live greatly improve. If all's well with the world, men feel it is pointless to be indifferent toward it; instead, they feel they should enjoy it. Stoicism arose when the world of the Greeks was in a state of collapse, and it offered useful advice for withstanding the rigours of life at that period. But once men came to feel that circumstances could be changed, Stoicism could not provide them with a positive programme for building a better world, and for this reason it was replaced by a more dynamic moral philosophy—Christianity. Like Stoicism, Christianity is a philosophy of consolation which offers guidance to men in time of trouble; but unlike Stoicism, it also suggests constructive measures which they can take to overcome their difficulties.

CHRISTIAN ETHICS

When one studies the history of Christianity, one is quickly impressed by the variety of doctrines which have been subsumed under that name. It soon becomes evident that there is no *homogeneous* philosophy which can simply be labelled as 'Christian ethics', without considerably distorting the facts, or at least without considerable qualification. For this reason, it would be an almost impossible task to trace the many and often subtle differences among these doctrines. A discussion of heresies alone would fill a tome, not to mention any attempt to follow the variations within orthodoxy itself. But even conceding that such a multiplicity exists, it seems possible, without undue violence to the subject-matter, to distinguish three main streams of ethical thought which can be labelled as 'Christian', and we will turn to a discussion of these now.

Let us call the first type of Christian ethical thought **'pastoral Christian ethics'**. This name refers to the moral views of certain early Christian sects—views which developed out of **Judaism** and **Persian mystical religions.** They emphasize the **Decalogue** (i.e., Ten Commandments), **ritualistic** practices (e.g., baptism), and the **moral teachings of Christ.** Christ is considered to be a holy prophet, giving divinely inspired guidance for living (e.g., 'As ye sow so shall ye reap.'). We call this sort of outlook 'pastoral' because it has little connection with abstruse philosophical speculation. The subtle controversies which we find in the later writings of the church Fathers are almost entirely unrepresented in early Christianity. Instead, the emphasis is upon **morally correct behaviour.** Metaphysics, when it occurs, is mainly restricted to the beliefs in a supernatural order, a personal God, and immortality. But in all these cases, systematic speculation about the beliefs themselves is lacking—or at least is negligible when compared with later developments.

The second type of Christian ethics is much more analytic than the 'pastoral' standpoint we have just considered. It appears only after the Catholic Church has developed as a social and political, as well as a religious, institution. We may call the ethics of this period 'Church Ethics'. But even Church Ethics, it should be mentioned, has undergone profound and numerous changes in its long history. These changes are due to a number of factors. For example, the influence of Plato and Aristotle upon the Christian Fathers altered the entire Christian conception of 'other-worldliness', bringing to it a metaphysical interpretation which was lacking in pastoral Christianity. Again, the concept of the soul changes from the time of ORIGEN, who regards it as being the same in all human beings, to the time of ST. THOMAS AQUINAS, who considers every soul to be unique. This had important consequences for the **doctrine of immortality**. Other causes of the change in Church Ethics are the following: (*a*) The rise of religious institutions such as the monastery and nunnery led the Church officially to favour **asceticism** and this view greatly affected its doctrines concerning sexual morality. (*b*) The growth of the Church as a factor in political and social life caused its ethical doctrine to vary depending upon the state of the continuing conflict between Church and State over the direction of men's lives. (*c*) Difficulties about the interpretation of Scripture of the sort which finally resulted in Luther's withdrawal from the Church (The Protestant Reformation) also caused some alteration in the official doctrine.

As a result of these influences, the ethical views of ST. AUGUSTINE, which could be regarded as expressing official church philosophy in the fourth century, were considerably revised by St. Thomas in the thirteenth century, and differ so radically in certain respects as to constitute almost a new ethical outlook. A major difference for example was the shift from a moral philosophy based upon Neo-Platonism (in St. Augustine) to a philosophy based upon Aristotle (in St. Thomas).

Finally, the third great change in Christian ethics came about with the Reformation and the development of Protestantism. Protestants rejected the ethical views of Catholicism (as represented by St. Thomas) in many respects (whether the clergy could marry, for example), but even within Protestantism no consistent ethical system has prevailed. It is perhaps not an exaggeration to say that there are nearly as many variations in ethical doctrine among Protestants as there are Protestant sects.

In spite of this considerable diversity, however, all these moral doctrines possess certain features in common which serve to distinguish them from other religious codes such as Judaism, Buddhism and Mohammedanism. Because of the existence of these pervasive traits, we are justified in speaking of 'Christian Ethics' as a single and distinct doctrine. But in doing so, we wish to emphasize that our description will be a highly general one, which does not serve to distinguish the various ethical strains within Christianity from each other; instead, its main function is to bring to light certain basic features which form a common doctrine to which all adhere.

All such ethical views, as can be called 'Christian', assume the existence of a divine being, and they further assume that this being is in some manner identified with Christ. Because of the latter assumption, Christianity can be sharply distinguished from Judaism, for example. Christian sects vary in the powers they ascribe to the divine being, and they also disagree about the exact relation the divine being has to Christ. In some it is the relation of simple identity; in others this is not so (e.g., the conflicts that arose between the Monophysites, the Nestorians and orthodox Christians). Similar differences exist with respect to an interpretation of the nature of Christ (to what extent He is human, to what extent divine).

However, even those early Christian sects which denied that Christ was identical with God agreed at least that God made His will known by means of Christ; hence the preachings of Christ about the proper way for men to live are assumed by all Christian moral theories to be the expressions of the divine will.

The preachings of Christ, together with certain other ethical prescriptions such as the Decalogue and certain of the writings in the New Testament, are regarded as forming a moral 'code'. A man is considered by all Christian doctrines to be behaving rightly in so far as he behaves in accordance with the code, and immorally in so far as he violates any of its provisions, such as 'Thou Shalt Not Steal'.

Christian ethics may thus be summarized as the view that there is a divine being who has laid down certain rules for moral behaviour, and that correct conduct consists in acting in accordance with these rules and incorrect conduct consists in violating them.

In actual practice, however, Christian sects are not in agreement about which rules make up Christian conduct. For example, the practice of birth control is regarded as immoral by Catholics but is not so regarded by most Protestant sects. In order to understand why Christian religions can differ in practice, even though they all agree to the above theoretical picture, we must refer to a distinction between what has been called 'ethical theory', and what has been called 'casuistry'. Roughly speaking, casuistry is applied ethics. Once one decides what is good or bad in general (and this is the function of ethical theory—Hedonists, for instance, decide that pleasure is the sole good), then one can go further and compile a list of things which are conducive to the production of goodness and things which are conducive to the production of badness. **Casuistry is the practice of compiling such lists.** Now the difference between the various Christian moral codes concerning practical conduct can be regarded not so much as a difference in theory as it is a casuistical difference; they all agree that God has ordained a system of rules which must be followed; but they disagree as to which rules belong to the system, and this latter disagreement may be regarded as **one of casuistry, not of theory**. Of course, not all disagreements between various forms of Christianity should be regarded as differences about which rules belong to the system; quite frequently, they may agree that a certain rule belongs, but still interpret it differently. This kind of difficulty often arises when one tries to apply teachings of the past to those problems of the present (such as the problem of birth control) that were not envisaged when the original statements of the doctrine were made.

We cannot, of course, here follow out the casuistical differences between the forms of Christianity, but in order to indicate the nature of casuistry, as opposed to ethical theory, we shall examine some of the pronouncements of St. Thomas concerning sexual morality. These pronouncements still form the orthodox outlook of the Catholic Church upon such matters. According to St. Thomas, there are certain general ways in which men should behave—for instance, they should love God and their neighbours. There are also certain specific ways in which they should not behave. For example, the moral code disapproves of adultery. It also forbids sexual relations between husband and wife save for the purpose of procreation—that is why birth control is prohibited. Divorce is not allowed because the father is essential in the education of the children.

Turning from these injunctions to more theoretical matters, the general view of Christian ethics (regardless of sect) is that the good life for man consists in the love of God, and that this good life can be attained by behaving in accordance with God's precepts (i.e., by behaving in accordance with the rules ordained by God, as interpreted by the clergy).

In speaking of Christian ethics, we have not stressed what is perhaps its most important element from a standpoint of theoretical ethics: its **authoritarianism**. The church regards the moral code as an **objective and infallible** guide to correct behaviour, which cannot therefore be questioned. This is because **the code is regarded as an expression of God's will.** Anyone who deviates from its precepts is by definition behaving immorally.

In practice, Christian sects have divided over how one is to discover God's will. 'Fundamentalist' sects stress the written word, as found in the Bible, as literally revealing God's will. Catholics hold that the Church is the 'vicar' of God, and that His will is expressed through the edicts of the Church. Protestants who refuse to accept this doctrine maintain that the relation between man and God is a *personal* one, requiring no intermediary; and that finally in deciding what God wishes, one must consult his own conscience. The theoretical exposition of a 'conscience theory' is to be found most clearly stated in the writings of BISHOP BUTLER.

CRITICISM OF CHRISTIAN ETHICS

The success of Christian ethics can be measured both by its endurance through immense social and political changes over a period of almost 2000 years, and by the fact that it has been widely accepted all over the world. In the latter respect, Christianity is strikingly more successful than Judaism, which is similar in its ability to persist through difficult times. But many philosophers have had serious reservations about Christianity, for reasons which we shall consider now.

The major difficulty with Christian ethics stems from its assumption that the moral code expresses God's will. A violation of the code is thus equivalent to disobedience towards accepted authority. Immorality in this view is equated with disobedience. Some philosophers have pointed out that this is an acceptable moral position only if it can be shown that God is good. Why obey the prescriptions of a divine being who may be evil? And why is disobedience in itself bad if one is disobedient towards a malevolent authority? At this point, Christian ethics is faced with a dilemma. Either it must be *proved* instead of being *assumed*, that God is good, or one must attempt to justify God's precepts on purely ethical grounds, rather than on theological ones. Both tasks offer major difficulties. For example, the existence of evils such as pestilence, plague, cruelty, premature death, disease seem powerful arguments against the unqualified goodness of God; if one adopts the other alternative and attempts to justify Christian ethics on non-theological grounds then he seems to be sacrificing what is distinctive in the theory.

However, there is another argument that is put forward by many people to stress the need for a non-theological justification of Christian ethics. We have seen the importance Aristotle placed on understanding and his insistence that an action is moral only if done from free choice and in full knowledge of the situation. Many people feel that this is an essential prerequisite of any moral action. This view of the nature of morality precludes actions done out of obedience—even to the will of God—from being regarded as truly moral. To act morally we must do something **because it is right** and not merely because God says we must. Hence some non-theological justification of Christian ethics seems necessary.

This becomes apparent when we consider the effects of arguments which deny or at least question the existence of God. If God does not exist, then it is impossible to justify the moral code as expressing His will. Philosophers who were atheists or agnostics, such as the British **Utilitarians**, could not accept this sort of justification. They frequently agreed with many of the particular moral laws of Christianity (e.g., 'Thou Shalt Not Steal'), but felt they had to be justified ultimately on non-religious grounds.

A third difficulty arises, even within Christianity, over how we can decide what God ordains. If we accept the writings in the Bible as evidence of God's will, then God's will can be shown to be inconsistent. To avoid these inconsistencies some interpretation of the Bible is required—and this is in any case necessary if we are to show how the teachings of the Bible relate to present-day problems—but then it is open to a critic to challenge the authority of the interpretation. If we take the Catholic position that the Church knows God's will, we fall into similar difficulties, and if we finally abide by the authority of conscience, then when men's consciences differ, we have as many authorities as we have differing intuitions. Who is to decide whose conscience really expresses God's will?

Puzzled by such questions, some philosophers have felt that it was necessary to think about ethical problems independently of any official doctrine. This led, in some cases, to systems which were incompatible with Christianity. We turn to one such now—the philosophy of BARUCH SPINOZA.

THE PHILOSOPHY OF SPINOZA

The estimation of Spinoza as a philosopher has varied considerably since his death in 1677. Some critics unhesitatingly label him as the greatest of all ethicists. Others who read the intricate body of discourse in which most of his ethical opinions are found, *The Ethics*, consider it to be a collection of muddles. They hold that it is confused in two ways: first, because it uses the geometrical method of Euclid to attempt to arrive at ethical conclusions which these critics contend is a method not fitting to moral subjects. Second, they argue that the system is poorly constructed. The definitions of crucial terms are often not clear, and certain proofs of the theorems do not go through. But both of these opinions are now regarded by the majority of philosophers as extreme. The consensus seems to be that, even granting the defects of his methodology, Spinoza must be reckoned one of the towering figures in the history of Ethics. Those who adhere to this appraisal say it is no overestimation to rank him as **one of the two or three greatest writers on morals to appear in the European tradition since the time of the Greeks.**

Spinoza was born on November 24, 1634, in Amsterdam, where his family had settled as Jewish refugees from the Inquisition in Spain and Portugal (his name was originally spelled 'de Espinoza'). Spinoza was brought up in both the Jewish and secular philosophical traditions. Biblical and Talmudic studies formed the core of his early education and he is known to have been familiar with the works of certain medieval Jewish philosophers, such as ABRAHAM IBN EZRA, MOSES MAIMONIDES, as well as with non-Jewish philosophers such as DESCARTES. As a result of his studies in secular philosophy, Spinoza rejected the teachings of the Jews and was excommunicated from the Jewish community. The excommunicating document reads, in part, as follows:

> The heads of the Ecclesiastical Council hereby make known that already well assured of the evil opinions and doings of Baruch de Espinoza, they have endeavoured in sundry ways and by various promises to turn him from his evil courses, But as they have been unable to bring him to any better way of thinking: on the contrary, as they are every day better certified of the horrible heresies entertained and avowed by him, and of the insolence with which these heresies are promulgated and spread abroad, and many persons worthy of credit having borne witness to these in the presence of the said Espinoza, he has been held fully convicted of the same. Review having therefore been made of the whole matter before the Chiefs of the Ecclesiastical Council, it has been resolved, the Councillors assenting thereto, to anathematize the said Espinoza and to cut him off from the people of Israel, and from the present hour to place him in Anathema with the following malediction . . .
> Let him be cursed by the mouths of the Seven Angels who preside over the seven days of the week, and by the mouths of the angels who follow them and fight under their banners. Let him be cursed by the Four Angels who preside over the four seasons of the year,

and by the mouths of all the angels who follow them and fight under
their banners. . . . Let God never forgive him for his sins. Let the
wrath and indignation of the Lord surround him and smoke forever
on his head. Let all the curses contained in the book of the Law fall
upon him. . . . And we warn you, that none may speak with him by
word of mouth nor by writing, nor show any favour to him, nor
be under one roof with him, nor come within four cubits of him,
nor read any paper composed by him.

Driven out by the Jews, and feared by Christians who regarded him
as an atheist, Spinoza spent the remainder of his short life in poverty.
He ground lenses for a living (in fact, he is supposed to have died of a
lung infection contracted from glass dust) and wrote philosophy in
his spare time. In his personal life, Spinoza of all the great philosophers
comes closest to being a saint: on the day of his death he was calm
and unafraid; in his life, in spite of vicious attacks made upon him,
he never became angry, never lost his reasonableness.

In order to understand the attraction which Spinoza's philosophy
has had for subsequent thinkers, we shall here quote at length from
the opening of his unfinished treatise called, *On the Improvement of
the Understanding*, which is one of the most brilliant pieces of philosophical writing in existence. The undogmatic, honest attempt to discover the good life, comes through to the reader with a tremendous
impact. Spinoza writes:

After experience had taught me that all the usual surroundings
of social life are vain and futile; seeing that none of the objects of
my fears contained in themselves anything either good or bad, except
in so far as the mind is affected by them, I finally resolved to inquire
whether there might be some real good having power to communicate itself, which would affect the mind singly, to the exclusion of
all else: whether, in fact, there might be anything of which the
discovery and attainment would enable me to enjoy continuous,
supreme, and unending happiness. I say 'I *finally* resolved,' for at
first sight it seemed unwise willingly to lose hold on what was sure
for the sake of something then uncertain. I could see the benefits
which are acquired through fame and riches, and that I should be
obliged to abandon the quest of such objects, if I seriously devoted
myself to the search for something different and new. I perceived
that if true happiness chanced to be placed in the former I should
necessarily miss it; while, if, on the other hand, it were not so
placed and I gave them my whole attention, I should equally fail.

I therefore debated whether it would not be possible to arrive
at the new principle, or at any rate at a certainty concerning its
existence, without changing the conduct and usual plan of my life;
with this end in view I made many efforts but in vain. For the
ordinary surroundings of life which are esteemed by men (as their
actions testify) to be the highest good, may be classed under the
three heads—Riches, Fame and the Pleasures of Sense: with these
three the mind is so absorbed that it has little power to reflect on
any different good. By sensual pleasure the mind is enthralled to the

extent of quiescence, as if the supreme good were actually attained, so that it is quite incapable of thinking of any other object; when such pleasure has been gratified it is followed by extreme melancholy, whereby the mind, though not enthralled, is disturbed and dulled.

The pursuit of honours and riches is likewise very absorbing, especially if such objects be sought simply for their own sake, inasmuch as they are then supposed to constitute the highest good. In the case of fame the mind is still more absorbed, for fame is conceived as always good for its own sake, and as the ultimate end to which all actions are directed. Further, the attainment of riches and fame is not followed as in the case of sensual pleasures by repentance, but, the more we acquire, the greater is our delight, and consequently, the more we are incited to increase both the one and the other; on the other hand, if our hopes happen to be frustrated we are plunged into the deepest sadness. Fame has the further drawback that it compels its votaries to order their lives according to the opinions of their fellow-men, shunning what they usually shun, and seeking what they usually seek.

When I saw that all these ordinary objects of desire would be obstacles in the way of a search for something different and new—nay, that they were so opposed thereto that either they or it would have to be abandoned, I was forced to inquire which would prove the most useful to me: for, as I say, I seemed to be willingly losing hold on a sure good for the sake of something uncertain. However, after I had reflected on the matter, I came in the first place to the conclusion that by abandoning the ordinary objects of pursuit, and betaking myself to a new quest, I should be leaving a good, uncertain by reasons of its own nature, as may be gathered from what has been said, for the sake of a good not uncertain in its nature (for I sought for a fixed good), but only in the possibility of its attainment.

Further reflection convinced me that if I could really get to the root of the matter, I should be leaving certain evils for a certain good. I thus perceived that I was in a state of great peril, and I compelled myself to seek with all my strength for a remedy, however uncertain it might be—as a sick man struggling with a deadly disease, when he sees that death will surely be upon him unless a remedy be found, is compelled to seek such a remedy with all his strength, inasmuch as his whole hope lies therein. All the objects pursued by the multitude not only bring no remedy that tends to preserve our being, but even act as hindrances, causing the death not seldom of those who possess them, and always of those who are possessed by them. There are many examples of men who have suffered persecution even to death for the sake of their riches, and of men who in pursuit of wealth have exposed themselves to so many dangers that they have paid away their life as a penalty for their folly. Examples are no less numerous of men, who have endured the utmost wretchedness for the sake of gaining or preserving their reputation. Lastly, there are innumerable cases of men who have hastened their death through over-indulgence in sensual pleasure. All these evils seem to have arisen from the fact that happiness or unhappiness is made wholly to depend on the quality of the object which we love. When a thing is not loved, no quarrels will arise concerning it—no sadness will be felt if it perishes—no envy if it is possessed by another—no fear, no hatred, in short, no disturbances of the mind. All these arise from the love of what is perishable, such as the objects already mentioned. But love towards a thing eternal and infinite feeds the mind wholly with joy, and is itself unmingled with any sadness, wherefore it is greatly to be desired and sought for with all our strength. Yet it was not at random that I used the words, 'If I could go to the root of the matter,' for, though what I have urged was perfectly clear to my mind, I could not forthwith lay aside all love of riches, sensual enjoyment, and fame. One thing was evident, namely that while my mind was employed with these thoughts it turned away from its former objects of desire, and seriously considered the search for a new principle; this state of things was a great comfort to me, for I perceived that the evils were not such as to resist all remedies. Although these intervals were at first rare, and of very short duration, yet afterwards, as the true good became more and more discernible to me, they became more frequent and more lasting; especially after I had recognized that the acquisition of wealth, sensual pleasure or fame, is only a hindrance, so long as they are sought as ends, not as means; if they be sought as means, they will be under restraint, and, far from being hindrances, will further not a little the end for which they are sought, as I will show in due time.

I will here only briefly state what I mean by true good, and also what is the nature of the highest good. In order that this may be rightly understood, we must bear in mind that the terms good and evil are only applied relatively, so that the same thing may be called both good and bad, according to the relations in view, in the same way as it may be called perfect or imperfect. Nothing regarded in its own nature can be called perfect or imperfect; especially when we are aware that all things which come to pass, come to pass according to the eternal order and fixed laws of Nature. However, human weakness cannot attain to this order in its own thoughts, but meanwhile man conceives a human character much more stable than his own, and sees that there is no reason why he should not himself acquire such a character. Thus he is led to seek for means which will bring him to this pitch of perfection, and calls everything which will serve as such means a true good. The chief good is that he should arrive, together with other individuals if possible, at the possession of the aforesaid character. What that character is we shall show in due time, namely, that it is the knowledge of the union existing between the mind and the whole of Nature. This, then, is the end for which I strive: to attain such a character myself, and to endeavour that many should attain to it with me.

The essence of Spinoza's moral philosophy is contained in the above quotation, but in a highly condensed form. Let us try in what follows to expand and perhaps clarify it.

To begin with, **Spinoza is a rigid determinist.** As he says, 'All things which come to pass, come to pass according to the eternal order and fixed laws of Nature.' In holding this view, **Spinoza was in the metaphysical tradition of the Stoics and of Descartes.** No man is free to act capriciously or by chance; all actions are determined by his past experience, his physical and mental constitution, and by the state of the laws of Nature at that moment. Secondly, **Spinoza is a relativist. He holds that nothing is good or bad in itself, but is only so in relation to someone.** Thus, it makes no sense, he avers, to say that castor oil is inherently good; it is good relative to a given person in particular circumstances. If one is ill and castor oil helps him recover, then in those circumstances it can be declared to be good for that individual. But if one is suffering from an inflamed appendix and takes castor oil, and if doing so should kill him, then it would not be good under those conditions for him. Since the same thing (e.g., castor oil) may at different times affect the same person differently, the goodness or badness of such a thing cannot be considered as an *inherent* property of it, like its density, but only as a property which comes into existence depending upon what relation it has to a human being. This view of goodness or badness is important, because it leads Spinoza to the position that riches, fame and sensual pleasure are not *inherently* worthwhile. They are not worth acquiring for their own sakes, **but only as means to making human life more happy.** When these things affect men in desirable ways, they are good; but when they affect them in undesirable ways, they are bad. As Spinoza says. 'There are many examples of men who have suffered persecution even to death for the sake of their riches, and of men who in pursuit of wealth have exposed themselves to so many dangers that they have paid their life as a penalty for their folly.'

Given, therefore, the two facts that all events are determined by natural laws so that men are not free, and also that things are not good or bad in themselves, then what does the good life for man consist in? According to Spinoza, such a life consists in the possession of a certain attitude towards the world. This attitude is in part emotional and in part rational. **The rational part of it consists in the recognition of the truth that all events are determined; the emotional part in an acceptance of this fact.** It is, as he says, 'the knowledge of the union existing between the mind and the whole of Nature'.

To put it otherwise, **Spinoza is arguing that a man will be happy when he comes to understand that there are limits to human power; by understanding that everything which happens must happen necessarily, one will no longer dissipate his energy in struggling against these events.** If a friend dies, it is pointless to give vent to emotion; it is part of the natural pattern. By looking at every event as part of a larger system ('in the context of eternity', to use his phrase), one will no longer be upset and frightened by the events that occur in his life. In this way, he can live a happy life.

Spinoza's philosophy can thus be interpreted as offering guidance to men which, if followed, will enable them to avoid fear, anxiety and unhappiness. These arise only when we become slaves to our emotions

—the man who does not take the broad view is a man 'in human bond-age'. But he can liberate himself by understanding that the course of nature is predestined and also by understanding that 'nothing is good or bad in itself', but that it only becomes good or bad according to how it affects us. By adjusting our outlook, we can finally develop an attitude towards the world which will liberate us from our emotional slavery to it—and when this happens we will be living the good life.

As we have already pointed out, Spinoza's masterpiece is *The Ethics*. This great work is regarded by many philosophers as one of the most difficult philosophical texts to understand; hence any interpretation of Spinozistic philosophy, such as the one we have given above which is in part based on *The Ethics*, must be considered by the reader as a brief introduction rather than as a definitive account.

The Ethics ends with a famous passage, which briefly summarizes the book. Spinoza writes:

> I have finished everything I wished to explain concerning the power of the mind over the emotions and concerning its freedom. From what has been said we see what is the strength of the wise man and how much he surpasses the ignorant who is driven forward by lust alone. For the ignorant man is not only agitated by external causes in many ways and never enjoys true peace of soul, but lives also ignorant, as it were, both of God and of things, and as soon as he ceases to suffer ceases also to be. On the other hand, the wise man in so far as he is considered as such, is scarcely ever moved in his mind, but, being conscious by a certain external necessity of himself, of God, and of things, never ceases to be and always enjoys true peace of soul. If the way which, as I have shown, leads hither seem very difficult, it can nevertheless be found. It must indeed be difficult, since it is so seldom discovered, for if salvation lay ready to hand and could be discovered without great labour, how could it be possible that it should be neglected almost by everybody? But all noble things are as difficult as they are rare.

CRITICISM OF SPINOZA

Spinoza's ethics has difficulties similar to those we find in Stoicism. To begin with, **Spinoza did not effectively resolve the conflict that exists between determinism and freedom.** He believed that if a man could come to understand that what comes to pass *must* come to pass, he could learn to accept this fact and in this way could achieve 'peace of mind'. But if all events in nature are determined, then one is essentially powerless to alter his attitudes. Either he will be determined to have the sort of attitude Spinoza suggests or he will be determined not to have it. But if the latter, there is nothing he can do about acquiring it.

A second difficulty concerns the Spinozistic doctrine of taking the broad view of human life, or the view '*sub specie aeternitatis*', as he puts it—'in the context of eternity'. At times this is useful advice to follow; men do become enslaved by their emotions in trivial causes. But at other times this is not so. Plain men believe there are occasions when they should feel deeply about the things that happen to them; to suggest that men should never feel this way would be *to eliminate some of the most profound of human experiences*. If followed, such an ethic might, for example, make artistic creation impossible. Moreover, in a significant sense, it would seem to violate human nature, since some men are temperamentally so constructed that it is psychologically impossible for them to adopt the Spinozistic outlook. For these reasons, such an ethic could not be expected to have a widespread and permanent appeal—and this has indeed been the fate of Spinoza's system.

UTILITARIANISM: JEREMY BENTHAM AND J. S. MILL

Utilitarianism has had a long and vigorous existence as a moral theory. It is still accepted by many American and British philosophers, although the original form of the theory has been somewhat modified in current versions. One of the earliest exponents of Utilitarianism was FRANCIS HUTCHESON, who is known to have advocated it in 1725; DAVID HUME's moral theory has also been interpreted as being a form of Utilitarianism. The most famous exponents of it, however, are JEREMY BENTHAM (1748–1832) and JOHN STUART MILL (1808–1873).

Both Bentham and Mill had very interesting lives. Bentham was an extremely shy and sensitive person, who always felt insecure in the company of strangers. He wrote voluminously but published practically nothing of his own volition; friends would literally force him to publish material and when he refused, they would surreptitiously publish it for him. Yet this man became one of the most controversial figures of the nineteenth century in England. In spite of his recluse tendencies, he became the head of a group of reformers called 'The Philosophical Radicals' who were to a great extent responsible for social and political changes in England; the British criminal code, for instance, was considerably improved because of the efforts of Bentham and his group.

Bentham opposed both monarchy and hereditary aristocracy, advocated complete democracy, including women's suffrage, and opposed British imperialism in India and the other colonies. In matters of religion he was an atheist.

John Stuart Mill is perhaps the most incredible prodigy in the history of philosophy. His father, JAMES MILL, who was a disciple and friend of Bentham, was greatly influenced by the Benthamite doctrine that a man's character and even his intellect can be completely determined by his education. As a result, John Stuart Mill was not allowed to go to public school, but was very carefully educated from infancy under the tutelage of his father. His achievements were amazing: at the age of eight he had mastered several languages, and by the time he was twelve, had worked carefully through many of the great literary and philosophical classics. Mill's *Autobiography*, which is mainly concerned with relating the story of his education, is a fascinating document revealing the psychological effects of this kind of training upon a young man.

The Utilitarians conceived of their philosophical work as **an attempt to lay down an objective principle for determining when a given action was**

right or wrong. They called this maxim the **Principle of Utility. The Principle states: an action is right in so far as it tends to produce the greatest happiness for the greatest number.** Bentham interpreted this principle as a form of Hedonism by identifying happiness with pleasure. Interpreted in this way, the principle states that an action is right if it is productive of the greatest amount of pleasure for the greatest number; otherwise it is wrong. However, it is not necessary to interpret Utilitarianism in this way, and as we shall show later, many modern philosophers who are Utilitarians are not Hedonists. **The essence of Utilitarianism as a philosophy is that it lays stress upon the effects which an action has. If an action produces an excess of beneficial effects over harmful ones, then it is right; otherwise it is not.** The fundamental point is this: the *consequences* of a given action determine its rightness or wrongness, not the *motive* from which it is done. We all know of cases where men act from the best intentions yet do something which has horrible consequences. Hitler may well have acted from a desire to improve Germany by killing the Jews, yet his acts led to torture, pain, genocide, and to the ultimate destruction of Germany itself. The Utilitarians would thus condemn his behaviour on the grounds that the effects of his actions produced a balance of pain over pleasure, and hence were wrong for that reason.

They regarded this principle as being completely objective. In terms of it, anybody could measure whether an action was right or wrong. For example, if we accept Hedonism, it becomes a purely scientific matter to determine whether a given action caused an excess of pleasure over pain for the greatest number. We merely calculate the amount of pleasure the act caused, and the amount of pain, and we have our answer as to whether it was right or wrong. Bentham even went so far as to develop in detail a method of making such calculations, which he called **The Hedonic Calculus.** This calculus has seven ingredients which allow one to measure the amount of pleasure or pain an act causes —ingredients such as the *intensity* of the pleasure, its *duration*, and so on.

The main result of Utilitarianism as a moral theory is to separate the rightness or wrongness of an action from the goodness or badness of the agent who performs the action. A man may be morally good in the sense that he may always act from good intentions (e.g., he may always act from a sense of honesty or from the desire to tell the truth). But the worth of the *action* is to be distinguished from the worth of the *agent*; for as we have indicated a man may be morally good and yet do something which has undesirable effects. If so, Utilitarians would pronounce the action wrong in spite of its being done from good motives.

Utilitarianism has often been regarded as a **political philosophy which entails democratic government as a political institution.** Whether this is so or not is a difficult question to answer briefly, but it is easy to see how the belief arose. To begin with, the great Utilitarians were democratically minded. They fought for civil liberties and for women's suffrage, for the conduct of government by law, and so on. This served to identify their philosophical doctrines with democratic causes. Secondly, in regarding each man as of equal importance in calculating the amount of pleasure and pain an action evoked, their views came to be identified with the democratic tenet that each man counts equally before the law. And finally, the rightness or wrongness of an act is to be determined by how it affects the majority—and this seemed to point to rule by the majority, another provision of democracy.

CRITICISM OF UTILITARIANISM

Let us turn now to some of the objections which have been made to Utilitarianism:

There are both theoretical and practical difficulties about how to determine how much happiness (i.e., pleasure) an action causes. For example, it is assumed by Bentham that in computing the amount of happiness or unhappiness an action creates, each man will count equally for one unit of happiness. Thus, we add up the number of men who are made happy by the act, add up the number of those made unhappy, and presumably we can then determine whether the act produces an excess of happiness over unhappiness. Some philosophers, such as NIETZSCHE, objected violently to this assumption. Nietzsche believed that **some people were inherently more important than others;** their happiness or unhappiness counted for more than the happiness or unhappiness of the average man. He described John Stuart Mill as a 'blockhead' for this presupposition. Nietzsche wrote about Mill as follows:

> I abhor the man's vulgarity when he says 'What is right for one man is right for another.' Such principles would fain establish the whole of human traffic *upon mutual services*, so that every action would appear to be a cash payment for something done to us. The hypothesis here is ignoble to the last degree; it is taken for granted that there is some sort of *equivalence in value between my actions and thine.*

A second and perhaps more serious difficulty is this: it is assumed in Utilitarianism that it is the *total* number of effects which must be taken into account before an action can be determined to be right or wrong. If we merely count the immediate amount of pleasure and pain we may be mistaken, since the long-range effects may give different results. Thus, the development and explosion of the A-Bomb upon Japan may have had beneficial effects in ending what could have been a longer war, yet the long-range effects of such weapons may be highly undesirable. But this leads to a theoretical difficulty, for if we can never assess the rightness or wrongness of an act until we know *all* of its effects, we shall have to wait infinitely long before declaring an act to be right or wrong, since there may be an infinite number of effects. The Principle of Utility was developed as a practical test for deciding whether an action is right or wrong, but if we cannot apply the principle until *all* the effects are known, **then its practical value is** useless, particularly as what we require of a moral principle is that it should help us to decide in advance what the right course of action is.

The objection we have just mentioned is usually countered by Utilitarians who say the rightness or wrongness of an action can be determined with a high degree of probability without waiting for all the consequences to happen. Thus, a man should do the act that seems most likely, according to probability theory, to have desirable consequences in the long run. But when we interpret the theory in this way, we introduce another difficulty which the theory was expressly created to avoid. The rightness or wrongness of an action now apparently depends upon *subjective* considerations. It seems to depend upon a man's belief that the act in question is *likely* to have desirable consequences. A man may believe this, act in accordance with the best scientific information about the probable consequences of his action, and yet the act may not have the effects he believed it would have. He may be mistaken, as future events will show. Are we then to say he acted wrongly in acting upon the best probabilities, or are we to say he acted rightly? Either answer has difficulties for the theory. If we maintain he acted rightly—but was mistaken—then we have given up the view that a right action is one which *in fact* has the most desirable consequences in the long run; on the other hand, if we adopt the position that he acted wrongly in acting from subjective considerations, we seem to be saddled with a criterion which cannot be used for practical purposes.

Another objection to Utilitarianism is that it violates the beliefs of plain men who frequently think our actions cannot be properly evaluated apart from some concern about the *motives* from which they are done. Men hesitate to say that an act is right when it is done from an evil motive (such as the intention to cheat someone) just because it has desirable effects. One consequence of Utilitarianism is that a world in which everybody acted from evil motives and yet had all their acts turn out to be desirable would be a good world; but the thought of actually living in such a world would be highly repugnant to men of common sense. Thus, the theory if pushed to the extreme seems to have implications which many men would not accept.

Some philosophers have accordingly rejected Utilitarianism on the ground that consideration in assessing the moral worth of an action must be given to the motive from which it was done. Let us turn to one such view now—the moral theory of IMMANUEL KANT.

KANTIAN ETHICS

Although Kant is mainly famous for his work in the theory of knowledge and in metaphysics, he believed that ethics was the most important subject in philosophy. He even used ethical arguments to establish the existence of God after showing that all proofs derived from so-called 'pure reason' are invalid. His argument is that the moral law requires that men be rewarded proportionately to their virtue. Since in everyday life men who are not virtuous may often be happier and more successful than men who are, such rewards evidently are not assured in this life. He therefore infers that there must be another existence where men are so rewarded, and this leads him to the conclusion that there is a God and an eternal life.

Like his work in metaphysics and epistemology (the theory of knowledge) Kant's contribution to ethical theory is of a very high order; but as one who has glanced at Kant's writings in those areas might expect, his writings in ethics are difficult to understand, and even more difficult to summarize. This is in part due to the compactness of his style, to the use of many technical terms, and in part to the awkwardness of his mode of expression; but it is also due in part to the subtle cast of his ideas, and to the fine distinctions he draws. Nevertheless let us try here to state the main points of his theory as simply as possible, illustrating these points with relevant quotations.

The main question which Kant's moral theory was designed to answer is: **'What is the nature of morality?'** This question can also be put in different ways: **'What is a moral action as contrasted with a non-moral one?'**, or again, 'What is the difference between a man who acts morally and one who does not?' Kant believed that this question, or set of questions, could be answered and that the key to it lay in distinguishing between **acts done from 'inclination' and acts done from a 'sense of duty'.** What then is meant by these terms?

Men often indulge in a certain course of action because they are forced to. For instance, if I am waylaid by a thief, I will be forced to turn my money over to him if I have any, or if I refuse, I am forced to suffer the consequences. In such a case, we would not ordinarily describe my actions as being 'voluntary actions', or 'actions done because I wanted to'. Nor would we say that I was 'doing my duty'. In this instance, I am not a free agent; I am properly described as not acting either from 'inclination' or 'from duty' but rather as 'being compelled to do so'. Hence, it is a requisite of any act's being done from 'inclination' or from 'duty' **that it be the act of a free agent.** Now obviously men are often free in the above sense—nobody is forcing them to behave in a certain way, or otherwise constraining their behaviour. For instance, I am free tonight either to go to a movie or to stay home and read a book, or even to continue to type this chapter. In a significant sense, it is up to me which of these I will do. But which of these *ought* I to do? If I have promised my publisher to finish this chapter tonight, then I am under an 'obligation' to continue to work on it. On the other hand, if the matter is not pressing, if there exists no 'demand' on me, we could say that it is a matter of 'taste' or 'inclination' which I should do. I should do that which I want to do, or which it pleases me to do, provided, of course, that no obligation exists which it is my duty to do. Now, as can be seen from this example, **'inclination' is to be distinguished from 'obligation'. An obligation is that which a man ought to do despite his inclinations to do otherwise.** Once under an obligation, a man ought to attempt to fulfil it. If no obligation exists, then it becomes a matter of inclination or of taste which he should do.

Now some philosophers have held that in matters of morality one should act upon his inclinations. He should do that act which pleases him, or which he wants to do in those circumstances; but Kant strongly rejects such an account of morality. He feels that **a man is acting morally only when he suppresses his feelings and inclinations, and does that which he is obliged to do.** Thus 'doing one's duty', is doing something which one is not inclined or willing to do, but which he does because he recognizes that he ought to do it; an obligation exists and he must fulfil it. Thus a man who does something merely because he is afraid *not* to do it (such as the fear of being imprisoned for not repaying a debt) is not a moral person: nor is a man moral who repays a debt merely because he wants to, or inclines towards doing that rather than something else. It is only when a man recognizes that he *ought* to repay a debt because he has incurred an obligation that he is genuinely a moral person. **Thus morality, as Kant sees it, is closely bound up with one's duties and obligations.**

One further point must be made before we can proceed to other elements of Kant's moral theory. It is important to distinguish actions which are 'in accord with duty' from those done 'from duty', as Kant puts it. The former are not necessarily moral acts, but the latter are. For instance, most parents are inclined to take care of their children; they may be so inclined because they are fond of them, or because they fear police action if they neglect them. But anyone who takes care of his children for these reasons is not acting morally. He is acting 'in accord with duty', but not 'from duty'. He would be acting from duty only if he recognized that he has a special obligation to his children because they are his children. A man who understands the nature of this obligation and acts upon it is moral; otherwise he is not. Kant explains this brilliantly in the following passage from his *Theory of Ethics*.

I omit here all actions which are already recognized as inconsistent with duty, although they may be useful for this or that purpose, for with these the question whether they are done *from duty* cannot arise at all, since they even conflict with it. I also set aside those actions which really conform to duty, but to which men have no direct inclination, performing them because they are impelled thereto by some other inclination. For in this case we can readily distinguish whether the action which agrees with duty is done *from duty* or from a selfish view. It is much harder to make this distinction when the action accords with duty, and the subject has besides a *direct* inclination to it. For example, it is always a matter of duty that a dealer should not overcharge an inexperienced purchaser; and wherever there is much commerce the prudent tradesman does not overcharge, but keeps a fixed price for everyone, so that a child buys of him as well as any other. Men are thus *honestly* served; but this is not enough to make us believe that the tradesman has so acted from duty and from principles of honesty; his own advantage required it; it is out of the question in this case to suppose that he might besides have a direct inclination in favour of the buyers so that, as it were, from love he should give no advantage to one over another. Accordingly, the action was done neither from duty nor from direct inclination, but merely with a selfish view.

On the other hand, it is a duty to maintain one's life; and in addition, everyone has also a direct inclination to do so. But on this account the often anxious care which most men take for it has no intrinsic worth, and their maxim no moral import. They preserve their life *as duty requires*, no doubt, but not *because duty requires*. On the other hand, if adversity and hopeless sorrow have completely taken away the relish for life; if the unfortunate one, strong in mind, indignant at his fate, rather than desponding or dejected wishes for death, and yet preserves his life without loving it—not from inclination or fear but from duty—then his maxim has a moral worth.

As can be seen from the above quotation, Kant differs sharply from the Utilitarians in stressing that **the essence of morality is to be found in the motive from which an act is done.** All such motives reduce to one —that a **man is moral when he acts from a sense of duty.** A man who keeps promises by accident, or who repays debts to avoid punishment, or who feels that it is to his advantage in the long run to do so, is not a moral man. He is moral if and only if he understands that he must keep promises and repay debts because it is his duty to do so —regardless of the consequences which doing so or not doing so will bring. Thus, the good man is a man of 'good *will*', i.e., a man who acts from a sense of duty. As Kant puts it in a famous phrase, **'Nothing can possibly be conceived in the world, or even out of it, which can be called good without qualification, except a Good Will.'**

In criticizing Utilitarianism for confusing the results of men's actions with the motives for committing such actions, Kant develops a distinction between **'prudential action'** and **'moral action'.** A man who repays debts because he fears the legal consequences acts from a sense of prudence; he is not a moral person. He would be moral only if he acted from the sense that he has incurred a monetary obligation and thus is 'duty bound' to repay it. Kant's criticism of Utilitarianism is contained in the following passage:

A good will is good not because of what it performs or effects, not by its aptness for the attainment of some proposed end, but simply by virtue of the volition, that is, it is good in itself, and considered by itself is to be esteemed much higher than all that can be brought about by it in favour of any inclination, nay, even of the sum total of all inclinations. Even if it should happen that, owing to special disfavour of fortune, or the niggardly provision of a step-motherly nature, this will should wholly lack the power to accomplish its purpose, if with its greatest efforts it should yet achieve nothing, and there should remain only the good will (not, to be sure, a mere wish, but the summoning of all means in our power), then, like a jewel, it would still shine by its own light, as a thing which has its whole value in itself. Its usefulness or fruitlessness can neither add to nor take away anything from this value. . . . Let the question be, for example: May I when in distress make a promise with the intention not to keep it? I readily distinguish here between the two significations which the question may have: Whether it is prudent, or whether it is right, to make a false promise? The former may undoubtedly often be the case. I see clearly that it is not enough to extricate myself from the present difficulty by means of this subterfuge, but it must be well considered whether there may not hereafter spring from this lie much greater inconvenience than that from which I now free myself, and as, with all my supposed cunning, the consequences cannot be so easily foreseen but the credit once lost may be much more injurious to me than any mischief which I seek to avoid at present, it should be considered whether it would not be more *prudent* to act herein according to a universal maxim, and to make it a habit to promise nothing except with the intention of keeping it. But it is soon clear to me that such a maxim will still be based on the fear of consequences. Now it is a wholly different thing to be truthful from duty, and to be so from apprehension of injurious consequences.

In short, we may summarize Kant's answer to the question: 'What is a moral action as contrasted with a non-moral one?' as follows: A moral action is one done **from a respect for duty,** and correspondingly, a moral person is a person who acts **from duty,** not from **inclination** or even **in accord with duty.**

With the above distinctions, Kant has outlined the sphere of morality for us. He has indicated the difference between behaving morally and not behaving morally; but this outline does not complete his system of morals. A man may still not *know* what his duty will be in a given situation. Is there any test for determining what one's duty will be in a particular set of circumstances? Kant answers that there is. Since human beings are rational creatures they ought to behave in a rational way, and for Kant this means that one ought always to behave as if one's course of conduct were to become a universal law. That is, **every action must be judged in the light of how it would appear if it were to be a universal code of behaviour.** This is why lying, even if it is expedient, cannot be accepted as moral under *any* circumstances; for if we were to regard lying as a universal law to which people ought to conform, we could see that morality would be impossible. On this point, Kant writes as follows:

The shortest way, however, and an unerring one, to discover the answer to the question whether a lying promise is consistent with duty, is to ask myself, should I be content that my maxim (to extricate myself from difficulty by a false promise) should hold good as a universal law, for myself as well as for others? and should I be able to say to myself, 'Everyone may make a deceitful promise when he finds himself in a difficulty from which he cannot otherwise extricate himself'? Then I presently become aware that while I can will the lie, I can by no means will that lying should be a universal law. For with such a law there would be no promises at all, since it would be in vain to allege my intention in regard to my future actions to those who would not believe this allegation, or if they over-hastily did so, would pay me back in my own coin. Hence my maxim, as soon as it should be made a universal law, would necessarily destroy itself. I do not, therefore, need any far-reaching penetration to discern what I have to do in order that my will may be morally good. Inexperienced in the course of the world, incapable of being prepared for all its contingencies, I only ask myself: Canst thou also will that thy maxim should be a universal law? If not, then it must be rejected, and that not because of a disadvantage accruing from it to myself or even to others, but because it cannot enter as a principle into a possible universal legislation, and reason extorts from me immediate respect for such legislation.

The Categorical Imperative. Kant invented a phrase, **'the categorical imperative'**, which makes the above point in a different way. He distinguishes **'the categorical imperative'** from so-called **'hypothetical imperatives'**. A hypothetical imperative is a directive to the effect that if you wish to achieve such and such an end, you must act in such and such a way. Hypothetical imperatives are thus concerned with **prudential action.** For example, if you wish to drive to Liverpool from London by the shortest route, directions for doing so can be given to you by means of a hypothetical imperative: 'If you wish to drive to Liverpool by the shortest route, take roads X, Y and Z'. On the other hand, the categorical imperative enjoins action without any ifs, or without regard to the effect such an action may have. It enjoins you to do such and such *without qualification*. It thus lays down **a rule which, if followed, will ensure that the person behaving in accordance with it is behaving morally.**

Kant formulates the categorical imperative in several different ways, the first of which is this:

'There is therefore but one categorical imperative, namely this: **Act only on that maxim whereby thou canst at the same time will that it should become a universal law.'**

As we have pointed out, Kant means by this statement that a man should always act as if every action were to become a universal law. Thus no man should steal, because if he were to steal and if everyone were to steal (if stealing should become a general rule) then moral relations based upon the possession of private property would become impossible. Similarly with regard to telling lies. One should never lie, since if lying were to become a universal law, all human relations based upon trust and the keeping of promises, would become impossible. In short, the view is that all acts should be entered into as if they were to become general laws—this is what the 'categorical imperative' tells us. If an act which one commits can pass the test of thus being universalized, it will be a moral act.

Another, and equally famous, formulation of the categorical imperative is the following:

'So act as to treat humanity, whether in thine own person or in that of any other, in every case as an end withal, never as a means only.'

This formulation of the categorical imperative has a long tradition in the history of ethics. It is another way of stating such maxims as

'Do unto others as you would have them do unto you.' It is an injunction to us to respect other people because they are rational beings like us. We should treat others as ends in themselves because that is how we regard ourselves. To treat another man **only** as a means to achieving what we want is to disregard his humanity, to treat him like a **thing** and to fail to show due respect for his status as a rational being. Consequently this doctrine has had important consequences for democracy. It supports the democratic view that 'all men are created equal', where this is interpreted to mean that no man should be discriminated against before the law. Certain criticisms directed against this formulation of the categorical imperative have been based upon misunderstanding. If this version of the categorical imperative is interpreted literally, it might be thought to mean that no man's interests and desires should be suppressed. But with such an interpretation, the view has the consequence that when conflicts between men arise it would be impossible for the courts (say) to decide between them; for by deciding against one of the men they would be acting against his interests. Such an interpretation of Kant's view would lead to a form of anarchy, thus making moral life inconsistent with life in society. However, as we have pointed out, such an interpretation of Kant is mistaken. In saying that each man should be treated as an end in himself, Kant is not implying that each man's interests should be granted or acceded to. He is merely saying that in any sort of conflict between men each man must be counted as being of *equal value* in the conflict. Regardless of a man's history, his present social status, or his present economic worth, he is not to be discriminated against. He must be treated equally with other men in the eyes of the law.

CRITICISM OF KANT

Kant's moral view may be regarded as an attempt to save what is valid in such conflicting accounts of the nature of morality as **Platonism** and **Hedonism**. The Platonist stresses the *objectivity* of moral standards, a thesis which Kant accepts (the categorical imperative represents an action as objectively necessary). At the same time, some account of human motives must be taken into consideration in assessing the moral worth of an action. The mistake of the Platonist, on the one hand, is to divorce goodness and badness from human motives in his desire to seek objectivity; the mistake of the Hedonist is to identify moral motivation with the search for pleasure. The Kantian theory is an interesting and plausible one because it attempts to do justice to both of these factors: (*a*) that morality to some extent depends upon human motivation and (*b*) that morality is not merely a matter of inclination or of taste or preference, but is something objective.

Common sense recognizes that morality involves both of these elements. If objectivity is identified, as the Utilitarian would have it, with the kind of effects a man's actions have, then according to Kant common sense would not identify morality with such objectivity. It makes a difference what intentions a man has when he acts. If he acts from 'the best will in the world', but makes a mistake, we do—ordinarily—tend to excuse him. The surgeon who operates upon a patient and kills him through a mistake is not *morally* blamed. He is, as Kant says, regarded as inefficient, as a bungler; but we do not consider him an immoral person merely because he has failed. This shows that some consideration of human motives is necessary in assessing an act as right or wrong. At the same time, Kant points out that morality is not entirely a matter of human motivation if human motivation is regarded as stemming from desire, caprice, or inclination. Some motives are wrong motives (e.g., the search for pleasure). It is only when one acts out of a respect for duty that we regard him as a moral being—and in such cases, he is acting *against* his inclinations.

A further argument in favour of the Kantian view is the common-sense outlook that **to behave morally one must behave consistently, i.e., 'universalize his behaviour'.** It is a legitimate objection to a draft dodger to tell him 'What if everybody behaved as you do?' We do feel that one ought to behave in a consistent way—it is not morally wrong at one time to evade paying your taxes, and morally right at other times to do so. We feel that one should always pay his taxes if he is obliged to do so—one should behave in accordance with a universal rule or maxim.

These considerations show that the Kantian ethic is a highly plausible one. What criticisms can be directed against it? There are three main criticisms which have been made of Kant's view. The first holds that although Kant tried to prove that the moral worth of an action depends only upon the motive from which it is done, in fact he surreptitiously introduces considerations of the *consequences* which an act has into a determination of its rightness or wrongness. For, according to this objection, he is tacitly showing that the *effect* of not behaving in accordance with the categorical imperative would be to make human life as we now know it impossible. For instance, he says, 'Then I presently become aware that while I can will the lie, I can by no means will that lying should be a universal law. For with such a law there would be no promises at all, since it would be in vain to allege my intention in regard to my future actions to those who would not believe this allegation, or if they over-hastily did so, would pay me back in my own coin.' In citing such an example, Kant is referring to the *consequences* of lying (e.g., 'being paid back in my own coin'), so that his theory seems inconsistent in so far as he has not held to his original claim that he is concerned solely with *motive*.

The second major criticism which has been made of Kantian ethics is that it does not handle cases where we have **a conflict of duties**—and these seem to be some of the most pressing and serious types of moral perplexity. Suppose I promise to keep a secret, and then someone else asks me about it. I cannot both tell the truth and keep my promise—yet according to the Kantian position, I should do both. In such a situation, I cannot, logically, universalize my behaviour; if I tell the truth, I will break my promise to keep the secret. If I keep my promise, I will not tell the truth.

A third difficulty, analogous to the above, is that Kant is urging too strong a claim when he insists that we should never tell lies, or never break promises. According to more moderate versions of objectivism, no claim as strong as this need be made. Moral rules are to be interpreted, this objection urges, as *generalizations*, rather than as *categorical* propositions without exception. In general we should tell the truth, but there may occur circumstances where we would feel morally obliged to lie. For example, if a maniac, armed with a revolver, comes looking for a relative in order to kill him, we would consider it highly immoral to inform the maniac of the whereabouts of the relative, merely because one ought to tell the truth. Telling the truth, keeping promises, repaying debts are obligations which one should keep, provided that no other overriding factors are present. W. D. ROSS has called such obligations, **'prima facie duties'**. One is obliged to perform such obligations, provided that no other overriding factors are present; or provided that all other conditions are equal. Such a criticism still allows room for an objective morality, without adhering to what runs contrary to common sense, i.e., that one must *always* tell the truth, *always* keep his promises, *no matter what* circumstances or conditions obtain. Would we not morally disapprove of the captured soldier who gave away military secrets on the ground that he was following the categorical imperative?

With this brief discussion of Kant, we come to the end of the classical views we shall deal with here. The above disquisition should not be regarded as containing a complete discussion of all classical philosophers, but only as a set of introductory remarks to some of the more famous moralists. Such writers as BUTLER, HERBERT SPENCER, NIETZSCHE, SCHOPENHAUER, HUME, LOCKE, HOBBES, ROUSSEAU and LUCRETIUS have not been treated, mainly because they hold views which are either variants of those we have considered, or because they are not now regarded as of first importance.

We turn now to a consideration of modern ethics.

MODERN ETHICS

Definition of 'Modern Ethics'.

As we pointed out in an earlier discussion, so-called 'classical' ethical theories are characterized by their efforts to answer two questions: 'What is the good life for men?' and 'How ought men to behave?' If we examine these questions from a slightly different perspective, we might interpret them as requests for advice by people who are puzzled by certain aspects of daily living. And the various answers which the classical theories give can be regarded as statements of advice to the individual. Thus Hedonism can be regarded as telling men that the good life consists of a life of pleasure, and further that they *ought* to act so as to acquire pleasure.

It is assumed in asking such questions and in giving such answers that the meaning of the questions and the meaning of the answers is clear. But in recent years, philosophers have come to realize that many of these questions and answers are not clear at all; that before we can give an answer to them we must find out *precisely* what they mean. To discover what they mean requires that the questions be clarified. The process of clarifying the meaning of questions and answers is called **philosophical analysis.** The use of this process persistently in modern ethics causes it to differ enormously from ethics pursued in the classical tradition. **The main difference is that one can engage in philosophical analysis without necessarily being committed to giving any sort of advice for living**—for instance, one may analyse a theory like Utilitarianism without necessarily advocating that doctrine. Of course, it is assumed that the process of analysis is not an end in itself; once one becomes clear about the meaning of the crucial terms and statements which occur in moral theories, it is assumed that he will be in a better position to decide which of them he ought to adhere to. Thus, 'modern ethics' is not regarded as an alternative to propounding ethics in the classical tradition so much as it is regarded as a preparation for the further study of such theories.

We might therefore define 'modern ethics' as that branch of philosophy which applies analysis to moral theory. In order to state somewhat more clearly what this definition implies, let us give both an ethical and a non-ethical example of philosophical analysis. Consider, to begin with, a simple word like 'brother'. What does it mean when it occurs in a sentence like 'John is the brother of Joan'. (It will have a different meaning, of course, in a sentence like 'all men are brothers'). In order to answer this query, an analysis of the term 'brother' is required. In order to analyse the meaning of the term, we must find a set of characteristics which belong to all those people who are brothers and only to those. Thus the property of 'having blonde hair', while attributable to some brothers is not a quality which every brother must have in order to be a brother (many things, such as women and dolls, may possess this trait without being brothers). On the other hand, every brother must be male. But being male, it should be noticed, is not sufficient to determine whether someone is a brother or not, since a given person may be male and yet be the only child in the family. If so, he would not be a brother. To be a brother requires not only that he be male, but also that he be a sibling, i.e., stand in the relation to some other person of having a common parent. The complete analysis of 'brother' reveals that it means the same as 'being a male sibling'. In more technical language, 'being a male' and 'being a sibling' provide the correct analysis of the term 'brother' because they give us the **necessary and sufficient conditions** which a person must satisfy in order to be such. To say that 'being a male' is a necessary condition means that no one who is not a male can be a brother. This condition plus the other necessary condition of 'being a sibling' *together* are sufficient conditions for being a brother—anyone who has both characteristics will be a brother. **Philosophical analysis is frequently considered to be the search for the necessary and sufficient conditions which determine the meaning of a term, although this is not its only job.**

Sometimes the phrase 'philosophical analysis' is used to refer to any process which attempts to clarify the meaning of a term, whether or not this process results in the sort of definition we have just

considered (i.e., in a definition which leads to the discovery of necessary and sufficient conditions). Let us now illustrate this sense of
'philosophical analysis', considering an example from ethics.

Suppose we are asked: 'Should Communism be taught in Universities?' Before we attempt to answer this question, we should make a
serious effort to find out what it means. We can do this by fixing on
the main terms which occur in it, such as 'Communism', 'taught', and
'Universities'. For example, the word 'Communism' can refer to the
doctrines advocated in Plato's *Republic*, Marx's *Das Kapital*, Engels'
Anti-Duhring Papers, the present writings of the Soviet Press, and so
on. We thus have here several questions which might be spelled out
as follows: 'Should the writings of Karl Marx be taught in Universities?' or 'Should the writings of Plato be taught in Universities?' and
so on. Again, the word 'teach' requires analysis. Does it mean the
same as 'neutrally expound', or 'advocate', or 'critically assess', or
'attack', or what? As one can see from these examples, a question
which appears at first glance to be simple turns out upon analysis to
be highly complex. One might wish to answer certain interpretations
of it affirmatively but others negatively. **The function of analysis
here is to make the question precise so that we will know how to reply
to it.**

Upon examination, classical moral theories like Hedonism, Utilitarianism, Stoicism, Christianity and so forth, turn out to be highly
complex doctrines. Before we can assess the merits of the advice they
give, we require first of all to understand the advice—and this can be
achieved only if we first analyse the meaning of the terms they use,
such as 'good', 'bad', 'right', 'wrong', 'ought', and so on. Modern
ethics, as contrasted with classical ethics, stresses this task—the task
we have called 'analysis'. Many modern philosophers believe that this
process of analysis shows that the methods of the classical moral philosophers have been mistaken, that the questions they asked were not
sufficiently clearly formulated and that, as a result, their answers have
not the validity they have claimed for them. In other words, many
philosophers now feel that in attempting to give us positive moral
guidance the classical theorists were attempting the impossible and
that the most any moral philosopher can do is to attempt to clarify for
us the implications of the language we use when we are expressing
moral judgments. This is the most important way in which what has
been called the twentieth century revolution in philosophy has affected
moral theory.

If any one philosopher is responsible for this revolution in the
approach to moral philosophy it is G. E. MOORE who claimed in his
Principia Ethica, published in 1903, that the classical theories were
attempts to deduce moral precepts from theological, metaphysical or
scientific premises and that such arguments are fallacious, since one
cannot argue from premises of one logical type (i.e., descriptions) to
conclusions of a different logical type (i.e., prescriptions). This is a
point which David Hume had made much earlier, but Moore developed it to show that what was involved was an attempt to define
moral words like 'good', 'bad' and so on in non-moral terms, in terms

of descriptive statements about God, about some metaphysical entity called 'goodness' or about human nature, i.e., to make 'good' synonymous with 'approved by God', 'conducive to the greatest happiness of the greatest number' and so on. To do this, he claimed, was to leave out of consideration the essential moral or prescriptive element in the meaning of such words. This is what he means when he tells us that 'good', like all moral words, is indefinable and that goodness is a simple, unanalysable property. To attempt to define it is to commit what he called the **Naturalistic Fallacy,** since any attempted definition of moral words will be in terms only of their descriptive meaning and the moral element, which is what we are primarily concerned with, will be lost.

Many philosophers have taken this as an indication that a new approach to the problems of moral philosophy is needed, an approach based on an analysis of the language of morals rather than an examination of factual statements about God, about 'goodness' or about human nature, and they have come to see that moral statements are not analogous to theological, metaphysical or scientific statements but have a peculiar logic of their own.

Let us now turn to a discussion of some modern theories, beginning with various classifications of them.

Classification of Modern Theories. Modern theories are now commonly classified in three different ways. They may be classified (*a*) as either **subjectivist** or **objectivist** or (*b*) as **naturalistic, non-naturalistic** or **emotivist** or (*c*) as **motivist, deontological** or **consequence theories.** In this section we shall briefly define each of these terms and then show why the classifications are important for an understanding of modern ethical theory.

SUBJECTIVISM AND OBJECTIVISM

In beginning a discussion of this classification, it is important to reiterate that **modern ethical theories are primarily concerned with the analysis of the language of morals.** Therefore, a theory will be classified as either subjectivist or objectivist (but not both, of course) depending upon how it analyses ethical language. We **can define the term 'objectivist' by saying that any theory which is non-subjectivist is objectivist.** This raises the question of defining 'subjectivism'.

There are two characteristics which determine a theory to be subjectivist:

(*a*) If the theory holds that what are ordinarily called ethical judgments such as 'Stealing is wrong' are **neither true nor false,** it is subjectivist.

(*b*) If the theory holds that ethical judgments are true or false, but that they are always about the psychology of the person who utters them and only that person, then again it is subjectivist. HOBBES's moral theory is usually interpreted as being subjectivist, because he held that such judgments as 'This is good,' can be analysed into 'I desire this.' Moral language, in his view, merely uses another form of words to speak about one's desires, inclinations, feelings, and so forth. The

moral theory of Kant is also subjectivist according to some interpretations because it analyses ethical judgments into commands, and
commands are neither true nor false (e.g., it makes no sense to say
that 'Right Face!' is either true or false).

Both Platonism and Utilitarianism are objectivist doctrines according to the above definition. Plato held that moral judgments *are*
true or false in exactly the same sense as judgments like 'two plus two
equal four'. Likewise, he held that such statements as 'This is good,'
are not about anyone's psychology, if true, but are about a certain
feature of the world called 'goodness'. Utilitarianism resembles Platonism in both of these respects. Judgments such as 'This is right',
mean 'This will produce an excess of pleasure over pain,' and on this
translation are simply ordinary *scientific* judgments; likewise, although
these judgments are about psychological entities, such as pleasures
and pain, they are not about the speaker's psychology *alone*—but
about the psychology of a number of people. For this reason, such
judgments go beyond the speaker alone, and refer to a group of individuals. In this sense, moral language is not subjective, but objective.
It is important to note, however, that such theories are based on a
view of moral statements as analogous to scientific statements.

This classification is extremely important because it draws attention
to the status of moral standards. If moral standards are merely subjective (like tastes) then there seems to be no way of settling disputes
about whether behaviour is immoral or not. If something tastes sour
to me, and sweet to you, we cannot say I am wrong or that you are
wrong—this is just the way things are. Likewise, if in saying that
'Stealing is wrong,' I am merely asserting 'I dislike stealing,' and if in
saying 'Stealing is right,' you are merely asserting that you like stealing, there seems to be no way of showing that one of us is wrong, the
other right. You feel about it one way, I the other and that is all
there is to it.

The question whether moral judgments are merely subjective pronouncements or not is thus an important one—and we shall consider in the next section arguments for and against both subjectivism
and objectivism.

NATURALISM, NON-NATURALISM AND EMOTIVISM

The classification of theories into those which are naturalistic, non-
naturalistic or emotivist, raises issues which are more academic, but
which are still important. Let us define these terms now, and then
show why the issues they raise are of considerable moment.

A theory will be regarded as **naturalistic** if it holds **both that moral
judgments are true or false, and also that such judgments are reducible
entirely to the concepts of some natural science (usually psychology).**

A theory will be defined as **non-naturalistic** if it holds that **moral
judgments are true or false, but that they are not reducible to any natural
science.**

A theory will be called **'emotivist'** if it contends that **moral judgments
are neither true or false, but are merely expressive of the feelings** of those

who utter them and evocative of the feelings of those who hear them. Since all the judgments of science are *either* true or false, it follows that if the emotivist analysis is correct, moral judgments cannot be reduced to scientific ones.

The importance of the issue which is raised by these classifications is this: is ethics a unique discipline, with laws of its own, or is ethics merely a branch of some science like psychology? If the latter, in order to make valid ethical judgments one would be advised to study science; if not, there is an autonomous body of human knowledge which must be studied in its own right.

Utilitarianism and the Hobbesian moral doctrine can be seen to be naturalistic theories; both contend that **moral judgments are really disguised ways of making psychological assertions** (they merely differ over the question of whether the judgments are subjectivist or not).

Platonism and Christian ethical theories are non-naturalistic doctrines. Plato believed that the world contained **moral entities** (goodness, rightness, etc.) in the same way as it contains *natural* entities, like chairs and tables. Moral judgments, when true, are about these entities and not about the entities found in nature; hence ethics which is the discipline which concerns itself with moral entities, cannot be reduced to one of the known sciences. The same considerations hold for Christian ethics, which regard moral judgments as being expressions of the divine will; these expressions are true or false, but they cannot be confirmed or refuted by scientific experimentation—hence Christian ethics again is non-naturalistic. However, in both Platonism and Christian ethics moral statements, although not being in themselves empirical scientific statements, are nevertheless analogous to statements of this kind since they are assertions about something, i.e., they are **descriptions** of something.

The **emotive theory**, which is supported by a number of modern philosophers—A. J. AYER, C. L. STEVENSON, RUDOLF CARNAP, to mention a few—avers that *both* naturalism and non-naturalism are mistaken. This theory takes up Moore's point and asserts that moral statements are not analogous to scientific statements in that the moral element in them is not an assertion or a description of anything. It agrees with non-naturalism that **moral judgments cannot be verified or falsified by scientific procedures,** and also agrees with naturalistic forms of subjectivism (like Hobbes's position) in holding that **moral judgments are about one's feelings**—but the sense in which they are 'about' these feelings is not that which traditional naturalistic theories have claimed. For moral statements are not descriptions at all. They are not even descriptions of one's feelings. Rather they are expressions of feelings, much as a grunt of pleasure after eating is an expression of satisfaction. Since one would not say that grunts are true or false, **it is a mistake to say that moral judgments, which express feelings, are true or false.**

We shall consider arguments for and against these views in the next section.

MOTIVIST, DEONTOLOGICAL AND CONSEQUENCE THEORIES

The classification of theories into motivist, deontological and consequence doctrines also raises issues of extreme importance. After defining these terms, we shall proceed to a discussion of the issues in question.

A theory will be called a **'motivist ethical theory'**, if it holds that **the rightness or wrongness of an action depends upon the motive from which the act was done.** Kant's ethics is an example of such a theory.

A theory will be called **'a consequence theory'** if it holds that the **rightness or wrongness of an action depends entirely upon the effects which the action has.** Utilitarianism is a classic example of a consequence theory. It is worth mentioning that consequence theories usually fall into two groups: **Hedonistic consequence theories** and **Agathistic consequence theories.** The former hold that the rightness or wrongness of an action depends upon whether it produces consequences which are painful or pleasant; the latter hold that goodness is not to be identified with pleasure, or badness with pain, but is something unique, just as redness is unique and cannot be reduced to anything else. Such a theory was held by G. E. Moore who himself maintained that the rightness or wrongness of an act depends upon the amount of goodness or badness the act produces. It is thus a consequence doctrine, but of a non-Hedonistic sort.

Deontological theories (held by W. D. ROSS, A. C. EWING and H. PRICHARD among others) reject both motivist and consequence theories. They claim that the **rightness or wrongness of an act depends neither upon the motive from which the act was done, nor upon the consequences of the act—but solely upon what kind of an act it was.** Thus, it is right to keep one's promises, because in making a promise one has performed an act which by its very nature obligates one to carry it out, regardless of one's inclinations or the effects which carrying it out will have. Because they stress the notions of 'obligation' and 'duty', deontological theories are often described as 'duty ethics'.

The disagreements among these doctrines have important practical consequences. Consider for instance, the question of punishment. How can we justify punishing criminals? According to motivist theories, we can justify punishing a man if his intentions were evil. If a man kills someone accidentally, we do not punish him; but if his *intentions* were to kill someone whom he hated, we punish him because he acted from bad motives. Consequence theories deny this. They argue that the only justification for punishment is to prevent further crime. If we leave a killing unpunished, then everyone will feel free to kill those whom he hates. We punish men because the *effect* or *consequence* of punishing them will be to deter further crime. Deontologists disagree with both positions. Their view, put roughly, is that we punish men for crimes because the acts they performed were wrong. It is inherently wrong to commit a crime, so that by punishing a man for the crime, we are acting justly. A man who does a good deed deserves to be rewarded; a man who commits a crime, deserves to be punished, and this is the only reason for imposing sanctions upon him.

With these definitions explained, let us now consider some of these issues in greater detail. Let us consider, as a specimen case, the arguments for and against subjectivism and objectivism.

ANALYSIS OF SUBJECTIVISM AND OBJECTIVISM

SUBJECTIVISM

Arguments for. The main argument for subjectivism is the argument based on an analysis of the language that we use to make moral judgments. As we have already seen, such judgments are more than statements or **descriptions** of something. They are also **prescriptions**. They are imperatives—commands to someone—and they are evaluations—expressions of one's own personal values. It is the latter which are the truly moral elements in such judgments and, since these elements are not descriptions, it does not make sense to ask whether they are true or false. Consider what I am saying when I tell a child, 'Stealing is wrong.' I may be telling him that stealing is forbidden by the law of the society we both live in, but this is far from all that that sentence contains. For I am also saying to him **in the same words**, 'Do not steal!' and, in addition, I am expressing my own disapproval of stealing. It does not make sense to ask whether the sentence, 'Do not steal!', is true or false, since it is not an assertion but a command, and equally it is not sensible to ask whether my feelings are true or false. Hence it would appear that all moral judgments must be subjective.

The second argument which supports subjectivism may be called the **Argument from Sentience.** Imagine a world in which there were no creatures which had feelings, desires, appetites, attitudes, knowledge—in short, a world in which there were no sentient beings. All the objects which made up such a world would be inanimate. Would it really make sense to say that anything good or bad could happen to the things in such a world? Would it be 'bad' for water to erode away a rock, or for a landslide to fill a valley with boulders? The subjectivist answer is that it would not make sense to ascribe such predicates as 'good' or 'bad' to these occurrences. It is only if some sentient being is affected by these events, or could be affected by them, that it makes sense to say that they are 'good' or 'bad'. Goodness and badness thus seem to depend upon the feelings, attitudes and desires of sentient beings. If we continue to reflect upon the problem, the subjectivist goes on to say, we can see that ultimately what is good or bad depends upon the individual psychology of the person who has certain attitudes towards events, such as liking or disliking them. From considerations such as these, it is argued that some form of subjectivism must be true.

A third argument in favour of subjectivism is the **Egoistic Argument.** This is used to reject objectivist theories such as Utilitarianism. What is the point of working for the greatest happiness of the greatest number if *you personally* become unhappy by so doing? In the final

analysis, who can be more important than *you*? If a course of action
leads to the well-being of others, but not to *yours*, can it really be
good? The subjectivist answer is a firm 'No!' We can justify working
for the good of the many only if we at the same time or at least in
the long run increase our own good; otherwise doing the action is
wrong.

Arguments against. The first argument against subjectivism is that
if we accept such a theory we can never settle any moral dispute. How
can we say that 'Hitler was wicked in killing 6,000,000 Jews,' if we
accept subjectivism? All this would mean would be: 'I disapprove of
Hitler's killing 6,000,000 Jews.' But if Hitler objects to this and claims
he did right in murdering these people, then he will mean by such a
judgment, 'I approve of killing 6,000,000 Jews.' We thus have no real
conflict, for he is saying: 'I approve of this action,' and we are saying,
'I disapprove of it.' It turns out that we are both merely talking about
how we feel: we are not talking about the act of killing these people.
Both of us are expressing our feelings: I disapprove and he approves—
but if so there is no real conflict between us. Plain men think that such
a consequence makes subjectivism as a moral theory undesirable. In
ordinary life, we seem to be talking not only about our feelings when
we say 'Hitler was wrong,' but about Hitler and about the acts he
committed. But to say that such a theory is undesirable is not to say
that it is untenable nor that plain men are not mistaken in what they
think they are asserting in such contexts.

A second difficulty in subjectivism is this. Plain men believe that
words like 'good', 'bad', 'right', 'wrong', and so on, have more or less
the same meaning for everybody who knows how to use the English
language. If they did not, it would be impossible to communicate
with other people. Since we obviously can communicate with them,
these words must have some interpersonal meaning. But it seems to
be a consequence of subjectivism that two different people would
never mean the same thing when they utter these words. For if I say
'That's good,' I mean the same as 'I like it,' whereas if you say 'That's
good,' you mean that you like it. The word 'good' in the first use refers
to a different person from the word 'good' in the second use. If this
is indeed a consequence of subjectivist theories, then plain men
would reject such views on the ground that these words do have
common meanings in the ordinary employment of daily English. It is
not, however, a necessary consequence. For the subjectivist will not
want to deny that the complexities of words like 'good' are such that
they can carry both of these meanings at the same time. When I say
that something is good, I am not only expressing my approval of it;
often I am also drawing attention to the fact that most men approve
of it too.

The third difficulty with subjectivism is that such theories cannot
give a justification of the concept of 'doing one's duty'. This is obviously an important notion in morals. One may often, in everyday life,
be faced with issues which involve one's duty. The man who has
pacifist inclinations and also believes it is his duty to defend his
country may suffer moral agony in trying to decide which of these

courses he should follow. The notion of 'doing one's duty', seems to involve acting against one's inclinations at least some of the time. One may desire to drink alcohol, but it may be his duty (if he is a doctor 'on duty' let us say) to remain sober. In short, the plain man feels that at least sometimes it is right for an individual to do that which he does not want to do, or like to do—and if so, it is difficult to see how subjectivistic theories can explain such a concept if they reduce all moral behaviour to liking and disliking.

OBJECTIVISM

Arguments for. The main argument in favour of objectivism is that it provides a **theory which corresponds more closely to the views of men of common sense about moral matters** than subjectivism. Consider the question of moral disagreement. Subjectivists hold that what *seem* to be moral disputes, if we judge merely from the sentences that each party uses (A saying 'That's good,' and B saying 'That's bad,') turn out upon analysis not to be such (A means 'I like it,' and B means 'I dislike it,'—and each can be right). Now **objectivists contend that there is no essential difference between a dispute about moral matters and a dispute about factual ones.** In both cases, there can be genuine disagreement in which one faction is right and the other is wrong. Thus, if I say, 'There are canals on Mars,' and you deny this, one of us is right and one wrong. Similarly, the objectivists say, if I assert 'Stealing is wrong,' and you deny this, one of us is right and one wrong. We are not simply talking about ourselves and how we feel about stealing, but we are talking about stealing, and whether that is right or wrong. In short, **our sentences have an objective reference** in exactly the same way as sentences about Mars do.

Now the plain man believes this too. He believes that it is not just a question of individual preference as to whether Hitler was right or not, but that in some objective sense, anybody who tortures and murders people is committing deeds which are wicked. Hitler may have defended his behaviour on the ground that he was acting properly, but all this shows is that either he did not understand the right way to behave, in which case he lacked moral knowledge; or if he did and acted against it, he was simply an immoral person. Objectivist theories allow us to account for the strong feeling we have that there are *genuine* disputes about moral matters.

Secondly, such theories allow us **to explicate the nature of 'duty'.** Plain men feel that there are certain duties in their lives which must be performed, regardless of whether one wants to or not. These duties are objective facts, which exist whether one chooses to ignore them or not. Thus, if I am a doctor and see a man injured in an accident, it is my duty to treat that man, even if it should prove highly inconvenient to do so. I may have another course of action in mind (I may be going to a party, say) which is much more pleasant; yet if I ignore the injured individual and proceed to the party, I am behaving wrongly. Sometimes there are things we *have* to do even though we do not *wish* to—and in stressing this fact, objectivism seems more in accord with common sense than subjectivist theories. It must be pointed out, however, that the subjectivist is not committed to a denial of the fact that we have feelings of duty and obligation; it is merely that he cannot accept that such feelings have any objective status.

Arguments against. The main difficulties with objectivism centre about **how we establish or prove** that a certain action is right or wrong. The objectivists claim that there is no real difference between the method of establishing a scientific hypothesis and a moral one; but critics of objectivism deny this. What seems essential in proving a scientific claim is (a) the acceptance by both sides of a common method, sometimes called the experimental method, and (b) the willingness of both sides to accept the judgments of disinterested observers after they have examined the evidence. Both of these characteristics seem lacking in the case of moral disputes. For example, it is difficult for the disinterested observer of a moral conflict to know what counts as evidence for or against either side. Supposing one side holds that 'euthanasia' was right in a particular case, the other that it was wrong. Both sides may completely agree about the facts of the case; they both agree, for instance, that the patient was dying of a disease which has no known or foreseeable cure; the patient was in great pain; he insisted that he be killed to relieve him of his agony; it is further agreed that the killer was acting from the highest motives (i.e., to relieve pain). But none the less one side holds that he did wrong in killing someone, the other side that he acted rightly. What further facts could be relevant to deciding this dispute? If the evidence in scientific matters is not decisive so that no one has any more reason to believe any scientific hypothesis than its denial, the proper course of action is the suspension of judgment—but, if we are members of a jury trying the killer, can we actually take this course? It seems we must decide, but how? The subjectivist answer at this point is that we finally examine our feelings and preferences and we decide in terms of them—this is the only possible answer. The objectivist claims that this will not do, but he is hard put to it to tell us what evidence would show one side to be right, the other wrong. This is the kind of difficulty that leads the subjectivist to believe that moral statements are not like scientific statements and cannot, therefore, have the same objectivity.

We conclude this section by suggesting to the reader that although considerable thought and energy has been applied to moral problems for more than two millennia, many of the difficulties still remain unresolved. Ethics is not a finished and complete subject and, because of its nature, it may never be; much work still remains to be done, and much work is still being done on these problems by philosophers, some of it extremely fruitful in suggesting ways of solving these problems. But that is another and perhaps more complex subject.

Ethics 55

SUGGESTED FURTHER READING

History of Ethics:

Sidgwick, H., *Outlines of the History of Ethics for English Readers*. Macmillan: London, 1962. (This is an excellent short history, whose main defects are its involved style and neglect of modern ethical theories.)

Broad, C. D., *Five types of Ethical Theory*. Routledge & Kegan Paul: London, 1930. (Excellent account of the moral views of Spinoza, Butler, Hume, Kant and Sidgwick.)

Classical Works in Ethics:

Plato, *Lesser Hippias, Crito, Protagoras, Gorgias, Republic, Philebus, Laws*. (These works range from brief dialogues such as the *Crito*, to long works such as the *Republic* and *Laws*.)

Aristotle, *Nicomachean Ethics*. (Aristotle's greatest work on ethics, dedicated to his son Nicomachus.)

St. Augustine, *The Basic Works of St. Augustine*.

Spinoza, *Ethics*. (One of the greatest classics in the field, but difficult reading.)

Butler, Joseph, *Fifteen Sermons Upon Human Nature*.

Price, R. A., *A Review of the Principal Questions in Morals*. (An excellent early account of non-materialism.)

Paley, W., *The Principles of Moral and Political Philosophy*. (A discussion of utilitarianism.)

Kant, I., *Critique of Practical Reason*. (A motivist theory of ethics.)

Modern Works in Ethics:

Carritt, E. F., *The Theory of Morals*. Oxford University Press: London, 1928. (Defence of non-naturalism.)

Hare, R., *The Language of Morals*. Oxford University Press: London, 1952. (A modern approach to ethical problems.)

Nowell-Smith, P. H., *Ethics*. Blackwell: Oxford, 1957. Paperback edition published by Penguin Books. (Another modern approach to ethical problems.)

Ross, W. D., *The Right and the Good*. Oxford University Press: London, 1930. (Deontological ethics.)

Stevenson, C. L., *Ethics and Language*. Yale University Press: 1944. (Emotive theory.)

Warnock, G. J., *Contemporary Moral Philosophy*. Macmillan: London, 1967. (An outline of the main features of the current modern 'schools'.)

Warnock, M., *Ethics Since 1900*. Oxford University Press: London, 1966. (Very good initial summary of the developments that have taken place in moral theory during the present century.)

CHAPTER II

POLITICAL PHILOSOPHY

Definition of 'Political Philosophy'.

It is difficult to formulate a precise definition of 'political philosophy' because political philosophy seems to have no special subject matter of its own. Its main tasks are in part to describe past and existing social organizations, in which respect it seems to duplicate the findings of economics, political science, anthropology, biology and sociology; and in part to evaluate these organizations, in which respect it is like ethics. For example, it describes the essential features of various types of governments (democracy, monarchy, fascism, etc.) and at the same time asks such questions about them as **'What is the ultimate justification for the existence of any form of government?'** The answer to such a question seems most naturally to emerge from ethical theory (e.g., a Utilitarian might answer 'to provide the greatest amount of happiness for the greatest number') and for this reason, political philosophy has sometimes been charged with being merely 'applied ethics'.

But even though political philosophy has intimate connections with the social sciences and with ethics, it would be a mistake to conclude that it does not have **distinctive problems of its own.** It deals, for example, with such issues as **'What are (or ought to be) the proper limits of governmental power over the members of society?' 'Is it possible to have rigid control over the economic affairs of people without curtailing their political freedom?' 'Should elected representatives to a legislature be allowed to vote as they see fit, or should they merely reflect the majority opinion of their constituency?'** and so forth. No doubt, these issues in part involve moral considerations, but it should also be remembered that they pose special difficulties of their own as well.

We can further characterize political philosophy by dividing it, like ethics, into **'classical'** and **'modern'** theories. **Classical political theories may be defined, roughly, as those which offer advice for achieving an ideal society. Modern theories, on the other hand, are primarily devoted to what we have called 'philosophical analysis'**, i.e., to the purpose of clarifying the meaning of this advice and of the terms we use in political discussions. Modern theories deal with such questions as 'What is meant by the phrase "universal human rights"?' as this appears in the Charter of the United Nations. 'What is the correct analysis of the word "state"?' and so forth. These issues raise questions which are often extremely subtle, but the attempts by philosophers to deal with them should not be regarded as mere quibbling. Rather they should be looked upon as initial moves towards the clarification of problems of political philosophy, so that the merits of the advice given in classical theories can more adequately be assessed and so that we can achieve greater clarity in our discussions of present social and political problems. To illustrate this, we shall briefly indicate the practical importance of providing a correct and rigorous analysis of such a term as 'The State'.

Some philosophers, notably HEGEL, have been greatly impressed by the fact that 'The State' is something different from any individual who belongs to it. For one thing, he noticed that we can describe a state as 'populous' but that it would be nonsense to ascribe this property to any individual citizen. From the fact that some characteristics belong to states which do not belong to the individuals, **Hegel inferred that The State was a separate, distinct entity which (so to speak) had an existence of its own. He also inferred that The State was more important than any individual citizen** not only because it united all citizens into a particular culture, but also because its persistence guaranteed the continuance of the culture even though its individual members perished. From this, it was a natural step to the glorification of The State. This glorification resulted in a political philosophy whose practical effects come down to us in such maxims as 'Deutschland Über Alles'. Philosophers who reject the doctrine that The State is more important than the individual often do so on the ground that the above analysis of The State is incorrect. They point out that what is called The State is a fictitious entity—it is merely a convenient way of talking about a group of individuals who are related in certain ways (living in a common area, having the same government, abiding by certain laws, and so forth). There is thus no separate existing thing called 'The State', apart from certain individuals and the relations they have to each other. Hence to glorify the state at the expense of its citizens is simply wrong-headed philosophy. This attack is closely connected, of course, with the **democratic view that the individual is more important than the state**—and in this respect, philosophical analysis may be regarded as having the important function of showing us that certain kinds of advice ('Die for the Fatherland') may be mistaken, i.e., philosophically and logically untenable. In analysing such terms as 'The State', or 'inalienable rights', political philosophy reveals itself to be a special discipline, which cannot be reduced entirely to the social sciences and to ethics. But for a fuller comprehension of its nature and functions, let us turn to some famous political theories and consider them in greater detail.

PLATO'S POLITICAL PHILOSOPHY

One of the most difficult and perplexing questions in political philosophy is: 'Who should rule?' Almost all the classical theories have dealt with it, and almost all of them can be classified according to how they attempt to answer it. If one holds that 'the people should rule themselves', he is advocating democracy (JOHN LOCKE); if he holds that one man should, he may be a monarchist (THOMAS HOBBES); and so forth. For Plato, this is the crucial question which every society must face, and his entire political philosophy can be understood as an attempt to answer it. Roughly, the Platonic answer is that a specially trained group of intellectuals should rule. Plato himself called his view 'aristocratic'. This was because he believed that the intellectuals were best fitted to rule; indeed the Greek words 'ariston' and 'kratos' together mean 'the rule by the best'. But it is perhaps a clearer characterization of Plato's political theory to designate it as **'authoritarian', i.e., as defending the granting of absolute authority to a special group for the purpose of ruling the society.**

In order to see why the question 'Who should rule?' is of fundamental importance for Plato, it would be fruitful to refer to the social conditions which prevailed in Greece at that time. Greece was composed of a number of small city-states, which had autonomous governments. These states engaged in constant warfare with each other, and even with such large, powerful nations as Persia. Most of them also suffered from a great deal of internal strife. Life for the average citizen was precarious. Dissatisfied with this state of affairs, Plato attempted to outline a society which would be free from such defects, in which men could live peacefully with each other, and in which every man could develop to his fullest capacity. This led Plato to ask: 'What would an ideal society be like?' if it could be brought into existence. The answer, he believed, depended to a great extent upon who ruled such a society.

In trying to describe the perfect society, Plato was greatly influenced by psychological and biological theories of the time. He assumed, accordingly, that there was an analogy between an individual person and the society in which he lived. The only real difference was one of size—a society is nothing but 'the individual writ large'. If so, the question of what an ideal society would be like can be reinterpreted as the question 'What makes an ideal or perfect man?' And Plato's answers to this query came in part from the then current theories of psychology and biology.

The psychology of the day held that every man is composed of two different ingredients: his body and his soul. Thus, what makes an ideal man is a matter both of physical and of psychological perfection. By 'perfection' Plato here meant the same as 'health'. To describe such a man, therefore, is to describe men who are physically and psychologically healthy. A man is physically healthy if he is not suffering from disease; but to determine when he is psychologically healthy is somewhat more complicated. Plato's reply was that the human soul was divided into three parts—what he called **'the rational element', 'the spirited element'**, and **'the appetitive element'.** The rational element is that part of a man's soul which enables him to reason, to argue, to deliberate and so forth. The 'spirited' element is what makes a man courageous or cowardly and gives him strength of will, and the appetitive element consists of his desires and passions, such as the desire for food, drink, sex and so on. In terms of this three-fold division of the soul, Plato argued that a man will be 'psychologically healthy' **if the three parts of his soul function harmoniously.** Reason should be in command of the appetites and the spirited element should with its strength support the dictates of reason to ensure that the appetites are kept under control. The appetites should not be repressed completely but should be satisfied only when reason says that it is appropriate. If a man is too exclusively controlled by reason, his emotional life will be impoverished. James Mill, if we can trust the reports of his son, John Stuart Mill, seems to have been a man whose rational life dominated his emotional life to the detriment of the latter. On the other hand, men are frequently dominated by their appetites: in order to satisfy their desires, they engage in conduct which is detrimental to themselves and to others. They are controlled by their passions, their feelings, and in this sense could be described as 'unbalanced'. In common-sense terms, a man is regarded as being 'sound in mind' when he is not unbalanced, i.e., if all the parts of his soul function harmoniously, each of them playing its role without dominating the other or without being so dominated. Thus, the Platonic answer to the question: 'What makes a healthy or ideal individual?' is 'An individual is healthy if all of the elements of his soul function harmoniously with each other'.

Since the state is nothing but the individual 'writ large', the same analysis can be applied to it. An ideal state would be composed of three classes: the rulers to administer it; warriors to defend it; and all other citizens to provide the essentials of life, such as food and shelter. Each of these classes corresponds to a division of the individual soul: The ruling class is the rational element of the society; the soldiers are its spirited element; and the other citizens are its appetitive element. Like the ideal individual, the ideal society will be one in which all these elements function harmoniously, with the warriors assisting the rulers to keep the rest of the citizenry under a benign but firm control. It would have no conflicts within it, and each class by doing what it is best fitted to do, would be happy and contented.

But the fundamental problem which the establishment of such a society raises is 'Who shall rule it?' since it is the rulers who ultimately will decide which individuals belong to which class; and it is they who must formulate the laws by which the society functions. Poor leadership will lead to poor laws; a wrong decision in placing someone in a given class will lead to unhappiness, or worse, to rebellion. It is thus essential that proper rulers be chosen if the society is to be ideal.

Plato gave careful directions for choosing rulers, and for making sure, once chosen, that they would not work for their own advantage. All children should be raised communally—i.e., by The State—until they are about eighteen. At that time, they will be subject to three types of test in order to determine prospective rulers from those who are to become warriors and artisans. These tests were to take two years. They would be in part physical (since ruling imposes a severe physical strain upon men and also because Plato believed that physical health was a prerequisite of mental health), in part intellectual, and in part moral. If a man cannot withstand moral temptation, then he might sacrifice the interests of the society in order to satisfy his own interests. The individuals who passed these tests would be carefully isolated for further training—most of it intellectual. They would be schooled in the abstract sciences. They would study arithmetic, geometry, solid geometry, astronomy and harmonics to prepare them for the abstract thinking necessary for their subsequent study of philosophy. The study of philosophy or 'dialectic', as Plato calls it, is the culmination of their theoretical preparation for the task of ruling, since it will lead them finally to a complete knowledge of the Good. As we saw in discussing Plato's moral theory in the previous chapter (see page 3), once they have this knowledge their actions must be good and they will always, therefore, make decisions which are in the best interests of the state. They will in fact be 'philosopher-kings'. The second part of their schooling would be practical: these men would be appointed to administrative posts of a lesser order and constantly observed in the performance of their duties. Anyone who failed to achieve competence in any of the above subjects would be dismissed as a potential ruler. After all the tests had been passed, the rulers would take part in the active administration of the society. But in order to avoid any chance of their placing their private interests over the public welfare, they would not be allowed to have private families, or to possess private property or wealth. Plato felt that family interests and the desire for riches were the two great obstacles to unbiased and impartial leadership. With these motivations which work against the public good eliminated, the guardians were to be given absolute authority in running the society. No one from the 'lower' classes was allowed to intervene in the administration of the government; for the members of the lower groups were not experts, as the rulers were. Plato justified giving the rulers absolute powers on the ground that ruling is a skill, just as medicine is a skill. In order to rule properly, one had to be trained for it; just as in order to practise medicine properly one required special instruction. To allow an untrained person a voice in the direction of the government was as foolish, in Plato's eyes, as to allow an untrained person to give advice for the proper conduct of a surgical operation.

Plato's philosophy leads, by natural steps, to an anti-democratic, authoritarian philosophy. It is government for the people, but not by the people. It is assumed that the rulers will know better than the people themselves what laws and policies will be in their best interest, just as a doctor can decide better than the layman can whether or not one needs a certain course of treatment.

CRITICISM OF PLATO

Plato's argument, when generalized, is perhaps the most powerful argument ever directed against democratic government. Let us first state it carefully and then see what can be said for and against it. The argument goes as follows:

Premise 1: Ruling is a skill.
Premise 2: Men differ innately in their capacities or abilities to exercise various skills.

Premise 3: Those who exhibit the greatest capacity for ruling should be trained in this skill and when trained, they ought to be made rulers of the society.

Premise 4: Because they have the greatest skill in ruling, they ought to be given absolute authority so that their laws will be put into effect.

It can be seen that the basis of the argument is that ruling is a skill. Plato proves this by appealing to common sense; do not plain men often decide that the ruler made a mistake in passing such and such a law? But to say that one can make mistakes is equivalent to asserting that ruling does involve knowledge, i.e., is a skill which can be learned. If one possesses knowledge he will not commit blunders; just as the doctor who is properly trained will not make an incorrect diagnosis. If we grant this premise, then it seems that the rest of Plato's argument follows. For if it is admitted that some have a greater capacity for

ruling than others, is it not the case that they should be trained to rule? Moreover, once so trained, will they not have the greatest skill in ruling, and if so, ought they not be given absolute authority to institute the laws they pass? Plato's point can be put very simply, and can be summed up in the question: Do you want those who are not either fitted or properly trained for ruling to rule? Will they not make mistakes and thus produce the tribulations which we find in existing societies because the rulers lack the knowledge to govern? One who opposes the Platonic theory at this point seems pinned on the horns of a dilemma. Either the trained must rule or the untrained must rule. But if the untrained rule, one will have improper government. If the trained rule, one will have authoritarian and non-democratic government. Hence, one seems committed either to non-democratic government or to improper government. Is there any way out of this impasse?

There are several ways of rebutting the argument, some of them stronger than others. The first is to deny that ruling is a skill in the way in which medicine is. Ruling is not simply reducible to a science in the way medicine is. One who prescribes for his subjects is doing something different from one who prescribes for his patients. The difference might be put as follows. The physician *directs* the conduct of the patient when he prescribes for him; he does not directly take account of the wishes and desires of the patient; instead, he prescribes a course of action which the patient must take if he is to regain his health. But the ruler of a society ought to have a different function from the physician. Instead of *directing* the interests and activities of the citizenry, his function (it has been argued) is to reflect these interests and to make their achievement possible. This is a view which has been sponsored by democratic theorists. Substantially, it states that men's interests differ; there is a wide diversity in their aptitudes, abilities, desires, attitudes and so forth. What will be good for one man may not be good for another. A good society is one which allows for the full expression of all such interests. The function of the ruler is not to direct the citizens' interests or behaviour along particular lines, and thus to impose *his* standards upon the members of society, but only to make it possible for them to live together as far as possible in accord with their own standards. We must remember, however, what we saw of Plato's moral theory in the previous section. For Plato there are absolute standards of goodness and, as we have just seen, the philosopher-king knows what these are. In ruling according to them, therefore, he is not imposing his own personal standards on the other members of society but directing their behaviour in those ways he *knows* to be right. An adequate refutation of Plato's argument, there-fore, requires a denial that such knowledge is attainable by anyone so that we can really show that ruling is not a science based on know-ledge in the way that medicine is.

A second and more powerful objection to the Platonic argument attempts to show that the conclusion to the argument does not follow from its premises. Thus, for instance, even if it is admitted that ruling is a skill, that men differ innately in their abilities to exercise such a skill, and even if it is agreed that such individuals ought to be selected as rulers, it still does not follow that these rulers ought to be given absolute authority. They should always be responsible to the people for their actions, and hence authority is to be vested in the people, not in the rulers. This objection stems from the long experience of tyranny which people have suffered at the hands of absolute rulers. As Lord Acton is reported to have remarked, 'Power corrupts, but absolute power corrupts absolutely.' In spite of the safeguards which Plato envisaged, experience teaches us that men who are intelligent can always find ways of circumventing such safeguards and of mis-using their authority. The best way, it seems, of preventing rulers from misusing their power is to invest them with as little of it as possible. Again we are rejecting Plato's basic beliefs that knowledge of the good is possible and that it will necessarily lead to virtuous behaviour.

A third objection to Platonism is that a society run by a few will stultify the development of most of the people who live in it. This objection is closely connected with the objection that we have already referred to. The Platonic view is that rulers can be trained in such a way as to become infallible judges of what is best for the people. Modern democratic theories hold that no man is infallible; and if no one is infallible, it is pointless to have someone else making mistakes for you. There is a good reason why one should be allowed to make his own errors. By doing so, he learns from experience; and by learning, he will become a more mature person and hence a better citizen. The Platonic conception of the relation between the ruler and the citizen is that of a parent-child relation. The ruler is essentially a parent who directs the life of his child-citizen. But if one's life is always directed by some other person, one will never grow up; one will always remain a child. The result will be a society composed of immature people who will never realize their capacities because they will never be given the responsibility to act on their own initiative. As we saw in Plato's moral theory (see page 6), in such a society most of the citizens will never be able to make their own choices and decisions; they will never achieve the kind of moral autonomy that we believe is an essential feature of mature, responsible adulthood. In short, this objection contends that self-government is essential to the development of a mature citizenry ('self-government' here meaning, of course, that the ultimate responsibility *ought* to rest with the people).

THE POLITICAL PHILOSOPHY OF THOMAS HOBBES

Not all philosophers have believed that the abuse of authority is the worst possible social evil. **Thomas Hobbes is an example of a philosopher who preferred the evils of absolute power to the evils of life in a society which did not contain such an authority.** It is easy to account for the Hobbesian dread of living in a country without a powerful sovereign. Born in 1588 (it is said prematurely when his mother was frightened by the report of the Spanish Armada), Hobbes lived through some of the most unsettled years in English history. He witnessed the rebellion against King Charles, the resulting civil war in 1642, and finally was forced to flee to the Continent, where he remained in exile for eleven years. But he was not safe there, either. In danger of assassination by his political enemies, he returned to England only to see his writings condemned as subversive. In 1662, on the threat of imprisonment, he was ordered to refrain from further publication about social and political problems. Against this background of turmoil, **it is understandable that what Hobbes feared most of all was a chaotic society.** In such a society no man's life or property or family is safe. The only way to assure domestic tranquillity lay in *compelling* people to obey the laws of the society, and in *punishing* them if they did not. But laws are only as effective as the enforcing agency makes them. A sovereign without absolute power to enforce laws is no sovereign at all in the last analysis, according to Hobbes; for he could not settle disputes which might arise among the citizenry unless he had such authority. In order to have a peaceful society, it is therefore required that the ruler have absolute control over it. Whatever abuses arise from his possession of such power, the society will nevertheless remain a peaceful one—and hence the abuses of such power are to be preferred to living in chaos.

It might be asked in questioning Hobbes's outlook, 'Why should a society without an absolute authority necessarily be chaotic?' **Hobbes's answer depends almost entirely upon a psychological theory about the nature of man. According to this view, man is by nature selfish and egoistic.** He is motivated by selfish desires which require satisfaction if he is to be happy. For example, all of his actions can be explained in terms of the attempt to gratify some desire, such as the desire for sex, for food, for shelter, for fame, for riches and so forth. If men lived alone, or in small groups, this fact would not have important implications; when they band together into larger and larger groups, it becomes of paramount significance in explaining their conduct toward each other. For two or more men may have desires which they want to satisfy, yet cannot because the desires are incompatible. Two men may desire the same woman, and therefore (assuming monogamy) both cannot be satisfied. As a result, when men herd together in large organizations, conflicts will break out among them in the effort to satisfy their desires at the expense of others. Life becomes a battle in which the strong will win—but only temporarily; for even the strong will finally succumb in the conflict (a defeated man may organize a group against the victor, for instance). This is the picture of the life of 'natural man', or as Hobbes called it, the picture of 'life in the state of nature'. In a famous sentence, Hobbes sums up the horrors of such an existence, telling us that the life of man in the state of nature **'is solitary, poor, nasty, brutish and short'.**

Such a state of affairs cannot continue indefinitely if men are to survive. The development of what we call 'society' is a way of ending 'the war of each against all'. Men finally realize that in order to survive the conflicts of the state of nature, they must abandon all efforts to satisfy their egoistic impulses. **Society is thus a compromise** which men enter into: in order to achieve peace, they must give up the attempt to satisfy their desires. No man wishes to compromise; every man would rather satisfy his desires; but the compromise is necessary if he is to survive.

Hobbes is one of the most important of the political theorists who used the theory of the 'social contract' to explain society and the basis of a man's obligations within society. **The compromise, or 'covenant' as Hobbes called it, consists of an agreement among men to abide by a certain set of rules, or 'conventions'.** These constitute what we now call the 'laws of the society'. Men agree to abide by these laws in order to avoid being harmed in conflicts which would rage were there no laws in existence. But, as Hobbes points out, laws are effective if and only if they are enforced. And the enforcing agency can enforce them only if it is granted absolute power. If it does not have such power, then it cannot prevent conflict. On this ground, Hobbes argued that the sovereign authority of any nation must be absolute.

Hobbes also suggested that the sovereignty be in the hands of one person—a king. In this respect, he is a monarchist. His reasons for advocating monarchy over other forms of government, such as oligarchy, or aristocracy, are these: If the sovereign consisted of a group, then this group might have conflicts within itself. Thus, the power of enforcement would be divided, and instead of a peaceful society, conflict would again break out. On the other hand, a monarch cannot be divided against himself. Secondly, a single ruler has more secrecy of counsel. Large groups invariably develop 'leaks' and important information may filter down to the people, again causing dissension among them. Finally, a monarch's decisions are 'only as inconstant as human nature, but a group has that plus the inconstancy of number'. For instance, the absence or presence of a few men can alter the decision which a government will take in framing laws. This can never happen with a monarch. Furthermore, there is no reason to believe that the monarch will work for his own good at the expense of the public welfare. As Hobbes put it, 'The King is only as rich as his country.'

Although the power of the monarch is to be absolute, Hobbes also wished to grant (perhaps this is an inconsistency) the subject certain 'liberties'. These liberties he defines as **'those things the subject may justly refuse to do even though commanded by the sovereign'.**

Since **sovereignty is created by a covenant or contract, the subject has left to him all those natural rights which cannot be transferred by covenant.** To put it differently, since the subject entered into the contract to preserve and protect his life, he is entitled to refuse to obey the sovereign when to do so would place his life in danger. For instance, the monarch's command to the subject to kill, wound or maim himself, or not to resist those who assault him, can be justly disregarded by the subject. Further, he is not bound to testify against himself in a criminal action (it was around this time, incidentally, that the historical precedent of the Fifth Amendment to the U.S. Constitution was established). A command for dangerous military duty may be refused if the intention of the sovereign in issuing it was not to preserve the peace (but no man can justly object to defending his country when it is attacked by an outside aggressor). Liberty does not include the defence of any man against the sovereign. Thus rebellion is *always* unwarranted, according to Hobbes; and, similarly, protection of a criminal from the officers of the law is likewise unjust (this tenet has also come down to us from Hobbes and is embodied in most legal codes). Men always have liberty to defend their lives against the sovereign; but if they are offered a pardon and refuse, then they are unjust. In a controversy with the sovereign, the subject has the right to sue (another provision which is found in American law). The obligation of the subjects to the sovereign lasts only so long as the sovereign is able to protect them: **'the end** [i.e., the purpose—A. S.] **of obedience is protection'.** Thus, a prisoner captured by the enemy has the liberty to become an enemy subject if the sovereign is unable to protect him.

The powers of the sovereign are imposing. According to Hobbes, no subject can make a new covenant or rebel against the monarch (provided that the monarch is capable of protecting him). No breach of the covenant is possible by the sovereign, for according to the Hobbesian theory, he has not contracted with his subjects. They have agreed among themselves to abide by certain laws, and have appointed him the agency for enforcing such laws. Once appointed, he has absolute authority. **It follows from this that a dissenting minority must now acquiesce to the dictates of the sovereign or be destroyed.** Further, no matter how the sovereign behaves, he cannot—by definition— act unjustly toward anyone. **'Just' behaviour consists, according to Hobbes, in abiding by the laws of the community; but since the sovereign makes the law, whatever he does will be law;** hence in a significant sense **he is above the law** and cannot violate it. The sovereign has **absolute right to control all opinions** (for it is his decision whether or not the expression of an opinion will cause chaos in the commonwealth). Further, **he is to make all civil laws and also to adjudicate disagreements involving the law.** He has the power to make peace or war with other nations, and to levy taxes in order to conduct such wars.

CRITICISM OF HOBBES

Since the above doctrine is composed of a psychological theory about the nature of man and also a political theory about who should govern society, each of these parts should be evaluated separately.

Some philosophers have interpreted Hobbes as attempting to give a true description of the *origin* of society. According to this interpretation, Hobbes is asserting that men originally lived in groups without laws regulating their behaviour. When it was discovered that life led in this way turned into a war of each against all, men fabricated an agreement among themselves to give up the satisfaction of their egoistic impulses in order to achieve peace. When Hobbes is thus interpreted, the theory may be attacked on the grounds that there is no historical or anthropological evidence to support it. The earliest information we have about primitive humanity comes only after men had reached a fairly high degree of social organization. What life was like before societies were formed, nobody knows; hence there is no reason to accept Hobbes's imaginative portrayal of 'life in the state of nature' as being accurate.

But such an interpretation of Hobbes is exceedingly superficial and misses the main significance of the theory. Hobbes is not trying to give an exact historical or anthropological account of the development of societies; instead he is trying to give **a philosophical justification for the existence of a certain type of government.** In other words, the notion of the social contract is an analogy designed to illustrate the basis of political allegiance, to show us why we should obey the law. Whether men in fact behaved in this way or not at some early historical moment is irrelevant to the significance of his account. **What is important is his analysis of human nature and the necessity of having an absolute authority in order to curb the excesses of human nature.** In part, therefore, his account may be regarded as psychological, in part as philosophical. Let us treat each of these independently, beginning with the psychological theory.

The Hobbesian view is that men are basically motivated by the drive to satisfy their desires. From this, he infers that men are by nature egoistic. Is the inference justified? Suppose we grant that men are motivated by desire, does it then follow that all their desires are egoistic? The answer depends in part upon what is meant by saying that 'men are motivated by desire'. To begin with, one might mean that it is the non-rational aspects of human beings which motivate them; that is that emotions, feelings and attitudes cause people to act as they do, not reason. So one might hold, as both Hume and Hobbes do, that although reason can reveal various alternatives for possible conduct, and also something about the probable consequences of selecting any of the alternative courses of action, reason does not itself initiate action. The choice of a given alternative, or of a given course of action, is—according to this view—a matter of emotion or feeling. Now if this is what is meant by the phrase 'men are motivated by desire', it does not follow that all desire is egoistic. Men may indeed be motivated only by non-rational factors—but these, such as the feeling of sympathy, may motivate them to act for the good of others. On the other hand, one might mean by saying that 'men are motivated by desire', that one is always motivated to act for one's own interest, and only his interest (regardless of whether it is reason or emotion which so motivates one). But if this is what Hobbes intends, it can be seen that from a psychological standpoint Hobbes is incorrect. Men may desire to contribute to the happiness of others as well as to their own. Do we not often sacrifice our interests for the interests of our families, wives, children, country? This can be put by saying that some of our desires are 'altruistic', rather than 'selfish'. We sometimes desire to contribute to the well-being of others, and if so, it is false that all desires are egoistic. What makes Hobbes's psychological account of human nature attractive is his vacillation between these two different accounts of motivation; but if we accept the former, egoism does not follow from it; and if we accept the latter, egoism is clearly false. Suppose however that we did accept the latter, i.e., the position that all men are motivated by egoistic desires (i.e., desires which work only for their own advantage), would it follow then that only the creation of an absolute authority would make for peaceful living in a society? The answer here, again seems to be 'no'.

Man's interests are diversified and they change from time to time. A ruler who is given absolute power will generally not reflect this change in men's interests, but will impose his own standards upon them. What seems required for satisfactory living in society is not that there should be *no* conflict at all within the society, **but only that the amount of conflict should not be such as to make certain other goals impossible of achievement.** The Hobbesian view would rule out all conflict, but it would also prevent the realization of many fundamental desires. A sovereign power which does not have absolute authority may yet have enough authority to eliminate most conflicts and still allow for the satisfaction of a wide range of interests. For this reason, it does not seem requisite—as Hobbes's account suggests—that absolute authority is necessary in order to achieve a good society. We may thus reject the philosophical part of the theory as well as the psychological part.

Hobbes's political philosophy is essentially an expression of defeatism. It is a 'peace at any price' philosophy. On this ground alone, it would be unacceptable to men of a less submissive temper. Compare, for example, the ringing words of Patrick Henry, 'Give me liberty or give me death!' or those of Thomas Jefferson, 'The tree of liberty must be refreshed from time to time with the blood of patriots and tyrants!' **Hobbes, in attempting to avoid the evil effects of internecine conflict, was willing to submit to the evils of tyranny and to surrender liberty in return for security.** For him these were the only choices which a citizen faced. But as Locke was to show these were not the only alternatives; it is possible to have both law and order and the absence of tyranny.

THE POLITICAL PHILOSOPHY OF
JOHN LOCKE

It is accurate to say that John Locke is the theoretical architect of democracy as it exists in the western world today. His ideas, as expressed in his famous *Second Treatise on Civil Government*, were influential in forming the political philosophy of the founders of the American and French Republics. A careful study of the Declaration of Independence and the American Constitution reveals both documents to be replete with phrases such as 'All men are created equal', 'Life, liberty and the pursuit of happiness', 'We hold these truths to be self-evident', and so forth, which are culled almost literally from the *Second Treatise*.

Like Hobbes, Locke lived in a period of great social unrest. Involved in intrigue against the King, he was forced to flee England twice during his life, once in 1675 and again in 1679. But these events did not sour his outlook on human nature. Both in this respect, and in his theory as to the proper function of government, he is diametrically opposed to Hobbes. Let us examine this theory in some detail.

Like Hobbes in the *Leviathan*, Locke begins the *Second Treatise* with what seems to be an historical account of the origin of government, using, like Hobbes, the notion of a social contract. The account begins with an important distinction which was undoubtedly directed at Hobbes: the distinction between life in a 'state of nature' and life in a 'state of war'. In the state of nature, men live on the whole peaceably. They own private property, such as land, and also have private possessions, such as cattle and sheep. Men by nature are not wholly selfish; they sometimes work for the good of others and they co-operate with each other; but sometimes, on the other hand, they do act egoistically. What property they own they may dispose of without asking the permission of anyone. The only law which governs them is what Locke calls 'the law of nature'. This is the provision that **'no one ought to harm another in his life, health, liberty or possessions'.** Now although life in the state of nature is as a rule peaceful, men occasionally may transgress the law of nature; they may attempt to kill someone, or to steal his property. When this occurs, the injured party has the right to punish the transgressor. **There would be no reason for men to leave the state of nature and to form societies, except that difficulties arise in applying punishment to those who transgress the law.** These difficulties are three in number: (*a*) Each man in the state of nature is his own judge of what is right or wrong, and this leads him to make biased judgments. One man may claim that he was injured, another may deny it. Who is to decide the merits of the dispute? (*b*) Even where it is plain that someone has violated the law, we may not have adequate force to punish him. (*c*) Moreover, the degree of punishment will vary for the same crime. A man who steals a loaf of bread may be hanged by one group of individuals; but another man may merely be fined. In order to overcome these impairments in the state of nature, men require (i) a judiciary which will administer the law impartially, (ii) an executive who can enforce the law when it is broken, and (iii) a legislature to lay down consistent and uniform laws. **Society originates in the attempt to develop such institutions for the purpose of remedying the defects of life without organized society. Men create a society by a voluntary agreement among themselves to erect these institutions.**

Now all this, Locke argues, is entirely different from a state of war. Locke's state of war is like the Hobbesian 'state of nature'. It is characterized by one man or a group of men seeking absolute domination over others. In such a case, there is want of a 'common judge' and there consequently exists a struggle for survival. Men will assault and maim each other, and life hangs by a thread. But it is an error to confuse this picture with that of life in the state of nature. This, according to Locke, was Hobbes's fundamental mistake. The state of nature (and for that matter even civil society) may become a state of war under certain conditions; but it is a fallacy to *identify* them. The conditions are that someone or some group will attempt to gain control *of an absolute sort* over others. When this happens, such a person creates a state of war between himself and those whom he attempts to dominate. **Opposition to him is not only justified, but even required**; for if men were to submit to him, they would in effect be giving up the advantages of social life for the difficulties which they previously encountered in the state of nature. On this ground alone, monarchy may be rejected, Locke argues, since the monarch by seeking absolute domination over the citizenry has established a state of war with them.

The above account when expanded can be seen to contain most of the important elements of democratic theory as we now know it. To begin with, it stresses that **law, not force, is the basis of government. A government without law will be tyrannical.** This is characteristic of monarchy. A king can issue a decree stating that so and so is under arrest. There may have been no previous regulation to cover the alleged crime; the person may not have known that he was doing something which would evoke the wrath of the monarch. Yet the ruler can fabricate at will regulations for the purpose of imprisoning someone whom he does not like. **Such a government operates by caprice, and the society which it controls will be correspondingly unstable.** In a properly conducted government (such as a democracy) such a state of affairs will be ruled out. **Democracy is government by laws which are arrived at after long deliberation by properly chosen representatives of the people, and which are promulgated so that all men may become acquainted with them.** All of this is sharply at variance with government by decree.

Secondly, according to Locke, **there are certain areas of human conduct which are immune from governmental interference.** Locke calls these **'rights'. This doctrine is the direct ancestor of the famous Bill of Rights in the American Constitution.** The Bill of Rights maintains that the government is powerless to abridge certain types of conduct of the citizenry: such as the freedom to speak, to worship as one pleases, and so forth. The main right which Locke emphasized, however, was the right to own private property. He believed that no government can justly take away a person's private property. This is because private property is, to a great extent, the fruits of a person's own labour. In a significant sense, part of the person is invested in his property (in fact, Locke often uses the word 'property' to refer to a man's life and liberty as well as to his possessions), and to take it from him is tantamount to an assault upon his physical person. Hobbes and Rousseau both strongly disagreed with this doctrine. They held that **property is a creation of society.** Before society exists, to quote Hobbes, there is 'no thine or mine'. A man owns what he can hold by force; he has no *right* to anything. This view, as we have seen, is strongly rejected by Locke. His outlook has had profound influence not only upon the creation of such a document as the Bill of Rights, but also in the creation of the democratic belief 'that all men are created equal by nature'. **Locke argued that all men are equal in the sense that they have rights which are anterior to those given them by society, and since they are not given to them by society, they cannot be taken away by society either.** In our time, this doctrine has been interpreted as the view that each man, regardless of his station in life, is to be accorded **equal treatment before the law**—'due process' is an application of it.

But the most important democratic element in Locke's theory is his attitude towards government. Society is created in order to eliminate the defects of the state of nature. When men leave the state of nature in order to enter society, they thereby give up the power of punishment to an executive whom they appoint. But the crucial fact which Locke emphasizes here is that the executive is *appointed* by the people, and therefore is *responsible to them*. As he says, 'The whole purpose of government is to make laws for the regulation and preservation of property, and for the defence of the community against external aggression, all this only for the **public good.**' Locke's theory is that the government is, so to speak, a glorified secretary. We entrust it with powers to do those things which we find it inconvenient or impossible to do ourselves, just as we appoint a secretary to handle our affairs if we are busy. But if the secretary violates our trust (if he embezzles money, say) we can fire him; and if the government violates our trust by attempting to usurp our rightful authority, we can dismiss it. **Ultimately, the source of authority lies with the people who appoint the government. It is merely a means for carrying out their will.**

In order to safeguard the people against the concentration of power, **Locke envisaged a government divided into three branches, each of which would function as a check upon the other.** Locke called these divisions the Executive, Legislative and Federative branches of government. The executive and legislative branches would have much the same function as they do in our own government, but the duties of the federative branch consisted in carrying on negotiations with foreign powers.

Locke greatly feared the possible concentration of authority in the executive. Consequently, he sharply restricted its powers. To begin with, **the legislature is to be the supreme authority in the ideal commonwealth.** It and only it has the power to make laws; the executive merely has the function of enforcing them. It cannot punish anyone unless this person has violated an explicitly promulgated law, and even this punishment is to be reviewed by an impartial judiciary. Further, the executive's right to obedience stems only from the fact that it is the person or body vested with the power of the law. It has no authority of its own and cannot claim obedience except when it is enforcing the law of the society. In this respect, Locke's system resembles British parliamentary government. The executive may be removed immediately from office if the legislature, or the people, feel that it has violated the limits of the power given it.

At the same time, in order to carry out the duties of his office, the executive is to be given certain powers. For one thing, he can dismiss the legislature, and also invoke it. In order to avoid the possibility that he will refuse to call it up, there is a limit upon the length of adjournment; he must call it within those limits or be dismissed. **If he refuses, the people have the right to use force against him.** Locke felt that it was not necessary to have the legislature always in session, since it is not necessary to make laws continuously; but the executive must always remain at his post, since it is always necessary to enforce the law. During those times when the legislature is not in session, should a national emergency arise, the executive is given the power to deal with it. **This is the famous doctrine of 'prerogative'. Prerogative is defined by Locke as 'the power to act, according to the discretion of the executive, for the public good without the prescription of the law, and sometimes even against it.'** Locke admitted that the use of executive prerogative could be dangerous; but he felt in view of the other safeguards his theory provided, any serious violation could be countered by the other branches of government, and by the people.

CRITICISM OF LOCKE

In the *Second Treatise*, Locke tried to show that men can live amicably together without submitting to a ruler having absolute authority. This state of affairs can be attained through government by law. Laws arrived at openly, and widely promulgated, make for a stable society; yet they are not absolute. If these laws prove eventually to be inadequate, they can be changed. Hobbes, on the other hand, assumed that the only alternatives were anarchy or despotism. Either men faced a war of each against all or they gave up their rights to an absolute monarch. But it was Locke's genius to see that the Hobbesian theory failed in an essential respect: by giving up their rights to an absolute sovereign, men were no more secure than they had been in the state of nature; for now they were subject to the whims, and caprices of the monarch. Once again, they lived precariously—but this time the danger came not from their fellow men but from their ruler. Instead of exchanging, as Hobbes thought, anarchy for stability, they merely traded one form of chaos for another.

In perceiving that stability and self-government were not incompatible, Locke became the source of inspiration for democratic societies which have existed successfully now for more than two centuries. His arguments in one form or another have frequently been repeated in the struggle for self-government. Abraham Lincoln, for example, opposed those who wished to keep the suffrage as small as possible, with words that are almost a paraphrase of the *Second Treatise*:

A majority held in restraint by constitutional checks and limitations, and always changing easily with deliberate changes of popular opinions and sentiments, is the only true sovereign of a free people. Whoever rejects it does, of necessity, fly to anarchy or despotism. Unanimity is impossible; the rule of a minority, as a permanent arrangement, is wholly inadmissible; so that, rejecting the majority principle, anarchy or despotism in some form is all that is left.

In part, Locke's reasons for rejecting the Hobbesian doctrine depend upon his theory of human nature, but also in part they depend upon the construction of an entirely new theory about political relations among people, involving such notions as 'rights', 'the law', 'the proper end of government', and so forth. In rejecting the Hobbesian account that men always act egoistically, Locke was doubtless correct. But leaving aside this psychological question, which we have already discussed, what can be said for and against the political theory of Locke?

Two main criticisms have been directed against it: one against the doctrine of 'rights', and the other against the notion of majority rule. Both of these doctrines, it is held, suffer from difficulties. Let us consider the question of rights first.

The main objection to Locke's doctrine of rights is that it is based on the idea of 'natural rights', i.e., rights that men enjoyed in the state of nature before the emergence of organized society. The objection is that such a claim is incomprehensible, since it is difficult to know how rights could exist before there existed a government and a system of law to grant them and to uphold them. Examination of the term shows that it does not have this kind of *descriptive* meaning; it makes a *prescriptive* claim that men *ought* to have these rights. This must cast some doubt on the validity of Locke's argument, which seems to be based on a belief that in a state of nature men do have these rights in some literal, descriptive sense.

Even if we agree with Locke's claim and accept that these are rights that men ought to have, there are still difficulties to be overcome. For example, the rights we feel men ought to have may be incompatible with the notion of 'the public good'. Locke had held that the purpose of government is to preserve certain rights and at the same time work for the public good. But there may be cases where we cannot do both, if we are the government. Consider the famous case of a man who shouts 'fire'! in a crowded theatre, knowing that there is no fire. People may be stampeded in an effort to get out of the theatre; some will be injured and others may be killed. If we accept the doctrine that a man has the 'right' to free speech, we cannot penalize him for speaking freely. But the exercise of free speech is obviously in this case incompatible with the public good. Such a man is a menace to the general public, and in punishing him for his action we do so on the ground that he has acted against the good of all. But it is clear that by so doing, we abandon the view that he has the absolute right to free speech.

Democratic philosophers who have puzzled about this question have, on the whole, been willing to abandon the doctrine of rights in such cases. They have agreed that men cannot have *absolute* freedom against the state; but, they argue, from this it does not follow that the state has absolute authority over men. A more moderate interpretation of 'rights' is demanded. **Rights, in this view, are those areas which can only be infringed with majority consent—when the public welfare is genuinely at stake.** Otherwise, men may remain free to speak. This more moderate doctrine qualifies Locke's views of rights, but still does not condone tyranny. **It holds that what is a right is a matter of degree;** certain areas of human behaviour can be interfered with only in times of great crisis, otherwise they must be left untouched. This still allows men very considerable freedom within society, even if it does not allow them *absolute* freedom. In any case, freedom can never be absolute. Complete absence of control is not freedom but licence. The notion of freedom is perfectly compatible with the existence of restrictions on our behaviour. The real problem is what kind of restriction can be justified.

The second main criticism that has been directed against Locke's political theory concerns the notion of majority rule. In raising the question 'Who should rule?', **Locke, unlike Plato and Hobbes, has been on the side of the people as opposed to the few.** On the whole, this doctrine has had salubrious effects. The few traditionally have been the wealthy, and the privileged, and in ruling they have worked for their own interests, or for the interests of a special class, against the interests of the majority. **But what Locke never realized is that the majority itself can become a tyranny; it can prove to be a despotism as fierce as any monarch in submerging the minority.** Democratic government is not merely government by majority rule, it is also government in which *minority* rights must be equally protected. Unless this latter provision is stressed, rule by the majority becomes despotic and democratic government turns into government which in practice is indistinguishable from an oligarchy. Locke emphasized majority rule as one of the basic tenets of democracy; and in so doing he was right. But at the same time, **no government can be a democracy without allowing for the protection of minorities, and it was Locke's great critic,** JOHN STUART MILL, **who completed democratic theory** by emphasizing the latter facet. We turn now to a discussion of Mill.

THE POLITICAL PHILOSOPHY OF
JOHN STUART MILL

Every student of history has been struck, at one time or another, by the paucity of civilizations which have granted political liberty to their citizens. Freedom has indeed been a precious thing. It existed only feebly in the Ancient World, not at all during the Middle Ages, and even today the societies which grant it are in the minority. Most attacks upon freedom traditionally have come from the 'right'; from societies which have been dominated by tyrants or by small groups of people. Today liberty is also threatened from the 'left', from so-called

communist societies. These threats, although menacing, are obvious
—and the measures for fending them off can easily be developed. But
some dangers to freedom are more insidious. They come from within
democracy itself. One such is the power which the majority has in a
democratic state. When this power is allowed to develop unchecked,
it may lead to a form of tyranny as evil as any kind of despotism, **a
tyranny of the majority over minority groups.** Mill's classic essay *On
Liberty* can be regarded as an attempt to find a method for eliminating this threat.

Mill begins the essay *On Liberty* by pointing out that he is talking
about **civil liberty (i.e., the limits of the power of society over the individual)** rather than about freedom of the will. The question of
authority versus liberty, like the problem of freedom of the will, is an
ancient one. Originally, 'liberty' was thought of in negative terms—as
the protection which the subjects had against the authority of their
rulers. Political thinkers conceived of the ruler as being necessary to
the well-being of society, but at the same time as being dangerous to
it. He was necessary to defend the society against external and internal enemies; but in preserving the peace, he might overstep his
legitimate authority and become a tyrant. **The aim of early libertarians,
therefore, was to set limits to the power of the ruler over his citizens.**
This was to be done in two ways: (*a*) by a doctrine of rights, which
if infringed by the sovereign justified rebellion against him, and (*b*)
by constitutional checks upon him in certain important matters—
such as the declaration of war.

However, with the development of democratic societies, political
theorists refused to accept the position that the ruler's interest was
opposed to that of the people. The ruler, on their view, was a represen-
tative of the people, and his authority was revocable at their pleasure.
Since the rulers are delegates of the ruled, it is not important to limit
their power; and indeed, to do so is equivalent to limiting the power
of the people themselves.

Mill points out that although this standpoint is theoretically correct,
a study of the actual development of the institutions within democracy
has shown the practical **need for certain limitations being imposed upon
the powers of the government.** 'Self-government' does not express the
true state of the case. **The people who exercise power are not the same
as those over whom it is exercised.** They not only develop their own
interests, but they are frequently influenced by pressure groups (such
as lobbyists) to work against the welfare of the people. The notion
of the limitation of the power of the ruler is thus still important,
even though the rulers *theoretically* are accountable to the people.

Even more dangerous, however, than the threat to freedom from
the rulers is the tyranny which the majority of people may exercise
over minorities. **One of the basic elements of democracy is that it
allows considerable latitude to its people in behaving as they wish;
in developing interests which differ from those of the majority, and in
satisfying such interests.** All of this can be summarized under the
name of 'individualism'. Now the majority may develop **a kind of
tyranny which prevents the development of individualistic behaviour.**

This tyranny can work in two ways: (*a*) **through pressure upon the government** (or originating within the government) **to adopt laws which operate against idiosyncratic or non-conformist or dissenting individuals, even though these individuals may be harmless** (e.g., the seventeenth century 'witch hunts' in New England), and (*b*) **merely by the pressure of public opinion.** Even though no law may exist, public opinion against a non-conforming individual may be so strong as to **deprive him of the usual benefits of the society.** In the first case, the doctrine of rights can to a considerable extent prevent the formation of laws which infringe upon areas an individual may regard as sacred and therefore inviolable (such as free speech, etc.), but the great danger to him comes from public opinion. **And public opinion is notoriously susceptible to error;** it may reflect ancient prejudices, be dominated by superstition and tradition. Consequently, Mill argues, public opinion ought not to be a law which individuals must conform to, even an unwritten law. It should be possible in a properly run democratic society, for the individual both to have the protection of the law against the prevailing sentiments of society, as well as to act freely in the face of majority opinion where no laws, but only customs, exist. The problem which faces any democratic state can be put this way: some types of behaviour by certain individuals obviously cannot be tolerated (e.g., criminal behaviour) and yet all non-conforming behaviour must not be suppressed, so that the problem is to find the legitimate extent to which the majority can interfere in the affairs of individuals or minority groups which do not conform to the behaviour of the majority. As he writes:

Like other tyrannies, the tyranny of the majority was at first, and is still vulgarly, held in dread, chiefly as operating through the acts of the public authorities. But reflecting persons perceived that when society is itself the tyrant—society collectively, over the separate individuals who compose it—its means of tyrannizing are not restricted to the acts which it may do by the hands of its political functionaries. Society can and does execute its own mandates: and if it issues wrong mandates instead of right, or any mandates at all in things with which it ought not to meddle, it practises a social tyranny more formidable than many kinds of political oppression, since, though not usually upheld by such extreme penalties, it leaves fewer means of escape, penetrating much more deeply into the details of life, and enslaving the soul itself. Protection against the tyranny of the magistrate is not enough: there needs to be protection also against the tyranny of the prevailing opinion and feeling; against the tendency of society to impose by other means than civil penalties, its own ideas and practices as rules of conduct on those who dissent from them; to fetter the development, and if possible, prevent the formation of any individuality not in harmony with its ways, and compels all characters to fashion themselves upon the model of its own. There is a limit to the legitimate interference of collective opinion with individual independence: and to find that limit and maintain it against encroachment, is as indispensable to a good condition of human affairs, as protection against political despotism.

Mill's answer to the question: 'What are the legitimate powers which society has over the individual?' is as follows:

> The object of this Essay is to assert one very simple principle, as entitled to govern absolutely the dealings of society with the individual in the way of compulsion and control, whether the means used be physical force in the form of legal penalties, or the moral coercion of public opinion. That principle is, that the sole end for which mankind are warranted, individually or collectively, in interfering with the liberty of action of any of their number, is self-protection. That the only purpose for which power can be rightly exercised over any member of a civilized community, against his will, is to prevent harm to others. His own good, either physical or moral, is not a sufficient warrant. He cannot rightfully be compelled to do or forbear because it will be better for him to do so, because it will make him happier, because, in the opinions of others, to do so would be wise, or even right. These are good reasons for remonstrating with him, or reasoning with him, or persuading him, or entreating him, but not for compelling him, or visiting him with any evil in case he do otherwise. To justify that, the conduct from which it is desired to deter him must be calculated to produce evil to someone else. The only part of the conduct of any one, for which he is amenable to society, is that which concerns others. In the part which merely concerns himself, his independence is, of right, absolute. Over himself, over his own body and mind, the individual is sovereign.

Mill put certain limitations on this principle. For one thing, he assumed that the principle would not apply to children. Being immature, they must be guided. Similarly, certain 'backward states' required paternal government. These states, if allowed self-government, would merely fall into chaos. The assumption throughout is that the principle should be applied only to mature and rational persons; but unlike Plato, who believed that only a specially trained few satisfied the requirement of rationality, Mill specifically states that in his opinion, in all modern nations all citizens have arrived at this state.

In order to show how the principle would operate in practice, Mill takes as a test case the suppression of opinion and discussion. He gives three reasons why it would be wrong to suppress any opinion. Let us consider each in turn:

First, it is wrong to suppress an opinion which the majority does not approve of because the suppressed opinion may be true. We all know of cases where the majority of men hold false beliefs; if the contrary belief is suppressed men may never learn the truth—and this in the long run may prove harmful to them (an example of a widely held belief which was false was the belief that the world was flat). **A false opinion is frequently corrected through open discussion.** A wise man is one who will listen to all sides of a question, examine the evidence for or against each, before making up his mind as to which side is the true one. But if the contrary opinion to the received view is never allowed to be expressed, he will never get the chance to exchange falsehood for truth.

To deny others the right to express their opinions is to assume one's own infallibility. But no man is infallible, and if so, it is always possible that the opinion he holds in a given case is mistaken. Some might object to this point on the ground that in actual practice it is necessary for men to assume that they are not mistaken in pursuing a given course of action. If one believes that it is necessary to wage war against an aggressor, should he suspend his judgment? This would be impractical. Mill's answer to this objection is one of the famous remarks in the history of liberalism. He says:

> There is the greatest difference between presuming an opinion to be true because, with every opportunity for contesting it, it has not been refuted, and assuming its truth for the purpose of not permitting its refutation. Complete liberty of contradicting and disproving our opinion, is the very condition which justifies us in assuming its truth for purposes of action; and on no other terms can a being with human faculties have any rational assurance of being right.

The second argument which Mill gives for not suppressing contrary opinion is this. Let us assume that the contrary opinion is mistaken, and that we do in fact hold the true view. Nevertheless, even a true opinion can be held in different ways: it can be held openly by a mind which is always willing to change its point of view depending upon the evidence, or it can be held as sheer prejudice. Now when we hold the true opinion, but are not willing to listen to contrary opinions, we hold it in the wrong way—as a prejudice. To hold an opinion in this way may be harmful, for **by reflecting upon all the arguments against it, and by thus being forced to think of ways of rebutting them, we actually come to understand our opinion more fully.** A man who fights for democracy, but does not understand what he is fighting for, could in other circumstances be fighting against it. He is merely reflecting the majority sentiments of the society he lives in, without making any attempt to justify the validity of such sentiments. He thus may be fighting for democracy but he may be fighting for it for the wrong reasons, or what is even worse, for no reason at all, except that his society commands him to do so. All this is an obstacle to future progress; **what we require in a democratic society is an enlightened individual, who will be mature and responsible because he reflects upon the issues which face him.** If he does not consider the opposing opinion seriously, he cannot become such a person; and this is why we must not suppress the opposite point of view without giving it a chance to be heard.

Mill writes on this point:

> To abate the force of these considerations, an enemy of free discussion may be supposed to say, that there is no necessity for mankind in general to know and understand all that can be said against

or for their opinions by philosophers and theologians. That it is not needful for common men to be able to expose all the mis-statements or fallacies of an ingenious opponent. That it is enough if there is always somebody capable of answering them, so that nothing likely to mislead uninstructed persons remains unrefuted. That simple minds, having been taught the obvious grounds of truths inculcated on them, may trust to authority for the rest, and being aware that they have neither knowledge nor talent to resolve every difficulty which can be raised, may repose in the assurance that all those which have been raised have been or can be answered by those who are specially trained to the task.

Conceding to this view of the subject the utmost that can be claimed for it by those most easily satisfied with the amount of understanding of truth which ought to accompany the belief of it; even so, the argument for free discussion is in no way weakened. For even this doctrine acknowledges that mankind ought to have a rational assurance that all objections have been satisfactorily answered; and how are they to be answered if that which requires to be answered is not spoken? Or how can the answer be known to be satisfactory, if the objectors have no opportunity of showing that it is unsatisfactory? If not the public, at least the philosophers and theologians who are to resolve the difficulties, must make themselves familiar with those difficulties in their most puzzling form; and this cannot be accomplished unless they are freely stated, and placed in the most advantageous light which they admit of. The Catholic Church has its own way of dealing with this embarrassing problem. It makes a broad separation between those who can be permitted to receive its doctrines on conviction, and those who must accept them on trust. Neither, indeed, are allowed any choice as to what they will accept; but the clergy, such at least as can be fully confided in, may admissibly and meritoriously make themselves acquainted with the arguments of opponents, in order to answer them, and may, therefore, read heretical books; the laity, unless by special permission, find them hard to be obtained. This discipline recognizes a knowledge of the enemy's case as beneficial to the teachers, but finds means, consistent with this, of denying it to the rest of the world: thus giving to the *élite* more mental culture, though not more mental freedom, than it allows to the mass. By this device, it succeeds in obtaining the kind of mental superiority which its purposes require; for though culture without freedom never made a large and liberal mind, it can make a clever *nisi prius* advocate of a cause. But in countries professing Protestantism, this resource is denied; since Protestants hold, at least in theory, that the responsibility for the choice of a religion must be borne by each himself; and cannot be thrown off upon teachers. Besides, in the present state of the world, it is practically impossible that writings which are read by the instructed can be kept from the uninstructed. If the teachers of mankind are to be cognizant of all that they ought to know, everything must be free to be written and published without restraint.

The third reason for requiring that the opposite opinion to our own should not be suppressed without being heard first is that even if it is neither wholly true nor wholly false, it may contain elements of the truth. Political theories are extremely complex. A political theory we do not agree with may be mainly in error, yet it may contain elements of the truth within it, and if we do not hear such an opinion, we may lose the opportunity to discover even this much truth.

CRITICISM OF MILL

As we have remarked previously, **Mill can be regarded as completing democratic doctrine.** Locke set down the main elements in democratic theory, such as government by promulgated law, the doctrine of 'natural rights' and, most important of all, the rule by the majority of the people. Mill added to this framework the proviso that the minority must be protected against possible tyranny by the majority. Since he did not accept the doctrine of natural rights, he attempted to justify limitations on the power of the majority on Utilitarian grounds. Roughly his argument is that **interference in personal matters will in the long run prove harmful to a democratic society. The development of individual initiative and a mature citizenry will both be prevented if the majority's likes and dislikes are allowed to become so powerful that they act as unwritten laws.** This doctrine, since the publication of the essay *On Liberty* has been accepted by most democratic theorists; but it has also been attacked on the grounds that it is impossible to put into practice.

Mill held that the majority could legitimately interfere in the affairs of the minority only when minority behaviour proved harmful to the fabric of society. But this raises the difficult problem: How can we tell when such behaviour will or will not be harmful? Ultimately, these critics assert, the choice will rest with a majority decision, expressed through the framing of laws by an elected legislature. Thus, in the last analysis, minority safeguards will always crumble under attack by the majority. From a standpoint of realistic politics, the minority is only as safe as the majority will let them be; and if so, there is no area of human conduct which is (or even ought to be) immune from such interference.

Had Mill lived to answer this objection, he might have agreed with it in part. If the majority feels that an individual or group of individuals is behaving in a way which is harmful to society, it can pass laws which will restrict such behaviour. Mill does not mean to deny the rightful authority of the majority in a democratic society. For example, it is necessary for the protection of the majority that we pass laws against the sale of adulterated food and drugs. But even in such cases, he would argue, the burden of proof is upon the majority to show that their interference is legitimate. They cannot justly interfere simply because they do not approve of an individual's conduct; they must show further that it is harmful to society. If this cannot be shown, the minority ought to be allowed to behave as it wishes. In practical terms, what Mill's philosophy reduces to is that **in any legal issue**

D

between an individual and the state, the burden of proof for showing tha an individual's behaviour is undesirable, always rests upon the state, no upon the individual. This presumption, once accepted (as it has bee in Great Britain and the United States), will provide the individual wit considerable security against majority interference, even if it does nc guarantee him complete immunity.

The history of political philosophy can fruitfully be looked at i terms of the question 'Who should rule?' Plato, Hobbes—and in fac most political theorists up to Locke—argued that individuals or specia groups should rule, Locke, on the other hand, gives powerful argu ments in favour of the rule 'by the people', where this is interpreted a rule by the majority. Mill, like Locke, believes that the majority shoul rule because on the whole they will be less threatening to the freedor of mankind than any single ruler or group; but even within democracy checks must be put upon the rule of the majority to safeguard persona liberty. We now turn to a philosopher who, like Mill and Locke, wishe to see the 'people' rule—KARL MARX—but whose philosophy has ha practical consequences which are inimical to freedom.

THE POLITICAL PHILOSOPHY OF
KARL MARX

Karl Marx was born in Trier, Prussia, in 1818 and was reared i a comfortable, fairly conventional upper-middle-class atmospher which proved a far cry from the conditions of unrelieved poverty i which he spent most of his mature years. He was sent to the Unive sities of Bonn and Berlin and graduated with distinction, receivin the degree of Doctor of Philosophy. In the normal course of event given this background, he might have been expected to pursue an aca demic career—and accordingly to have vanished into history in cloud of cross-references and footnotes, as is the fate of most di tinguished professors. But such was not the case. Even at that earl date, Marx was regarded as being too radical for academic life, an consequently he chose to take a job on the *Rheinische Zeitung*, left-wing newspaper which strongly opposed the policies of the gover ment. When the newspaper was suppressed, Marx left Germany an went to live first in Paris, and later in Brussels, until the Revolutio of 1848 when he returned to Cologne. When the Revolution faile Marx again departed from Germany, this time settling in Londo which became his home for the remainder of his life.

In England, Marx renewed his friendship with Friedrich Enge whom he had known in Europe, and who had been his collaborate

in the publication of the *Communist Manifesto* in 1847. Engels's fathe was a prominent manufacturer of cotton goods in Manchester and, a is so often the case with fathers who have radical sons, was highl conservative. Engels worked for his father, and with part of h income supported Marx who at that time was living in incredib poverty. In 1870 Engels moved from Manchester to London, and wi Marx founded the International Workingmen's Association (som times known as the First International)—an organization designed better the lot of working people. Marx died in 1883, and Engels—working from Marx's notes—completed the final volumes of *Capital*, Marx's political masterpiece. Engels died in 1895.

Marx's political philosophy is a highly complex doctrine which contains at least three distinct elements. The first is a **metaphysics,** which Marx inherited from Hegel, and in which **he attempts to prove that political, social and economic events are to be understood in terms of certain general laws of history, called 'the dialectic'.** The second is an **economic theory,** in which Marx offers **a defence of Socialism as opposed to Capitalism;** and the third is an **ethic,** which stresses **human values as opposed to the values allegedly existing in material goods.** Let us consider each of these in turn, beginning with the metaphysical part of the doctrine.

Marx's Metaphysics: The Influence of Hegel. G. F. HEGEL was, by all odds, the most important German philosopher of the nineteenth century. Like most young intellectuals of the period, Marx was greatly influenced by his writings, especially his writings on the Philosophy of History. Later on in his life, Marx was severely to criticize Hegelianism, but he never really succeeded in shaking off its hold on him. Indeed, to a considerable extent, Marx's political doctrines can be understood only in the light of Hegel's metaphysics, as we shall now attempt to show. Roughly, the influence was this: **Marx believed that Hegel had found a general historical law, called 'the dialectic', but he thought that Hegel's use of it was metaphysical, rather than scientific.** He accepted the existence of the dialectic, but attempted to make it materialistic by explaining the historical process in economic rather than metaphysical terms and by applying it to **classes rather than to nations. He thus tried to explain history in terms of the struggle between classes** instead of the struggle between nations, as Hegel had done.

As we have intimated above, the essential notion in Hegel's works—a notion which Marx utilized, but applied differently—is what Hegel called 'the dialectic'. Hegel had borrowed the term 'dialectic' from Plato, but gave it a much broader signification. In Plato, 'dialectic' is regarded as a certain kind of logical process. It is a method of argumentation, employing what modern logicians call 'the method of the contrary case'. It is used for the purpose of eliciting from someone to whom it is applied, information which he possesses, but of which he may not be aware. Thus, by questioning a slave boy, Meno, who had never studied geometry, Socrates elicits from him certain theorems of Euclid, or again, by questioning Cephalus, Polemarchus, and others in *The Republic*, Socrates attempts to extract from them a true account of the nature of 'justice'. The method operates as follows: someone proposes a thesis about the nature of justice. For example, *The Republic* opens with Cephalus suggesting that 'justice' means the same as 'telling the truth and paying one's debts'. The next step in applying the method is to find a contrary case to the thesis—i.e., a case which we would ordinarily say involved justice, but did not involve telling the truth. This is called by Hegel the **'antithesis'.** The reconciliation of thesis and antithesis produces a **synthesis** which itself becomes a new thesis at a more advanced level. By continually applying this method, by proposing **thesis and antithesis,** a true account of the nature of justice is finally arrived at—an account which **encompasses and reconciles** both thesis and antithesis.

To give an example of this process, taken from *The Republic*, consider the following: Cephalus proposes that 'justice' means 'telling the truth and paying one's debts'. Socrates then produces a contrary case. He points out that if you have borrowed a weapon from a friend who subsequently goes out of his mind and demands it back, you would not feel it right or just to give it back to him. Justice in such a case requires that you ought not to pay your debt. If so, justice is sometimes compatible with not paying one's debts and the thesis that 'justice' means 'paying one's debts' is false. We are thus forced to produce a new definition which will include both the original thesis, and the contrary case. When found, this will be a **synthesis** of the original definition and the objection to it.

For Hegel, the term 'dialectic' has much the same meaning that it has in Plato. **It is a logical process, which proceeds from thesis to antithesis, and to a synthesis which combines them both.** But Hegel regards the dialectic as more than merely a logical process in the sense in which verbal argumentation is a logical process. For him, it is an **actual process which events in the world follow. All change, especially historical change, takes place in accordance with the law of the dialectic: a thesis is produced, it develops an opposition (its antithesis), a conflict between them ensues, and the conflict is resolved into a synthesis which includes both thesis and antithesis.**

Hegel, as we have mentioned, thought that history could best be understood by observing the development of nations in the light of the dialectic. A given nation can be regarded as occupying a position in the dialectic which is analogous to the position occupied in an argument by the thesis or hypothesis which the argument is supposed to establish. As the nation develops, it produces opposition to itself. An opposing nation may be regarded as its antithesis. Finally, the two conflict, and from the struggle, there emerges a new civilization which is of a **higher order** than either of the previous ones. **It synthesizes what is of most value in each.** This new nation now becomes a new thesis, which in turn will develop its antithesis, and so forth, ad infinitum. Furthermore, Hegel believes that this is a process that is leading to perfection. It is through this process that a state progresses towards the realization of what he calls its 'Spirit'. The end or aim of the development of the essential nature of every state is what he calls 'The Idea' or 'The absolute Idea'. Thus, for Hegel, the dialectical process is a spiritual or metaphysical process.

Hegel believed that in discovering the dialectic he had discovered a *necessary law* of nature. It was not merely the case that nations sometimes opposed each other; but it was *logically necessary that by its very nature* every nation will ultimately breed its opposite, will conflict with it, and then proceed through the remainder of the dialectic. In short, **the course of history is determined by the dialectic and nothing can alter this course.** Men suppose that through social action they can change the course of history, but they are simply mistaken through a lack of historical knowledge. Men are merely pawns of historical necessity—it is really the dialectic which controls the course of events.

Marx accepted Hegel's analysis of historical change as proceeding in accordance with the dialectic. But he did not like the metaphysical explanation of this process and he thought that Hegel's application of the dialectic to nations was essentially superficial. Marx prefers a materialist dialectic; he prefers to explain the dialectical process of history in economic rather than metaphysical terms. The reason why nations change is that the classes of men within the nation begin to oppose each other. The history of the world should not be regarded as a history of the rivalry between states, but more fundamentally as a history of the rivalry between classes.

Professor Barnett Savery has put this point very well. He writes:

> The Marxists explain the doctrine of opposites in the following way: Everything contains two main opposing forces, one is called the thesis, the other is called the antithesis. These two forces destroy each other, but from the destruction arises a new situation which is called a synthesis. Eventually, this synthesis breaks down into its opposites—and we have a new thesis and a new antithesis. And then out of these opposing forces arises a new synthesis—and so on. The Marxists, as we shall indicate, make use of this idea in order to demonstrate that communism, as a society, is ethically superior to all previous existing societies.

The historical King-state society, according to the Marxists, broke down into its opposites—the King-rulers, on the one hand, and the dispossessed and slaves on the other hand. From the struggle between these opposites, a synthesis was formed, and the feudalistic society came into being. Feudalism, then, broke down into its opposing forces, the lords and the serfs; and this struggle was synthesized and modern capitalism was born. And, now, the Marxists claim that capitalism has broken down into its opposites; the employers, on the one hand, and the employees, on the other hand. The new society, according to the Marxists, will be Marxian socialism. The Marxists argue that each new society is ethically superior to the society that existed before. Feudalism, they claim, is superior to the King-state; capitalism to feudalism; and communism to capitalist societies.

This aspect of Marxism indicates what is meant by the class struggle; it is the doctrine of opposites as it reveals itself in societies. The Marxists claim that they do not create the class struggle; they claim, rather, that they merely show its existence, and then make use of it in order to foster the growth of communism. The additional belief of the Marxists, that each distinctly new society is ethically superior to the old social forms, makes excellent propaganda for Marxism. Undoubtedly, many people become adherents to communism because they believe that they are working for a world that is better than anything that has ever existed.

Let us show in somewhat more detail how Marx applied the dialectic to classes, and what inferences he drew from such an application. To begin with, Marx felt that every person belongs to a certain socio-economic group within the society. Such a group is called a 'class'. The system of classes that a given culture has is completely determined by the **economic means and conditions of production** in the culture. Thus, each period of economic development has a corresponding class system. For instance, during the period of hand-mill production, feudalism was the system of classes which prevailed. When hand-mill production was replaced by steam-mill production, capitalism replaced feudalism. Capitalism is an economic system with three main social classes: those who own or control the means of production, called by Marx 'the capitalists'; those who are entirely dependent for their livelihood upon the earnings they get while working for the owners—the working class; and certain other groups, such as small businessmen, or white-collar workers (lawyers, doctors, professors, etc.) who may not fit exactly into either scheme—the middle class.

Marx's thesis was that all class relationships are independent of men's wills, and in fact are really determined by the prevailing economic system. Men think they can choose the class they wish to belong to, but such opinions are merely self-deceptive. **Classes are really determined by the means of production,** and the class a person falls into will depend upon where he stands relative to the means of production. Since the means of production themselves follow the pattern of history, i.e., the dialectic, every such means will generate its own opposition and this will lead to a conflict. The conflict will itself engender new relations between people and the means of production, with a resulting change in the class arrangement of the culture. Classes being determined by their relation to the means of production, they too will be subject to the domination of the dialectic. The result is that history can be succinctly described as taking the course which class conflict takes.

To illustrate what Marx means by class conflict, let us consider a specific example, the rise of socialism as a result of class conflict within capitalistic society.

According to Marx, because of technological advances in a capitalist society, there will be a constant increase in the productivity of that society. This tendency toward an increase in productivity means that there will be a corresponding increase of wealth in the class which owns the means of production. At the same time, the conditions of life in the working class will become worse, and instead of having more money the workers will have less. In fact, finally most of the money in the society will be concentrated in the hands of the few who own the means of production. The intermediate classes will be wiped out, and capitalism will present a picture of two classes highly opposed to each other—a small but very wealthy class ('the bourgeoisie') and a large but indigent working class ('the proletariat'). Tension and hatred will develop between these classes and finally a revolution will take place, which will lead to a **classless society,** in which there is no exploitation of the worker. This is Socialism as Marx pictured it. The steps of the dialectic are easily perceived in this picture: capitalism presents a thesis—that one ought to work in order to realize a profit. The thesis if followed leads to a state in which a few own the means of production, and everyone else is subject to the control of those few. But if followed, the thesis produces antagonism between the large, indigent class of workers and the small capitalist class. This is the stage of the dialectic called the 'antithesis'. Finally, an open conflict breaks out and the capitalist class is submerged. A new classless society arises (the 'synthesis').

We may summarize Marx's metaphysics as follows: Marx accepts the Hegelian doctrine that world history follows a pattern of opposing forces, called 'the dialectic'. Hegel believed that the pattern primarily applied to nations, but Marx showed that it applies to classes. Classes are determined not by men's wills or inclinations, but by the means of production which exist in that particular culture. Classes produce their own oppositions, leading to conflicts and finally to an overthrow of the particular class system. In the case of capitalism, the overthrow will lead to a classless society, or Socialism, in which the means of production are controlled by the workers (i.e., everyone in such a society).

We have designated Marx's theory, as adumbrated above, a '**meta-physical' theory because it rests upon the thesis that all change takes place through conflict, and moreover, conflict of a curiously logical sort.** Marx himself, of course, believed that he had discovered a scientific law which applied to classes, and which explained history. He thought this law was scientific because it referred to materialistic considerations (such as economic factors) in explaining the movement of events; whereas Hegel thought that nations were motivated by what he called 'spirit'. Marx rejected an explanation in terms of 'spirit' as unsatisfactory, and instead attempted to give a 'hard-headed' account of the nature of change. But, as we have shown, his explanation, like Hegel's, may itself be charged with being metaphysical, **since it deduces the nature of change from purely logical considerations.** In terms of this doctrine, Marx predicts the coming of a classless or socialist society. But even though this prediction is based upon metaphysical assumptions, some at least of Marx's attack upon capitalism is based upon a careful descriptive account of how capitalistic societies have worked. This attack attempts, on economic grounds rather than on logical or metaphysical ones, to show that capitalistic societies will inevitably collapse. Let us turn now to Marx's economic theory to see how it reinforced his metaphysical views with regard to the prediction that capitalism must inevitably fail and give way to a socialist economy.

Marx's Economic Theory: The Attack Upon Capitalism. The basic notions in Marxian economic theory are **The Labour Theory of Value, The Theory of Surplus Value,** and **The Concentration of Capital,** and the coming of Socialism as a result of that concentration. Let us begin with the Labour Theory of Value.

The Labour Theory of Value is not original to Marx. It was propounded by many famous economists who preceded him, among them, for instance, DAVID RICARDO and ADAM SMITH. The point of the theory is to determine what is meant by 'economic value'. Marx's version runs something like this: There is a distinction between the 'use value' of a commodity and its 'exchange value'. A commodity may be useful to us, but it may have no value if we try to exchange it for something else. For example, air has use value: we require it in order to live. But if we try to exchange it for a book, no one will accept it. This is because it is readily available to anyone who wants it. What makes a commodity have exchange value is that it can be obtained only at some cost. This cost is what Marx calls its 'economic value'. More basically, what makes a commodity costly is the amount of **labour power** that goes into its production. In order to save labour power men will accept for exchange items which require labour power in order to be produced. Thus 'economic value' is defined in terms of 'the quantity of labour necessary for its production in a given state of society, under certain social average conditions of production, with a given social average intensity, and average skill of the labour employed'.

The Theory of Surplus Value. According to Marx **the ordinary worker, lacking capital, is forced to sell his labour, and thus in a sense, himself, as a commodity.** Roughly, the amount of money which an employer pays to the worker is an estimation of the economic value of the labourer regarded as a commodity which the employer must purchase. But the labourer normally produces items having much more economic value than is represented by the wages he receives. The difference between the amount of economic value he produces and the amount he receives for his work is called 'surplus value' by Marx. The employer does not pay him for this—in fact, the employer takes the surplus value of a labourer's efforts and utilizes it in various ways, the most important of which is profit. Thus, according to Marx, workers actually produce the wealth through the amount of labour they contribute, but the capitalists take a considerable amount of it without rewarding the worker correspondingly. This is the source of their profit.

The Theory of Surplus Value allows us to pinpoint the source of conflict between capitalist and worker. The capitalist wishes to accumulate as great a profit as possible. This will be possible only if he pays the lowest possible wages and sells his commodities for the highest possible price. On the other hand, the worker's demands are exactly the opposite: to receive the highest possible wages for his work and to buy produced goods as cheaply as possible. Thus, within capitalism we have a fundamental inconsistency, and strife between these classes is unavoidable.

The concentration of capital and the coming of Socialism. According to Marx, capitalism as an economic system enjoins one to seek the highest possible profits from his investment. For the capitalist, this means engaging in constant competition with other businessmen, since profit depends upon the amount of goods which can be sold. Now in order to sell a large volume of goods, it is necessary to sell them as cheaply as possible. In effect, this means that one must constantly try to undersell his competitor. But since the cost of production is relatively similar for goods of similar quality, the only place where an employer, in the long run, can significantly cut his costs lies in his using the most inexpensive labour. As the power of the capitalist grows, this becomes even more important. For after freezing small businessmen out of business by underselling them he will finally be left in competition with a few large-scale producers, like himself. At that stage, in order to meet their competition and in order to acquire greater and greater profits, he will have to pay the worker less and less. He will demand a greater surplus of the worker's productivity. The result of this tendency, according to Marx, is that in the later stages of a capitalist society, the worker will become increasingly poorer and the capitalist increasingly richer. Tension is bound to develop between them when the worker realizes that he is being exploited (this realization is called 'becoming class conscious')—and finally conflict will break out. As a consequence of this conflict, the worker will take over the means of production, and a new thesis will be inaugurated—the age of the classless society, or Socialism.

Apart from the defects in capitalism which the above economic analysis indicates, there is an even more serious fault to be found with it. According to Marx, **capitalism engenders relations among men which are ethically immoral ones. Humanity disappears in the treatment of men by each other, and is replaced by an inhuman drive for profits.** Thus, in arguing that capitalism was not a workable system, Marx was in part basing his contention upon an ethical theory, as well as upon economic and metaphysical doctrines. Let us consider briefly his views on morality in concluding this section.

Marx's Ethical Views. Marx maintained that **industry and technological discoveries develop much more rapidly than do the techniques for controlling them.** As he puts it:

> In our days everything seems pregnant with its contrary; machinery gifted with the wonderful power of shortening and fructifying human labour, we behold starving and overworking it. The newfangled sources of wealth, by some strange weird spell, are turned into sources of want. The victories of art seem bought by the loss of character. At the same pace that mankind masters nature, man seems to become enslaved to other men or to his own infamy. Even the pure light of science seems unable to shine but on the dark background of ignorance. All our inventions and progress seem to result in endowing material forces with intellectual life, and in stultifying human life into a material force.

Thus, even though industrial expansion should have made it possible for men to live more comfortably together, with greater security, exactly the opposite is taking place. The capitalist system in order to maintain profits for those who own the means of production induces one war after another; children are forced into labour; the conflict between classes is intensified. All this, according to Marx, is due to two factors: to what he calls **'self-alienation'**, and to what he calls **'fetishism'**. Socialism will remedy both. 'Self-alienation' is a term Marx uses to describe man's plight in the modern industrial world. Instead of finding industry helpful, instead of finding that it improves men's relations with each other, we find exactly the opposite. **Men are cut off from other men; are isolated and made fearful and insecure.**

This is not merely alienation from the world, but *self*-alienation; for man is alienated from his own true nature. He creates a highly technical world, but he cannot control it—and thus, he alienates himself from all those things which he prizes most and which this technology was designed to achieve for him: security, comfort, friendship, leisure, culture and so forth. Self-alienation is accompanied by 'fetishism', the worship of the products of labour. For instance men produce motor cars by their labour; and once having produced them, men become ruled by such inanimate things. It is the *things* which are given value, not the *person* who creates them. As Marx writes:

> The object which labour produces, its product, is encountered as an *alien entity*, a force which has become independent of its producer. The more the worker toils the more powerful becomes the alien world of objects he produces to oppose him, and the poorer he himself becomes.

The most terrible effect of capitalism has been to depersonalize the relations between men; to make men more like machines and machines more like men. It is this tendency which Marx is arguing against. Socialism, he feels, will not only remedy the economic affairs of men, but will introduce a new morality as well—a morality based upon human values, not upon machine values.

With these remarks, we conclude our exposition of Marx's political philosophy. Let us now turn, briefly, to some critical remarks.

CRITICISM OF MARX

As we have pointed out, political philosophies may be classified according to how they answer the question 'Who should rule?' As we have seen, Plato and Hobbes are advocates of the doctrine that a few should rule. Marx, on the other hand, like Mill and Locke, is unashamedly on the side of the many. Marx's political philosophy can without distortion be interpreted as holding that in a capitalistic society a few will rule, i.e., those who own the means of production, and that this is basically wrong. In stressing that it is the majority which is important, Marx is firmly in the tradition of liberal and democratic philosophers. Further, many contemporary thinkers are inclined to agree with Marx's ethical outlook, which lays stress upon the importance of human values as opposed to the world of the machine which modern industry has created.

The main criticisms of Marxist theory are aimed at its philosophy of history and at its economic theory. The Marxist conception of history has been attacked on two fronts. In the first place, it is argued that there can be no justification for any attempt to establish broad general laws of history. This may be a useful way of understanding the past but it cannot provide any valid basis for predicting the future, as Marx tries to do. Marx sees historical development as an inevitable process which will ultimately lead in all states to the establishment of the classless society. There must be serious doubt about the validity of this kind of interpretation of history and of the claim that the process will stop at that point. The second criticism of his philosophy of history is levelled at the introduction of a **moral evaluation** of these stages of change. Each one, Marx tells us, is **ethically superior** to the one that precedes it and the final stage, the classless society, is perfection. In other words, this is a theory of historical **progress** rather than of mere historical **change**. There must be some standard by which we evaluate this progress so that to speak in this way is to appeal to an absolute moral criterion which Marx himself will not admit the validity of in his other discussions of morals. For elsewhere he tells us that moral values are not expressions of 'eternal truths' but are relative to the society in which they are held. The objective ideals of his conception of history are not compatible with his subjective view of social morality. This inconsistency lies at the very root of Marxism.

Marxist economic theory has been criticized by defenders of capitalism on empirical grounds, that is by an appeal to facts which seem to disprove it. **According to Marx, the capitalistic system will inevitably produce periodic depressions and will finally culminate in the accumulation of wealth by the owners of the means of production, and in the increasing misery of the workers.** |All this will lead to revolution, and to

the development of a socialist, classless society. Now, defenders of capitalism attack this thesis on two counts: **They point out that the prediction of increasing misery in capitalist societies has not been confirmed.** In fact, the lot of the worker is better than ever. He works fewer hours, has more money, and in general lives on a higher standard than workers did a century ago. Instead of producing lower standards of living, and instead of exacerbating the relation between employer and employee, capitalism has produced higher standards of living, and better relations between owner and worker. They also point out that **capitalism has shown itself amazingly inventive** in solving difficulties which appear within it. Such developments as the growth of Trades Unions, anti-trust laws, social-security measures, have all proved beneficial in contributing to the economic stability of capitalist societies. For example, Trades Unions have thwarted the tendency to sell labour power more and more cheaply by fixing the rates for the use of labour time. Such measures as these, according to critics of Marx, will constantly be discovered by capitalist countries and hence the prediction of increasing misery will not be fulfilled.

The Marxian answer to both of these charges is the following: Although the standard of living in some capitalist countries is higher than it used to be, this is not true of all capitalist countries. Furthermore, Marxists contend, the spread of socialism throughout the world has been greater in this century than ever before. This, they argue, is evidence that socialism is the preferred system and that capitalism is slowly losing its hold. Against the view that capitalism is imaginatively able to solve its problems, Marxists argue that many of the measures which are used are socialist measures. For example, deficit spending in a time of crisis is a socialist device for avoiding a depression; the growth of Trades Unions in order to restrict the size of the labour pool is likewise another instance of tampering with the normal development of capitalism. Marxists say that such devices as these are necessary in order to save the system from destroying itself.

This concludes our brief outline of Marxist theory and of some of the objections to it. With it we come to the end of this section in which we have tried to draw attention to some of the major political problems that philosophers have concerned themselves with and some of the difficulties they have encountered in doing so. The reader will see for himself how many of these problems continue to be unsolved, open questions. We hope we have stimulated him to further enquiry into some of them. A bibliography of selected readings follows.

SUGGESTED FURTHER READING

Classical Authors:

Plato, *The Republic*. (The most famous exposition of an authoritarian society.)

Aristotle, *Politics*. (A great classic of political theory.)

Machiavelli, *The Prince*. (Advice to the ruler by a shrewd politician.)

More, Thomas, *Utopia*. (An attempt to work out a perfect society.)

Hobbes, T., *The Leviathan*. (A defence of absolute monarchy.)

Locke, J., *Second Treatise on Civil Government*. (A classic statement of democracy.)

Rousseau, J. J., *Social Contract*.

Mill, J. S., *Essay on Liberty*. (A defence of freedom.)

Hegel, *The Philosophy of History*. (German Idealism which influenced Marx.)

Marx, *Capital*. (Analysis of capitalism.)

Modern Authors:

Benn, S. I. and Peters, R. S., *Social Principles and the Democratic State*. Allen & Unwin: London, 1959. (A modern discussion of some of the major problems of political theory.)

Foster, M. B., Jones, W. T. and Lancaster, L. W., *Masters of Political Thought*. 3 vols. Harrap: London, 1959. (Good summary of the history of political thought, with many long quotations from the original texts: a very useful introductory work.)

Plamenatz, John, *Man and Society*. 2 vols. Longmans: London, 1963. (A detailed critical examination of the most important social and political theories from Machiavelli to Marx.)

Popper, Karl, *The Open Society and Its Enemies*. 2 vols. Routledge & Kegan Paul: London, 1962. (A discussion of the threat to democracy of the totalitarian implications of the theories of Plato, Hegel and Marx.)

Sabine, George, *A History of Political Theory*. Harrap: London, 1963. (An outstanding history of political thought.)

CHAPTER III

METAPHYSICS

What is Metaphysics? Of all the branches of philosophy, none sounds more alarmingly abstract than metaphysics. In ordinary usage a theory or view is called 'metaphysical' if it seems complicated beyond comprehensibility. Or, the term 'metaphysical' is used as synonymous with 'fanciful', or 'imaginary'.

Actually, metaphysics, in the ordinary Greek, meant simply 'that which comes after physics'. It has been speculated that the word entered the philosophical lexicon when the treatises of Aristotle, now called his **Metaphysics,** were found untitled among his papers. Since they appeared among the manuscripts after the work entitled *Physics*, they were simply called 'Metaphysics', 'meta' being the Greek word for 'after'.

But there is another, a philosophical sense in which metaphysics means 'after physics'. Many of the early Greek philosophical writings were entitled 'Concerning Nature' (the Greek term for nature being 'phusis'). These works usually dealt with what we would now consider physical science, but they were also speculations about the meaning and nature of the universe—that is, with questions which arise *after* the physical problems have been resolved, or which are concerned with what lies *after* or *beyond* the physical world of sensory experience.

Pluralism and Monism. To explain this, let us consider an example of a metaphysical question with which the ancient Greeks were concerned. After developing a crude system of scientific 'explanation' in terms of earth, air, fire and water, they asked whether these were the fundamental elements of the natural universe, or whether something else accounted for the four elements and the events of nature.

Some of the early metaphysicians were **pluralists** who held that **more than one** feature of the universe accounted for scientific knowledge of it; others were **monists** who insisted that there was **one and only one basic feature.** What should be stressed is that the questions posed by the early metaphysicians were ones that arose *after* physical problems had been considered, and that these answers undertook to evaluate and interpret the physical theories in other non-physical terms.

Scope of Metaphysics. Beyond these speculations, the metaphysician attempted to work out hypotheses that would account for (make intelligible) all scientific knowledge as well as everything else that we may know or believe about the universe. These metaphysical explanations purport to encompass the most general and fundamental characteristics of the cosmos, both physical and mental (or spiritual).

In order to survey this vast and all-encompassing branch of philosophy, we will first consider some of the basic metaphysical problems that have persisted throughout the ages. Then we shall examine some of the most famous metaphysical systems in the history of philosophy. Lastly, we shall glance at some of the criticisms directed by certain philosophers at the value of metaphysical investigations.

THE PROBLEM OF PERMANENCE AND CHANGE

The first metaphysical problem to be considered is one of the earliest in the history of philosophy, **the problem of permanence and change.** Beginning with the first philosopher we know of, THALES, Greek thinkers were impressed with two basic features of the world— **the occurrence of natural change, and the continuance of certain apparently permanent conditions.** The earliest theories attempted to account for both the persistent and the changing features by portraying the world in terms of certain stable, constant elements (or element) which constitute the 'real', or permanent aspect, while the rest was flux in the world of 'appearance'. The latter might continually alter, but the former always retained the same basic, unchanging aspects.

However, certain difficulties appeared which suggested that the changing and the permanent features of the universe were incompatible. On the one hand, it was pointed out, if everything changed there could be nothing permanent; and on the other hand, if there was a permanent element of the universe, it could not change, could not account for alterations, and therefore could not be part of a system that involved change.

Heraclitus and Cratylus. The early Greek philosopher, HERACLITUS, was the theoretician of change. **Everything alters and changes,** he insisted. One can never step twice into the same river, since it does not remain the same. The only permanence was not some 'stuff' or substance that remained constant, but rather the **principle of law of change.** Everything in the cosmos was in flux. It came into being and it passed away. Only the universal principle that everything changes remains unaltered.

A later disciple of this philosophy of change, CRATYLUS, saw that if one took this theory seriously, no permanence would be left, not even the permanence of the law of change. If everything changes, even the words we use, the meanings they have must be in constant flux, so that we cannot even have a constant language with which to describe the world in which we live. So, Cratylus concluded, one cannot even step into the same river once, because by the time one steps into it, it has changed. In fact, if everything is constantly changing, one cannot even discuss anything, since by the time one finishes speaking, the speaker, the words, the meanings, and the listener have all altered. Hence, all that Cratylus felt he could do in this world was wiggle his finger when he was addressed, to indicate that he had heard. But it would be futile to try to make the universe stand still long enough to make any response. Thus, if one took the notion of change literally, one could not make sense out of it, because there would be no lasting features which one could seek to understand.

Parmenides. If those who emphasized change as a fundamental characteristic of the cosmos encountered great difficulties, so did their opponents who argued for permanence. The early Greek philosopher, PARMENIDES, made an analysis of what could validly be said of the fixed, unchanging and unchangeable features of reality. If the universe consisted of some permanent, immutable base, Parmenides pointed out, then this constant element could not alter, move, divide, separate, and so on, since any of these properties would indicate change. Further, if the subject of investigation is some fixed Being or Reality, then this permanent element can have no properties other than existence, since any other properties would suggest change or mutability. The sole truth that could be discovered about the permanent Being is that it *is*.

Everything else in the world of flux, Parmenides claimed, cannot belong to the real world, or the world of permanent Being. Anything that can alter changes from not existing to existing to not existing again. The Permanent cannot change into anything without ceasing to be permanent. What is, cannot change into what is not, without passing out of existence. Hence, the Permanent, the Real, *is*, and cannot be part of Reality or become part of Reality. What is permanent must remain forever the same. It is what it is, and to become something other than this would involve the contradiction that it became what it is not. The changing world is what the Real or Permanent world is not. The only property the fixed aspect of the universe has is **that it exists.** Thus, the changing aspect cannot be part of existence, since it does not belong to the real, unchanging aspect, and must, therefore, be non-existent. As Parmenides concluded in a famous phrase, **'Being is, Non-being is not'** and only the unchanging belongs to the world of Being.

Zeno. As if Parmenides had not gone far enough in asserting what happens when one claims permanent features for the world, his disciple, the famous ZENO of Elea, went still further. Zeno (not to be confused with the Zeno whom we have already discussed as the founder of Stoicism) sought to show that not only did the changing world have nothing to do with the Real, Permanent world, but that the concept of change itself was impossible. Zeno was not disputing that we experience change in the course of our daily lives—in seeing things grow, move around, and change qualities. Rather, he claimed that any attempt to **explain** change or motion would lead to contradictions, and would thus compel acceptance of the Parmenidean philosophy that only the Permanent and Unchanging was real. The rest could be dismissed as an unfortunate illusion that we can only ignore.

Zeno's 'Paradoxes'. The arguments of Zeno, which still play a role in metaphysical discussions, are his well-known **paradoxes** concerning motion. By these he tried to show that starting with an ordinary situation in which we suppose something to be moving or changing, it could be shown that such motion cannot possibly occur. The most familiar of the Zeno paradoxes concerns Achilles and the tortoise. If Achilles can run ten times faster than the tortoise, and the tortoise has a ten yard lead at the outset—then when Achilles has run ten yards to catch up to the tortoise, the latter has moved ahead one yard. When Achilles runs this yard, the slow tortoise has moved on one tenth of a yard. Each time Achilles reaches the position where the tortoise had been, the tortoise has moved on some small distance, so that Achilles will never catch up, even though he moves so much faster.

Another of Zeno's paradoxes holds that for an object to move from one place to another, it first must move half of the distance involved. But to move half of the distance, it must move half of the half, and so on infinitely. Also, for it to move to each stage will take some time, no matter how slight. Thus, not only will the object go through any infinite number of distances, it will also require an infinite number of time intervals. Therefore, for an object to go from one place to another, no matter how small the distance, will require forever, and, according to the argument, in no finite time will it ever be able to traverse the distance.

The last of the Zeno paradoxes that we will mention here is the argument that for an object, like an arrow, to go from one place to another, it must move either where it is, or where it is not. If it moves where it is, it will be standing still. If it moves where it is not, it cannot be there. Therefore, the object cannot move. A version of this argument was offered to show that it was impossible for a person to die. Someone dies either when he is alive or when he is dead. If he dies when he is dead, then he must have died twice. If he dies when he is alive, then he must be dead and alive at the same time. Therefore, he cannot die. (There is an amusing account that has come down to us of the Zenoist who was haranguing a crowd in ancient Athens about why nothing can move, and in the course of emphasizing his point with some wild gestures, he dislocated his shoulder. A doctor who was in the audience examined the shoulder, and told the Zenoist that the circumstances were impossible, because he either dislocated his shoulder where it was, or where it was not. If the former, then his shoulder was not dislocated since it was still in the same place. If the latter, his shoulder could not be there to be dislocated. The patient, we are told, gave up his views at this point, and demanded that the doctor fix his shoulder, no matter how it got there.)

Each of these arguments attempts to show that when one tries to explain the common-sense fact of change or motion, one is led to the paradoxical conclusion that either nothing can move, or that if it does move, it takes an infinite time to traverse any distance. There is a vast literature analysing Zeno's arguments, and propounding solutions to them. But, in their day, regardless of one's opinions as to the ultimate merits of the reasoning, the Zeno paradoxes produced a crisis among both scientists and metaphysicians. The former were horrified to find that the best mathematical account of moving objects seemed to lead to such paradoxical conclusions. In Greek mathematics, there are ingenious attempts to construct different theories of motion in order to avoid the Zenoist conclusions. Among the metaphysicians, the problem became one of discovering some intelligible explanation of how the two basic features of change and permanence could be reconciled in a consistent theory about the ultimate nature of the universe. Heraclitus' views seemed to eliminate permanence as a characteristic of the world, and the arguments of Parmenides and Zeno appeared to show that change or motion could not be a real aspect of the world.

Democritus' Solution. One of the most important metaphysical theories in the ancient world was the **materialism of Democritus,** who tried to resolve the conflicts that had arisen between the theories of change and permanence by offering a new conception of the fundamental characteristics of the real world. **The basic features of the Democritean universe were both unchanging and unchangeable in one sense, and also constantly in flux in another.**

According to Democritus, the ultimate constituent of the real world was an indivisible physical unit, the atom (which originally meant 'that which has no parts', or 'that which cannot be divided'). Each atom had fixed characteristics of form, shape, etc., which remained permanently and perpetually the same. Thus, the Democritean atoms had the immutable property that Parmenides had insisted must belong to the world of Being.

But, in addition to their unchangeable nature, the atoms were supposed in continual change of position, constantly moving through empty space. For all time, they fell through space, colliding with other atoms and being thrown into different courses and arrangements. Thus, although one could always describe the form and shape of each atom in the same manner, since it had a permanent character, one could also attribute to it a never-ending change of position, or a permanent impermanence of location.

With this compromise between the totally fixed and unchanging universe of Parmenides and Zeno, and the constantly changing one of Heraclitus, **Democritus believed he could develop a theory about the nature of reality that could account for all we know about the cosmos.** On the one hand, the eternal, immutable features of the atoms would provide a basis for the permanent features of the universe, a stable structure to which no changing properties could be attributed. The constant motion of the atoms, on the other hand, accounts for alteration in an unchanging world. The world of atoms always remained the same; but the position and distribution of the atoms could be altered without affecting the permanent, stable characteristics. In this way, Democritus sought to explain apparent changes in terms of changing combinations of atoms—for example the change of colour of a leaf, the movement of visible objects. The changes we perceive do not actually take place in reality, but something else does, which does not alter the permanent structure of the universe, but which produces, in conjunction with our atomic constituents, the apparent changes of our experience. Thus, Democritus agreed with Parmenides to the extent of insisting upon the unchangeable nature of reality, and the illusoriness of apparent change, while, at the same time, claiming that a type of change (that of position) is a basic feature of the real universe, and accounts for our experience of reality.

Aristotle's Solution. Another of the great metaphysical theories to resolve the problem of change and permanence was that of ARISTOTLE.

For him, neither experienced change, nor permanence could be sacrificed in constructing an adequate theory of the fundamental characteristics of the world. Even the apparent changing qualities had to be taken seriously, and not simply dismissed as they had been in the writings of Democritus.

Accordingly, in Aristotle's analysis, one had to recognize two basic elements in any possible natural event. The first of these is that there must be **something which remains the same, and yet is somehow subject to variation.** The other is that there occur **genuine changes of qualities.** Thus, for example, when an acorn grows into an oak, there must be some permanent feature that has at one time the qualities that we call an acorn, and later, those that we call an oak. Unless this were the case, we could not even properly describe it as a change, since there would be no relation between the former state and the latter. But, if there is some fixed aspect, there must be another that changes, there must be something different between the acorn and the oak, or there would be no genuine alteration.

Matter and Form. The two features, Aristotle said, are **matter and form.** Matter, in its pure state, would have no characteristics whatsoever. But matter is that which is capable of being 'informed'—of assuming various forms. The **matter** of the acorn and oak (which is not really pure to begin with) has the **potentiality** of receiving different forms, of having one form at one time, and another at a later time. The **form** of the object at any given time is its **actuality, what it has become at that particular moment.**

Each and every object in this world has thus a permanent nature which persists through its realization or acquisition of different forms. Each and every object can be understood only in terms of **both its matter and its form, and the processes by which it grows, alters, or moves, that is, replaces one form with another.** The permanent aspect of an object (with one exception that will be discussed later) never exists independently, or without assuming some form. **The object always is in some state and is in process of reaching some other state.** Thus, the **formal,** changing aspect, and the **material,** permanent aspect of any object are always present and always constitute the basis for any explanation of what is occurring.

In the analysis of Aristotle and Democritus, an attempt was made to resolve the metaphysical problem of change and permanence. Each tried to develop some way of accounting for two of the basic features of the universe without being led into contradictory or paradoxical views. Each sought to construct a general explanation of the characteristics of the objects of the world which would provide a broad basis in terms of which all scientific information could be portrayed or understood.

The problem of permanence and change, like the other metaphysical problems that we shall examine next, is one of the persistent problems that any general system of the nature of the universe has to confront. Those who wished to construct a metaphysical framework in order to interpret or evaluate our knowledge and beliefs have found that the task centres around finding some consistent set of answers to the difficulties that have arisen from the beginning of philosophy. As we shall see, these problems are to some degree interrelated. The question that we shall consider next, the mind–body problem, in some measure involves the theory of permanence and change.

THE MIND-BODY PROBLEM

The mind–body problem has been a major concern of metaphysicians, especially since the rise of modern philosophy in the seventeenth century. In the form in which we shall discuss it, this problem has arisen as the result of certain views of the great French philosopher, RENÉ DESCARTES. In spite of our increasing knowledge about the behaviour of the mental and the physical world, this metaphysical question continues to plague philosophers.

Basically, the problem involves answering the questions, **'What is the fundamental nature of mind and body?'** and **'How are mind and body related?'** An elementary consideration of what we know about mental and physical events might well lead one to suspect that the most general characteristics of each are different from the other, and yet that they seem to bear some relation to each other, or some influence upon each other.

Our scientific knowledge would seem to suggest that the physical world is inanimate, purposeless, yet determined or fixed in the order of events within it. The mental world, on the other hand, involves consciousness, planning, willing, desiring, etc. Yet, though these worlds may be different in many respects, our experience appears to indicate that they are interrelated or interconnected. When something happens in the physical world, this affects the mental world, and may change one's thoughts, wishes, etc. Similarly, a desire that one may have can alter events in the physical world, as when one decides to strike a match. This decision, an event in the mental world, is then followed by a physical event of a match being struck and a flame being lit. Given the apparent differences between mental and physical events, and their apparent relationships with each other, various metaphysicians have tried to construct theories about the nature of mind and body and the connections between them.

Cartesian Theory. Descartes, who is often blamed for having created the difficulties that arose from this problem, asserted that mind and body are two totally different types of entity. They are different **substances.** From a careful scrutiny of the 'clear and distinct' idea that he had of his own mind and of physical objects, he decided that the basic feature of the latter was their geometrical qualities (size, shape, and so on) and the basic feature of the former was **thinking.** In each case, these seemed to him to be the inseparable properties that accounted for all the other features of these two entities.

In his work, *The Principles of Philosophy*, Descartes summed up his theory as follows:

> But although any one attribute is enough to give us knowledge of a substance, there is always one chief property of a substance

that constitutes its nature and essence, and upon which all the others depend. Thus extension in length, breadth and depth makes up the nature of physical substance; and thought makes up the nature of thinking substance. For, everything else that may be attributed to bodies presupposes their extension, and is only a form of this extended thing; just as everything that we find in mind is only some form of thinking. Thus, for example, we can not conceive of a figure except as an extended thing, nor of movement except as taking place in an extended space; and in the same way imagination, feeling and will occur only in a thinking thing. But, on the other hand, we are able to conceive of extension without figure or action, and of thinking without imagination or sensation, and so on, as is quite clear to anyone who examines the matter carefully.

Thinking and Extension. Thus, according to Descartes, the essential property of a mind is that it thinks, and the essential property of body that it is 'extended'. All of the forms that bodies occur in involve only various extensional features, never mental ones. Similarly, no form of thought involves extension. The realms of thought and extension are completely different. Then, if all this is accepted, how can mental events have anything to do with physical ones and *vice versa*, since the one occurs in space and the other is unextended thought with no physical properties whatsoever? To make the question more difficult, Descartes claimed in his physical theories that all physical action occurs by the impact of one extended object upon another. Since mental events are not extended, how can there be any impact or contact between that whose nature it is to occur in space, and that which does not occur in space? How can an idea move a hammer, or a hammer strike upon an idea?

Conflicting Evidence. In spite of the complete separation in his theory between mind and body, Descartes was impressed by the common-sense and scientific evidence that indicated the reciprocal influence of mental and physical events. A pin jabbed into the physical, extended finger is followed by a thought or a pain in the unextended mind. But, a studious examination of the medical and psychological evidence convinced Descartes that the mind is only aware of physical events in the brain. Various motions can take place in the body without being followed by mental events, unless the physical motions first cause movements in the nervous system and then in the brain. Similarly, just by producing certain physical motions in the brain, without affecting the rest of the body, one can stimulate thoughts. The example which most impressed Descartes was that persons who had lost a limb could be led to think that this 'limb' was being moved, or pained, merely by stimulating parts of the nervous system. This sort of information led Descartes to the conclusion that there must be some kind of contact between the mental and physical worlds, and that the contact must take place in the brain.

On the basis of this conclusion, Descartes developed a theory that the interaction between mind and body took place in the pineal gland, which is located at the base of the brain. Here, presumably, some sort of impact occurred between the physical, extended brain, and the unextended, thinking mind, which allowed physical events to lead to thoughts and thoughts to alter the direction of the motions of extended objects.

When it was pointed out to him that his solution to this metaphysical problem was quite unsatisfactory, because he had still not explained plausibly how it was possible for mind and body to interact upon one another, if they were really of two totally different natures, Descartes became more and more vague about the matter. He insisted that the fact of interaction was known to everybody; we experience it all the time. But how mind and body were united, he admitted, was most difficult to explain. The pineal gland theory actually produced more problems than it solved, since one could ask whether this gland was physical, and if so how it could be next to something which did not occupy space. If it were mental, how could it be next to any part of the brain? And so on. In a letter, written late in his life to one of his admirers, the Princess Elizabeth of the Palatinate, Descartes threw up his hands in despair, and told her that the union of mind and body is best understood by not thinking about it, and that it is just one of those mysteries that has to be accepted without being comprehended.

The Materialist Theory. Other metaphysicians were not willing to give up as easily as Descartes, and suspected that the difficulties in the problem arose from the initial separation of mind and body in the Cartesian metaphysical system. If one refused to grant that mind and body were really different kinds of entity, then one would not have any trouble accounting for their interrelations. One way of avoiding some pitfalls of the Cartesian theory was to adopt a completely **materialistic metaphysics,** and claim that both mental and physical events could be accounted for in terms of purely physical concepts and laws.

This type of theory which was advanced in Descartes' time by his belligerent opponent, THOMAS HOBBES, and in our own day by some **behaviourist psychologists,** maintains that **what we call mental events are really, like physical events, only various combinations of matter in motion.** The physical movements that occur in the brain are what we call thoughts, and these are produced by other events in the material world, either outside our bodies, or inside, and, in turn, can produce further physical motions in ourselves or outside of ourselves. Every idea—of pain, of perception, of memory, and so on—is nothing but a set of physical occurrences in our higher nervous system and brain. When we say that we have a sensation of yellow, for example, this is explained as the result of certain light waves stimulating the optic nerve, which in turn causes a certain pattern of motions in the brain.

The very simplicity of the materialist solution to the mind–body problem makes it appealing. Moreover, the vast body of evidence accumulated about the physical basis of mental events by psychologists, psychiatrists, physiologists and other scientists, also makes this theory seem most plausible. However, it raises certain fundamental difficulties which have led many metaphysicians either to attempt to modify it, or else to abandon it.

If one examines an idea and asks if this is actually the same as what we mean by a physical event, one discovers a problem. The experience of seeing or hearing something, and the bodily events that occur in the nervous system and the brain at the same time, do not seem to be identical. For instance, if a person were watching a television show, and a scientist were at the same time examining the viewer's brain, they would each see different things. The viewer would see a series of pictures, while the scientist would see a series of 'readings' of various measuring devices. It is conceivable that our information about the physiology of the brain may reach the point where the scientist can tell what the viewer is seeing, that is, from the physical reactions in the brain, he might be able to construct the sequence of events that comprised the television show. Even so, it would still be the case that each of them would be seeing directly something else.

Criticism. What this seems to indicate is that our immediate awareness, our consciousness, even if it is causally related to various physical events in our environment and in our bodies, is still something different from the physical events that may be open to direct or indirect public inspection. The materialist theory, in its simplest form, denies any distinction between our mental life and the physical developments in our brain. Nevertheless, the critics stress the fact that one's immediate experience seems to belie this claim. One is aware of all sorts of sensations, feelings, etc., and not a series of physical occurrences in the brain. Even if the latter are the cause of the former, it still remains the case that they are different and distinguishable. Hence, the critics claim, the materialists cannot successfully reduce the mental world to the physical world simply by asserting that all mental events are actually nothing but a series of physical occurrences.

Another criticism of the materialist solution to the mind–body problem is that if it were true, the materialist theory itself, which presumably is a mental event in somebody's life, would turn out to be nothing but one more set of physical events in the brain. Similarly, any alternative theory would merely be some other physical event. In that case, how can one set of motions in the brain be said to constitute the truth, whereas others would constitute a falsehood? If any metaphysical theory is just a physical occurrence in somebody's head, why should one of these occurrences be taken seriously, and the others discounted as wrong?

Finally, the materialist solution also carries serious implications for ethics. If our thoughts are physical occurrences in the brain, they must be ultimately explicable in scientific terms; it must be theoretically possible to explain our thoughts in the same way as we explain events in the physical world, i.e., in terms of cause and effect. This leaves no room for evaluation of a situation, for consideration of its implications, for decisions reached after careful **thought.** In other words, such a theory must lead to a completely deterministic account of human behaviour. It must lead to an explanation of human behaviour in terms not of **free choices** based on careful appraisal but in terms of **physical cause and effect, stimulus and response.** This is in fact the kind of explanation favoured by the behaviourist psychologist, but its implication for ethics is that no such thing as a moral choice is possible. We shall consider this problem in greater detail later in this chapter.

Epiphenomenalism. Because of such problems, a modified form of the materialistic theory of mind and body has been developed—**epiphenomenalism.** This view admits that our thoughts, feelings, etc. are not merely physical states in our brain. Instead they are adjudged to be a by-product of the sequence of physical occurrences, something like the smoke given off by fire. The significant events which occur in the world are only those of matter in motion. But along with this, for reasons not yet known to us, each time there is a certain sort of physical situation in the brain, a thought occurs, which is caused by material events.

The epiphenomenalistic solution may overcome some of the difficulties in the simple version of materalism, but it does not do justice to our mental life. As we have just suggested, we take our thoughts seriously, are bothered by them, brood about them, seem to initiate actions on the basis of them. If they are nothing but a vague by-product of the material events which occur in our brains, bearing no actual relation to them, it is strange that they should play such an important part in our lives.

Idealism. If the materialist theory in one form or another has its difficulties, the opposite alternative, **idealism, which insists that everything is basically mental rather than physical,** may be even less credible. This metaphysical theory (which will be considered later in this chapter) when applied to the mind–body problem, has the disadvantage of flying in the face of our common-sense beliefs, and being in apparent conflict with scientific evidence. Even before reflecting on these matters, we seem to be convinced that there are physical events which influence our behaviour. Scientific data concerning the influence of, say, drugs and surgery on our mental life suggest that a mentalist, or idealist, approach to the mind–body problem is difficult to accept, unless the arguments in its favour can far overweigh the initial conflicts with our ordinary beliefs.

The Theories of Malebranche, Leibnitz and Spinoza. In the seventeenth century some interesting alternative theories were offered to resolve the problem of the relationship between mind and body, by some of the great metaphysicians of the period, NICHOLAS MALEBRANCHE, GOTTFRIED VON LEIBNITZ and BARUCH SPINOZA. Malebranche, a Catholic priest, was a follower of Descartes, but much more consistent than his mentor. Where Descartes accepted apparently conflicting theories in order to avoid denying or challenging our ordinary experience, Malebranche insisted on reaching a *consistent* conclusion, no matter how implausible it might be.

Occasionalism. Malebranche's theory, which is called **Occasionalism,** insists on the Cartesian distinction between mind and matter. Each is totally different—one is composed of nothing but ideas, the other only of extended events. (In fact, they are so different, that Malebranche claimed that mind cannot even know body. All that mind can know are ideas. When we think of bodies, what we are thinking of is something called intelligible extension, rather than physical extension. The sole evidence that bodies exist, Malebranche found in the opening lines of the Book of Genesis, which proclaim that God created a physical world. Were it not for this, we would never even know that there are any material objects.) If these two realms are so distinct, Malebranche insisted, then there cannot be any interaction or connection between them.

What actually happens, according to Malebranche, is that although mental events have nothing to do with physical ones, whenever anything happens in one realm, God makes something corresponding occur in the other. The events in one are not the **causes** of events in the other, they are only the **occasions** of God's actions. Thus, when I hear the ring of the telephone, this is not due to the occurrence of sound waves, which are part of the physical world and have nothing to do with thoughts that I may have. Instead, when the events take place in the mechanism of the telephone, God produces a thought in me of ringing. Since one has nothing to do with the other, He might just as well have produced the taste of a pear in me, or the idea of the number 7. But, through the inscrutable wisdom of God, He has decided to order my mental life and the series of physical events so that when a specific event occurs in one, He makes something else occur in the other.

Criticism. No matter how peculiar Malebranche's theory may appear it has the advantage that it avoids the difficulties of Descartes' speculations, and no experience can possibly disprove it. Descartes had insisted upon holding both to the complete separation of mind and body and to their interaction. By eliminating the latter, Malebranche is able to hold to the former without encountering contradictions. The theory can be made to account for literally everything. No matter what experiment one might devise to show that mind influences body, or body influences mind, it can always be explained in Malebranchian terms, as God producing a certain effect in one realm when something else happens in the other. On the other hand, no matter how consistent Malebranche's theory may be, it remains extremely unconvincing in the light of our ordinary experience, which we naturally interpret in terms of some relation between mental and physical events. Moreover, Malebranche's conception of God as being constantly involved in producing all effects in this world, as engaged in producing sounds, tastes, smells, and motions in the physical world—is hardly in keeping with most 'acceptable' concepts of the Deity.

A further difficulty arises when we ask how God achieves these effects, how God acts causally on both mind and body. The source of the mind–body problem lies in the fact that physical substance and thinking substance cannot interact. The definition of substance that the Cartesians had used logically precludes the interaction of one substance with another. Two substances must by definition have nothing in common with one another. For if they have anything in common they cannot be separate substances. Now, as Spinoza tells us, 'If two things have nothing in common with one another, then one cannot be the cause of the other; for since there would be nothing in the effect that was also in the cause, everything that was in the effect would have arisen out of nothing.' How, then, does God act causally on mind and body, on thinking substance and on physical substance? If God Himself is either thinking substance or physical substance, then there is only one of these substances that He can act causally on. The Cartesians, however, regarded God as neither, but as quite separate from both—in other words, as a third substance. On this account it is logically impossible for Him to act causally on either mind or body. This was one of the inconsistencies in Cartesianism, as developed by Malebranche, that Spinoza seized on, as we shall see.

Leibnitz. Leibnitz's theory of the relations between mental and physical events is not much more plausible than Malebranche's view. According to Leibnitz, every entity, whether characterized as mental or physical, is independent, and constitutes a **monad.** Each monad is determined or fixed in its properties according to its nature. Everything that can possibly happen to a monad follows from its own essential characteristics, and not from the influence of any other entity.

'Pre-established Harmony.' What accounts for the apparent relationships between different monads—in Leibnitz's theory—is that though they have no influence on each other, there is a **pre-established harmony** between the monads. They have been so constructed that events occurring in one are harmonious with the others. In the example used earlier, monads of the telephone and of my mind are such that when certain physical occurrences take place in the former, I hear a ringing sound. This is not owing to the fact that the telephone caused me to hear anything, but rather that our monads are in perfect order. Mine is so set that at a given time, I have the idea of a certain sound, and at just that time a physical clapper is beating on a physical bell in the telephone. The following illustration may clarify this theory: if there were two clocks that kept perfect time so that when one pointed to the hour the other rang a bell, it might be the case that this is because the clocks have some connected mechanism **(Descartes' theory)**, or that some outside intervention makes one ring when the hands on the other reach a certain point **(Malebranche's theory)**, or that the clocks had been made perfectly at the outset, and, although they had no relation whatsoever to each other, they each kept perfect time **(Leibnitz's theory).** Thus, each monad is so created by God that it is in perfect harmony with every other for all eternity, and the events in the career of one are bound to be in perfect accord with the others. Brutus did not kill Caesar because of anything Caesar did; instead, each monad was so constructed by God, that at the same moment that Brutus's monad had certain thoughts, and performed certain actions, Caesar's was such that he was in a certain locale, and dropped dead.

Leibnitz's theory, like Malebranche's overcomes the difficulties in Cartesian metaphysics, by giving up any claim that there is a relationship between mind and body. Also, like Malebranche's, Leibnitz's view, though it may not contain any inconsistencies, is incredible from the point of view of our ordinary, common experience.

Spinoza. The last of these seventeenth century accounts of the mind–body problem that we shall consider is somewhat different. Spinoza decided that the difficulty in the Cartesian theory came from its total separation of mind and body and, as we have seen, the total separation of both from God, although this difficulty had not been appreciated by the Cartesians. To overcome this, he did not wish to adopt the materialist or idealist solution of subordinating one of these realms to the other, but, instead, insisted that they were both aspects of the same thing. This theory, sometimes called the **dual-aspect theory, claims that mind and body are both attributes of one and the same entity,** which Spinoza named God, Substance or Nature.

If the mental world and the physical world are both aspects of the same entity, then what is the relationship between one and the other? According to Spinoza, there is no influence between one and the other, but there is a **parallelism,** so that for everything that happens in one realm, a corresponding event occurs in the other. This is due to the fact that the physical and mental worlds are really two different ways of looking at the same thing, God or Nature. Hence, **Spinoza contended the logical order of the mind was identical with the physical order of Nature.** For every thought there is a corresponding physical event, and *vice versa.* Thus, the ringing of the telephone that I hear and the physical motions that are taking place in the mechanism are not two different things, but are two different aspects of the same thing, or two different ways of looking at the same thing, as it occurs in God or Nature.

Spinoza's metaphysical solution may not lead to the same kind of unbelievable views as those of Malebranche or Leibnitz, or the inconsistencies involved in Descartes' view; however, it led to certain conclusions regarding the nature of God, which most of his contemporaries found completely unacceptable. (Some of these will be considered in the chapter on philosophy of religion.) As a result, it was not until the time of the nineteenth-century German metaphysicians, that Spinoza's views were treated seriously.

The theories regarding the relationship between mind and body illustrate the difficulty the metaphysician has in trying to develop an explanation of this fundamental feature of our experience. The first metaphysical question that we considered dealt with the general character of the universe, and the second, with the relationship between two of the basic features of it. Before examining some of the major metaphysical theories that have attempted to account for all of the chief characteristics of the cosmos as we know it, we shall look at one further problem that metaphysicians have debated throughout history —**the free will problem.**

THE PROBLEM OF FREE WILL AND DETERMINISM

The problem of free will deals primarily with the human element in the universe—whether or not it is the 'captain of its fate' to any degree. In our experience of our own behaviour and own decisions we find two opposing features. The first of these is our awareness of our own freedom, of our own ability to decide for ourselves, to deliberate about what to do in various situations, and to come to our own conclusions about what to believe and what to do. On the other hand, the second element is that we discover that in many cases what we believed at the time to be a free decision had been influenced by various personal and social factors, so that we did not actually decide the question 'freely'. The more we learn about the workings of human nature, the more we come to realize that a great deal of what we do and think is the result of our upbringing, our education, our environment, our biological nature, etc. Hence, metaphysicians have been concerned with the problem of **whether, in view of the information at our disposal, human beings can be said to be free agents, or whether their activities and thoughts are determined completely by the many influencing factors that impinge upon them.**

Complexities. In most of our judgments about people we assume that, in some sense, they chose freely to do what they did, or to believe what they do. We punish, condemn, or blame individuals for making certain choices and decisions, and insist that they ought to have done something else, and if they had they would then be deserving of rewards and praise. Much of the basis for our legal system presumes that people can be held responsible for what they do, because, to some degree or extent, they could have done otherwise.

At the same time that we conduct ourselves morally and legally on the basis that human beings are free agents, and can make decisions of their own free will, we are being made more and more aware that this sort of assumption is very often erroneous. We are shown many forceful indications of the way in which human nature can be guided and influenced by propaganda, advertising, parental training and so on, so that individuals are often more victims of circumstance and deter-

minations beyond their control than responsible agents. Psychiatrists testifying at criminal trials have tried to show that the defendant cannot be held morally responsible for actions which resulted from determining factors beyond the control of the individual, so that it is meaningless to hold that the person freely decided to commit the actions for which he is being tried.

This conflict between our ordinary assumption of human freedom and our often grudging recognition that this is not always the case, has been brought sharply to public attention in discussions about the culpability of soldiers who are captured in war, and who aid the enemy. Some of those who were tried had evidently performed actions which were not in the best interest of their country, and actions which are declared criminal in military codes. But were the soldiers in question responsible for what they had done, and can they responsibly be judged morally guilty? When it is made clear that they had been subjected to all sorts of pressures, direct and indirect, that either forced them to perform the actions, or altered their conscious moral framework so that they 'chose' to perform the actions, can they then be considered free agents?

We are much less inclined to judge harshly when it is revealed that someone's actions were involuntary. If a man is compelled to commit actions by direct force, we do not hold him responsible. If torture, coercion, threats result in actions that in ordinary circumstances we would judge wrong, we are willing to excuse this behaviour because extraordinary circumstances prevented the person from deciding and acting as a genuinely free agent.

We often apply the same criteria to personal factors that prevent due deliberation and decision. If someone commits certain actions when under the influence of alcohol, narcotics, or extreme emotional stress, we are willing to take these conditions into account, and again conclude that the individual was not a free agent who can be held morally responsible. Thus, we distinguish between types of crime and degrees of guilt according to whether there are mitigating factors that might have influenced or determined one's behaviour at the time the deeds were committed.

The striking evidence of the effects of 'brainwashing' and of psychological 'conditioning' in general create a problem of judging to what extent we can ever hold anyone responsible as a free agent for what he has done. When we learn that there are methods, some relatively simple, by which a person's attitude and outlook can be altered so that he can be made to 'wish' to perform certain actions which are condemned by society, is a person so conditioned actually responsible? Even if some soldiers voluntarily aided the enemy, were they actually free agents if they had first been subjected to influences which controlled their attitudes toward events and the choices they made?

The problem of judging the extent to which our so-called voluntary choices and actions really are voluntary, in the sense of being completely free, becomes even more difficult to decide when further evidence about human psychology is considered. The findings of modern psychoanalysis seem to indicate that our attitudes, our standards of judging, and even our choices have been determined by a host of conditioning processes. Our parents, our social group, our teachers, our employers, all influence us, so that when we seem to be acting voluntarily, we may actually be making the choices that we must make, given the factors which influenced our development.

By pursuing this sort of discussion, one can discover more and more areas in which our 'voluntary' behaviour can be shown to be the product of various influences. Even though we may be able to choose our actions, the framework in which we choose, that determines which of several alternatives we will select, may be something entirely beyond our control. We may not be responsible for this framework, and hence, are not really free agents. The framework has been imposed upon us by all sorts of psychological, social, biological and other factors.

In view of all this, the metaphysical problem of free will seems to revolve about determining how far a belief in human freedom is consistent with our experience, our knowledge and our views about human nature. **On the one hand, there is a point of view which insists there actually is no human freedom—the view called determinism. As against this, there is the claim that in some manner, and to some degree, there is some free element in human behaviour.**

The Arguments for Determinism. Although most of the familiar evidence for determinism consists of scientific findings about human behaviour, long before the rise of modern science forceful arguments were constructed to support this position. In fact, the area in which perhaps the greatest battles were fought between determinists and those who believed in free will was that of theological controversies. In many religious traditions, a form of **divine determinism has been advocated, claiming that God Himself is the sole causal agent in the universe, and determines all actions, human and natural.**

The Religious View. One form of divine determinism has argued that since God is all-powerful and all-knowing, He is able to control everything that occurs, and to know beforehand (predetermine) everything that takes place. If there were any event, whether a human thought or the movement of a leaf, that God did not know in advance, then there would be a limitation on Divine power. Since (in this theory) such a limitation is unthinkable, prior to the Creation of the world, God must have known all that would take place in the future. This being the case, He must have known every choice that we would ever make in the course of human history. Thus, **everything that anyone does is predestined and predetermined by God's prior knowledge and prior decisions.**

If one claims that God is the ultimate cause of whatever takes place, and that God has foreknowledge of everything that occurs, but that we are still able to choose freely, the theological determinists, like the great American Calvinist, JONATHAN EDWARDS, argued that this is a spurious form of freedom. We may think that we are choosing freely, but our choices in fact have been determined in advance, so that we cannot actually make an original decision. Even though we may engage in elaborate deliberations about what choice to make, the ultimate decision is fixed, since God already knows it. Though we willingly make the choice that God expects, our willingness is merely another item that God controls, has foreseen and foreordained.

The Metaphysical Basis. In addition to the theological argument for determinism, there is a metaphysical basis for this view, deriving from the maxim, **'Every event must have a cause'.** If one accepts this principle then not only physical events, but also mental events, such as our decisions, must have causal explanations. To apply the principle to everything except human wishes seems entirely unjustified and arbitrary.

If we accept the causal maxim as applying to the physical world because we feel that there must be some explanation of where the physical order comes from and why it functions as it does, then the mental world, and especially the world of our deliberations and choices, seems also to require a causal explanation. Why should I choose this instead of that? Why should I want this instead of that? How did I come to develop this sort of a mental outlook instead of some other? All these are perfectly reasonable questions. The answers appear to require a deterministic theory about our nature, our character and our behaviour, a theory which will account for one's performing certain acts and not others. Even if one insists that one's choices and decisions are due to factors within one's own nature, one is conceding that some sort of causal or deterministic explanation is possible.

In David Hume's account of causality (discussed in the chapter on the theory of knowledge) the same kind of patterns of constant con-junction, or regular sequence, can be found with regard to our volitions as well as other things. How people will choose, or what they will want, can be predicted with considerable accuracy. Not only can trained scientists, such as psychologists and psychiatrists, discover laws of human volition so that they can predict the probable course of human affairs on the basis of certain concomitant events, but even in the more 'practical' world of business, there seem to be reliable clues about human volition. Manufacturers are able to foretell with im-pressive accuracy how many people will buy their product, given certain stimuli in the form of advertising, etc. If this sort of prediction were not possible, it would be extremely risky to manufacture any-thing save items that are necessary to the preservation of human life. Thus, even if we do not observe the force that makes people de-cide as they do (and, as Hume pointed out, we don't observe the force that makes physical actions occur either), we find that there are **patterns of constant conjunction between our voluntary decisions and other events, and that these patterns provide adequate clues for making reasonable or probable guesses about the future course of human choices, within a limited range of accuracy.**

Apart from the theological and metaphysical arguments for deter-minism, of course, the strongest and most convincing evidence at the present time is the almost overwhelming mass of scientific information about the factors that influence or determine human behaviour. So many discoveries have been made in psychology, physiology, neuro-logy, pharmacology, etc., that we appear to be fast approaching the determinist's dream of being able to predict *all* human behaviour, not only the actions a person will perform, but his thoughts and feelings as well. It may soon be the case that a thorough examination of the biological and psychological characteristics of an infant, may enable scientists to write his autobiography before he lives his life, although they would probably have to write it in conditional terms, such that, *if* certain things happened in the world around him, *then* he would have certain thoughts and feelings, make certain decisions, and perform certain actions. Most of us would prefer to think that this grim prospect is more science-fiction than science.

In the face of the scientific evidence now available about the laws of human motivation, and the ways in which human attitudes can be affected, the case for determinism appears to be extremely strong. Anyone nowadays who would want to argue that human beings are really free agents, in spite of all the knowledge we have to the con-trary, would be hard pressed to discover an area of human behaviour in which there is not already some information indicating that there are influencing or determining factors which account for the actions and volitions of men.

Arguments for Free Will. Regardless of the apparent strength of the arguments and evidence for the determinist theory, the opponents of this view have been able to formulate perhaps equally powerful argu-ments, and to point out that there are experiences and attitudes of human beings that would make no sense at all unless men were free agents. First of all, the libertarians claim, everybody is aware of his own freedom. Even if someone can predict the choices I am going to make, when I make these choices, I feel that I am free. The proponents of free-will insist that no determinist arguments can eliminate or account for the actual experience of freedom which we all sometimes have when we make our choices. (Of course, the determinists can point out that even if one grants that we have this experience, it in no way denies that in spite of how we may feel about it, our volitions are nonetheless determined.)

Free Will and Science. In recent years, the libertarians have also tried to enlist the support of a discovery in modern physics. This discovery is the **Heisenberg uncertainty principle** which asserts that there is a fundamental indeterminacy in our knowledge about physical particles. If the position and velocity of a particle are to be experimentally determined, it is found that all experimental methods of so doing will give us the the position accurately at the expense of error in the velocity determination; or will give us the velocity accurately at the expense of error in the determination of position. It is not possible to determine both quantities without uncertainty.

The interpretation that has been made of this scientific law in relation to the free-will question is that **there is an element of indeterminacy in nature.** This is taken to suggest that there is a degree of freedom of action on the most basic level of physical existence, and by analogy, that such freedom occurs on higher levels, such as the human one. But the Heisenberg principle is actually irrelevant to the main issues involved in the argument between the libertarians and the determinists. It may show that a certain formulation of complete determinism is no longer adequate, or in keeping with present day physical theory. But this does not indicate in the slightest that because we may never be able to discover all the determining factors in the physical world, that therefore human volitions are free. The Heisenberg principle has not led to any conclusion concerning the indeterminacy of our knowledge above the level of particle motions, which, in fact, are predictable in large numbers, but not in individual cases. Indeterminacy on the lowest level of physical action certainly does not show that free will is involved, or that any decisions have been made by the particles to act the way they do. Hence, no serious analogy between the results of modern physical science and the basis of human volition seems possible.

The free-will case is stronger when it points to those features of our moral and legal judgments which make sense only if human beings are in some sense free agents. Some opponents of theological determinism, and now of scientific determinism, argued that most religious views of the world are silly or trivial if man cannot make free choices. The whole point of God's condemning man for original sin, and His later offer of salvation for man if he accepted or believed in certain principles, seems to require a free participation from man's point of view. Otherwise, the theological drama, at least of the Judaeo-Christian tradition, becomes a puppet-show which we are trapped in, rather than a message which we can do anything about.

Free Will and William James. This argument when conducted on the ethical level becomes, perhaps, more forceful. As William James insisted, in his essay on 'The Dilemma of Determinism', there are two striking features of our moral experience which are intelligible only if we assume that men are free agents. The first of these is the occurrence of remorse. Over and over again people express the view that they regret that they did, or believed, certain things, and wish that they had done or believed otherwise. If human actions or thoughts could not be otherwise, then what possible point can there be in regretting what might have been, especially since nothing else could have occurred?

Besides the fact that regret or remorse would be meaningless if we were not in some sense free, James also pointed out our attribution of responsibility to men, and our punishing them for not exercising it properly make no sense if we are all completely determined. We do not condemn and punish determined physical objects like stones and cars for the things they do, because we do not think that they are responsible free agents. Why then do we punish people if they also could not have done otherwise? If we punish them because we are determined by all sorts of factors to behave in this fashion, then punishment loses all moral significance, and becomes only an indication of the influencing factors that determine the punishers. If we punish people in order to alter the factors that condition their behaviour, then are we, the judges, free in our decision to punish, or merely determined by other factors? If the latter, then punishment is nothing more than inflicting the standards of the group in power on the minority, and has no moral or ethical significance. If the former, then the libertarian has made his point, by showing that someone must be assumed to be free in order that morality shall be meaningful.

A last form of argument that can be cited in favour of the free-will theory is that arguments about the question assume that people are able to judge and decide these matters freely, according to the evidence. If the determinist's theory is true, then instead of propounding arguments, he ought to find out what factors produce philosophical decisions, and then employ these, whether they be cricket bats, alcoholic beverages, or whatever. But the fact that he continues to use argumentation suggests that he, too, suspects there is some element of freedom in human behaviour. Also, if one takes determinism seriously, anyone who believes in free will is determined to accept that theory, so what possible good could reasonable discussion accomplish?

Conclusion. The metaphysical problem of the freedom of the will, which has been argued for centuries, may indicate the role of the metaphysician more clearly. In trying to work out a general account or explanation of the elements of our experience, we find that there is **overwhelming evidence suggesting that human beings are completely determined** in what they do and think. On the other hand, some of the presuppositions that we employ in our moral life seem to require that we accept **some degree of free agency on the human level.** The libertarian may be able to show that complete determinism is incompatible with certain aspects of our experience and belief, but, when he tries to specify in what our freedom may consist, he seems to be unable to find any type of human behaviour for which there is no scientific evidence of its source. The metaphysician, faced with these two poles of explanation, is obliged to develop some general theory about the nature of the universe which can account for the evidence on both sides of the question.

TYPES OF METAPHYSICAL SYSTEM

Having considered some examples of the kinds of problem that metaphysicians deal with, we shall now turn to some of the major metaphysical theories that have been constructed in the history of philosophy. Since their number is large, we shall consider only some of the basic ones, first of antiquity, and then of more recent philosophy, that is, since the Renaissance. It has been claimed that all of the kinds of metaphysics are actually merely permutations of the views of Plato and Aristotle. Since that is in some degree the case, we shall start our survey with them.

Plato's Metaphysics. In a later discussion of the theory of knowledge, we shall see how some of the basic elements of Plato's metaphysical theory developed from his attempt to work out an explanation of what true knowledge we have, and what it is about. Fundamentally, Plato's picture of the universe is that the real, stable, permanent part is the world of Ideas or Forms. The world of ordinary experience is an illusory, transitory, unimportant sequence of events which take place in the physical world, the realm of appearance rather than of reality.

The relationship between the supersensible world of Ideas and the visible, but only apparent, world of material things is set forth in Plato's dialogue, the 'Timaeus'. Both realms are described as if they are eternal. But the world of Ideas is responsible for, or is the cause of, whatever order occurs in the material world. This is due not to any direct action by the Ideal World, which does not appear to involve any sort of change or activity, but rather to some kind of agent who is able to introduce some shadow or copy of the Real World into the chaos of the material or sensible universe.

On the one hand there is a world of perfection, which is the permanent realm of Ideas, comprising the meanings or definitions of things. On the other hand there is some amorphous, incoherent 'something' which is able to some extent to receive various aspects of the Forms. But, in order to explain how one of the realms comes in contact with the other, Plato conceived of an agent, called the **Demiurge,** who is able to exist on the borderline of both worlds. The Demiurge tries to impose the various forms on the chaotic material world, introducing triangularity, circularity, brownness, and so on, until there is some sort of order in the visible world. But, the material world is not able to support or sustain these unchangeable Ideas, and so can only partake of them for limited periods of time. Hence, there is bound to be the constant flux of the visible world as the temporary order it receives from the world of Ideas dissipates.

Later Developments. Later Platonists in antiquity emphasized more

E

and more the creative agency of the world of Forms, changing it from a static world of perfection into the source of all power and reality in the universe. In the process of the absorption of Platonic metaphysics into Christian theology, the Ideal world was finally made into the Divine Creator not only of the temporary order in the universe, but of the physical universe itself as well. Thus, from PLOTINUS in the third century, A.D., to SAINT AUGUSTINE, one hundred and fifty years later, there was a movement to transform the Ideas into active agencies, and finally into the Divine power itself, which creates the physical world out of nothing, and organizes it according to the Divine pattern of the Forms.

Mind-Body-Soul. The human world, in Platonic metaphysics, is conceived of as a borderline condition, somewhat akin to the position of the Demiurge. Man is part of the physical world in that he has a **body,** receives sense-impressions, and so on. But at the same time he also has an immaterial **mind** which is capable of knowing Forms. He also has a directing agency, the **soul,** which is portrayed as a chariot rider, guiding and being guided by two horses, mind and body. The former wants to soar into the heavenly realm of the Ideas and to contemplate them. The latter wants to immerse itself in the affairs of physical life. The human soul is caught between these two opposing forces, trying to steer while it is trapped in its prison house, the body.

Somehow, in these circumstances, what the soul is able to accomplish in bringing about harmony remains afterwards—after its liberation from bodily life. In terms of this metaphysical picture of human nature, we are supposed to be able to rid ourselves of complete determination by bodily needs. Most people, at present, have no freedom, because their lives are completely fixed by their physical requirements. One's soul, however, can liberate itself from this bondage, and direct one's human life both in terms of one's physical circumstances, as well as one's intellectual desires. Then, after the end of bodily existence the soul can soar upward to the eternal, perfect world of Ideas.

The Infusion of Mysticism. This side of Plato's metaphysics, though possibly not so intended by its author, has led to an otherworldly and mystical view, which is usually part of what is called **Platonism.** (As the term, Platonism, is ordinarily employed in philosophy, it is a serious question as to whether Plato was himself a Platonist.) By stressing that aspect of Plato's theory (i.e., that which deals with the desire of the soul to escape from its prison house in the body) many Platonists have insisted that whatever is valuable in the universe is to be found only in the Ideal world, not in the physical world. Somehow, they have insisted, we can enter into the higher metaphysical realms only by rejecting completely all material concerns, and contemplating the eternal characteristics of the perfect world of Forms.

Neo-Platonism. In the extension of Plato's views known as **Neo-Platonism,** the metaphysical theory propounded by Plotinus, the otherworldly point of view is distinctly emphasized. The Neo-Platonists maintained that, metaphysically speaking, one could become part of that level of the universe with which one was concerned and understood. Thus, one could change one's fundamental nature by renouncing interest in the physical world, and being concerned instead solely with the Ideal world. If one finally reached the point of being able to contemplate the Idea of Ideas, the One, a mystical union would take place between oneself and the One. We are told that Plotinus was so convinced of this otherworldly and mystical side of Platonism, that he tried to avoid showing even enough interest in his physical life to take a bath, and instead devoted himself to his studies and to contemplation so as to achieve this mystical union.

Aristotle's Metaphysics. In contrast to the dual nature of Plato's universe of the world of Ideas and the shadowy world of physical things, Plato's student, ARISTOTLE, constructed a metaphysical system devoted primarily to explaining **the natural world as the real world.** Starting from the conviction that the natural world we are all acquainted with in our daily life can be accounted for, made intelligible without appealing to some metaphysical realms beyond human experience, he constructed a theory based on what he regarded as the fundamental characteristics of nature. Besides those that we discussed earlier (matter and form) **Aristotle included also the notion of purpose.**

Teleology. All the objects of our experience consist of formed matter moving or changing in a pattern that is usually purposeful, or **teleological, i.e., the motions or changes occur in order to achieve some goal.** As indications of this, Aristotle pointed to persistent patterns of development. Acorns always grow into oak trees, never into anything else. Children grow into adults. Stones always fall down until they reach a state of rest on the surface of the earth. In all these instances the motions or changes seem to be directed towards the achievement of specific results, which appear to be the same, or nearly the same, for all members of the group or species.

Further, the examples one can think of that violate this claim of fixed purposeful direction of change or motion, actually constitute evidence for a more general thesis, that there is purposefulness which pervades all natural events and explains the course of nature. The instances in which objects do not change or move to accomplish an end are those in which objects have been interfered with by some outside agency. The acorn that is eaten by a squirrel, the stone that moves upward instead of downward, the child who fails to grow up because he is killed in his youth, are all instances of violent, or, as Aristotle would call it, **unnatural interference** with the object. But, when the object is left to develop naturally, we note that it tends in a certain direction in order to arrive at some final result, which seems to be the same for all members of the same species.

The way in which this natural purposefulness or teleology exhibits itself is through the forms which objects tend to acquire in the course of their development. Every object in its natural history seems to be trying to realize or obtain a certain form proper to it, and its actions are all directed towards this goal. The acorn, for instance, normally goes through a series of developments, culminating in its losing its original form and taking instead the form of an oak. When it achieves a certain size, it seems to have reached the goal towards which its changes were tending. The stone when it falls to the surface of the earth also appears to have completed a series of changes which result in achieving its desired form, a resting place.

Matter and Goal. Put in most general form, the Aristotelian contention is that every object in this universe, with the exception of God, is composed of some form of an underlying stuff called 'matter'. The matter of each kind of object has the potentiality for acquiring a form proper to the object, called its 'end' or 'goal'. The process of change or motion is the actualizing of the potentiality of the object. There is a natural tendency or teleology which leads each and every object to seek the achievement of its natural goal, or final form. The alterations that every object undergoes cannot be understood except in terms of the purposes involved.

Pure Forms. There is **a relative goal** for every object, that of realizing the form proper to its species. There is also an **ultimate goal** of every object, that of realizing a state of complete rest from which it will be absolutely impossible to change. But everything, in so far as it is composed of matter, always has some potentiality, some capacity for change, movement, or alteration. Hence, only by becoming **pure form** entirely devoid of matter would it be possible for an object to arrive at this final state.

As we look around the universe, we observe that to varying degrees different species are able to achieve some aspect of permanence, or immutability, or rest. The closest approximation to this state, Aristotle thought, was to be found in the heavens. The stars and the planets, as far as he could tell, changed in only one respect, that is, they changed only their position. Their shape and size remained forever constant; they neither decayed nor grew. The only manner in which they appeared to seek for their ultimate form was in their continually circling around the sky. In their movement, they always seemed to repeat the same orbit, indicating that they were so close to complete rest that all that separated them from this goal was the regular, circular movement in which they engaged in their unending quest for the state of being pure form.

However, compared to the near-perfect state of the celestial objects, those on the surface of the earth are much further removed from the achievement of the ultimate goal. All living things approach it only to the degree that the species remains forever the same, even though the individual members change, and finally decay and die. Since Aristotle was not an evolutionist, he regarded the form of the species as forever constant. Hence, it is through reproduction of the group, he claimed, that living things participate in 'the eternal and the divine'. But humans can come closer to the ultimate state than any other organism. They are able to accomplish this through **contemplating pure form.** To the extent that we can manage to reach such **pure thought, our minds acquire or realize a state of form alone, a conception of perfection.**

The Unmoved Mover. Since, in one way or another, every object in the world aims to achieve a state of pure form, there must be an actual entity which is this goal of all change or motion. This object is called the **Unmoved Mover,** because, although it itself undergoes no change (since it contains no matter at all, and hence, has no potentiality), it is the reason why everything else in the universe moves. All things—from lowly stones to men and heavenly bodies—go through the kind of developments they do because of a natural tendency or desire to become like the Unmoved Mover. Thus, it is out of love for the perfection of pure form that the natural world goes endlessly about its movement, alteration and change. In Aristotle's metaphysical scheme, the Perfect Being, the Unmoved Mover, does nothing, and plays no part in the activities of the world, but only serves it by being its purpose and goal. This teleological universe, in which everything in nature happens purposefully, and can be accounted for in terms of the relative and final ends being pursued, also has a frustrating aspect. Although all natural objects, except the Unmoved Mover, undergo change in order to actualize their potentialities, they are bound to fail because they never can become pure form. Even the heavenly bodies, so close to achieving perfection and rest, never do so, but instead revolve forever in their circular orbits. The world, thus, is seen by Aristotle as an eternal series of processes, always pursuing the same goal, and never arriving at this end.

Epicurean Metaphysics. In sharp contrast to the Aristotelian conception of the universe explained entirely in terms of purposeful action is **the materialist view** of EPICURUS. This theory, originally proposed by the early Greek philosopher, Democritus, and best known through the *De Rerum Natura* by the Roman poet, LUCRETIUS, portrays a **universe containing nothing but variously shaped atoms moving through empty space.** The conception of the indivisible atom as the fundamental feature of the universe, having no purpose, no qualities except its size and shape (and possibly weight), suffices, the Epicureans claimed, to account for all that we know about the world.

Physical Theory. The permanent aspect of the universe is the physical atom, uncreated and unchangeable. The Epicureans considered the atoms as solid particles, which could not be broken down into smaller units, and which occurred in an unlimited number of sizes and shapes. There were, according to this theory, cube-shaped atoms, pyramid-shaped atoms, hooked atoms, spherical ones, and so on. Every object in the world is nothing but a combination of atoms disturbed in empty space. This includes living things, and even the human mind, as well as inanimate objects like stones and tables. Though the atoms are eternally the same, their combinations alter, and hence, the objects which we experience may change and disappear, but the atoms themselves never do.

Movement is a fundamental feature of the atom, which never had a beginning, but has been going on for all time. In the original theory of Democritus, the atoms all fell downwards at different rates of speed. Because of varying velocities, the faster-moving atoms overtake the slower ones, and a collision occurs. Owing to their differences in shape, the colliding atoms are sent off in various directions, causing other collisions, and so on. As a result, all sorts of atomic combinations are formed and later broken up. **This version of metaphysical atomism is completely determinist** in that from the initial position of atoms in the universe, and from the directions in which they are moving, it is possible to predict exactly the entire future course of the movements of all atoms. Hence, every event in the world, including thoughts, volitions and all mental events, is completely determined solely by the locations and motions of the basic physical particles.

Indeterminacy. However, Epicurus, for various ethical reasons, was oppressed by the thought of a totally fixed universe, and, therefore, modified the ancient atomic theory by introducing an indeterminable element into the atomic world. According to him, besides moving straight downward and colliding, the atoms also occasionally have 'a gentle swerve' which alters their course. The swerve, supposedly, occurs for no discoverable reason, but, whenever it takes place, it disrupts the fixed determined character of the atomic universe, and prevents us from accurately predicting what will happen in the world.

Both the determinist and indeterminist versions of atomism are examples of a completely materialist metaphysics. According to both Democritus and Epicurus, **everything in the entire universe can be accounted for solely in terms of the notions of matter and motion.** All physical action can be explained in terms of 'the fortuitous concourse of atoms'. Mental events, it is claimed, can also be characterized as the result of the collisions of a very fine type of spherical atom, called a soul atom. Living things possess these atoms, whereas inanimate objects do not. When living things die, what happens is that the soul atoms depart from this particular combination.

Purposelessness. Totally unlike the Aristotelian theory of the cosmos, Epicurean metaphysics portrays a world that is completely purposeless. It does not seek for causal explanations of natural events in the end or purpose towards which they are aiming; the explanation for why anything happens can only be in terms of the **prior events in the atomic world.** On both the cosmic level and the level of human events, nothing occurs in order to achieve any goal, but solely because certain atomic collisions have taken place. Man's habit of regarding the world as made for him, and the events in it as part of a plan in which he plays a central role, is condemned as an erroneous point of view. As far as our hopes, wishes, desires, thoughts are concerned, they have nothing to do with the actual course of events. Things have to happen because of the patterns existing in the world of atoms, not because we or anyone else want them to occur, nor because of any advantages that might result from their occurrence.

This completely materialist metaphysics also rules out as important or relevant to the world's affairs the thoughts and ideals of mankind. These are only the results of atomic events within us, and rather than being guiding clues to the nature of events, or bases for comprehending the universe, they are merely the effects of certain material causes. The worlds of Platonic Ideas, of Aristotelian purposes, are nothing but illusory visions taking place in the human brain and hence not deserving of serious consideration or of serving as the basis for our highest hopes.

The Epicurean vision of a purposeless, material cosmos is one of the great metaphysical systems. In spite of its sharp rejection of man's spiritual hopes and goals, this theory has contributed an all-encompassing scheme which provides a way of accounting for our experience. It has also served as an antidote to some of the grandiose metaphysical systems by returning men to an examination of the material world as a way of understanding their experience. It is quite understandable that during the great religious era, the Middle Ages, Epicureanism was almost totally neglected, but in the beginnings of modern science, in the sixteenth and seventeenth centuries, there was a strong revival of interest in ancient atomic metaphysics.

Stoic Metaphysics. The last of the major classical metaphysical theories that we shall consider is that of the leading opponents of the Epicureans, the **Stoics.** Like the former, they held to a materialist conception of the world. But the Stoics also contended that the **material world was pervaded by a dynamic force, which acted not mechanically but purposefully,** in order to maintain a universal rational pattern throughout all nature.

Matter and Reason. The fundamental elements of the Stoic cosmos are **matter and reason,** which are found everywhere. **Matter** is not a series of atomic units, but a continuous amorphous stuff, which is pervaded by a rational force that gives it its characteristics. Physical objects, according to this theory, represent various states of tension of matter owing to the action of the rational forces that exist throughout the physical world. The dynamic quality of these rational forces brings about all the changes that take place.

The element of **reason** is sometimes called **the soul of the universe, sometimes the rational seeds within it, sometimes Universal Reason or God.** It is conceived of as a cosmic power that organizes and governs the entire universe, not from outside, but from within. As a totality, it is the guiding principle of the world, and considered individually it is the rational element or seed within each separate thing which governs or directs it.

Stoic Determinism. Since, in the Stoic metaphysic, everything that happens, happens for a reason, and the reason is the plan of the cosmic rational element, there is complete determinism in nature. But this determinism is not the result of previous developments in the physical world; rather it is due to the purpose of the cosmos, the end result that Universal Reason works towards. Everything must be as it is because its occurrence is rationally dictated by the all-pervasive Reason in accordance with its rational purpose. Thus, **every event is rational and necessary in this completely rational world.** For anything different to take place than what does, there would have to be some reason. But there cannot be any, since Universal Reason directed the occurrence of what does happen, and hence this must be the sole rational possibility.

Fatalism and Optimism. This theory of the Stoics leads to a **complete fatalism and a cosmic optimism.** The fatalistic view results from recognizing that **everything that happens must happen and there is nothing we can do about it.** Since the causal agency is beyond our control or influence, instead of brooding about the course of events, past, present and future, we ought to accept the prevailing state of affairs—**what occurs, must occur.**

The only area in which anything can happen that is not necessary is in the realm of thought. One can either accept or reject, in the mind, the course of events. The person who acquiesces in the universal law of nature and of reason, can be at peace with the world. On the other hand, the person who cannot or will not accept this fatalistic view is unhappy and at war with the world. He spends his life disturbed at what happens and wishing it were otherwise. Since it cannot be, all that results is unhappiness, while the course of nature remains the same.

The optimistic side of the Stoic metaphysical outlook arises from **equating the necessity and rationality of what occurs with its goodness.** Since Universal Reason directs the activities of the world, they must be directed in order to achieve some cosmic purpose. This purpose would only be the goal if it were **the right goal** for the entire universe. No matter what happens, it is the result of the necessary actions guided by the Universal Reason pervading all of nature—therefore this must be the best of all possible worlds.

The optimistic claim leads to the view that the universe can only be judged as a whole, and in terms of the direction in which it is moving. To regard a part as significant, and to evaluate it, is to miss the essential point that the purpose of Universal Reason is expressed and worked out throughout the entire cosmos. Thus one who cannot understand how a basically good universe can contain such awful events as earthquakes, famines, plagues and wars does not realize that the entire material world is interrelated and interdirected. Even the parts of the whole that we may not approve of represent some aspect—a necessary one—of the rational scheme of things. If the parts are seen in terms of the larger context, then one, supposedly, will accept them as required features of this best of all possible worlds, and not as defects.

Stoic metaphysics, then, represents a combination of a pure materialism and a type of teleology. Nature is conceived of as entirely physical, and also as pervaded by some rational cosmic force. As a result, instead of arriving at a deterministic, purposeless picture of the world, as the Epicureans did, the Stoics make their determinism the consequence of the universal guiding spirit; and the physical events that occur are necessary and good parts of a necessary and good world, moving towards the most reasonable, and hence best, of all possible conclusions.

Cartesianism, Modern Metaphysics. Turning from the ancient metaphysical systems, which form the basic patterns of the later ones, we shall next consider some post-Renaissance theories. With the beginnings of modern science, and the realizations that the older accepted systems of thought, especially medieval Aristotelianism, were no longer adequate to account for man's new knowledge, philosophers sought new metaphysical theories which might be more appropriate to this new situation.

The philosophy of Descartes provided this kind of metaphysics. (In calling it 'new', this is not to ignore the fact that much of Descartes' fundamental outlook was based upon certain theories in the Platonic tradition, especially those of the great Christian Platonist, St. Augustine.) It is from the views of Descartes that most of the metaphysical systems of the last three centuries begin, trying to improve upon them, or to overcome what they regard as difficulties in the Cartesian system.

The Three Substances. In Descartes' metaphysics, as we have seen, there are three basic components in the universe, called substances—**God, Mind and Matter.** Everything else is a modification, or particular example of these. God is the creative substance, who has made the other two. The mental substance has, as its essential property, that **it thinks,** whereas the essential property of matter is that **it is extended.** Everything that happens in either the material or the mental realm is entirely dependent on the Will of God, which orders and controls them.

The physical world is conceived of as a vast, world machine, which operates according to God's constant laws. God constantly conserves and controls a physical order in which various portions of extension move others by contact, producing the regular world that modern science describes. According to Descartes, everything that is extended is part of this machine, including all of the animal world, which he thought of as a series of smaller machines, operating entirely by mechanical principles, but, possibly, more complicated than inanimate objects.

The only aspect of the created world that is not part of world machine is—mind. Mind is completely unextended, and hence not in contact with the material world. Mind engages in mental activities like thinking, willing, and the like. As we have seen earlier in this chapter, one of the gravest problems in Cartesian metaphysics is to explain satisfactorily how the mental world and the physical world can be in any way related and how God can be said to act causally on either of them.

Descartes' mechanism, **in denying completely any purposeful tendencies in the physical world,** provided a satisfactory metaphysical basis for the new physical theories of such scientists as Galileo. But, at the same time, the sharp division of the created world between the mental and the physical substance gave rise to many difficulties in constructing a consistent theory of the entire universe. Also, the Cartesian conception of the overpowering role played by God seemed to tend towards a kind of mysticism, rather than provide a basis for scientific knowledge. If all power rested in God alone, then neither aspect of the created world—mind or matter—could have any causal efficacy. Any account of natural events would ultimately reduce to saying 'it happens because God so wills'. Hence, instead of employing mental or physical terms, the end result would be to convert all questions into Divine mysteries, which mortals can never comprehend.

Because of problems which appear to arise out of Descartes' rigid separation of the basic components of the universe, various metaphysicians sought to construct theories which would modify the Cartesian view by simplifying its fundamental conceptions. On the one hand, some philosophers felt that by eliminating the material substance from the metaphysical system, a more satisfactory theory could be developed. Others insisted that the solution lay in denying the mental or spiritual components of the Cartesian world, and working out a more advanced form of mechanism. Thus, out of the original Cartesian metaphysical theory two divergent kinds of metaphysics have developed, one **mentalistic,** called **idealism,** and the other **a modern form of materialism.**

Idealism. The metaphysical meaning of **idealism** has little to do with the ordinary meaning of the word. Instead, its philosophical usage relates to **a theory which holds that the most important element in the nature of reality is mind or spirit.** After Descartes, some philosophers developed a Cartesian system without the notion of a physical substance. The full flowering of this kind of theory appears in the metaphysical views of the Irish philosopher, BISHOP BERKELEY (discussed more fully in the chapter on the theory of knowledge).

Bishop Berkeley. Berkeley's contention is that there is no such entity as a physical world, or matter, in the sense of an independently existing object. Instead, all that we ordinarily call physical objects are actually collections of ideas in a mind. A table is the set of perceptions that I have when I touch, look, and so on. But this is not to say that things are really different from what they appear to be. **Berkeley insisted that all that we can ever know about objects is merely the ideas we have of them. The appearances we experience are the very objects, and the appearances are sensations or perceptions of a thinking being.**

Mind and God. But what accounts for the series of ideas that occur, and the regularity of the patterns? According to Berkeley, ideas themselves are only passive effects of something, unable to produce or cause any further ideas. We, the perceivers who are aware of the ideas, are only able to influence or affect a very small number, if any, of the ideas that we have. Whether we will it or not, when we open our eyes, we perceive certain ideas. When our finger is pricked, even though we may not enjoy it, or wish it, we experience a painful sensation, and so on. Therefore, Berkeley claimed, the order of ideas must be due to some mind other than ours, who constantly perceives all the ideas, and at various times makes us perceive the particular group of them which constitutes our experience. **This universal mind which always perceives is God.**

Further, according to Berkeley's theory, **mind is active,** and is an agent, while **ideas are only the passive effects of mental activity.** In fact, the only sort of power which can produce anything exists solely in mind, either in the finite spirits which are ourselves, or in the Infinite Mind of God. **The entire, magnificent world of nature, with its wonderful scientific harmony is nothing but an expression of the ideas in the Divine Mind.** As he suggested, **the natural world was presented to us as a kind of sign language for interpreting God's Mind.**

Thus, the cosmos, in Berkeley's metaphysics, consists of spirits, or minds, some finite, and one infinite, which are all active agents. In addition, there are the passive effects—ideas—which have the degree of permanence that they exist as the constant perceptions in the mind of God. They also, at various times, are the experiences of human beings. These ingredients, mind and ideas, Berkeley claimed, provided a completely adequate basis to account for all our knowledge about the world, whereas a metaphysical system including another independent ingredient—matter—would create all sorts of difficulties and problems.

Solipsism. The Berkelian theory, which its author called **immaterialism** (the world conceived without matter) led to further extensions—**subjective idealism and solipsism. The latter view is that the universe, as far as one can ever tell, is nothing but myself, my mind, and its ideas.** This view develops from Berkeley's argument that the only things that we can know to exist are those that we can experience. This theory eliminates any other mind but my own, and any other objects but my ideas, and leaves the universe nothing but the sequence of thoughts which occur in me.

J. G. Fichte. Besides the implausibility of solipsism, there is the problem in such a view of accounting for the origin or cause of one's ideas. In order to work out a more satisfactory theory of idealism, the German metaphysician, JOHANN GOTTLIEB FICHTE, at the end of the eighteenth century constructed his theory of **subjective idealism.** This view differs from Berkeley's and the solipsist's by insisting that mind is a continuously creative and evolving entity, somehow generating the various features of the world that we know.

Before expounding his theory, Fichte pointed out that there **were** two major metaphysical outlooks: **materialism**—the view that **everything** is to be accounted for in terms of material causes; and **idealism** —the view that the explanation must be in terms of mental causes. Neither of these theories can be proven or disproven, and each can develop arguments against the other. The philosopher who wants to meditate on metaphysical matters must first decide which outlook he accepts, and then proceed to construct his theories.

Ego and Non-Ego. Having made his choice for the idealistic outlook, Fichte envisaged the universe as the outpourings of the fundamental substance, called the Ego. From this source, he claimed, two aspects emerged, **the self that I am aware of, and the non-Ego, the things that I regard as other than myself.** Both of these depend upon, arise from, are intelligible in terms of, the underlying creative agent behind the scenes. Thus, by the time one develops any awareness or consciousness of the meaning or nature of one's experience, it is already in the form of **object** (the outside world) and **subject** (oneself). The subjective idealist comprehends this two-sided world in relation to a mental source or agent who created it, or who provides the grounds or foundation for making it understandable.

The person of idealistic tendency tries to probe beyond and behind the immediate features of his world in the quest for some explanation for them. The characteristics of the so-called physical world, as we know it, and of our individual mental worlds, as we are conscious of them, are both known as effects of something. The entity which could account for both the objective and subjective aspects of our experience must lie behind both. Thus, the Ego of Fichte's metaphysics is not simply the mind of the solipsist, transformed into a creative agent who generated the entire universe. Instead, the Ego is more impersonal, a creative agency from whom each individual mind is derivative. Each person, and the world which he is aware of, is an expression of something more general, of the creative activity of the Ego. In his efforts to avoid criticism from orthodox religious quarters, Fichte sometimes stated his theory so that he almost gives the impression that he is talking about the traditional notion of God, rather than a transcendent, super-personal mind, as the source of all aspects of the universe.

Objective or Absolute Idealism: Hegel. Perhaps the most famous modern metaphysician is Fichte's successor, GEORG FRIEDRICH WILHELM HEGEL, whose views dominated metaphysical thought throughout the nineteenth century, and who has become somewhat of a villain for most twentieth century philosophers. The abstruse complexities of his writings have made Hegel a professional joke, so that when somebody wrote a book entitled *The Secret of Hegel's Philosophy* a reviewer pointed out that the author had kept the secret very well. Perhaps it is not possible to make complete sense out of the entire Hegelian scheme. In this brief sketch, we shall not attempt to enter into much of the involved structure of Hegel's system, but only to indicate a few of the central themes.

World and the Absolute. One of the main Hegelian contentions is that everything in the universe can be understood only in terms of an **objective or absolute Mind** which has been evolving throughout the world's history into a transcendent, self-contained Being. As we saw in the chapter on political philosophy (see page 82), each stage in the world's development is the expression of the inner struggle of the Absolute to achieve complete self-realization. In the process of evolving, it has been striving towards a stage of complete understanding and intelligibility.

Hegel claimed that the earlier phases of the history of the Absolute could not explain or account for the events of nature and history. Every attempt to construct a system that would provide a complete account of the source, the nature, and the meaning of the universe, proved to be incomplete or unsatisfactory. (In Hegel's terms, each of these attempts contains contradictions, or contradictory elements.) The Absolute itself was constantly striving to overcome this predicament by rendering itself, through its expression, the World, intelligible and consistent. Hence, the world that has appeared in the historical realm has represented a successive series of approximations on the part of the Absolute towards realizing its goal of making itself a complete, comprehensive and rational foundation of the totality of world experience.

To clarify this, let us consider Hegel's picture in terms of the evolution of the world. The universe commenced as a series of discrete particles, providing no explanation of how they were related, why they were here, and so on. Any attempt to describe this almost chaotic state of the universe would encounter difficulties, because any characteristics that were present in the world would be insufficient to describe the whole Universe. Thus, if one asserted that squareness is a characteristic of the universe, this would be contradicted by other characteristics of the world. The Absolute, in order to make itself more intelligible, synthesized the elements into a describable pattern—the physical system of the world.

Even so, this physical account was inadequate to explain why this takes place, or to answer all the questions that could be asked. One could still find contradictory elements, or at least conflicting or apparently incompatible ones, in the attempt to work out a completely rational explanation of the world. So the Absolute evolved to a higher stage, the chemical one, and then the biological one, and finally the human one. These stages represent the 'march of reason through the world', the realization of a fuller expression of the Absolute or Objective Mind, so that it can become a more consistent explanation of the universe.

The Dialectic. In the Hegelian conception, this process of the Absolute is a type of 'logical' one, transformed in our experience into a historical one. The 'logical' development is the famous Hegelian **dialectic, wherein each attempt to formulate something about the universe (a thesis), is contradicted by another formulation (an antithesis), and the conflict between the two is resolved in a proposition which incorporates the partial truth of both of them (the synthesis).** What is frequently presented as a conflict of thesis and antithesis is actually an example of two incomplete accounts which are then synthesized into a more general formulation. Thus, the attempt to explain all physical processes quantitatively is opposed by the purely qualitative physical events, requiring an explanation that encompasses both.

The Absolute is portrayed by Hegel as striving constantly to overcome, or resolve, this dialectic of thesis and antithesis by higher and higher syntheses, until it will finally achieve complete self-realization in an all-encompassing synthesis, which will include all partial truths in one vast truth. At this point the inner logical struggle will be over, as will the history of the world. Since each stage of dialectical ascent is expressed outwardly in terms of some stage in the development of the historical world, when the Absolute reaches completion, so will the cosmos. The latter will then be a completely coherent entity, which can be entirely understood.

As the dialectical struggle goes on, and the universe develops, so does our understanding of it. Until the world becomes completely intelligible there can be only limited comprehension of its structure, since the developments themselves are not yet completely rational. The intelligence of any individual can reach only that degree of understanding and coherence that the Absolute is then expressing. Therefore the entire structure of the universe can be stated in a metaphysical system only when the Absolute has reached full self-realization. At that point thought and being will become identical, since full comprehension and the full state of the universe will be one and the same thing.

The Hegelian Culmination. Hegel's **objective idealism** is the final culmination of transforming the Cartesian metaphysic into a theory where only mind is real, and only mental actions and effects can form a basis for accounting for the world of our experience. Moving from Berkeley's static world of ideas, as the persistent thoughts in the Divine

Mind, to Fichte's creative Ego, generating both the subjective and objective features of the universe, **Hegel completely objectified thought and mind into the basic independent entity,** devoid of all personality, and all subjective properties. **The Hegelian Absolute Mind becomes the real universe, manifesting itself outwardly as world history, and inwardly as the rational dialectical process, marching toward full self-realization.** Somehow the metaphysical system, when properly understood, is not just a description of the objective universe, but actually is the Absolute, intellectually expressed.

Materialism. In contrast to the idealist's approach, the **materialists sought to develop a modified Cartesianism, eliminating mind, and possibly God, from the basic metaphysical scheme, and attempting to explain everything in terms of material events.** Beginning with THOMAS HOBBES in the seventeenth century, and continuing with the French materialists of the Enlightenment, the type of theory developed does not differ substantially from the Greek materialist theories except in details.

Impact of Science. Instead of employing the crude, speculative atomism of Democritus and Epicurus, the modern materialists tried to show in more elaborate terms, based upon the general discoveries and theories of modern physical science, that a purely materialist account can be given of everything we know. Using first the physics of Descartes and of his contemporary atomist, Gassendi, and later the theories of Isaac Newton, the materialists tried to show that all events in the universe could be explained as the results of mathematically describable motions of extended, solid features of the universe.

The rapid growth of the physical sciences, of physics and astronomy, gave an initial appeal to the materialist theory in the minds of a great many forward-looking thinkers, who had become exceedingly sceptical of previous metaphysical theories. The difficulties in a complete materialism seemed to arise in extending the already triumphant pattern of material explanation from physical things to living and thinking things. The beginnings of the social sciences in the eighteenth century, the development of modern chemistry in the nineteenth century, and the tremendous progress in biology and psychology in more recent times have all given greater authority to the materialist in his belief that even if it has not yet been accomplished, it will soon be possible to account for all events solely in terms of physical concepts and laws.

But from the time of Descartes, certain problems in developing a complete materialism had arisen. The Cartesian metaphysic contains a materialism about the natural world, both animate and inanimate, but also recognizes that this cannot be extended to the mental world. In order to extend it to the world of living things, Descartes had to claim that animals are really 'automata', small machines. Since Descartes' day, the materialists have had to try to make good the claim that all living processes, like digestion, growth, reproduction, can be explained in a purely mechanical fashion, and that similar kinds of explanation can be offered for the events of one's mental life.

Biology. As a result, there has been a running battle between two opposing groups of theoretical biologists, the **vitalists** and the **mechanists.** The contention of the latter is that it is gradually being shown that various processes of animals and plants can be explained in physical and chemical terms, and that there is no reason to suspect that this cannot ultimately be done with all biological questions. On the other hand, their opponents claim that either it is already the case that one has to abandon purely materialist concepts and introduce certain other ones, like 'life-force', that cannot be reduced to physical or chemical notions, or that this will occur. Without such non-materialist ideas, the vitalists assert, it will not be possible to give a satisfactory account of the information we already possess about the behaviour of living things.

Psychology. Similarly, in psychological theory a battle has been, and is being waged, between those who believe that some sort of materialist science of human behaviour can be, or is being, developed, and those who insist that the evidence indicates that this is not, or cannot be the case. Here, the issues involved are extremely complex, and much of the merit of each case will depend upon the future course of experimental research in establishing whether or not a satisfactory explanation of human and animal psychology can be developed along materialist lines.

Physics. However, as modern physics moves further away from the simple mechanical conceptions of Newton's theory, the original materialist metaphysic has begun to lose some of its force and appeal. If the picture of the physical world presented by the scientists is no longer one of simple physical particles in motion, as the cause of all physical events, then a theory about the basic characteristics of reality based on an outmoded scientific theory is not as acceptable. As scientific theorists move further away from a view that science provides accurate accounts of the intimate secrets of physical reality, **to a more empirical conception of science as a hypothetical model of what the world may be like, that suffices for predicting the future course of experience,** a materialism based on the developments in scientific research has become less attractive. Those who base their theories about the fundamental character of the world upon an interpretation of our scientific knowledge have tended to adopt a **positivistic or pragmatic, or less materialistic form of naturalistic theory, than the classical forms of materialism.**

Dialectical Materialism. Although the type of materialism advocated by KARL MARX is discussed in detail in the chapter on political philosophy, it is relevant to say something about it here, before leaving this subject. **Marx's materialism is based on 'standing Hegel on his head', and transforming the Hegelian idealistic pattern into a theory about the natural world.** Instead of attributing the dialectical scheme to some Absolute or Objective Mind, **it is in Nature alone that the processes of overcoming contradictions take place.**

Everything in the universe is interpreted as being the result of physical forces in operation. But these forces, rather than operating merely in a mechanical pattern, proceed in a dialectical fashion, achieving or evolving more and more consistent and coherent features.

All the processes of nature can be explained as dialectical processes of this type, but, as we have seen (page 83), Marx emphasizes the economic aspect of his dialectical materialism. The human world, which is, of course, the chief concern of the theory, **contains a type of materialistic being, whose way of existence is determined by the material factors involved in his attempts to produce sufficient material goods for his survival.**

Economic Theory. Each type of economy that has evolved in history contains conflicting, or contradictory elements (a thesis and an antithesis) which have been resolved in a synthesis, a new type of economy, which in turn has involved new conflicting elements, and so on. The conflict between slave and master, serf and lord, has finally given rise to the present material system of production—capitalism. **At each stage, the entire culture, the intellectual and artistic forces, are an expression of the then existing materialistic base which determines and accounts for human societies.**

The 'Synthesis' of Communism. According to Marx, the present form of material life, based on a capitalist economy, contains a final conflict that is to be resolved, a conflict between the producer, the worker, on the one hand, and the employer, the owner of the means of production, on the other. This will ultimately be synthesized in an economy in which this separation between employee and employer disappears, and with it all conflict. At this point, the Hegelian dream of the complete realization of the Absolute will take place in the natural world instead, with the elimination of all contradictions and the achievement of a totally rational social order—for Marx, a communist society.

Naturalism. The last type of modern metaphysics that we shall consider is **naturalism.** In this theory, it is claimed that all the features of the universe can be explained or accounted for in **natural or experiential terms.** Materialism is a restricted form of naturalism, in which only basic physical concepts, of matter and motion, are thought requisite in order to explain everything. **Naturalism can allow for the employment of any of the concepts that arise from our study of nature and experience, and not merely the concepts of physical science.**

The naturalists contend that beginning with the Cartesian system an artificial division has been imposed upon our conceptions of the world which has continually engendered unsatisfactory results. After Descartes completely separated mind and matter, metaphysicians have tried to undo the damage by eliminating either mind or matter, or attempted to reduce one category to the other, with unfortunate consequences. Instead, it is suggested, one should recognize that both are aspects of our experience, and ought to be interpreted in these terms.

The Influence of Science. There have been many different types of naturalist account of the universe, usually modelled on the prevailing scientific motifs of the time. The basic natural or experiential conceptions have been, by and large, drawn from the dominant scientific discoveries of the time, in physics, biology, etc. In the nineteenth and twentieth centuries, the most common expressions of naturalism have been attempts to work out consistent accounts of all of our knowledge about the world in terms of biological and psychological themes, especially in the light of the evolutionary aspect of the natural and human world brought to the fore in nineteenth century geology, biology, history, psychology, etc. Such philosophers as HENRI BERGSON, FRIEDRICH NIETZSCHE, WILLIAM JAMES, JOHN DEWEY, and others, have attempted to construct general theories about the nature of reality in purely naturalistic terms, extending the insights provided by these sciences into metaphysical theories.

Experience. In the most common versions of naturalism, the fundamental category is taken to be experience itself. Out of this, two aspects are distinguished, the objective and the subjective. These are not separate entities, the external world and the mind, but rather different ways of looking at, or regarding, **the relationships or processes that take place in experience.** On the basis of these aspects, further discriminations or selections are made, which encompass other aspects in terms of scientifically organized patterns, human values, purposes.

The evolving, developing character of experience becomes the basis for regarding the describable or understandable world, both objective and subjective, as **indeterminate to some degree.** Future possibilities are open as to what further natural properties, orders and tendencies may appear. Hence, there is also a degree of openness in naturalistic explanation, that **any attempted explanation is always an approximation of the characteristics of the universe, rather than a fixed and final description,** which is bound to be correct for all times and all places.

Some naturalistic theories develop some of the suggestive leads of Stoic metaphysics, in conceiving of the natural and experiential order as having a dynamic, emergent feature, which brings forth new facets in nature in the course of time. Such a natural dynamism would account for, these naturalists believe, the evolutionary character of our natural knowledge, without appealing to any supernatural agency. It would also provide a basis for the belief in both the openness of natural developments, or their indeterminacy at any given moment, and the need for revising one's estimates of the fundamental nature of the universe.

SOME CRITICISMS OF METAPHYSICS

These metaphysical theories attempt in one way or another to present some **general system that will account for the manifold characteristics of the world, our knowledge of it, and our beliefs, hopes, aspirations, and other aspects of our 'subjective' nature.** For over two thousand years, metaphysicians have debated as to which of these theories is more satisfactory, more plausible. After all this time, though many of these systems may appear as interesting speculations, there seems to be no general agreement amongst philosophers as to which of them is true, or at least truer than the others. Moreover, each school of metaphysicians appears to be able to show that there are serious difficulties in the views of all the others, but does not seem to be able to develop a satisfactory justification of its own views.

Because of this confusion, some philosophers have thought that the fundamental problem is that there is something wrong with meta-physical reasoning itself. If this be the case, the question is not the truth or plausibility of the theories, but rather what is wrong with the entire metaphysical enterprise, and why is it bound, by its very nature, to lead to unsatisfactory results. We shall consider the answers to this query of two of the most famous critics of metaphysical reasoning and system construction, DAVID HUME and IMMANUEL KANT, who both claimed to have discovered the basic limitations that prevent any successful solution to any metaphysical problem.

Hume's Criticism of Metaphysics. Hume's criticism of metaphysics derives from his empirical and sceptical point of view, and is summed up in the famous concluding passage from his *Enquiry Concerning Human Understanding*. There, he asked:

> When we run over libraries, persuaded of these principles [that is, Hume's empirical principles] what havoc must we make? If we take in our hand any volume; of divinity or school metaphysics, for instance; let us ask, Does it contain any abstract reasoning concerning quantity or number? No. Does it contain any experimental reasoning concerning matter of fact and existence? No. Commit it then to the flames: for it can contain nothing but sophistry and illusion.

The basis for the book-burning crusade is **Hume's contention that the only meaningful terms or ideas are either sense impressions or mathematical concepts.** Sense impressions are meaningful because they can be tested by experience and observation; mathematical concepts are meaningful because they express relationships between ideas that we can intuitively see to be true and certain. No other concept can be meaningful since we have no way of testing its validity. Hence, the key notions of the metaphysicians—e.g., 'substance', 'reality', 'mind', 'matter'—actually are meaningless since we are unable to define them in terms of anything that we know about. Therefore, the propositions that metaphysicians propound might sound impressive, but they have no significance.

Meaning and Experience. Further, the questions that the meta-physicians are seeking to answer are as meaningless as the concepts that they employ in trying to answer them. They wish to find out what is the nature of reality, what is the cause of the world's characteristics, what is the relationship of matter and mind, what degree of freedom does the human will exercise, what is the role of God in the affairs of natural and human existence, and so on. But, in terms of the sorts of relationship that we are capable of discerning in our experience, and in mathematics, none of these can be taken seriously. We would not even know what they are questions about, how one would go about answering them, or what a correct answer would look like.

Over and over again in his philosophical writings, Hume explained various metaphysical problems, and showed that when analysed in terms of his empirical criterion of meaning, the questions dissolved into meaninglessness. If our knowledge about the world is restricted to what we experience, plus the inferences we make as a result of the constant conjunctions of events, and our own habit of expecting the future to resemble the past, then how can we possibly tell if there is any permanent structure to reality above and beyond what we are aware of? There is nothing in our experience that suggests that our impressions belong to some object outside of experience, or that they can be explained in terms of such an object.

The Critique of 'Substance'. The basic principle of metaphysical explanation up to Hume's time, the notion of a 'substance', whether it be mental, physical or divine, which is the fundamental element of the universe, Hume found completely unintelligible. If our ideas come to us from our sensations or our reflections, where does this notion come from?

> If it be convey'd to us by our senses, I ask, which of them; and after what manner? If it be perceiv'd by the eyes, it must be a colour; if by the ears, a sound; if by the palate, a taste; and so of the other senses. But I believe none will assert, that substance is either a colour, or sound, or a taste. The idea of a substance must therefore be deriv'd from an impression or reflexion, if it really exist. But the impressions of reflexion resolve themselves into our passions and emotions; none of which can possibly represent a substance. We have therefore no idea of substance, distinct from that of a collection of particular qualities, nor have we any other meaning when we either talk or reason concerning it.

Not only do we have no impression or idea of this thing called 'substance', but when we look at what the metaphysicians say about it, we are further baffled. They say that a substance is something that can exist by itself, that is, something that can be conceived of apart from everything else, and requiring nothing else to account for itself. But, Hume pointed out, if this means anything, it applies to every perception that we can have. Each idea in our mind can be thought of separately and can be distinguished from every other idea. When we conceive of the idea apart from all others, it seems to meet the metaphysicians' meaning of 'substance'.

But, the metaphysical philosophers might say, Hume has missed the whole point of what metaphysical explanations are about. A substance is something entirely different from a perception, and is that which accounts for why the perception has the characteristics that it does, and is that to which the perception belongs or inheres. When presented with this view, Hume observed: 'We have no perfect idea of anything but of a perception. A substance is entirely different from a perception. We have, therefore, no idea of a substance.'

As to the second point, that a metaphysical account in terms of substances is necessary to explain the existence or nature of our ideas or perceptions, Hume again disagreed. We have our perceptions; our impressions occur. Nothing seems to be required to explain or support their existence. As far as we can tell, they simply are, and any question about why they are, and why they are what they are, seems both uncalled for and actually unintelligible. So Hume concluded: 'What possibility then of answering that question, Whether perceptions inhere in a material or immaterial substance, when we do not so much as understand the meaning of the question?'

When one looks further into these matters, Hume found, it only becomes worse. The concept of matter, and the physical world, as really composed of extended solid stuff in motion, Hume found as unintelligible as Berkeley did before him. If the qualities of immediate experience—e.g., colour, sound, taste, smell—were excluded from being features of the material world that supposedly existed independently from us, then Hume insisted, we could not possibly conceive of what this matter is like. All the qualities that the metaphysicians attribute to matter—extension, motion, and solidity—turn out to be just as subjective as the others, as Berkeley had earlier proved. But, once 'we conclude, that neither colour, sound, taste, nor smell have a continu'd and independent existence', and 'we exclude these sensible qualities', then 'there remains nothing in the universe which has such an existence'.

The Critique of Idealism. When one leaves the problems of the materialists aside, and examines the claims of the idealists, who would explain everything in terms of mind, the same difficulties arise. The concept of mind is just as unclear as that of matter. If we search for some impression that gives rise to such an idea, we find that there is none. We are not aware of some entity to which all of our thoughts belong. Instead we are acquainted only with the succession of our ideas. Hence, we do not know of any mental substance, nor do we find any way in which our perceptions or thoughts might belong to it.

The Mind–Body Problem. When one examines some of the specific problems that metaphysicians are concerned with, it appears that their concepts make no sense, and that the difficulties are all of their own making. Consider, for example, the mind–body problem, which had been so much debated in the hundred years between Descartes and Hume. The question of how a mental event can be related to a physical event, and vice versa, is a difficulty only if one first introduces the concepts of mental and material substance, and then asks how, if these two are entirely different, can there be any necessary connection between what happens in one and what takes place in the other? If one eliminates the meaningless concepts of the two substances, and the equally unintelligible idea of a necessary connection between events, then what is left? Only the question of whether it is possible that certain events that we call mental, such as tastes and smells, can be constantly conjoined with others that we call physical, such as the movements of extended objects? The answer, Hume insisted, was Yes. We experience this sort of conjunction all the time, between the taste of a pear, and the shape of a pear, between the sound of C sharp, and the striking of a certain key on the piano, and so on.

If it is pointed out that the mere fact that these constant conjunctions occur does not explain how the physical event produces the mental one, or vice versa, Hume can easily reply, 'So what?' In no other case, whether it be of two constantly conjoined physical events, like a hammer moving and pushing a nail, or two conjoined mental events, do we ever discover how one produces the other. No **causal**

relationship can ever be **observed**, even in the material world (see page 211). Thus, the special case of conjunctions between mental and physical events raises no new problem, unless it is complicated by the introduction of some meaningless or unintelligible metaphysical notions.

Free Will and Necessity. Similarly, Hume contended, if one examined the free-will controversy, one would find again that there was no real problem. The difficulties have been due entirely to metaphysical notions introduced by the philosophers, rather than to any grave, intricate matters concerning the notions of liberty and necessity. Thus, Hume claimed:

> If I be not much mistaken, we shall find, that all mankind, both learned and ignorant, have always been of the same opinion with regard to this subject, and that a few intelligible definitions would immediately have put an end to the whole controversy.

All that anybody ever meant by necessity, or necessary connection, is that two events have been constantly conjoined, and that when we see one of them, we automatically expect or predict the occurrence of the other. In this sense, there is as much necessity in human actions as there is in any other aspect of the universe. Everybody has always been aware that there exists a constant conjunction between our motives and our voluntary actions. If we examine human behaviour, both at the present time, and in past history, we find that there have been regular sequences, which have been repeated over and over again, of a certain motive followed by a certain action. Thus, Hume argued, in the ordinary meaning of 'necessity', there is a necessity in human behaviour.

Liberty. On the other hand, if one analyses what people mean by 'liberty', one will find that there is, and always has been, agreement, that there exists liberty in human actions.

> For what is meant by liberty, when applied to voluntary actions? We cannot surely mean that actions have so little connection with motives, inclinations, and circumstances, that one does not follow with a certain degree of uniformity from the other, and that one affords no inference by which we can conclude the existence of the other. For these are plain and acknowledged matters of fact. By liberty, then, we can only mean **a power of acting or not acting, according to the determinations of the will;** that is, if we choose to remain at rest, we may; if we choose to move, we also may. Now this hypothetical liberty is universally allowed to belong to every one who is not a prisoner and in chains.

But, in this common meaning of 'liberty', there is no conflict between saying that human actions are necessary, in that they are regularly conjoined with certain motives, and saying that human beings possess liberty, in that they can act as they wish, so long as they are not constrained. The wishes people have can still be their own desires, and also be conjoined with other factors. Thus, Hume insisted, as soon as one turned from the metaphysical constructions to a consideration of the problem in ordinary terms, the entire question that had been so long debated, disappeared.

Philosophers had complicated the issue by seeking either to establish that every event, including human volitions, has a cause, in the sense of something that necessarily produces the occurrence of the event; or, on the other hand, claiming that there could be an uncaused event, in the sense of an event that takes place without the influence of any other event in the universe. But since we can never tell from our experience whether events are necessarily produced by others, and, at the same time, every event we know of stands in some kind of relation of constant conjunction with some other occurrences, there really is no opposition of alternatives such as the metaphysicians had proposed. Thus, once this problem had been clarified, everyone could agree that, in an ordinary sense, **human beings are both free agents, in that they can do as they please when not constrained, and at the same time their actions are necessary, in that there are laws of human behaviour.**

These examinations of metaphysical problems led Hume to the conclusion that there was no point in trying to answer the questions. Instead he sought to show both why they are meaningless quibbles, and why it is that supposedly sane and intelligent people discuss them at such great length. **The study of metaphysics, for Hume, becomes the study of metaphysicians.** This type of investigation constitutes an inquiry into the possible causes of this strange kind of human aberration that has manifested itself in so many philosophers from ancient Greece to the eighteenth century. Many of Hume's comments on metaphysics are really research in the pathology of the metaphysical mind in operation.

According to one account Hume offered, one can discover psychological explanations for why certain people get snared into searching for solutions to metaphysical problems. In a case study that he presented of the Aristotelian philosopher, Hume first showed the series of mental steps involved by which the imagination of such a person creates the notions that he disputes about. Then, in comparing this sort of behaviour to normal thinking, Hume believed that there must be some sort of metaphysical idiosyncrasy that leads these unfortunates astray, into a wilderness of their own invention.

What happens is that the metaphysician, like any good philosopher, notices that there is something peculiar about some of the things that ordinary people believe. For example, practically everyone believes that they perceive a connection between objects that are constantly conjoined. But the metaphysician sagely observes that this simply is not the case—each object is entirely distinct and separate, and it is only as a result of people's habit of association, that they arrive at a contrary conclusion. The metaphysician, having begun by realizing that we do not see any necessary connection between events, nor the power that produces them, then sets off on a wild-goose chase, searching for this causal agency behind the scenes, seeking for some explanation for our ordinary experience.

They [the metaphysicians] have sufficient force of genius to free them from the vulgar error, that there is a natural and perceivable connection betwixt the several sensible qualities and actions of matter; but not sufficient to keep them from ever seeking for this connection in matter, or causes.

If the metaphysician were normal, he would accept his discovery calmly. He would realize that ordinary people are wrong, but that this is not terribly important. One can continue to live normally by recognizing, in theory, that we can only know the individual events of our experience, and also realizing that in practice we are led, naturally, to associate constantly conjoined events. The metaphysician goes astray by insisting that if the ordinary view of the causes of events is wrong, some other answer must be true. Then, he is tormented forever, looking for his answer. 'For what can be imagin'd more tormenting, than to seek with eagerness what for ever flees us; and seek for it in a place where 'tis impossible it can ever exist?'

But, fortunately for the forlorn metaphysician, Hume suggests, nature offers him some consolation. After he has invented his terminology, and used it long enough, he begins to think that he is talking about something. The terms, which to begin with 'are wholly insignificant and unintelligible', come to satisfy the metaphysician, just because he uses them all the time. (Hume suspected that these people imagine that the strange words they use have some secret meaning, which might be discovered by deep reflection.) Merely by talking to each other and themselves, Hume claimed, the metaphysicians think that they are saying something, and that they have found the answer to their quest.

> By this means these philosophers set themselves at ease, and arrive at last, by an illusion, at the same indifference, which the people attain by their stupidity, and true philosophers by their moderate scepticism. They need only say that any phenomenon, which puzzles them, arises from a faculty or an occult quality, and there is an end of all dispute and enquiry upon the matter.

The sort of inventive imagination that metaphysicians exhibit, Hume suggested, was also found in the beliefs of children, and the fictions of poets. But, Hume observed, in concluding his study of the metaphysician, 'We must pardon children, because of their age; poets, because they profess to follow implicitly the suggestions of their fancy: But what excuse shall we find to justify our philosophers in so signal a weakness?'

Kant's Criticism of Metaphysics. The great German philosopher, IMMANUEL KANT (1724–1804) took the metaphysical quest more seriously than had Hume. Kant felt that what was wrong with this intellectual enterprise was not some psychological defect in some philosophers, but a basic problem in the nature of what human beings could possibly know. Thus, from an investigation at the fundamental level, Kant thought, it would be possible to discover what certain knowledge we could attain, and thereby, also to discover the limitations which would prevent the uncovering of any metaphysical truths.

Mental Faculties. Kant began his study of human knowledge, in his *Critique of Pure Reason*, agreeing with the empiricists' claim that our knowledge begins with experience. However, as he stated at the outset, 'although all our knowledge begins with experience, it does not follow that it arises from experience'. It is also the case, Kant argued, that what we know is the product of our own thinking faculty. **Our contacts with the experiential world supply the content of our knowledge, but our faculties supply the form in which we know it.**

A Priori **Knowledge.** What Kant was primarily concerned with was to discover not what knowledge we derive from experience, but what *a priori* knowledge human beings could possess—that is, **knowledge that is universal and necessary and independent of experience.** He believed that both in mathematics and the study of nature (physics)— owing to the role played by the mind—there was some information which had to be true of all possible experience. But, he wanted to discover whether there could be any *a priori* **metaphysical knowledge, necessary and universal knowledge that was neither mathematical nor physical, and which went beyond ordinary experience.**

Analytic and Synthetic Knowledge. The types of *a priori* knowledge fall, Kant claimed, into two groups: **analytic and synthetic.** The former consists of propositions or judgments whose truth can be determined without reference to any experience, but solely on the basis of the terms employed. For example, the propositions 'A red rose is red', and 'All bodies are extended', Kant asserted, are necessarily and universally true, solely because of the definitions of the terms involved. This is the same point that we saw Hume making about mathematical concepts (see page 128). Such a proposition is true because what is predicated of the subject is already contained in the definition of the subject. It requires only the principles of logic to discover that these judgments are **analytic** *a priori* **truths.**

But, in the case of a **synthetic judgment, the predicate of the judgment must contain some information not contained in the subject.** The judgment must be the result of a **synthesis** of two quite separate notions, one being the subject about which the other, the predicate, is asserted. **Thus, the analysis of the concepts included in the judgment would not suffice to reveal whether it was true.** But Kant admitted after studying Hume, our ordinary empirical information, such as 'This piece of paper is white', though synthetic, in that the predicate contains a concept not included in the subject, **is not** *a priori*, that is, is not universal or necessary or independent of experience. To be an *a priori* **judgment a synthetic judgment would have to contain some information not purely of a logical nature, and yet not dependent on empirical or experimental information for its truth.**

In both mathematics and physics, Kant thought, there were judgments of precisely this character. Even the elementary proposition that $7 + 5 = 12$, he insisted, was a truth that was not merely true because of the definitions of the terms involved, but, rather was one that contained more information in the predicate than was included in the bare concepts of '7' and '5'. In combining these two concepts into another one which is their sum, a kind of intuition must take place, which introduces something new in the conclusion.

That 5 should be added to 7 was no doubt implied in my concept of a sum 7 + 5, but not that that sum should be equal to 12. An arithmetical proposition is, therefore, always synthetical, which is seen more easily still by taking larger numbers, where we clearly perceive that, turn and twist our conceptions as we may, we could never, by means of the mere analysis of our concepts and without the help of intuition, arrive at the sum wanted.

Similarly, in geometrical truths, Kant claimed, one finds the same sort of synthetic element, as for example, in the proposition 'A straight line is the shortest distance between two points', where the concept of 'straight line' does not include the notion of its being the shortest, and yet the statement is a necessary and universal truth. And, in physics, he contended, it is also the case that there are propositions like 'Every event has a cause', which are synthetic, and are also *a priori*.

Intuition. The general problem of understanding what we can know, especially what we can know that is necessarily true, requires answering the question, 'How are synthetic *a priori* judgments possible?' (Kant took it for granted that there were such judgments.) The first level of his explanation is the claim that the very order or form of our experience has an *a priori* character, which arises from the mind, and not the outside world. In order to have a recognizable, discussible experience, it must of necessity fall into a pattern. We find, for instance, that we neither do have, nor can conceive of, any possible experience except in spatial and temporal terms. Thus, it appears to be required that there be a formal character to everything that we are aware of, and, in view of Hume's arguments, that experience itself cannot supply any necessary reason for the features it has. Therefore, Kant claimed, there must be some forms of all possible experience, or, as he called them, the **forms of intuition,** which we impose upon everything that we are in contact with. We can be certain, in advance of any experience, that two sorts of *a priori* characteristics will be present in any awareness that we may have, that it will have temporal and geometrical features, and that the truths of mathematics will apply to everything that we discover about the world of experience.

Besides the forms of intuition, Kant believed, there must also be principles or concepts by which we organize the general content of any possible experience in order to recognize it as a coherent datum. Otherwise, the argument goes, we would merely have the awareness without any means of discussing or describing it. Hence, it must be the case, on Kant's theory, that since we are capable of attaining organized and intelligible information about the world, **we must have within ourselves the organizing principles.** Our minds structure and interpret the observations of our senses. (The objects of our experience cannot supply these factors, for once again, if Hume is right, there are no necessary features in the experiences themselves.)

Categories. These further conditions which are imposed upon the data of our sensations are those which are needed in order for us to be able to make any judgments at all. **Every judgment is a synthesizing of two concepts into a connected proposition.** This requires that the mind employ a certain formal apparatus in putting together what it is aware of, an apparatus such that its judgments must have certain **quantity** (that they be about 'All' or 'Some' or 'None' of something) and that they have some **quality** (positive or negative). Further, there must also be a general conceptual scheme by which the types of items that we are acquainted with are ordered and related. This last part of the intellectual framework consists of what are called the **categories,** which Kant listed in four groups of three, involving such notions as causality, substance and accident, possibility, etc. These are the 'original pure concepts of synthesis, which belong to the understanding *a priori*, and for which alone it is called pure understanding; for it is by them alone that it can understand something in the manifold of intuition, that is, think an object in it'.

Thus, Kant's theory is that **the world of our experience, the so-called phenomenal world, is the product both of something which we are presented with, and the *a priori* conditions supplied by the mind.** The mind is viewed as something like **a vast blank form which determines the kinds of answers that can be given, but not the specific content, which only experience can determine. The forms of intuition, the logical functions of judgment, and the categories fix the necessary conditions of both experience and knowledge, but the actual content arises only from something independent of us.**

Transcendental Inquiries. This theory is much like claiming that we look at everything with a complex set of coloured glasses which we cannot remove. We perceive the phenomenal world, the world of appearance. But what we experience has two parts. The form of the world of appearance is determined by the glasses, and hence, is 'necessary and universal'. On the other hand, the content of the phenomenal world is not in any way conditioned or determined by the glasses. Only the way in which we will have to see and interpret it is. We can investigate both the content and the form. Science studies the former, and what Kant called 'critical philosophy', can examine the latter, by **transcendental inquiries,** that is, investigations which seek to find out from our experience and our judgments, what the necessary features of these must be in all cases.

Critique of Metaphysics. Having claimed to have gone beyond Hume, by showing how we are able to attain necessary knowledge about the world, Kant then went on to agree with his predecessor that metaphysical knowledge about the general characteristics of reality was impossible to attain. When we try to expand our knowledge either inward or outward we come to a complete impasse. If we seek inside ourselves for what is the cause of, or the basis of, our mental machinery of forms and categories, we are unable to discover anything. Similarly, when we try to move beyond the phenomenal world, to the realm of things-in-themselves, we are again unable to proceed.

The difficulty which prevents us from developing any metaphysical knowledge is that we have no way of determining if our mental apparatus is applicable to anything beyond the world of possible experience, the phenomenal world. We possess no concepts, no forms of intuition, no logical schema, that we have any reason to believe apply to the Self, or to the **things-in-themselves,** the real objects that may exist behind the world of appearance. The *a priori* conditions that we can uncover are exclusively conditions of an experienceable world, not of one that may exist in another realm.

Our forms of intuition, first of all, restrict us to what can be experienced in a spatial and temporal context, namely, empirical objects. Our logical forms and our categories are organizing principles within this context. They constitute a set of necessary rules for thinking about items within, and, as far as we know, only within, the phenomenal world. Hence, the necessary conditions which allow us to acquire *a priori* knowledge about the world of appearance, cannot be extended to tell us about a possible trans-empirical world, unless we could discover some means of determining whether the metaphysical realm can and must be thought of in the same way as the phenomenal one.

The metaphysicians who try to build some sort of bridge from what we know must be true of the phenomenal world to what must be true of the **noumenal** (that is, non-empirical) world, always get into trouble. There simply is no basis for any inference either from the content of experience, or from its necessary conditions, to any metaphysical conclusion at all. To make his point, Kant examined what he regarded as the stock claims of the metaphysicians, and tried to show that either they committed some elementary logical fallacy in reaching their conclusions, or that they arrived at completely contradictory results.

Antinomies. As soon as the philosopher takes the *a priori* conditions of pure thought as objective conditions of the universe, all sorts of errors occur. The arguments built upon such an assumption to establish the nature of the mind or self necessarily commit certain logical errors, in order to move from some purely logical considerations to some claims of objective fact. The arguments which attempt to establish the nature of the noumenal world, the real world of things-in-themselves, result in what Kant called 'antinomies', **conclusions which can be both proven and disproven.** Thus, reasonings which purport to prove that the world is finite, has a beginning in time, and so on, can be attacked by showing that just as good arguments can be constructed to establish the denials of these contentions. Hence, we have no way of telling which of two contradictory views on these metaphysical questions is more likely to be true, or even plausible.

With regard to the ultimate metaphysical basis of experience, Kant claimed that all the evidence put forth actually established nothing at all. Although we shall later consider Kant's criticisms of the arguments for the existence of God, it can be stated here that Kant insisted that all the proofs that there must be some Being whose nature accounts for the fundamental characteristics of the universe, turn out, on careful inspection, to be inconclusive. Once again, the metaphysician tries to reason beyond his experience, and his conceptual framework, and, as a result, achieves nothing.

All in all, Kant concluded, **the metaphysical enterprise, in its traditional sense, is doomed to failure.** The summit of our understanding consists solely in our being able to discover the conditions that regulate our knowledge of the phenomenal world. But any attempt to go beyond this, to employ the necessary features of our judgments about experience, to discover the constituents of the real world, always ends in disaster. We can never tell if the noumenal world is spatial and temporal, but only that the world of appearance must be. We can never tell if the noumenal world contains substances, causally related events, and so on, but only that the sense world must be so interpreted. Hence, any effort to discuss and reason about the realm of the Self, the thing-in-itself, or God, becomes, for Kant, only an unfortunate dialectical illusion. The metaphysician who does not see this will merely waste his time meandering around in a maze of his own construction, arriving at all sorts of odd and incompatible results.

Conclusion. As a result of the criticism of metaphysics propounded by David Hume and Immanuel Kant in the eighteenth century, and revived in many forms in the present day, many philosophers have accepted the judgment that the sort of knowledge sought by the metaphysician is not attainable. They have either developed Hume's critique into the modern form of positivism (see pages 280–5), insisting that metaphysics is a disease to be treated, not a discipline to be investigated, or they have followed Kant and held that our knowledge cannot transcend the categories which we employ in thinking about our experience. Therefore, some of the latter thinkers have suggested (as Kant did in his *Critique of Pure Reason*) that one ought to abandon the traditional investigation and transform metaphysical research into 'categorical analysis', the study of the necessary conditions involved in knowing anything.

Others have refused to abandon the quest for metaphysical truths, for information about the 'real nature' of things. Some metaphysicians reject critiques of their undertaking while proposing new solutions to the old metaphysical questions. (Perhaps, the most famous of these philosophers in the twentieth century is the late ALFRED NORTH WHITEHEAD.) But, by and large, metaphysical interests have diminished in contemporary thought, and are just beginning to show some slight signs of revival in the English-speaking world.

SUGGESTED FURTHER READING

Classical Authors:

Plato, *Timaeus*. (Plato's metaphysical theory.)

Aristotle, *Physics* and *Metaphysics*.

Descartes, René, *Meditations on First Philosophy*. Dent: London, 1953. (The classical statement of the Cartesian system.)

Berkeley, George, *Three Dialogues between Hylas and Philonous*. Collins: London, 1962. (Berkeley's best presentation of his theory.)

Hume, David, *A Treatise of Human Nature*. (Hume's first work in which he developed his views at greatest length.)

Hume, David, *Enquiries Concerning the Human Understanding*. (A more popular presentation of his arguments.)

Kant, Immanuel, *Prolegomena to any Future Metaphysics*. (Kant's supposedly elementary statement of his theory.)

Modern Authors:

Blanshard, Brand, *The Nature of Thought*. 2 vols. Allen & Unwin: London, 1939. (A modern statement of the case for idealist metaphysics.)

Hampshire, Stuart, *Spinoza*. Penguin Books: London, 1967. (A good critical discussion of Spinoza's philosophy.)

James, William, 'The Dilemma of Determinism', in *Essays in Pragmatism*. Mayflower: London, 1957. (An interesting essay on the problem of free-will and determinism.)

Körner, S., *Kant*. Penguin Books: London, 1953. (A good critical discussion of all aspects of Kant's philosophy.)

Russell, Bertrand, *A History of Western Philosophy*. Allen & Unwin: London, 1939. (A good and very readable summary of the views of all the major European philosophers.)

Ryle, Gilbert, *The Concept of Mind*. Hutchinson: London, 1967. (A modern attempt to solve the mind–body problem.)

Warnock, G. J., *Berkeley*. Penguin Books: London, 1968. (A good critical discussion of Berkeley's views.)

CHAPTER IV

PHILOSOPHY OF RELIGION

The branch of philosophy called the **philosophy of religion** is not necessarily concerned either with justifying or disparaging any particular claims of any particular religion. Rather, the interest of this aspect of philosophy is **to examine the intellectual questions that arise in considering religious views.** These questions are usually either special problems connected with the **theory of knowledge as applied to religious knowledge, or metaphysical problems** involved in efforts to construct a satisfactory and consistent explanation of certain concepts employed by various religions.

Philosophy and Religion. The age-old concern of mankind with religious questions, many of which antedated the earliest beginnings of philosophy, has led various thinkers to inquire into the meaning of the claims made by different religions, the evidence upon which these claims are based, the standards that can be employed in evaluating their merits, and whether these claims can be made part of a general theory about the nature of the universe. Some of the philosophers who have raised these questions have been interested in showing the plausibility or reasonableness of certain religious views. Others have sought to disprove, or render doubtful, certain religious views. Some have regarded the problems involved neutrally, merely trying to ascertain whether any special kind of knowledge and concepts are involved in religious matters, and whether any special standards need be employed. Thus, for some philosophers, the philosophy of religion has involved an attempt to find a rational justification or explanation of their religions, for some it has been an attempt to justify or explain the grounds or basis of their disbelief, and for others merely an attempt to examine another area of human interest and experience.

In this section, we shall explore some of the problems of the philosophy of religion and some of the major theories that have been offered, including some views that have been used to justify or explain some of the major religious beliefs in the Judaeo-Christian tradition, and some of those which have been advanced in favour of atheism. We shall first deal with the problem of religious knowledge.

THE PROBLEM OF RELIGIOUS KNOWLEDGE

Various religions purport to possess some special and vitally important knowledge about the nature of the world and of man's role in it. But there is a wide divergence of claims among different religions and religious persons as to what this information is, and what assurance we have that it is true. If one examines the kind of information involved in religious knowledge and the kind of evidence for it, certain problems arise which indicate that religious knowledge is of a radically different sort from that which we find in other fields of human experience, especially in the various fields of scientific investigation.

The Problem of Revelation. In many religions, the sort of information that is regarded as crucial consists of reported revelations of the Word of God. If one asks, how did human beings discover this knowledge, and what guarantee do they have that it is true, one finds some remarkable differences between revealed knowledge and our ordinary knowledge. With regard to our knowledge about historical questions, scientific ones, and the like, we can give answers to these queries, which though they may be open to serious difficulties, present a basis for general agreement that does not seem to apply to our religious knowledge. No matter what theory of knowledge one holds to, one would usually agree that it is at least highly probable that water is composed of hydrogen and oxygen, and that Julius Caesar was assassinated. But the same type of agreement does not hold for religious information.

Well then, what is the difference? In our scientific and historical information, even if we cannot agree as to the ultimate basis for it, or the standards for evaluating its fundamental truth, at least there is, by and large, no serious disagreement as to what constitutes probable evidence. The appeal to experimental data, to records, to public experience, is sufficient to establish what we call 'the facts in the case'. This will not settle the issues outstanding in epistemology, but, except in special cases, will suffice to dispel any disagreement in the realms of our scientific and historical knowledge.

But, when one turns to religious matters, these methods no longer appear to be applicable. If one asks whether the Bible contains religious information, this is no longer a scientific or historical question. There are historical problems about when the various books of the Bible were written, who wrote them, and the like, but these are different sorts of problem from whether the Bible is a source of religious knowledge. The historical questions can be investigated by the standard techniques of historians, and within limits, can be given answers with a fair degree of probability. But, how can the other sort of problem be solved?

Investigating the history of Palestine two and three millennia ago may show that various statements in the Bible, reporting historical facts, such as the location and description of Solomon's palace, seem, to the best of present-day historical knowledge, to be true. But, even if every historical fact in the Old and New Testaments could be confirmed by careful examination of ancient records, archaeological findings, and so on, the question would still remain, how can we tell if the Bible contains any *religious* information?

Scientific and Religious Knowledge. Some people might suggest that this is an absurd question, since the Bible says clearly that it is not a mere record of some events in the history of ages gone by, but is also, and far more important, a statement of the Word of God. So all that one has to do to answer the question is to read the Book. But anyone can write a book and record in the text that this book contains religious information. The crucial question would be whether this claim is true. And merely by reading the book this could not be ascertained. The fact that the book contains a sentence asserting that it contains religious knowledge can be established; but the *truth-value* of the sentence, the problem at issue, cannot be.

No historical investigation can establish that any particular person had any religious information, or that any book contained it. All that historical inquiry can tell us is that certain people and certain books have made the assertion that they possessed religious knowledge. We may become reasonably assured that the historical personage, Moses, lived at a certain time, that he performed certain acts recorded in the Bible, and that he asserted that he had received certain important religious truths from God. But whether Moses was correct in his assertion is not a question that can be answered by historical investigation.

If one asks what differentiates the Bible from other ancient historical records, like the writings of Herodotus, the Greek historian, it is not a question of historical fact, but, rather that one of these documents is supposed to be a source of religious information, while the other is not. But the point of this discussion is that the difference indicates something peculiar about religious information. The standards that we apply to determine historical information and scientific information do not help us to determine if some particular book, or a certain person, possesses some religious information. What seems instead to be involved in the case of religious knowledge is **some element of belief, faith, or religious experience.**

Religious knowledge does not seem to be a type of our ordinary empirical knowledge in that we cannot examine and evaluate it in the same manner. Claims about plant life on Mars, cures for cancer, or anything else dealing with events within the world of our experience, can be discussed and examined by certain standards that we call scientific. But the merits of various reported items of religious information can only be discussed and examined in terms of certain beliefs, faith, or religious experience, even if the belief is that these reported religious truths have no religious significance at all.

To clarify this point, we might consider a hypothetical example. If some mountaineers, climbing Mount Everest, discovered a document purporting to contain the Word of God, how would we test whether the work did in fact contain religious information? An examination of the mountain climbers, the mountain, and the document, would all involve certain scientific tests and standards, and would give us some reasonably reliable information about the people in question, the place where they made their discovery, and the nature of the document. But such an examination would not decide whether the document was the Word of God, since this is not a feature or quality of the document that can be tested chemically, historically, or in any other empirical fashion.

Those who accepted this hypothetical document as a statement of some important religious information might offer as reasons for their view that there were certain extraordinary features of the work that led them to this conclusion, certain extraordinary signs, or even miracles, that led them to distinguish this document from ordinary ones. In this case, they would be asserting that above and beyond the available scientific information, there is certain special information that enables one to see, or realize, that there is a special significance to this document.

Others might claim that there are certain general theories about the nature of the universe which lead one to conclude that the views appearing in the hypothetical document contain genuine religious information. Here again, the basis for adjudging the information to be religious would not be simply observable and scientifically testable features, but rather **some metaphysical or ethical views that one has arrived at independently of the document.**

Lastly, one might state that certain beliefs, or personal experiences, convince one of the religious nature of the document. No appeal would be made to special conditions or signs outside of oneself, or to any general reasonings, which one could explain to others. Instead, the basis for accepting the document as a religious one would be one's personal conviction, belief, faith, or religious experience, that this document revealed the Word of God.

Natural and Revealed Religion. These varying responses reflect some of the major explanations that have been offered to explain the basis of, and warrant for, religious knowledge. These explanations can be divided, roughly, into the traditional distinction between **natural** and **revealed** religion. The contention of those who attempt to provide a **natural** basis for religious knowledge is that there are special events, facts, or other *reasons* that provide a foundation for religious conviction. On the other hand, the contention of revealed religion is that fundamental religious truths are known to us only by revelation, faith or personal experience. This distinction is not to suggest that there is any necessary opposition between revealed and natural religious knowledge. In fact, the claim of a great number of theologians has been that much religious insight can be gained by natural procedures —e.g., through recognizing certain signs or through reasoning—but that other religious truth can be gained only by faith or revelation. They have contended the two types of religious knowledge supplement, or complement, each other.

Since those claims regarding natural religious knowledge often involve the presentation of evidence, and argument about the nature and existence of a Divine Being, much philosophy of religion has dealt with an examination and evaluation of the merits of this sort of religious knowledge, and of the kind of support advanced in its favour. Therefore, we shall examine these claims, especially those regarding the natural evidence offered for the existence of God.

Natural Religion: The Argument from Design. Throughout the ages, those who believed that it is possible to discover religious knowledge by natural procedures have attempted to develop various proofs of the existence of God to show that the most fundamental religious knowledge—that there is a Divine Being—can be demonstrated by acceptable arguments. Among these arguments is one called the **argument**

from design, which is probably familiar to almost everybody in one form or another. This argument purports **to establish the existence of God from an examination of and induction from information that we have gained about the universe.** In fact, since the beginnings of modern science, various versions of the argument from design have been presented which **attempt to prove the existence of God from the latest findings in the physical and biological sciences.**

Hume's Argument. One of the classical statements of the argument from design appears in David Hume's *Dialogues on Natural Religion.* One of the characters, Cleanthes, states it as follows:

> Look around the world, contemplate the whole and every part of it: you will find it to be nothing but one great machine, subdivided into an infinite number of lesser machines, which again admit of subdivisions to a degree beyond what human senses and faculties can trace and explain. All these various machines, and even their most minute parts, are adjusted to each other with an accuracy which ravishes into admiration all men who have ever contemplated them. The curious adapting of means to ends, throughout all nature, resembles exactly, though it much exceeds, the productions of human contrivance—of human design, thought, wisdom and intelligence. Since therefore the effects resemble each other, we are led to infer, by all the rules of analogy, that the causes also resemble, and that the Author of nature is somewhat similar to the mind of man, though possessed of much larger faculties, proportioned to the grandeur of the work which he has executed. By this argument *a posteriori,* and by this argument alone, do we prove at once the existence of a Deity and his similarity to human mind and intelligence.

The central claim of the argument from design is that our studies of nature reveal an orderliness and a pattern in the features of the physical, chemical and biological aspects of the world. The more that nature is studied, the more impressed one becomes with both the intricate relationships within its parts, and with the general plan of the universe. The order and design of nature resembles greatly the order and design of human artefacts, such as houses and watches, in which each part is perfectly adjusted to each other in order to achieve some purpose or end of the whole object. Since the effects of human planning are so much like the effects that we discover in the natural world, the argument runs, we can therefore infer, or induce, that the causes which produce the effects in each case are alike. In the case of human achievements, the cause is thought, wisdom and intelligence. Therefore, there must be some kind of intelligent deity who is the author or cause of the effects in the universe. Since the amount of design or order in the natural world and its complexity far exceeds human ingenuity, the cause of this must also be of greater wisdom.

Even in ancient times, with the extremely limited information then available about the many kinds of regularities and patterns in the natural world, many were struck with the force of the argument from design. But after the beginnings of the scientific revolution in the sixteenth and seventeenth centuries, one finds more and more elaborate appeals to scientific findings as the basis for concluding that there must be some divine being or power who organizes and directs the complex order of nature. In our own day, there have been various attempts to show that the amazing unfolding of the secrets of nature by contemporary scientists has strengthened the evidence that there is some sort of intelligent guidance to the world scheme. Recently a great French biologist, Le Comte de Nouy, published a work entitled, *Human Destiny*, in which he argued that the intricate relationships found in biochemistry relating to the development of living organisms, and the general evolutionary history of plants and animals, suggest a plan which could not have occurred by accident, but must instead have had some overall direction and director to account for its orderliness.

In spite of the apparent force of the argument from design in terms of our ever-growing knowledge about the natural world, various thinkers have found many difficulties involved in this type of reasoning, which, if examined closely, may well vitiate entirely the seeming strength of the argument as a proof of the existence of God. Perhaps the best presentation of these difficulties occurs in a work already cited, Hume's *Dialogues Concerning Natural Religion*.

Hume's Criticisms of the Argument from Design. All his life, David Hume was concerned with the merits of various arguments which purported to establish the existence of a Divine Being. In his early notebooks and letters, he continually reflected about the problem, pointing out flaws or fallacies involved in the arguments of various religious writers. In various works, Hume made some incisive criticism of the reasoning employed by some of the religious philosophers. Possibly because of its currency in his day, one of his major undertakings was a thoroughgoing critique of the argument from design. He worked on this, off and on, for about twenty-five years, perfecting his famous *Dialogues Concerning Natural Religion*. Some of his friends urged him to abandon this work, to destroy what he had written, because it was too dangerous and irreligious. For long periods of time he set it aside. Then, when he knew that he was dying, he completed the work and made plans to ensure its publication after his death. He tried to induce his good friend, the economist Adam Smith, to guarantee to have it printed after he died, but Smith was unwilling, either because he feared the consequences to himself, or he did not see what would be gained by making public such seditious material. Similarly, Hume's printer, also an old friend, refused to agree to publish the book. Finally a nephew of the Scottish philosopher, who apparently had nothing to lose, published the work anonymously, three years after Hume's death. The publication of the *Dialogues* in 1779 brought to light one of the most important documents in the philosophy of religion, one that has been studied and argued about ever since.

In the *Dialogues*, the argument from design is examined and dissected from almost every possible angle. Hume began his attack by criticizing the analogy between human productions and nature. The works of man and those of nature do not resemble each other sufficiently so that we can have any strong reason to suspect that they have similar causes. As the sceptic in the *Dialogues*, Philo, puts it:

If we see a house, Cleanthes, we conclude, with the greatest certainty, that it had an architect or builder because this is precisely that species of effect which we have experienced to proceed from that species of cause. But surely you will not affirm that the universe bears such a resemblance to a house that we can with the same certainty infer a similar cause, or that the analogy is here entire and perfect. The dissimilitude is so striking that the utmost you can here pretend to is a guess, a conjecture, a presumption concerning a similar cause.

Critique of the Analogy. We have experienced the relationship between human planning or design and the achievements which result from this. In the case of nature, we have no experience of the cause, but only of the effect. The natural effects do not so resemble the man-made ones that we can be certain that similar kinds of causal factors must be operative in both. For all we know there may well be numerous causes of order and design other than thought.

For aught we can know *a priori*, matter may contain the source or spring of order originally within itself, as well as mind does; and there is no more difficulty in conceiving that the several elements, from an internal unknown cause, may fall into the most exquisite arrangement, than to conceive that their ideas, in the great universal mind, from a like internal unknown cause, fall into that arrangement.

In fact, it is the height of human vanity to rush headlong to the conclusion that since in the tiny part of the cosmos occupied by man the same factors that occur to bring about planned human achievements appear similar to the natural effects around us, that therefore these same factors are the dominating principles of the governance of the entire universe about much of which we have no information at all.

Hume concluded this first general criticism of the kind of analogical reasoning involved in the argument from design by observing through his sceptical spokesman:

And will any man tell me with a serious countenance that an orderly universe must arise from some thought and art like the human because we have experience of it? To ascertain this reasoning it were requisite that we had experience of the origin of worlds; and it is not sufficient, surely, that we have seen ships and cities arise from human art and contrivance. . . .

. . . Can you pretend to show any such similarity between the fabric of a house and the generation of a universe? Have you ever seen nature in any such situation as resembles the first arrangement of the elements? Have worlds ever been formed under your eye, and have you had the leisure to observe the whole progress of the phenomenon, from the first appearance of order to its final consummation? If you have, then cite your experience and deliver your theory.

Up to this point, Hume's criticism of the argument from design has been that **its fundamental contention that there is a great resemblance between the effects of human planning and natural effects, and that** therefore the universal causal agency must be like the cause of human artefacts, namely thought, is not convincing. We have learned from experience that human effects result from design, but we have no such experience with natural effects and how they happen to arise. The defender of the argument in the *Dialogues*, Cleanthes, retorts 'that it is by no means necessary that theists should prove the similarity of the works of *nature* to those of *art* because this similarity is self-evident and undeniable'. For the sake of the argument, Hume temporarily accepted this claim, in order to show that even if there were a strong resemblance between human and natural works there would still be basic defects or disabilities in the argument to establish the existence of a Divine Being.

Cause and Effect. The basic principle employed by those who believe the argument from design is that **like effects prove like causes.** The more like the effects are, the more like are causes. But even if we assume that there really is a close similarity between natural and human effects, then Hume showed that we would still have no grounds for coming to the traditional religious or theological conclusions about the nature of God.

First, by this method of reasoning you renounce all claim to infinity in any of the attributes of the Deity. For, as the cause ought only to be proportioned to the effect, and the effect, so far as it falls under our cognizance, is not infinite, what pretensions have we, upon your suppositions, to ascribe that attribute to the Divine Being?

Not only would the argument from design, if valid, prevent us from telling if God is infinite, it would also prevent us from concluding that He is perfect.

Secondly, you have no reason, on your theory, for ascribing perfection to the Deity, even in His finite capacity, or for supposing Him free from every error, mistake, or incoherence, in His undertakings. . . . At least, you must acknowledge that it is impossible for us to tell, from our limited views, whether this system contains any great faults or deserves any considerable praise if compared to other possible and even real systems. Could a peasant, if the *Aeneid* were read to him, pronounce that poem to be absolutely faultless, or even assign to it its proper rank among the productions of human wit, he who had never seen any other production?

But were this world ever so perfect a production, it must still remain uncertain whether all the excellences of the work can justly be ascribed to the workman. If we survey a ship, what an exalted idea we must form of the ingenuity of the carpenter who framed so complicated, useful, and beautiful a machine? And what surprise must we feel when we find him a stupid mechanic who imitated others, and copied an art which, through a long succession of ages, after multiplied trials, mistakes, corrections, deliberations, and controversies, had been gradually improving? Many worlds might have been botched and bungled, throughout an eternity, ere this system was struck out; much labour lost, many fruitless trials made, and a slow but continued improvement carried on during infinite ages in the art of world-making. In such subjects, who can determine where the truth, nay, who can conjecture where the probability lies, amidst a great number of hypotheses which may be proposed, and a still greater which may be imagined?

Anthropomorphism. If one takes seriously the similarity between human and natural effects, and the principle that like effects have like causes, then the result will be to conclude that the author or authors (since there is no reason for limiting the cause of nature to one agent on the basis of this argument) of nature are much like human beings. The more alike one insists that the effects are, the more human or **anthropomorphic** one will have to paint the portrait of the deity, until one is driven to a picture of God totally at variance with all religious traditions. On the other hand, if one denies that the causes—that is, God and man—are really alike, then one has no basis for drawing any conclusion about the nature of a Divine Being by means of the argument from design.

At best, Hume insisted, the evidence about the order and design in nature allows one

> to assert or conjecture that the universe sometime arose from something like design; but beyond that position he cannot ascertain one single circumstance, and is left afterwards to fix every point of his theology by the utmost licence of fancy and hypothesis. This world, for aught he knows, is very faulty and imperfect, compared to a superior standard, and was only the first rude essay of some infant deity who afterwards abandoned it, ashamed of his lame performance; it is the work only of some dependent, inferior deity, and is the object of derision to his superiors; it is the production of old age and dotage in some superannuated deity, and ever since his death has run on at adventures, from the first impulse and active force which it received from him.

One can go on endlessly inventing possible explanations in keeping with the basic claim of the argument from design, that there is a similarity between the order in nature and the order in human productions. Any explanation, hypothesis, imaginative theory which accounts for the occurrence of the degree of order that we find in nature is equally satisfying, if one accepts the argument from design as a valid argument for establishing that some sort of designer or designers of the universe exist.

Other possible analogies. As if he had not gone far enough in showing that the basic analogy is not really a sound one, and that if it were, one would either be led to conclude that God was just like a human being, or that an unlimited number of hypotheses were equally plausible, Hume offered another and perhaps more devastating assault on the argument from design. Starting with the same evidence about the order in nature—he reasoned—**totally different kinds of analogy can be equally well established which will yield totally different kinds of**

conclusion. Not only do some aspects of the natural world resemble the effects of human activities, but some also resemble the effects of the biological activities of animals and plants. One finds many similarities between the development of living organisms and natural events. The organic and functional relationships in the biological world can also be found in other aspects of nature.

One who accepts the argument from design asserts that the world

resembles the work of human contrivance; therefore its cause must also resemble that of the other. Here we may remark that the operation of one very small part of nature, to wit, man, upon another very small part, to wit, that inanimate matter lying within his reach, is the rule by which Cleanthes judges the origin of the whole; and he measures objects, so widely disproportioned, by the same individual standard. But to waive all objections drawn from this topic, I affirm that there are other parts of the universe (besides the machines of human invention) which bear still a great resemblance to the fabric of the world, and which, therefore, afford a better conjecture concerning the universal origin of this system. These parts are animals and vegetables. The world plainly resembles more an animal or a vegetable than it does a watch or a knitting-loom. Its cause, therefore, it is more probable, resembles the cause of the former. The cause, therefore, of the world we may infer to be something similar or analogous to generation or vegetation.

Like the vegetable world, or the animal world, the entire natural world may possess some inner principles of development and of order. There are sufficient similarities among biological entities to provide a different theory of the cause of natural order than the claim that there must be an intelligent designer of nature. Instead, there might merely be some sort of **inner self-regulation and growth,** as one finds in carrot seeds, that orders the direction of their development.

If one says that there is no evidence to support such an explanation Hume was perfectly willing to agree, *but* he also maintained that, by the same token, there is no evidence for the argument from design. All that we know is the evidence of patterns or regular orders in nature. What we see around us resembles to some extent the effects of human productions, but it also resembles still more the effects of biological organization. The crucial point is that

we have no data to establish any system of cosmogony [a theory about the origins of the universe]. Our experience, so imperfect in itself and so limited both in extent and duration, can afford us no probable conjecture concerning the whole of things. But if we must needs fix on some hypothesis, by what rule, pray, ought we to determine our choice? Is there any other rule than the greater similarity of the objects compared? And does not a plant or an animal, which springs from vegetation or generation, bear a stronger resemblance to the world than does any artificial machine, which arises from reason and design?

Materialist Hypotheses. In fact, if the only information that we have to judge by is the character of the events that we see, one could also offer a completely materialistic and mechanistic interpretation of nature. One could develop a hypothesis like that of the ancient Greek philosopher, EPICURUS, to the effect that the cause of natural events is nothing but the blind motions of solid, material atoms, moving through space, and occasionally colliding, without plan or reason. The small portion of the universe that we are able to observe has obvious features of order or organization. But, from what we can tell about, we have no more basis for assuming that the cause of this order is like the cause of the order in a ship or a watch, or in an ant, or an onion, or *even* the order due to pure chance. If one threw several thousand small pieces of iron into the air, in falling they would exhibit some sort of pattern or design, which we would not say was due to any ordering principle, but rather to accident or chance. Hume suggested that we cannot be certain that the so-called organized universe is not also the result of some blind, cosmic accident. We cannot even be sure that there is an agency that is responsible for the order in the world; hence, we certainly cannot conclude that the agency is an intelligent one.

Critique of Religious Traditionalism. As a final feature of his critique of the argument from design, Hume pointed out that the analogical reasoning employed in the argument **does not provide a basis for any conclusion about the moral attributes of the designer of nature,** even if one concludes that there is such a designer. The conception of a moral, just, good, deity does not follow from the comparison of natural and human effects. If the designer is supposed to be like the human designer, then we would have no reason to suppose that there is any special moral quality belonging to the author of nature. When one examines the product—i.e., nature—and observes all its unpleasant features, e.g., hurricanes, earthquakes, the wars of one part of nature upon another, can we conclude that the planning was that of a just and good intelligence?

After accumulating evidence of the unpleasant features of nature, Hume made his criticism in the form of an analogy to show that if one merely contemplated the character of the object presented to us, one would be hard-pressed to believe that it was designed by either a very wise or a very good planner.

Did I show you a house or palace where there was not one apartment convenient or agreeable, where the windows, doors, fires, passages, stairs, and the whole economy of the building were the source of noise, confusion, fatigue, darkness, and the extremes of heat and cold, you would certainly blame the contrivance, without any further examination. The architect would in vain display his subtilty, and prove to you that, if this door or that window were altered, greater ills would ensue. What he says may be strictly true; the alteration of one particular, while the other parts of the building remain, may only augment the inconveniences. But still you would assert in general that, if the architect had had skill and good intentions, he might have formed such a plan of the whole, and might have adjusted the parts in such a manner as would have remedied all or most of these inconveniences. His ignorance, or even your own ignorance of such a plan, will never convince you of the impossibility of it. If you find any inconveniences and deformities in the building, you will always, without entering into any detail, condemn the architect.

When this point is applied to a consideration of the world we know, the question can be asked:

Is the world, considered in general and as it appears to us in this life, different from what a man or such a limited being would, *beforehand*, expect from a very powerful, wise, and benevolent Deity? It must be strange prejudice to assert the contrary. And from thence I conclude that, however consistent the world may be, allowing certain suppositions and conjectures with the idea of such a Deity, it can never afford us an inference concerning his existence.

Thus, given the unfortunate, unpleasant and undesirable events that one witnesses, one is unable to infer that the design of the cosmos is benevolent, just, or good. This is not to deny that if we knew the nature of the cause of the world's order we might be able to explain satisfactorily these apparent ills. But if all our knowledge of this cause is supposed to result from an induction or inference from our observations, then, Hume insisted, we have no basis for judging that there is any moral guidance to the course of nature. In fact, Hume claimed, some other hypotheses are more plausible, such as that the directing force or agency in the world has no moral or immoral character, or possibly that there are two radically different directing forces in the universe, one good, and the other bad. (This latter theory is often called the **Manichaean** view.)

Conclusions. Hume demonstrated that the argument from design is based on an unsound analogy, that, if it were sound, it would lead to the conclusion that the deity is much like a human being, that many other theories are at least as likely, if based solely on experience, and that the evidence is insufficient to allow us to infer that the directing force or agency is infinite, perfect, or even moral. Hume finally concluded his criticisms by admitting that the argument from design, if not a valid argument, was still to some extent convincing. The order in nature, in spite of all that has been said, suggests, if it does not prove, **'That the cause or causes of order in the universe probably bear some remote analogy to human intelligence'.** Beyond this, we have no way to extend the argument in order to establish anything about the characteristics of this cause or these causes, or to develop any hypotheses about how they are related to us and our problems. As Hume had indicated earlier, beyond this 'one simple, though somewhat ambiguous, at least undefined, proposition', one can construct endless possible theories of nature. Unfortunately, if we are restricted only to what we can observe, we have no standards for evaluating or judging which of the many hypothetical possibilities may be the more probable.

152 *Philosophy Made Simple*

Thus, in his masterful analysis of the argument from design, Hume showed that this attempt to establish the existence and nature of a divine being was most inconclusive, and the more plausible or reasonable the argument might be made, the less it would tend to prove that there is any kind of divine agency or guidance similar to that taught by the various major religious traditions. Moreover, if our religious knowledge is to be derived from scientific knowledge, we would be able to find little or nothing that would lead us to conclude that there is some deity who governs the universe, and who is concerned in governing in our interest or in terms of certain ends in which we are, or may be, involved.

If Hume's analysis of the argument from design is sound, as many thinkers since have found it to be, then those who attempt to discover some kind of natural evidence or reasoning upon which to base religious knowledge will have to turn elsewhere. Other philosophers, therefore, have produced two different types of argument to establish the existence of a divine being, the **cosmological,** or **causal argument,** and the **ontological argument.**

The Cosmological (or Causal) Argument. This argument, like the argument from design, begins from the facts of our experience, from what we observe. We see things move, change, and so on. In order for these events to occur, **there must be a cause either in the sense of a prior event, or a reason for the occurrence of the event.** As we trace back from effects to their causes, we can either continue indefinitely, or there is some ultimate cause that requires no further causal explanation. **This ultimate cause is what is meant by God.** In order to rule out the alternative of an indefinite or unlimited succession of causes, it is argued that if it were possible to trace back the causal sequence indefinitely, then there would be no beginning to the series. If there were no actual beginning, then there could be no succession, since each cause must follow after its predecessor. If there is no first element to the causal sequence, then there could be no second, third, and so on. Therefore, the conclusion is that **there must be a first cause** of events, and this first cause is what is called God. Thus, from the experience we have of caused events we can prove the existence of a Supreme Being, or a First Cause.

Aristotle and St. Thomas Aquinas. This argument, often called the cosmological argument for the existence of God, has been employed for a long time by philosophers and theologians. In one form or another it is in the proofs offered by Aristotle, by St. Thomas Aquinas, and many others. Sometimes it is employed to establish that there must have been a first cause in the history of the universe, that is, a first event, from which all the others have followed. Others have used it to claim that there must be an ultimate explanation for the events in the universe, whether the cosmos had a beginning or has been eternal. Their contention has been that to account for the occurrences in the world, an explanation has to be made, and an explanation for that, and so on. Unless there is some ultimate explanation, they assert, there can be no other explanation, and nothing can be accounted for.

Although this argument has been subjected to severe criticism it is still accepted as valid and decisive by many philosophers of religion. In the form in which it occurs in the *Summa Theologica* of St. Thomas Aquinas, the cosmological argument is regarded as conclusive evidence for establishing the existence of a Supreme Being by the Roman Catholic Church. One finds, however, that with non-Catholic thinkers the argument has lost ground since the criticism of it by David Hume and Immanuel Kant.

Some Criticisms of the Cosmological Argument. If one agrees with the arguments Hume presented regarding the theory of knowledge (see discussion on pages 208–20) then the main premise and the conclusion of the cosmological argument lose their force. Hume maintained that if his claims as to what we cannot know are legitimate, then we are unable to establish that any particular being, whether it be God, or anything else, must, of necessity, exist.

I shall begin with observing that there is an evident absurdity in pretending to demonstrate a matter of fact, or to prove it by any arguments *a priori*. Nothing is demonstrable unless the contrary implies a contradiction. Nothing that is distinctly conceivable implies a contradiction. Whatever we conceive as existent, we can also conceive as non-existent. There is no being, therefore, whose non-existence implies a contradiction. Consequently there is no being whose existence is demonstrable.

Thus, according to Hume, no valid argument can establish the existence of a Supreme Being, or of anything else. Since we can always conceive what it would be like for any describable object to exist, to be part of the temporal and spatial world, or not to exist, then no demonstration that a specific entity must exist can be decisive. The denial of the conclusion of the demonstration cannot be disproven, and, hence, nothing has actually been established by any reasoning that purports to establish that some particular being must exist.

Critique of Causality. Further, Hume argued that we cannot prove or establish the fundamental premise of the cosmological argument, that every event must have a cause. If what is meant by a cause is something that produces an event, or something that explains or accounts for an event, then we cannot even tell whether it is the case that events have been produced by something, or can be accounted for. We can only determine what events occur in regular sequences with other events in our experience. But, on Hume's analysis, is there any reason to conclude that the sequence of constantly conjoined events must have a first term, or that there must be some ultimate explanation of the entire sequence? We can trace back the succession of events indefinitely, but why must we conclude that it has to have had a beginning?

In such a chain, too, or succession of objects, each part is caused by that which preceded it, and causes that which succeeds it. Where then is the difficulty? But the *whole*, you say, wants a cause. I answer that the uniting of these parts into a whole, like the uniting of several distinct countries into one kingdom, or several distinct members into one body, is performed merely by an arbitrary act of the mind, and has no influence on the nature of things.

Thus, **it is Hume's contention that the observable succession of events that we consider causes and effects, requires no ultimate beginning, since it can be conceived of as continuing indefinitely, forward or backward.** The entire causal chain requires no explanation; it can be regarded as merely an arbitrary fact of our experience, or an arbitrary act of the mind as it structures that experience, that we see events occurring in some orderly fashion, instead of occurring completely helter-skelter.

Finally, Hume argued, even if the cosmological argument were valid, it would still not establish what its supporters claim. If there had to be some first cause, **why could this not be the material, physical world rather than God?** If one answered, there has to be some explanation for where the world comes from, or why it has the properties it has, then Hume would retort that exactly the same is true of God. If one is willing to accept as a final explanation of the universe that God is its first cause, then an explanation that **the material world is its own cause** should be just as satisfactory.

Kant's Critique of the Cosmological Argument. The great German philosopher, IMMANUEL KANT, following after Hume's analysis of the problem of knowledge and applying Hume's conclusions to the problem of the existence of a Supreme Being, made a series of criticisms of the arguments for the existence of God in his *Critique of Pure Reason.* With regard to the cosmological argument, Kant contended that it contains invalid assumptions which prove nothing.

The first of these assumptions, Kant wrote, was that from contingent events we can infer that there must be a necessary cause of their existence. **The principle of causality, that every event must have a cause, applies, as far as we can tell, only to the world of sense experience.** But, in the cosmological argument, this principle about empirical knowledge is used to carry us beyond the world of sense experience to something that is supposed to transcend it. This extension, Kant insisted, is unjustified and illegitimate. We have no basis for assuming that the principles we employ in the analysis of our experience can be made to apply to anything beyond experience.

The Attack on 'First Cause'. Further, Kant pointed out, we have no justification for inferring that there must be a first cause. **The principles which we follow with regard to the use of reason do not support the argument in question, since we have no rational means for arriving at the end of our quest for causes and explanations, nor have we any way of determining when the series of causes and explanations have been completed.** Therefore, we can never be justified in claiming that we have found the first cause.

Basically, what Kant considered to be at fault in the cosmological argument for the existence of a Supreme Being is that it attempts to **reason beyond all possible experience, as well as beyond the limits for which we have any guarantee that our rational faculties are reliable.** By illegitimately extending principles—whose only known application and warrant is the realm of actual experience—to questions that transcend all possible experience, one creates these proofs and comes to conclusions about the necessary existence of some of our concepts. But once one has left the limits of the application of reason, all sorts of arguments can be constructed and things proved, and all sorts of paradoxes and dilemmas created. In this realm, we have no standards as to what is valid argumentation, and hence no way of determining when we have successfully established anything at all. All that we can do is recognize that all arguments that transcend possible experience, whether they be about God, or anything else, are entirely speculative, and fruitless, and prove nothing of which we can be certain.

The criticisms directed against the cosmological argument by Hume and Kant derive from their theories of knowledge. To the extent that the basic views of most modern philosophers are built upon the claims of either of these thinkers, the cosmological argument has found slight support in recent years. A great many philosophers assert that the argument is not conclusive and fails to establish the existence of a Supreme Being.

The Ontological Argument. Another argument that has been employed to prove the existence of God is the **ontological** argument. This proof tries to establish that **solely from the definition of a Supreme Being, it follows that He must necessarily exist.** No knowledge about the world is required in order to develop this argument, and hence, it is considered **as a purely** *a priori* demonstration. It has been a favourite of many of the great metaphysicians, such as St. Anselm, Descartes and Spinoza. Apparently they have preferred it above all other arguments for the existence of God for what to most non-metaphysically inclined persons may appear to be its most obvious defect, namely, that the argument bears no relation to our experience, but only to a concept or idea of a Supreme Being.

St. Anselm. The classical form of the ontological argument appears in the writings of the famous medieval thinker, ST. ANSELM. He contended that anyone who understood what was meant by the terms 'God' or 'Supreme Being', would see that such an entity must exist. God is that Being than which none greater can be conceived. Since I can comprehend this definition, I can conceive of God. Moreover, I can conceive of God as existing not only as a concept in my own mind, but also as **existing in reality,** that is, **independently of my ideas.** Since it is greater to exist both as an idea and as a real thing, than merely to exist as an idea, **God must exist both in reality and as an idea.** By definition God is that than which none greater can be conceived. Hence, God must exist in reality, or else something greater than God can be conceived (that is, an entity possessing all of God's properties, *plus* real existence); this, by the very definition of God or the Supreme Being, is impossible.

Spinoza. A briefer though probably less convincing presentation of the ontological argument appears in the *Ethics* of BARUCH SPINOZA, although it is worth remembering that the meaning Spinoza gives to 'God' is very different from its customary meaning, as we have seen (page 104). The eleventh proposition of Book I reads: **'God, or substance, consisting of infinite attributes, of which each expresses eternal**

and infinite essentiality, necessarily exists.' The evidence offered for this proposition is that 'If this be denied, conceive, if possible, that God does not exist: then His essence does not involve existence. But this is absurd (that is, it is contrary to the definition of God). Therefore God necessarily exists.'

Descartes. A more discursive version of the argument appears in Descartes' *Meditations*. There he reasoned:

But now, if from the simple fact that I can draw from my thought the idea of anything it follows that all that I recognize clearly and distinctly to pertain to this thing pertains to it in reality, can I not draw from this an argument and a demonstration of the existence of God? It is certain that I do not find in me the less the idea of him, that is, of a being supremely perfect, than that of any figure or of any number whatever; and I do not know less clearly and distinctly that an actual and eternal existence belongs to his nature than I know that all that I can demonstrate of any figure or of any number belongs truly to the nature of that figure or that number: and accordingly, although all that I have concluded in the preceding meditations may not turn out to be true, the existence of God ought to pass in my mind as being at least as certain as I have up to this time regarded the truths of mathematics to be, which have to do only with numbers and figures: although, indeed, that might not seem at first to be perfectly evident, but might appear to have some appearance of sophistry. For being accustomed in all other things to make a distinction between existence and essence, I easily persuade myself that existence may perhaps be separated from the essence of God, and thus God might be conceived as not existent actually. But nevertheless, when I think more attentively, I find that existence can no more be separated from the essence of God than the essence of a rectilinear triangle can be separated from the equality of its three angles to two right angles, or, indeed, if you please, from the idea of a mountain the idea of a valley; so that there would be no less contradiction in conceiving of a God, that is, of a being supremely perfect, to whom existence was wanting, that is to say, to whom there was wanting any perfection, than in conceiving of a mountain which had no valley.

Essence and Existence. In each of these presentations, the same basic theme occurs. From an examination of our concept of God as a perfect being, or that being than which none greater can be conceived, we can see that one of the elements of this perfection, one of the ingredients of the very definition of God, must be His existence. Hence, unlike any other concept, whose definition does not entail that it must exist, or does not include existence as one of its properties, the concept of God includes in its very nature that **God is an existent being.** Thus, merely from the idea of God, we can tell that He must necessarily exist, in the same way that from the definition of a triangle, we can tell that the sum of its interior angles equals 180°.

Before considering some of the many criticisms that have been levelled against this metaphysical argument for the existence of God, it should be pointed out that some philosophers who employed the argument did not do so as a means to establishing a fact (namely, that there is a God) but rather to explain **the nature of Divine Being.** Descartes, for instance, did not offer the ontological argument as a disproof of atheism, but introduced it only after he believed he had already established the existence of God by other means, by an argument of a causal type. Then, if one already accepted the fact that God existed, the value of the ontological argument was that it made clear what sort of a Being God is, as distinguished from all others. God, alone, of all the objects we know of, is such that the concept or idea of Him includes the idea of necessary existence, whereas no other thing that we can conceive of includes within itself, or within the definition of it, its necessary existence. **This showed, for metaphysicians like Descartes and Spinoza, that God alone is the cause of Himself, is a self-existent Being.**

Criticisms of the Ontological Argument. Ever since the original presentation of the ontological argument by St. Anselm in the Middle Ages, philosophers have attempted to show that there was something peculiarly wrong with this form of reasoning. The earliest critique was sent to Anselm by a contemporary of his, GAUNILON, a monk of Marmoutier, who wrote in defence of the 'fool', whom Anselm had claimed could say, but could not believe, that God did not exist, since as soon as he understood what the concept of God was, he would see that it followed from his definition that He existed. In order to demonstrate what was wrong with the ontological argument, Gaunilon pointed out that if this sort of reasoning were legitimate, one could also show that all kinds of unreal or imaginary objects must also exist. For example, if one could imagine that there is a perfect island somewhere beyond the point where any explorer could possibly go, it follows that if this island is perfect, or is that island than which none greater can be conceived, then according to Anselm's argument, the island must exist. If it did not, then it would not be perfect, or be that island than which none greater could be conceived. But since by definition it is perfect, and no greater island can be imagined, then from that concept alone, we can be sure that it must actually exist. By indicating that one could develop all sorts of ontological arguments about all sorts of ideas, Gaunilon sought to show that the argument contained elements which are absurd and contradictory. (Anselm, in his own defence, claimed that the ontological argument applied only to God, since no other concept could be that of a perfect object.)

St. Thomas. Another kind of criticism was made by St. Thomas Aquinas, who claimed that the error of the ontological argument was that it assumed we could know the nature of God, that He is a perfect being, before knowing whether He existed. Actually, **His Nature can be learned only after one knows His existence, and not vice versa.** In fact, the ultimate knowledge of God, the final understanding we can come to, according to St. Thomas, is the definition of God as He is conceived in the ontological argument. Hence, **first we must establish His existence** by other means, then study His properties, and, at the end of this investigation, we may know enough to define God, that is, to be able then to employ St. Anselm's argument. Until then, according to St. Thomas, the ontological argument is only an uninteresting hypothetical observation that if God is a perfect (that is, a necessarily existent) Being, then God necessarily exists.

Kant. Perhaps the best known criticism of the ontological argument is that of Immanuel Kant in which he undertook to demonstrate why **existence is not the kind of property that can be part of the definition of any concept.** The idea or conception that we have of anything involves a series of properties or predicates (e.g., that it is square, green, heavy). But can existence be such a predicate? If we conceive of something, and then conceive of it as existing, is our idea of the thing any different? In his famous illustration, Kant pointed out that the idea of £100 (Kant did not, of course, refer to British currency) and a real £100 contain the same monetary elements. The idea that I have in my mind is something that can be broken down into one hundred one pound notes, into coins, etc. Its economic value is the same, whether I am merely thinking of it, or whether I have the money in my pocket. One does not change the concept involved whether one merely thinks of it, or thinks of it as existing. As applied to the argument for the existence of God, **the force of the concept or idea of God or a Perfect Being is not increased by thinking of it as existing, or merely thinking about it.** Hence, no bridge can be built from the idea of a Perfect Being to the actual existence of such a Being. We can either prove something trivial, or nothing at all, by means of the ontological argument. Either it is shown that we can define the term 'God' in such a way, that the proposition 'God necessarily exists' can be derived from the definition (which only shows an interesting, but metaphysically unexciting fact about this definition, but nothing about what objects may or may not exist in the universe) or nothing is shown, since the idea of a Being than which none greater can be conceived is the same whether we are thinking of this object as something in our minds, or whether we are thinking of it as a real independent object.

Conclusion. Although many thinkers believe that the existence of God can be established by means of rational or natural evidence, other philosophers maintain that no satisfactory rational evidence can be adduced to prove God's existence. Some of the latter believe that no satisfactory proof is possible because the object in question does not happen to exist. Others have concluded that the difficulties involved in all the proofs are due to the nature of the subject, which is, perhaps, beyond our rational capacities. These thinkers have claimed that the problems involved in finding rational or natural evidence establishing the existence of God may indicate that one must seek another type of evidence entirely, and abandon the quest by means of reason.

Atheism. If there are no valid proofs for the existence of God, then three completely different conclusions seem possible. **The first of these is simply the outright denial that there is any Divine Being.** This atheistical conclusion does not, of course, follow as a logical consequence from the unsatisfactory nature of the proofs. The fact that adequate rational evidence cannot be found to establish that something exists, neither shows that it does exist nor that it does not exist. In fact, most of the criticisms that have been levelled against arguments purporting to prove the existence of God are equally cogent when levelled at the use of similar arguments to prove the non-existence of God. Therefore, the atheist attempts to claim too much for the criticisms that have been levelled against arguments for the existence of God, if he claims that they prove that God does not exist.

Agnosticism. A conclusion that may be more in keeping with the evidence is that of the **agnostic who contends that there is not sufficient rational evidence to establish either the existence or the non-existence of a Supreme Being.** Therefore, he declares that he simply does not know (which is the literal meaning of 'agnostic') and that he will withhold opinion until such time as there may be more decisive evidence to support one side or the other.

Fideism. Besides these irreligious or non-religious conclusions, there is also a religious conclusion that has recognized the inadequacy of the proofs for the existence of God. This is called **fideism, a view that our religious knowledge is not, and ought not be, based upon rational or natural information, but solely on faith.** The general contention of the fideists has usually been that **religious knowledge is beyond the limits of man's rational faculties and understanding.** Hence, what human beings must do in order to obtain religious knowledge is first to recognize the hopelessness of accomplishing this by rational means, and then seek knowledge of God by **faith alone.**

Fideism represents a combination of a complete scepticism about the possibility of human knowledge, at least in the area of religious knowledge, and an appeal to knowledge through faith, unsupported by rational evidence. In fact, the fideists have portrayed the attempts by human beings to comprehend God by their reason and their sense information as an impious and dangerous example of human vanity, trying to measure the divine world by the puny standards of man's imagination, understanding, and experience. Heresies have resulted, the fideists charge, from this human presumption and rashness, man's insistence on making his mental conceptions of the universe the measure of all truth. In order to avoid this, one should recognize, as Hume said (possibly with tongue in cheek, since he was more likely an agnostic than a fideist) that 'to be a philosophical sceptic is, in a man of letters, the first and most essential step towards being a sound, believing Christian.'

In nearly all leading religious traditions in the western world, there has been fideistic theorizing, usually by religious or mystical thinkers, who have regarded the attempt to comprehend religious knowledge by means of reason as a most dangerous trend. On the other hand, some of those who have made out the best case for the fideistic viewpoint have apparently been non-believers, who felt that this was the easiest or safest way to state their doubts. This rejection of rational evidence for religious knowledge appears in such religious thinkers as Pascal and Kierkegaard and such irreligious thinkers as Hume and Voltaire. In both the religious and the irreligious philosophers who have asserted the irrationality of religious belief very similar arguments occur.

What this appears to indicate is that the nature of fideism is such that it is based upon a sceptical theory of knowledge that leads either to a religious or to an agnostic conclusion, both of which are compatible with the philosophical arguments employed. If one is convinced that we have no rational evidence, and can have no rational evidence, regarding either the existence or nature of God, then what follows? The fideists claim that *because* of the lack of evidence, one ought to believe by faith alone. But, one could just as well arrive at the conclusion that because of the lack of evidence, one ought to suspend judgment, and reach no conclusion at all. The arguments indicate neither that the fideistic nor the agnostic conclusion is the correct one. The argument would be compatible with either one or the other.

Pascal. Perhaps this point will be clarified by a passage from the great seventeenth century French scientist and religious thinker, BLAISE PASCAL. After gaining fame as a scientific prodigy, Pascal suddenly withdrew from the world of affairs, retiring to the stronghold of an extremely fanatical religious group, the Jansenists, at the convent of Port-Royal. In an unfinished work, *Les Pensées*, he set down the reasoning that led him to his religious outlook. The work, as we now have it, is a series of comments on various themes about man, his understanding and his destiny. In one of the longest of these comments, Pascal discussed the relationship between scepticism and religious belief.

The passage begins:

The main arguments of the sceptics . . . are that we possess no certainty concerning any principles apart from faith and revelation, except in so far as we perceive them naturally within ourselves. But this natural intuition is no convincing proof of their truth; because we have no certainty, apart from faith, as to whether man was created by a good God, or a wicked demon, or chance, and these principles are true, false, or uncertain depending upon our origin. No person is certain, apart from faith, whether he is awake or asleep . . . [and so, the sceptics have shown that everything we know is uncertain. But, on the other hand, we find ourselves drawn by nature to believe all sorts of things. We are torn between an intellectual scepticism which renders everything doubtful, and a natural dogmatism which inclines us toward believing many things.—R. H. P.]

What then shall man do in this state? Should he doubt everything? Should he doubt if he is awake, if he is being pinched, or if he is being burned? Should he doubt whether he is in doubt? Should he doubt his own existence? We are not able to go as far as that; and I put it down as a fact that there never has been a completely thorough-going sceptic. Nature sustains our feeble reason, and prevents it from raving to that extent.

Should he then assert that he is in possession of certain truth—he who, when pressed at all, can show no title to it, and is compelled to let go his hold upon it?

What a chimera then is man! What a novelty! What a monster, what a chaos, what a contradiction, what a prodigy! Judge of all things, imbecile worm of the earth; depositary of all truth, a sink of uncertainty and error; the pride and trash of the universe!

Who will unravel this mess? Nature refutes the sceptics, and reason refutes the dogmatists. What then will become of you, O men, who try to discover by your own natural reason, what is your true condition? . . .

Know then, proud man, what a paradox you are unto yourself. Humble yourself, weak reason; be silent, foolish nature; learn that man infinitely transcends man, and learn from your Master what is your true condition, of which you are ignorant. Hear God.

This powerful passage from Pascal stresses our complete uncertainty, and our complete inability to understand anything. But, Pascal insisted, we are not able to rest in scepticism or agnosticism, but find ourselves impelled to believe. Since we cannot justify our beliefs rationally, we are therefore compelled to turn away from the unsatisfactory quest for knowledge by means of rational evidence, to knowledge based on faith alone. The sceptic or agnostic shares with Pascal the rejection of all knowledge supposedly based on natural or rational principles, but does not take the next step he proposed, that of pure belief. Instead, the sceptic or the agnostic has no belief, or has suspended judgment on all questions for which there cannot be satisfactory evidence. No argument or evidence can be given for determining which is the better or truer path, that of the fideist, or that of the agnostic, but both start out from the same sceptical basis. Hume's comment that scepticism is the starting point for true Christianity may be correct from the fideistic outlook, but it was also the starting point for the irreligious and agnostic outlook of Hume and Voltaire.

Revelation. Another conclusion that is often drawn from the criticisms of the arguments for the existence of God, sometimes as part of a fideistic theory, is that **religious knowledge cannot be based upon natural evidence, but is, instead, based upon revealed knowledge.** The contention here is that the philosophers who debate the merits of rational arguments miss the point. There is another source of knowledge that is the basis for our religious knowledge, and if one accepts this source, one will not be interested in whether a particular argument advanced by a philosopher or a theologian happens to be valid.

Those who advocate this conclusion usually insist that religious knowledge is of a different order from natural knowledge, and that the philosophers of religion have frequently failed to make this distinction. Hence, they have dealt only with natural religion, which may well be as unsatisfactory as Hume and Kant thought. But there is another area of religion, revealed religion, which is unaffected by the criticisms that have been levelled against natural religion.

Revelation is to be found either in certain documents which are accepted as the Word of God, or in certain experiences which are taken as communications or contacts with a Divine Being. The philosopher of religion may raise various questions about how one recognizes that certain knowledge is revealed, or how one distinguishes private experiences that are illusory from those which are said to be genuine. The believer in revealed religion can retort that he is as assured of the revealed character of this knowledge as of the knowledge itself. Even if he cannot prove by rational means that certain information is genuine revelation (which would be a problem in natural religion), he has access to certain knowledge and to certain assurances, which settle these questions as far as he is concerned.

THE PROBLEM OF THE NATURE OF GOD

Another question dealt with by philosophers of religion is that of **the nature of God.** By and large this is a metaphysical question, in which the attempt is made to develop a theory compatible either with our general information as given in certain religious traditions, our scientific knowledge about how the world operates, or our rational understanding of the character of the various aspects of our experience. Theories about the nature of God range from different forms of scientific atheism, contending that God is a figment of the human imagination invented for various psychological, sociological, economic, and other reasons, to very elaborate metaphysical theories purporting to explain the characteristics of the Divine Will, the Divine Intelligence, and the like.

Atheism. Atheism is the theory that either **there is no God, or if there is, He cannot in any way affect human existence.** To support this contention, evidence is offered consisting of our knowledge of the physical world and human behaviour, or some sort of materialistic or naturalistic metaphysics, or insoluble difficulties which confront those who affirm the existence of God.

In modern times, the increased understanding of the operations of the natural and human world has led many thinkers to claim that all problems can be resolved by natural, rather than supernatural, concepts, and that supernatural concepts can themselves be explained in natural terms. This view is, perhaps, summed up in the attitude of the mathematician, Laplace, who, when he was explaining to Napoleon his theory of how the astronomical universe came into existence, was asked where God fitted into his scheme. He replied 'I have no need of such an hypothesis.' The atheistical contention is that the questions that formerly were answered in terms of God can now be answered in terms of scientific knowledge.

In addition, the atheists contend, we now have information that explains why people hold religious beliefs, and this information suggests, if it does not show, that the role played by religious belief in human history has nothing to do with the actual existence of a God. Psychological theories developed by Nietzsche, Freud, and others suggest that religious beliefs have arisen because of certain human needs, a human desire to feel secure in such a vast cosmos, and the like. Thomas Paine, Karl Marx, and others have drawn attention to the role played by religious belief in securing certain institutions and keeping classes in social and political power. Some psychologists like Leuba and Freud tried to establish a connection between sexual problems and religious convictions. In this manner, the atheists have claimed that God as an actual entity does not exist, but is only a construction of the human mind, invented to meet certain needs.

Philosophical Basis of Atheism. A more philosophical basis for atheism is given by **any metaphysical theory which provides an adequate rational comprehension of what we know about the world by means of a system containing no supernatural concepts.** A materialistic or naturalistic metaphysics which attempts to account for our knowledge and experience in terms of a cosmos containing **nothing but material or natural objects** has been advanced as a rational justification of atheism. If one can satisfactorily account for everything without requiring the concept of a Divine Being, then, the atheist asks, why should we have need of, or believe in, such a Being?

As part of the philosophical justification for atheism, some philosophers have pointed out that no consistent or satisfactory theory of the nature of God explains how a Divine Being can have the properties usually attributed to Divinity and yet have anything to do with the human world. From ancient days, in the views of Epicurus, down to such twentieth-century thinkers as Bertrand Russell, philosophers have argued that there are paradoxes and contradictions involved in the notion of an all-powerful God, in the notion of a just God who governs an unjust universe, in the notion of an eternal, unchanging Deity who acts and creates the universe, and so on.

Pantheism. Another theory of the nature of God, which its opponents have regarded as merely another form of atheism, is **pantheism.** **This is the view that God is not a separate being, but is either the entire natural order or an aspect of the entire natural order. Either the universe as a whole is God, or the power or force that pervades the whole of the cosmos is God. God is everywhere, and is everything, or is in everything.**

Spinoza. Perhaps the most famous presentation of pantheism is the metaphysical system of Spinoza. As we saw in the previous chapter (page 104), he sought to establish that **God and Nature were one and the same substance** and that everything that exists or takes place in the world is an aspect, modification, or attribute of God, and that everything can be explained or accounted for by showing the manner of its derivation from God or Nature. Every physical or mental event in the universe was interpreted in Spinoza's great metaphysical system as an aspect of one of the two known attributes of God or Nature, **thought or extension.**

According to the Spinozistic view, God has no personal qualities, since He is not a being independent of or separate from the universe. Those views which describe the Divine Being as having properties analogous to those of human beings were dismissed as being merely anthropomorphic, and having nothing to do with the true nature of things. The proper attitude toward the universal Divine nature is what Spinoza called **'the intellectual love of God', the appreciation of the Divine character of everything, through understanding the nature of reality.** Thus, through comprehending the structure of the universe, by means of grasping the vast scientific system that determines the various specific events of the cosmos, one is expressing the intellectual love of God, and recognizing the pantheistic character of the world.

Deism. This theory of the nature of God maintains that **there is a Divine** Being or Divine Power separate from the physical world, which It has created or started, but that this Divine Being or Power exercises no direct influence or force on events occurring within the universe as it now exists. With the development of modern astronomical and physical systems in the seventeenth century, many thinkers saw that these scientific views suggested a picture of the universe as a self-contained mechanism, like a clock, and each successive state of affairs could be completely explained in terms of the previous state of the mechanism. In these terms, they developed the conception of the nature of God called **deism** to account for God's relations to this mechanical cosmos. God was pictured as the 'perfect watchmaker', who had created or regulated this mechanism according to the best rational principles, and then, having set the machine in motion, no longer played any role in the affairs of the natural world.

The deist theory finds no place for the relationships believed to exist between man and God by most religious traditions. Since God takes no active part in the affairs of the world, there is no point to prayer or supplication. In fact, assuming complete wisdom on the part of God, some of the deists claimed that this must be the best of all possible worlds, and that prayers to bring about certain changes in this world actually constituted a form of dangerous blasphemy against the perfectly ordained and ordered system of the universe.

Theism. The theory of the nature of God that best fits most religious traditions in the western world is that called **theism.** This is the view that there is a God, or there are Gods, who stand in some kind of **direct or personal relationship with human beings.** The theistic conception of Divinity can be either **polytheistic,** that is, that there are many gods—e.g., the theism of Greek mythology; or it can be **monotheistic,** that is, it can limit the conception of Divinity to one God, as is the case in the Judaeo-Christian tradition. But in either the polytheistic or monotheistic conception of God there are several further questions about the nature of God that have to be resolved.

The Nature of God. One of these is whether the God or gods are finite or infinite in power, knowledge, and other attributes. In ancient Greek polytheism, each of the deities was limited as to what he or she was able to accomplish. In the conception of God in the Judaeo-Christian tradition, the Deity has usually been portrayed as all-powerful, unlimited in what He is able to do. However, there have been several philosophers of religion, even within this tradition, who have thought that the only way of reconciling the conception of the Divine Nature with the evils that occur in this world was to portray God as lacking complete or absolute power or knowledge.

The Ethical Problem. Another question that has been much discussed by theists is the relationship between the Divine Nature and the standards of goodness, justice, morality, and the like. As the problem was put by Plato long ago, is something right because the gods will it, or do they will it because it is right? The question at issue is whether the standards of value are only the arbitrary pronouncement of God or the gods, or whether there are some universal standards of value which even the Deity accepts and obeys. On the one hand, there are theistic theories which conceive the nature of God as co-eternal with certain eternal truths, such as the ultimate standards of value and truth, which God accepts and employs in His relations with the world. On the other hand, there are theories, sometimes called **voluntaristic,** which assert that the power of the Deity is totally unlimited, and that it is within this Divine Power that God makes various things true or good. Anything which God so wills is, by the very fact that God has willed it, necessarily right and just.

As is evident, the range of possible theistic theories is very large. Conceptions of the number or character of the Divine Being can be adjudged in terms of their consistency and their coherence with our general understanding of the world. Most theistic theories have been developed in terms of how they fit in with certain religious traditions, which begin with what they believe to be certain knowledge about God and his relation to the universe. The theistic philosophers' achievements can then be evaluated according to how well they fit in with the view of God held by these traditions.

In the Judaeo-Christian tradition there has been a long history (dating from the *Book of Job*, the *Epistles* of St. Paul, the philosophy of Philo Judaeus, and other works) of attempts to develop a theistic point of view in harmony with the picture of the Divine Nature as revealed in Scripture. Those who were concerned with working out an intelligible and rational conception of God that was compatible with our other knowledge about the world, and who were also believers either in Judaism or Christianity, tried to construct philosophically acceptable forms of theism. The conceptions of the nature of God, or the gods, of Plato, Aristotle, and the Neo-Platonists have been studied, modified, combined, in order to present a rationally satisfactory version of theism that is also consistent with the Judaeo-Christian view of God's Nature. Philosophers and theologians have attempted to work out acceptable rational explanations of Creation, of the Trinity, of the immortality of the soul, and other doctrines.

Criticisms of Theism. Alongside the history of attempts to construct a rational theology, usually in theistic terms, there has been as long a history of either cynical opposition, or attack from mystics and fideists. Powerful objections have been made that the proposed theory does not meet the requirements of a rational mind. Various religious thinkers have tried to show that we cannot rationally know anything at all about the nature of God. (Some of the most extreme of the mystics and the fideists have presented a theory called **negative theology,** maintaining that God is beyond any of the classifications or categories that man can conceive. No statements that we can make can apply to God except negative ones that tell us what He is not. Thus, our sole knowledge about the nature of God is in negative terms, telling us, for example, that 'God is not an animal'.)

The theistic conception of God, since it best corresponds to the various revealed religious traditions, has of course been of great concern to philosophers of religion. Within nearly every Christian, Jewish and Mohammedan group there have been many attempts to develop a theistic theory which is consistent with the group's concept of God. In terms of such a theory, each group has tried to construct a satisfactory rational defence of its religion.

Conclusion. In view of the age-old concern of mankind with religious problems, this area of human experience constitutes a subject matter for philosophical analysis. The philosopher—in examining the problems of religious knowledge and metaphysical theories about the nature of God—is not necessarily concerned to argue for or against any particular religious belief or theory. Rather his interest is to analyse it, to raise questions about it in order to understand it rationally.

Although must philosophizing about religious questions has been of an apologetic character, that is, has been aimed at rendering various religious beliefs intellectually acceptable, it is just as likely that careful rational examination may result in doubts that an intelligible theory is possible. The philosophy of religion is not committed to developing evidence either for atheism or for religious belief. Instead, **its crucial concerns are to examine the knowledge-claims that are made in this area, to see if there are standards in relation to which they can be justified,** and to evaluate and interpret these claims within the framework of rational understanding. It is always possible that the best conclusion one may be able to reach is a fideistic or sceptical one—that no defensible rational comprehension can be gained in the area of religious knowledge and that no satisfactory rational interpretation or explanation can be made.

SUGGESTED FURTHER READING

Classical Authors:

St. Anselm, *Proslogium*. (The classical statement of the ontological argument.)

St. Thomas Aquinas, *Basic Writings*, edited by A. C. Pegis, 3 vols. Burns and Oates. (Selections from St. Thomas' writings, covering his most important theories.)

Hume, David, *Dialogues Concerning Natural Religion*.

Kierkegaard, Soren, *Training in Christianity*. Oxford University Press: London, 1941. (An exposition of the fideist point of view by one of the most important modern theologians.)

Nietzsche, Friedrich Wilhelm, *The Philosophy of Nietzsche*. New English Library: London, 1966. (Contains several works of Nietzsche in which his atheism is set forth.)

Pascal, Blaise, *Pensées*. Penguin Books: London, 1966. (One of the classical presentations of the problem of the nature of religious knowledge.)

Voltaire, *Candide*. Penguin Books: London, 1968. (A brilliant satire concerning the problem of evil.)

Modern Authors:

Copleston, F. C., *Aquinas*. Penguin Books: London, 1967. (A good critical discussion of the views of this philosopher by a modern Thomist.)

James, William, *The Varieties of Religious Experience*. (A classic in the psychology of religious behaviour and attitudes.)

CHAPTER V

THE THEORY OF KNOWLEDGE

One of the most important branches of philosophy is **epistemology** (theory of knowledge). Philosophers have attempted to discover the means by which our knowledge is acquired, the extent of our knowledge, and the standards or criteria by which we can reliably judge the truth or falsity of our knowledge.

We tend to be well satisfied with what we think we know about the universe and do not ask how we obtained our knowledge, or question its reliability. Occasionally we are shocked to discover that what we thought was certain is proved dubious or false. If this happens often enough we may become suspicious of all claims to certainty.

Suppose, for example, that someone whom we trusted told us that all the news in our daily newspaper was false. We might—in consequence—begin to distrust our friend, or distrust the newspaper, or distrust ourselves. We would certainly begin to think about the kind of evidence we would need to help us to discover what the truth of the case was. We would begin, in fact, to ask the sort of questions that have led philosophers to develop a theory of knowledge.

Perhaps the most fertile source material for developing a theory of knowledge has been the history of human opinions. No theory or belief has been so absurd that there has not been someone who believed it, and argued for it. The history of science is replete with theories that have been thoroughly believed by the wisest men and were then thoroughly discredited.

Repeatedly people have attempted to impose their beliefs on others and punish those who rejected them. The early Greek philosopher, ANAXAGORAS, was exiled from Athens for saying that the moon was a stone. In the twentieth century a teacher in Tennessee was punished for teaching the Darwinian theory of evolution. In the last twenty-five years there have been many martyrs whose 'crimes' were that they challenged the 'infallible wisdom' of the rulers of their society.

Philosophers are concerned to determine the basis of all knowledge-claims, and to agree upon standards for judging these claims. If so much of what had been taken as certain has instead proved false or doubtful, then how can we ever be certain?

RENÉ DESCARTES: THE PROBLEM POSED

The great French philosopher and mathematician, RENÉ DESCARTES, (1596–1650) posed the problem in most striking form. Descartes lived in a rapidly changing world, one marked by almost continuous religious conflict between the Catholics and the Huguenots, and by intense controversy between the advocates of Aristotle's views about the nature of the physical world, and those who supported the new theories of Copernicus, Kepler and Galileo. The fact that there were new theories suggested that there were other methods of seeking after knowledge than those that had been employed by the Greeks and by everyone else since that time; this encouraged philosophers to begin to inquire into the nature of these methods and the validity of the knowledge they led to. Descartes, trained in Aristotelian philosophy, set out to study the world for himself. After extended investigation he came to suspect all accepted views which claimed authority merely because they were ancient and honoured. When he returned to Paris in 1628 he found that the most independently thoughtful of his contemporaries were similarly agitated by the conflict between the older ideas which they felt they could no longer accept, and the new theories. Most of them despaired of finding certainty and turned to **scepticism —a view that doubts whether any of our beliefs can be supported by adequate or sufficient evidence.** Descartes, however, did not surrender to scepticism. He had an intense desire to be certain, to be so certain that no discovery could ever shake his beliefs again. He left Paris, a desperate man in quest of certainty. In his retreat in Holland, he tells us, he inquired into everything he knew to see what, if anything, he could accept as reliable knowledge.

Descartes felt that he could be certain only of knowledge which could never be false or doubtful. Most of what we accept, Descartes thought, could not meet this standard—despite our certainty, it still might be false. He determined to test the knowledge that he like anyone else ordinarily would accept—knowledge derived from our sense experience. The results of his test (if he is right) are so devastating that philosophers have been compelled ever since to investigate the problem of the foundation of knowledge.

Descartes' Test. Before examining some of their theories, we must first consider Descartes' test. He begins his *Meditations on the First Philosophy* (1640) by writing:

> It is now some years since I detected how many were the false beliefs that I had from my earliest youth admitted as true, and how doubtful was everything I had since constructed on this basis; and from that time I was convinced that I must once for all seriously undertake to rid myself of all the opinions which I had formerly accepted, and commence to build anew from the foundation, if I wanted to establish any firm and permanent structure in the sciences. . . .
> Now for this object it is not necessary that I should show that all of these opinions are false—I shall perhaps never arrive at this end. But inasmuch as reason already persuades me that I ought no less carefully to withhold my assent from matters which are not entirely certain and indubitable than from those which appear to me manifestly to be false, if I am able to find in each one *some reason to doubt*, this will suffice to justify my rejecting the whole. And for that end it will not be requisite that I should examine each in particular,

which would be an endless undertaking; for owing to the fact that the destruction of the foundations of necessity brings with it the downfall of the rest of the edifice, I shall only . . . attack those principles upon which all my former opinions rested.

That is, Descartes feels that there is no need to test *every* opinion that he formerly held—an 'endless undertaking'—but will instead consider general types of belief. **If there is any reason for doubt, then the entire category ought to be treated as doubtful and unreliable.** The first category to be treated is those opinions which we derive from sense experience.

All that up to the present time I have accepted as true and certain I have learned either from the senses or through the senses; but it is sometimes proved to me that these senses are deceptive, and it is wiser not to trust entirely anything by which we have once been deceived.

Reliability of Sense Data. Descartes assumes that everyone is familiar with the phenomenon of being deceived by his senses. One may see something at a distance which turns out to be quite otherwise when seen close up, or see things differently when they are in water from when they are out of it, e.g., when one is rowing, the oar appears to be bent. Since this sometimes happens, Descartes suggests we cannot really be certain it does not happen all the time. If one grants this is sometimes the case but objects that in most cases we can be quite certain that our senses are not deceiving us, Descartes presses his test:

But it may be that although the senses sometimes deceive us concerning things which are hardly perceptible, or very far away, there are yet many others to be met with as to which we cannot reasonably have any doubt, although we recognize them by means of the senses. For example, there is the fact that I am here, seated by the fire, attired in a dressing gown, having this paper in my hands and other similar matters. And how could I deny that these hands and this body are mine, were it not perhaps that I compare myself to certain persons, devoid of sense, whose brains are so troubled . . . that they constantly assure us that they think they are kings when they are really quite poor, or that they are clothed in purple when they are really without covering, or who imagine that they have an earthenware head or are nothing but pumpkins or are made of glass. But they are mad, and I should not be any the less insane were I to follow examples so extravagant.

Perhaps; but Descartes is beginning to shake our assurance. Can we be certain that we are not also subject to delusions? If his test has not already led to some doubt, Descartes raises another, more troubling problem:

At the same time I must remember that I am a man, and that consequently I am in the habit of sleeping, and in my dreams representing to myself the same things, or sometimes even less probable things, than do those who are insane in their waking moments. How often has it happened to me that in the night I dreamt that I found myself in this particular place, that I was dressed and seated near the fire, whilst in reality I was lying undressed in bed! At this moment it does indeed seem to me that it is with eyes awake that I am looking at this paper; that this head which I move is not asleep, that it is deliberately and of set purpose that I extend my hand and see it; what happens in sleep does not appear so clear nor so distinct as does all this. But in thinking over this I remind myself that on many occasions I have in sleep been deceived by similar illusions, and in dwelling carefully on this reflection I see so manifestly that there are no certain indications by which we may clearly distinguish wakefulness from sleep that I am lost in astonishment. And my astonishment is such that it is almost capable of persuading me that I now dream.

The problem thus posed is troublesome. How can we be certain that everything we see and do is not part of a dream? Any means that we employ as a check might, for all we can tell, also be parts of the dream. People have dreamt that they have pinched themselves to see if they are dreaming. Descartes concludes that no matter how we feel about it, there is no guarantee that our sense experience is not part of a dream. Therefore, we have grounds for suspecting the reliability—that is, the accuracy—of the knowledge we acquire through our senses. But even if it is all a dream, one might ask, are not some aspects of the dream trustworthy? Accordingly, Descartes proceeds with his test:

Now let us assume that we are asleep and that all these things, e.g., that we open our eyes, shake our head, extend our hands, and so on, are but false delusions; and let us reflect that possibly neither our hands nor our whole body are such as they appear to us to be. At the same time we must confess that the things which are represented to us in sleep are like painted representations which can only have been formed as the counterparts of something real and true, and that in this way those general things at least, that is, eyes, a head, hands and a whole body, are not imaginary things, but really exist. For, as a matter of fact, painters, even when they study with the greatest skill to represent sirens and satyrs by forms the most strange and extraordinary, cannot give them natures which are entirely new, but merely make a certain medley of the parts of different animals, or if their imagination is extravagant enough to invent something so novel that nothing similar has ever before been seen, and such that their work represents a thing purely fictitious and absolutely false, it is certain all the same that the colours of which this is composed are necessarily real.

Descartes, at this point, seems willing to admit that even if it were possible that the particular content of our experience might be a dream, still the dream itself must be based on something. All the objects that we are acquainted with—ourselves, chairs, tables, trees —might be part of a vast delusion or dream, but at the same time, the fantasy seems to be based on *something*. But on what? Descartes suggests that the particular objects that we experience, talk about, live with, may be part of a **continuous dream world.** We may invent in our dream the objects that populate it. But our invention, if it is such, follows certain patterns, and has certain fixed properties. Elephants are always bigger than butterflies, and squares never have round corners. Descartes concludes from these considerations that the actual items of our experience may be illusions, and the studies we make of them (e.g., Astronomy, Botany, Physics) may also be illusions if their objects are figments of our imagination which exist only in our dreams. Still, the world of our dreams—if we assume for the sake of the discussion that everything we experience is part of a dream-world— has some order and is constructed according to certain geometrical and numerical patterns. 'For whether I am awake or asleep, two and three together always make five, and the square can never have more than four sides, and it does not seem possible that truths so clear and apparent can be suspected of any falsity or uncertainty.'

The Question of Deity. But lest anyone think that the test is over, and we at last have something that we can rely on, Descartes raises a final and more devastating reason for doubting even the knowledge of which we are most certain:

> Nevertheless I have long had fixed in my mind the belief that an all-powerful God existed by whom I have been created such as I am. But how do I know that He has not brought it to pass that there is no earth, no heaven, no extended body, no magnitude, no place, and that nonetheless, I perceive all these things and they seem to me to exist just exactly as I now see them? And, besides, as I sometimes imagine that others deceive themselves in the things which they think they know best, how do I know that I am not deceived every time that I add two and three, or count the sides of a square, or judge of things yet simpler, if anything simpler can be imagined? But possibly God has not desired that I should be thus deceived for He is said to be supremely good. If, however, it is contrary to His goodness to have made me such that I constantly deceive myself, it would also appear to be contrary to His goodness to permit me to be sometimes deceived, and nevertheless I cannot doubt that He does permit this.

Having suggested the most harrowing possibility of all, that the world is commanded by a deity who deceives humanity, Descartes prepares to conclude his test. If, notwithstanding all our efforts, we cannot avoid being misled, then how can we trust *anything*? If when I add two and three, I am compelled to make a mistake that I am incapable of detecting, how can I avoid mistaken conclusions? Once the possibility of systematic deception is admitted, all appears lost, and even our most 'reliable' information seems dubious. Hence, Descartes concludes:

> At the end I feel constrained to confess that there is nothing in all that I formerly believed to be true, of which I cannot in some measure doubt, and that not merely through want of thought or

through levity, but for reasons which are very powerful and maturely considered; so that henceforth I ought not the less carefully to refrain from giving credence to these opinions than to that which is manifestly false, if I desire to arrive at any certainty in the sciences.

Doubt. Descartes' test appears to have ended in disaster. If we inquire into the truth of our opinions, seeking evidence which would guarantee that it is impossible that these beliefs are false, we find that such evidence appears to be lacking. Instead, reasons can be offered which suggest, whether plausibly or not, that **our most cherished and firm beliefs could be false.** Sense illusions, and fantasies due to insanity or drunkenness, cast some doubt on the reliability of our sense information. We may merely be 'seeing things'. The possibility that the whole of experience may be part of a dream leads to further doubts as to whether we are in fact seeing a world that exists, or even whether there is any world outside of our imagination. Lastly, the possibility that an evil genius is deceiving us leaves us entirely without assurance in the foundations of our knowledge.

Descartes' Purpose. The purpose of Descartes' test is not to promulgate science-fiction fantasies, but to illuminate a crucial problem. We are willing to take for granted a great deal that *might* be false or uncertain. In showing the difficulties that exist in establishing acceptable views, Descartes did not wish to convert us to scepticism and total doubt, to make us unwilling to accept an opinion for fear that it might prove false. Instead, he undertook to find a satisfactory basis for our knowledge, a basis so certain 'that all the most extravagant suppositions brought forward by the sceptics would be incapable of shaking it'.

THE PROBLEM OF KNOWLEDGE:
A CLOSER LOOK

The Problem. Let us now examine theories that Descartes and other philosophers have formulated about the nature of our knowledge, the foundation for it, and the extent of it. In order to make clear what their theorizing has been about, it is first necessary to understand **the nature of the problem of knowledge.**

When we say that we 'know' something, what sort of a claim are we usually making?

Popular Usage. In ordinary discourse we use the verb 'to know' loosely. When we say that we 'know' something, we usually mean we are sure that something is true, as when two people dispute about the F.A. Cup Final of 1933, and one says, 'I *know* that Everton won'— with complete assurance. Without help from Descartes, it is clear that when we use the word 'know' to express personal conviction, our claim may in fact be groundless. We are all acquainted with extremely opinionated people who are in fact—extremely mistaken.

There are still less positive usages of 'know', as when people use the word as equivalent to 'believe', 'think', and the like. When laymen say they 'know' that the Salk polio vaccine is effective, they in fact mean that they 'think so', having perhaps heard that this is the view of some authoritative persons. If one is asked if Smith is going to be at the party, and the answer is, 'Yes, I know that he is', this may merely be a convenient way of saying, 'I believe he is; at least, I heard him say that he was planning to be there.' One is not expressing complete assurance, but only a conviction. One would hardly be willing to guarantee the accuracy of such a statement on the mere basis of having heard Smith's plans. Clearly Smith may have to change his plans, or something may happen to prevent his attendance.

Of course, the word 'know' may be used to express what is nothing more than a hunch, or a hope, or a pig-headed opinion. The gambler who 'knows' the next number on the roulette wheel is merely guessing or acting on a 'hunch'. Politicians, during election campaigns, who 'know' who will win, and who 'know' what will happen to the country if they are wrong, are only expressing their hopes and fears. Similarly, the man who 'knows' that Oxford has a better rugby team than Cambridge, when Oxford has lost all its games, and Cambridge has won all, is simply expressing a fanatical loyalty that transcends, and is indifferent to, mere facts.

The Philosophical Sense. But the popular usages of 'know' are hardly what philosophers have been debating. 'Knowledge' of that order could not survive Descartes' test. Philosophers have been concerned to find out if we can really 'know' anything in the sense of possessing information that is not open to question. 'Knowledge', in this usage, is sharply distinguished from opinion. Many sceptics have claimed that people's 'knowledge' only expresses opinions which may or may not be true. Against this, some philosophers have insisted that there is obtainable information which is not mere opinion, but which is beyond question true. **It is the quest for this type of certain knowledge that has given rise to the problem of knowledge.**

To illustrate this usage, an anecdote may be helpful (a story which our informant insists is true). A philosopher and a friend were driving in a car. At an intersection the car was struck by another one, which had apparently driven through a red light, since the light facing the car with the philosopher and friend was green at the time of the accident. The friend owned the car, and sued the person who had struck him. The latter, at the trial, insisted that the light was green for him, and red for his accuser. In fact, he insisted that he *knew* he was right. (This was probably the usage of 'know' in the sense of hope, or believe.) To corroborate his friend's story, the only other witness, the philosopher, was put on the stand. The lawyer for the plaintiff asked the philosopher about the colour of the light and the witness answered that it seemed to be green. The lawyer asked him to be more precise, did he *know* the colour of the light? The philosopher said that he did not *know*, but it *looked* green, and he thought it was *probably* green. The more the lawyer pressed the philosopher-witness for a positive answer, the more the latter insisted that he did not *know*, he merely had an *opinion* which might be wrong. The jury and judge, faced with the absolute assurance of the defendant, and the uncertainty of the philosopher, could only decide against the philosopher's friend. The rub was that the philosopher insisted on using 'know' in the strict sense in which one who knows is *absolutely certain*—by Descartes' standard. In fact, our law courts usually avoid the philosopher's difficulties by seeking to establish the defendant's guilt 'beyond reasonable doubt', without seeking *absolute* assurance that a person *must* be guilty, and cannot *possibly* be innocent.

The philosophers who have sought to discover what sort of knowledge, in this strict sense, we possess—and what sort of evidence we can adduce, and what standards we judge it by—have offered various theories about the nature, source and basis of our knowledge. We shall now consider some of these theories. The first group makes positive claims to the effect that human beings can discover **absolutely true knowledge, knowledge that under no circumstances can be false, and that this knowledge can be acquired through the use of our rational faculties.**

ANCIENT GREEK PHILOSOPHY

The Sophists. One of the oldest positive theories of knowledge was developed in the early days of Greek philosophy. In the fifth century B.C. a group of wise men appeared in Athens called the **Sophists.** They were **extremely doubtful about the possibility of discovering anything that was really true.** Instead, they taught their followers how to 'get along' in the world, *without* certain knowledge. They taught their followers how to win disputes, how to speak well and convincingly and, generally, how to succeed. Their underlying theory developed from two remarks of two of the leading Sophists. PROTAGORAS, perhaps the greatest of the Sophists, said, **'Man is the measure of all things,'** and GORGIAS, another great Sophist, proclaimed, **'Nothing exists, and if it did, no one could know it, and if they knew it, they could not communicate it.'** From these statements the Sophists developed the view that knowledge in the strict sense was unattainable, and, therefore, man should not bother to seek what he can never find. Instead, the Sophists insisted, following Protagoras' dictum, everyone should 'measure' matters according to his nature and needs, since man alone was the measure of all things.

Socrates and Protagoras. Thus the Sophists proposed that man should accept the fact that all his alleged knowledge was only relative to man's outlook. Since no one, according to Gorgias' statement, can know any truth, or report it if he did know it, the Sophist solution was to train for success. In one of Plato's *Dialogues* called 'Protagoras', Plato describes a meeting between Socrates and the great Sophist, Protagoras. A friend, named Hippocrates, tells Socrates that Protagoras is in Athens, and they must rush to see him. When Socrates asks why, Hippocrates answers that he must become a student of the great Sophist and acquire his wisdom. Socrates asks his friend what he expects to learn. Hippocrates is unable to answer clearly and they go to see Protagoras to find out what he can accomplish. Socrates tells Protagoras that his friend, Hippocrates, is a well-to-do Athenian who desires to achieve political eminence, and 'who is desirous of making your acquaintance; he would like to know what will happen to him if he associates with you'. Protagoras answered: 'Young man, if you associate with me, on the very first day you will return home a better man than you came, and better on the second day than on the first, and better every day than you were on the day before.'

Socrates is baffled and inquires, 'When you say that on the first day on which he associates with you he will return home a better man, and on every day will grow in like manner—in what, Protagoras, will he be better? and about what?' The great Protagoras answers, 'You ask questions fairly, and I like to answer a question which is fairly put. If Hippocrates comes to me he will not experience the sort of drudgery with which other Sophists are in the habit of insulting their pupils; who, when they have just escaped from the arts, are taken and driven back into them by these teachers, and made to learn calculation, and astronomy, and geometry, and music . . . but if he comes to me, he will learn that which he comes to learn. And this is prudence in affairs private as well as public; he will learn to order his own house in the best manner, and he will be able to speak and act for the best in the affairs of the state.'

Criticism of Sophism. Socrates worried about such 'schools for success' (which resemble many present-day educational institutions). What troubled him is that people like Protagoras profess they do not possess genuine knowledge and yet presume to instruct people in worldly success. The students and the teachers might, after all, be doing the wrong thing, since they do not have any positive knowledge. Learning 'how to get away with it', Socrates thought, was not wise, unless one was sure that it was *right* to 'get away with it'. Being able to speak well, to convince people, to be a leader, is not enough, unless one also knows what to speak *about*, what to convince people *of*, and *where* to lead them. Otherwise, Socrates argued, the results of such skills may be disastrous.

What was dangerous about the Sophists, Socrates thought, was that neither they nor their students had any knowledge; hence the blind were leading the blind. But with the skills for success the Sophists had mastered, they became public menaces, unless they knew what was *right*. This they could be sure of only if they had genuine knowledge which could not possibly be false. If the Sophists prevailed upon people to accept their views, they might well follow them down a road to utter ruin, if the opinions were wrong.

PLATO

Socrates was convinced that one could act only on the basis of the truth. In various *Dialogues*, Plato, in his presentation of the conversations of Socrates, tried to construct a theory of knowledge—what knowledge was available, how we could obtain it, and why it was true.

Plato's view, put briefly, was that knowledge consists in the apprehension of those aspects of the world which never change, never alter. Plato believed that the world contained such constituent elements, which he called 'ideas' or 'forms'. What, then, are 'forms', and why does knowledge consist in the apprehension of them, rather than of changing things?

The problem may appear clearer if we consider a series of statements: (*a*) 'Rover is a dog', (*b*) 'Fido is a dog', and (*c*) 'Spot is a dog'. If Fido and Rover and Spot are all different animals, what are we saying about them? We are saying that they have something in common, and that each animal falls into a common classification (e.g., 'being a dog'). But what does the general term 'dog' refer to? If we were asked what 'Rover' referred to, we could simply point to that dog. But what would we point to in order to show what 'dog' referred to? If we pointed to Rover, and then to Fido, and then to Spot, would that make clear what the general term 'dog' referred to? We might be indicating that they all had tails, or spots, or all said 'Woof'.

Plato suggested that our ordinary statements include the use of general terms, and that in order for our ordinary statements to be meaningful, one must know what these general terms signify. To do this, Plato insisted, one must do more than merely point to various particular things. Those things would only be, at best, *examples* of things that fall into general classifications, but would not themselves be the classifications.

The 'Euthyphro'. In one of Plato's 'dialogues'—the 'Euthyphro'—Plato made this point forcefully. The dialogue is a discussion between Socrates, on his way to the courthouse, and a priest of Athens, Euthyphro. The latter tells Socrates that he is going to court to have his father tried for murder. When Socrates asks for details, we see that it is extremely doubtful whether Euthyphro's father is actually guilty; but Euthyphro insists that he should accuse his father because that is the holy thing to do in this case. Socrates asks him, what is holiness? Euthyphro responds, it is doing what I am doing. Socrates responds that Euthyphro's act may be an *illustration* of holiness; but to determine if the act is holy, one must know the meaning of the general term 'holiness'. When Euthyphro attempts to make clear what 'holiness' means, Socrates shows him that his definition is inadequate. Finally Euthyphro gives up, because, he says, each time he puts his words down, they get up and walk away.

Universals. To prevent the words from marching off, Plato claimed, we must discover the meanings of our general terms. If we employ these terms to classify items in our experience (e.g., to point out that we call this a dog, and that a cat) by virtue of the fact that they fall into certain classifications, then these remarks can only be meaningful if we know the meaning of the general terms, also called 'universals'. The general terms seem to refer to something different from the items of our experience, since they are the means for saying things about items in our experience. We call Rover a dog in virtue of certain characteristics. Plato's thesis is that only if we know what is required for something to be a dog, can we tell that Rover falls into this classification.

How can one discover what these general terms or 'universals' mean, so that one can tell if a certain item falls into some classification? Plato argued that, first of all, we could *not* know these universals (or as they are sometimes called, **Forms or Platonic Ideas**) through our ordinary sense experience. All that we discover by these means are *particular instances,* which keep changing all the time. Rover grows, sheds his hair, moves around, and so on. In these circumstances we cannot know the general nature or characteristics by virtue of which Rover is a dog. Our sense experience does not reveal universals or Forms, but only particular examples. Therefore, if we are to know Platonic Ideas, it must be by some other means.

SOCRATES' THEORY OF UNIVERSAL FORMS

In a dialogue called the *Meno,* Plato portrayed Socrates as claiming that **we cannot acquire knowledge through learning.** He argued that in order to learn something we must discover a truth that we did not previously know. But in that case, we could not recognize it. Thus, if one were taught something that one did not already know—such as the truth in Euclidean geometry that the area of a rectangle is equal to the height multiplied by the length of the figure—Socrates claimed that one could not tell that this proposition was true when one learned it unless one already knew it to be true. In brief, the Platonic thesis is that **one cannot learn what one does know since one already knows it. And one cannot learn what one does not know, since if one doesn't know it, one cannot recognize it as a truth when one learns it. Therefore, learning is impossible, and any knowledge that we can have we must already have.**

Recollection. Socrates concluded that we do not *learn* anything— we *remember* what we already know; **all the knowledge of Forms or universals is already in our minds.** Our sense experience can, at best, only have the incidental effect of jarring our memory, and bringing to our conscious attention information that is within us, but of which we have not yet become aware.

The 'Meno'. To demonstrate this theory of knowledge by recollection, Socrates, in the *Meno.* talks to a slave boy, who reveals that he has never been taught any mathematics. He is then asked to solve the following problem: If there is a square whose sides are each one inch long, how long are the sides of a square whose area is double that of the original square? The slave boy answers twice as long; that is, two inches long. Socrates shows him that this is incorrect by getting him to figure out the area of this new square (the height times the length) or 2 inches times 2 inches. Hence, the new square is four times the area of the original one. Without ever indicating the answer, but only by criticizing whatever the slave boy says, Socrates finally leads him to discover the right answer—a square built upon the diagonal of the original square. The fact that the slave boy, who had never studied or been taught mathematics, could recognize the right answer and be completely sure of it, and could find the right answer without being told, is offered as evidence that he must already, in some sense, have known the answer.

The Source of Knowledge. If we gain our knowledge through recollection as this theory holds, where does our knowledge of universals or

Forms or Platonic Ideas come from? According to the argument, it cannot come from experience, nor from education, since it is already within us. But when and how did it come within us? According to Plato, since we have never acquired the Forms in our life-time, they must have already been within us when we were born. To account for the fact that infants do not seem to know very much, we are told that the soul (which Plato believed must have existed prior to one's birth, in order to contain the Platonic Ideas) forgets its knowledge of Forms at birth, and must somehow regain consciousness of the knowledge that is already there.

The Philosopher-King. With this much of Plato's theory of knowledge before us, we may ask again, how can we gain knowledge of universals or Forms? How can one jar one's memory to recall the Platonic Ideas and thus come to possess real knowledge? An answer to this question is presented in Plato's great dialogue, *The Republic*. As we saw in Chapter II (pages 59–60), in the course of outlining the nature of the ideal state, Socrates is asked how this new and better world might be achieved. He answers: 'Until philosophers are kings, or the kings and princes of this world have the spirit and power of philosophy, and political greatness and wisdom meet in one . . . then only will this our State have a possibility of life and behold the light of day.' To show how one might become a philosopher, Socrates discusses the problem of how the intended rulers of his society may come to possess true knowledge, and to employ it in guiding the republic.

Kinds of Knowledge. There are, according to Socrates' account, two main types of information that we can possess—**visible or sensible (i.e., acquired through the senses) and intelligible.** The **visible or sensible information** is divided into images or shadows, and opinions. The lower level of our visible information is a vague, blurred conglomeration of patterns; the higher level is the clear patterns—with identifiable objects and coherently organized images. But none of this constitutes knowledge, because none of it is indubitable—it is not understood in terms of the Forms or universals. Hence all that we can report is how it *seems* to us, what it *appears* to be.

The **intelligible information,** on the other hand, deals with Platonic Ideas, and it is here that knowledge is possible. The lowest level is the use of Platonic Ideas as hypotheses without understanding their nature. If squares have certain properties, then we can draw certain conclusions about geometrical relationships. One assumes, but still does not know, the nature of these universals. The highest level, complete knowledge, occurs when one knows the Platonic Idea, in the sense of being fully aware of it in one's mind, and understanding its nature.

The Allegory of the Cave. This division, and the road to complete knowledge, is further explained by Socrates by means of a tale which is sometimes called 'The Allegory of the Cave'. It begins:

And now, I said, let me show in a figure how far our nature is enlightened or unenlightened: Behold! human beings living in an underground den, which has a mouth open towards the light and

reaching all along the den; here they have been from their child-
hood, and have their legs and necks chained so that they cannot
move, and can only see before them, being prevented by the chains
from turning round their heads. Above and behind them a fire is
blazing at a distance, and between the fire and the prisoners there is
a raised way; and you will see, if you look, a low wall built along the
way, like the screen which marionette players have in front of them,
over which they show the puppets.

I see.

And do you see, I said, men passing along the wall carrying all
sorts of vessels, and statues and figures of animals made of wood
and stone and various materials, which appear over the wall? Some
of them are talking, others silent.

You have shown me a strange image, and they are strange
prisoners.

Like ourselves, I replied, and they see only their own shadows, or
the shadows of one another, which the fire throws on the opposite
wall of the cave.

True, he said, how could they see anything but the shadows if
they were never allowed to move their heads?

And of the objects which are being carried in like manner they
would only see the shadows?

In such a world, Socrates claimed, 'the truth would be literally
nothing but the shadows of the images'. But what would happen if the
prisoners were suddenly released and no longer took the shadows
for the real objects?

At first, when any of them is liberated and compelled suddenly to
stand up and turn his neck round and walk and look towards the
light, he will suffer sharp pains; the glare will distress him, and he
will be unable to see the realities of which in his former state he had
seen the shadows; and then conceive some one saying to him,
that what he saw before was an illusion, but that now, when he is
approaching nearer to being and his eye is turned towards more real
existence, he has clearer vision—what will be his reply?

Obviously he will be confused by the increased light and the changes
in the quality of the objects of his perceptions.

And if he is compelled to look straight at the light, will he not
have a pain in eyes which will make him turn away to take refuge
in the objects of vision which he can see, and which he will conceive
to be in reality clearer than the things which are now being shown
to him?

True, he said.

And suppose once more, that he is reluctantly dragged up a steep
and rugged ascent, and held fast until he is forced into the presence
of the sun himself, is he not likely to be pained and irritated? When
he approaches the light his eyes will be dazzled and he will not be
able to see anything of all of what are now called realities.

This state of being blinded by real knowledge will not last long. Socrates claimed:

> He will require to grow accustomed to the sight of the upper world. At first he will see the shadows best, next the reflections of men and other objects in the water, and then the objects themselves; then he will gaze upon the light of the moon and the stars and the spangled heaven; and he will see the sky and the stars by night better than the sun or the light of the sun by day.
> Certainly.
> Last of all he will be able to see the sun, and not merely reflections of him in the water, but he will see him in his own proper place, and not in another; and he will contemplate him as he is.

Plato stated the essence of the allegory by having Socrates interpret it in terms of his theory of knowledge.

> The entire allegory, I said, you may append, dear Glaucon, to the previous argument; the prison-house is the world of sight, the light of the fire is the sun, and you will not misapprehend me if you interpret the journey upwards to be the ascent of the soul into the intellectual world according to my poor belief, which, at your desire I have expressed—whether rightly of wrongly God knows.

Making of a Philosopher-King. It is necessary to escape the jail of the cave (i.e., the world of visible information) and turn upward to the world of intelligible knowledge, to find the Forms or universals that are within us, and to grow accustomed to contemplating them, so that we may at last achieve real knowledge.

To achieve this goal, Socrates outlined a scheme of training for would-be philosopher-kings, so that they would arrive at the knowledge of Platonic Ideas. What must be done is to bring about 'the turning round of a soul passing from a day which is little better than night to the true day of being'. Those who genuinely desire knowledge must be trained to discover the Forms or universals in their minds. But, if, as had been previously claimed by Socrates, learning is not really possible, then the 'education' of the future philosopher-kings must be a peculiar process, which does not actually *teach* them. Instead, what will be done is to train them to *recollect* the knowledge that is, and always has been, within them.

The Use of Reason. The first step is to lead them to realize the inadequacy of sense information, and to notice the recurrence of certain oddities in the visible world. By observing the changing quality of the same object in the world of shadows, one begins to wonder. The fourth finger, for example, is large when compared with the little one, but small compared with the middle finger. Is the fourth finger large, or is it small? When one ponders such a problem, Socrates claimed, 'these intimations which the soul receives through the senses are very curious and require to be explained'. The eye saw the object as large, and also as small. To explain this, according to Socrates, the mind seeks to understand what 'largeness' and 'smallness' mean. Thus, the mind has begun the search for universals or Platonic Ideas.

Arithmetic. Having started the future philosopher-king on his journey towards understanding and knowledge through the use of reason rather than the senses, Socrates proposed a second, more lengthy and difficult step. This stage consists of training the mind to deal with abstractions, to reason about universals or Forms. To do this, the student is to be trained first of all in **arithmetic.** Here, instead of looking at shadows, he must look inward at his ideas and learn to deal only with thoughts and meanings rather than with visible objects. Socrates held that 'arithmetic has a very great and elevating effect, compelling the soul to reason about abstract numbers, and rebelling against the introduction of visible or tangible objects into the argument'. In learning to do sums 'in his head', instead of counting his fingers and his toes, the student will be liberated from the cave, and will catch a glimmering of the Forms within him.

Geometry. After he has become skilled in arithmetic, Socrates proposed to teach the would-be philosopher-king **geometry,** since 'the knowledge at which geometry aims is knowledge of the eternal, and not of anything perishing and transient'. Geometry will lead one to discover necessary truths about universals such as lines, squares, triangles and circles. When one discovers such truths not from looking at pictures or diagrams, but solely from ideas, then one will have acquired knowledge which can be demonstrated, and which is unchangeable. The pictures or diagrams may change, but the geometrical truths, depending only on the ideas, or the meaning of the terms, will not change.

Solid Geometry and Astronomy. From geometry the course of study proceeds to **solid geometry.** It is clear from what Plato says about this that very little research had been done in this field in his own day. However, he is convinced of the need to advance research in this area and to encourage his philosopher-kings to come nearer to the abstract Forms by proceeding from a study of two-dimensional figures to a study of those of three dimensions. This is a necessary preliminary to a study of **astronomy,** a study of the movements of solid bodies. The heavenly bodies may be the most perfect of **visible** things, but because they are **visible** they are greatly inferior to the true realities, the true objects of knowledge. But a study of their movements must be undertaken by the intellect rather than by the senses, so that such a study will again lead our philosopher-kings towards the unchanging, eternal truths.

Harmonics. The last stage of this course of studies is the study of **harmonics.** Just as the study of astronomy will help the philosopher-king to come nearer to abstract thought by starting from those things which are visible, so will a study of harmonics by starting from those things which are audible. Again the emphasis is not on a study of sounds themselves but on the relationships between them.

The Dialectic. The would-be philosopher-king is finally ready for the last and most important step—complete liberation from the shadows of the cave through the study of **dialectic.** Through this study one is not merely aware of, or familiar with, the Forms or universals—now one knows and understands them. Now one is able to recall completely the true, indubitable knowledge within oneself.

What does the study of dialectic consist in? Socrates pointed out that one could only answer this question accurately if one had already reached complete understanding. Negatively, the difference between the study of mathematics and that of dialectic can be briefly indicated, and positively its general characteristics can be stated. But the actual content of dialectic is what each person would know when he finally obtained real knowledge, 'when a person starts on the discovery of the absolute (i.e., Forms or Platonic Ideas) by the light of reason only, and without any assistance of sense, and perseveres until by pure intelligence he arrives at the perception of the absolute good'. Then 'he at last finds himself at the end of the intellectual world'.

Mathematics and Dialectic. The difference between dialectic and the various branches of mathematics is that the latter are based upon assumptions and hypotheses which the mathematician takes for granted without examining them to find out why they are true. The Forms or universals are employed, but the mathematician assumes their characteristics, without being able to explain what their nature is, or why they have it. Thus for example, in arithmetic, it is assumed that when equal quantities are added to equal quantities, the results are equal. (e.g., if $A = B$, and $C = D$, then $A + C = B + D$.) When Socrates asked the mathematicians what 'equality' meant, and how they knew that assumptions like these were true, he discovered they did not know, but had accepted a great many hypotheses from which they developed their subject matter. In the dialogue, *Theatetus*, in a discussion with one of the greatest of the Greek geometers, Socrates showed that he did not understand the basic concepts, and had never questioned or examined the basic assumptions of the subject. To this extent, then, mathematics is only what Socrates called 'dreams about reality'. It is not knowledge in the full sense.

If, on the other hand, one examined one's hypotheses and assumptions and concepts, until one had arrived at full and complete understanding of them, then one would be involved in the study of dialectic. **Mathematical studies prepare one for this understanding** by providing some facility in dealing with Forms or universals. But the last step, that of **understanding and grasping the nature of Platonic Ideas, is the work of the dialectic.**

> Then dialectic, and dialectic alone, goes directly to the first principle, and is the only science which does away with hypotheses in order to make her ground secure; the eye of the soul, which is literally buried in an outlandish slough, is by her gentle aid lifted upwards; and she uses as handmaids and helpers in the work of conversion, the sciences which we have been discussing (i.e., the various branches of mathematics).

The way to obtain complete and true knowledge, according to Plato, is, first, to give up any reliance upon sense information and turn instead to examining the intelligible world through the aid of one's reasoning power only. When one turns away from the sensory world, one begins to discover the Forms or universals in one's own mind. To become used to examining the world of ideas, one first learns to manipulate and relate various ideas in the light of several assumptions and hypotheses—those of the different branches of mathematics. When one is finally able to examine and understand the Forms or universals, and grasp their nature, then one has arrived at real knowledge, full recollection of the Platonic Ideas which are within oneself, and have always been there.

Appearance and Reality. To the question, what would one know upon acquiring this type of knowledge, Plato replied that one would know the real world and not merely the 'shadows' or 'images'. The Platonic Ideas, for him, are not mere items in one's mind—they are real things, which exist eternally, without change, apart from the visible, physical world. **Just as sense information is considered illusory by Plato, so are the objects that we encounter in our sense experience.** The real, the important, the valuable objects of this world are those that we discover when we have real knowledge. Thus Plato conceived of the universe as divided between **appearance and reality,** and our information about it as divided between **opinion and knowledge.** We can only have opinions about the world of appearance, but our souls can have true knowledge about the real world, the world of Platonic Ideas.

Plato claimed that we can possess knowledge in the strict sense, that is, knowledge of which we can be absolutely certain, but such knowledge is different from the sort of information in which we are usually interested. Knowledge in this strict sense can be obtained about universals or Platonic Ideas, but only through the arduous means of forcing one's 'memory' through an extended study of mathematics. When one becomes aware of the Platonic Ideas, the experience of knowing them makes one completely certain—that is, incapable of being wrong. But such knowledge, which seems to be guaranteed solely by the experience of having it, is nevertheless limited. What we know thereby is, according to Plato, **the real world, the world of Forms or universals. The visible world can never really be known.** The Forms which it partakes of, and which are copied in the shadowy appearances always before us, can be known; but we cannot know, in this strong sense of 'know', the world of shadows, since they are not the Forms, but merely reflections of them, often inaccurate ones. Our best knowledge—actually, our only complete and true knowledge—is that discovered through the study of dialectic—our knowledge of Platonic Ideas. Mathematics, the next highest, is not yet complete knowledge, but it does deal with the Forms. (Sciences like physics—Plato thought —could not involve true knowledge, since physics would be a study of the world of shadows, the changing world of appearance.)

DESCARTES' THEORY OF KNOWLEDGE

If we turn from Plato to a much later theory of knowledge, that of Descartes, we find another **positive theory claiming that we are capable of discovering absolutely true knowledge.** Descartes' views about the nature, source and basis of our knowledge in many ways resemble those of Plato.

The Quest for Certainty. At the beginning of this discussion, we examined Descartes' test for the reliability of our knowledge, and saw the devastating results he achieved in showing that *all* of our ordinary information—including scientific and even mathematical information—is open to challenge. Descartes' point in proposing such a catastrophic test was not just to introduce doubts about everything: 'I did not imitate the sceptics, who doubt only for the sake of doubting, and pretend that they are always uncertain. On the contrary, my purpose was only to obtain good ground for assurance for myself, and to reject the quicksand and mud so that I might find the rock or clay.' Descartes was seeking an absolutely certain basis for all knowledge. He felt that such a foundation could be secure only if one had first used his test in order to eliminate anything that might possibly be false or doubtful. Descartes writes:

> I shall go on setting aside everything which might, in the slightest degree, be supposed to be doubtful, just as if I had found out that it was completely false; and I shall continue to follow in this path until I find something which is certain, or at least, if I am unable to do anything else, until I have learned that it is certain that there is nothing in the world that is certain.

The Certainty of Existence. In this manner Descartes carried on his test in search of some information which would be indubitable and certain. If he could find such knowledge, he could use it as a starting-point for justifying the entire structure of human knowledge. After having cast doubt on our sense information, our scientific information, and on mathematics, Descartes continued his quest until he found exactly the kind of certainty for which he sought.

> I was convinced that there was nothing in the entire world, that there was no heaven, no earth, that there were no minds, nor any bodies. Was I not then also convinced that I did not exist? Not in the least. It was certain that I myself existed since I convinced myself of something (or just because I thought of something). But there is some kind of a deceiver, who is very powerful and very cunning, and who always uses his ingenuity in order to deceive me. Then, for certain, I exist also if he is deceiving me, and let him deceive me as much as he wishes, he can never make me be nothing as long as I think that I am something. So that, after having considered this well, and having carefully examined everything, we have to arrive at the definite conclusion that this proposition: 'I am, I exist' has to be true every time that I utter it, or that I mentally think about it.

'I Think, Therefore I Am.' The only piece of information which Descartes found had to be true was **'I exist.'** Whenever I think about it or try to conceive, according to Descartes' test, how it could possibly be false, I realize that in order to think about it, or in order to perform the test, **I must be.** No matter what the alleged 'deceiver' may do, no matter how hard he may try to deceive me, he cannot deceive me into thinking that I am, if in fact I actually do not exist. If I think, Descartes insists, then I can be absolutely positive that I exist. As soon as I try to conceive of any condition under which **'I think, therefore I am,'** (or in its famous Latin form, *cogito, ergo sum*) may possibly be false, I am completely assured that I exist. Any attempt to doubt or deny this is still another thought which confirms and assures me that I must exist in order to think. No matter how hard I try to disprove the statement 'I think, therefore I am,' as soon as I *think*, the truth of the statement has been demonstrated again.

Perhaps, one way of underlining Descartes' point is to consider the following story. A famous American philosopher, MORRIS RAPHAEL COHEN, was reported to have engaged in a discussion with a student after class. Professor Cohen had been teaching Descartes to his class and had developed all the reasons for doubting that have been outlined earlier in this discussion. Then he sent the students home to read Descartes' *Meditations*. The next day, according to the story, a very haggard student, unshaven, eyes bloodshot, came to Professor Cohen after class and said that he was very worried. He had been up all night studying and thinking about the assignment, trying to decide whether he really existed. 'Professor Cohen,' he said very anxiously, 'tell me, please tell me, do I exist?' Professor Cohen considered the question and then answered, 'And who wants to know?'

In any case, Descartes was convinced that he had finally discovered a truth that 'was so certain and so assured that all the most extravagant arguments brought forward by the sceptics were incapable of shaking it'. He hoped that, by examining this one absolutely certain truth, it might be possible to discover a rule or criterion by which to judge the truth of other statements.

> I am certain that I am a thing that thinks; but then do I not also know what is required to make me certain of a truth? Certainly in this fundamental knowledge, there is nothing that convinces me of its truth, except the clear and distinct perception of that which I assert, which would not, indeed, be sufficient to assure me that what I say is true, if it could ever happen that something which I conceived so clearly and distinctly could be false. And, therefore, it seems to me that I already am able to establish as a general rule that all things which I conceive very clearly and distinctly are true.

Descartes' contention is that by inspecting the one truth ('I think, therefore I am') we can discover a rule or criterion about *all* truths. Why am I so certain that 'I think, therefore I am' is true? According to Descartes, the only feature of this statement which convinces me that it is true, is that I clearly and distinctly see, or understand, what is being said. If this **clarity and distinctness** are the only conditions that produce my conviction, and they are not *general* conditions which all truths must have, then I might be mistaken in this case. If clarity and distinctness are not the standards or criteria of truth, and they are all that indicate that 'I think, therefore I am' is true, then that assertion may actually be false. Therefore, the argument concludes, **clarity and distinctness must be the marks of truth, the distinguishing characteristics by which you can tell the true from the false.** Hence the general rule can be formulated, 'Whatever is clearly and distinctly conceived is true.'

Clarity and Distinctness. But what are these characteristics of clarity and distinctness? In a somewhat baffling section of his *Principles of Philosophy*, Descartes gave as clear and distinct an explanation of what clarity and distinctness are as one can find in his works. The section reads as follows:

> What a clear and distinct perception is. There are even some people who, in their entire life, perceive nothing so accurately as to be able to judge of it properly. For the knowledge on which a certain and uncontestable judgment can be formed, ought not only to be clear, but distinct as well. I call that clear which is present and apparent to an attentive mind, just as we say that we see objects clearly when, being present to the perceiving eye, they operate on it with sufficient strength. But the distinct is that which is so precise and different from everything else that it contains nothing within itself but what is clear.

At first glance, this explanation may not seem to help very much; but careful consideration may aid in grasping Descartes' point. Apparently, an experience or a thought is clear if it is **so forceful, that we cannot avoid being aware of it.** The illustrations Descartes offered of a clear idea fall roughly into two types—one of **vivid sense experiences,** such as a toothache, and the other of **thoughts,** such as mathematical ideas, or mental activities like thinking, wishing, and so on. In both types, the mind is made aware of something either **mental or sensory.** But, as we are told soon afterwards, while an idea can be clear without being distinct, the reverse cannot occur. An idea that is clear, but not distinct, is an experience that is so vivid or forceful that we cannot avoid being aware of it; but at the same time we are not certain of *what* we are experiencing. The example which Descartes employed, in this connection is that of the toothache. The experience is clear. One is forced to be aware of it. Nevertheless, one is not certain of *what* the ache is, or *where* it is. One cannot tell whether the pain is in the tooth, or in the mind. (In terms of Descartes' theory of the relation of mind and body, which was examined in Chapter III (see pages 97–9), he was convinced that the pain could not be in the physical tooth, but only in the mind.) What is lacking here is an ability to distinguish what the experience is, from anything else in the world. If one could accomplish this, that is, **so define the experience that it could not possibly be confused with anything else, then it would be distinct as well as clear.** On the other hand, any idea which we could so define would of necessity also be clear, since in order to be able to distinguish it from anything else, we would have to be intensely aware of the idea.

Extensions of Certainty. Pursuing further the notion of clear and distinct ideas, Descartes asked what else is true besides the truth that I am a thinking being. In the course of this investigation, he developed a theory about the universe we can know with complete certainty, a theory which in the end would provide further justification for his criterion of true knowledge. In order to complete this discussion of his theory of knowledge, we shall briefly state the remaining argument of his *Meditations*.

Innate Ideas. When I examine my ideas in order to find which of them are clear and distinct, Descartes claimed, I discover that most of them are either unclear or indistinct, and that they either come from experiences I have had, or they have been invented by myself. These include ideas such as those of the sun, or mermaids, of the Cathedral of Notre Dame in Paris, and of goblins. In addition to such ideas, Descartes insisted that there is another type called **innate ideas,** which can come neither from experience, nor can they be constructed or invented in my imagination. As we shall see shortly, these innate ideas are the ones that are really clear and distinct.

God. The kinds of idea that Descartes believed must be innate are those of **mathematical objects,** like the idea of a circle, and also, and most important for his argument, **the idea of a Perfect Being, God.** These ideas have properties that do not appear in our experience. No circle that we see is perfectly round. But the one that we can think about, is. We ourselves are not perfect enough. Descartes claimed, to invent the sort of perfection that appears in some of our ideas, especially that of God. We are merely finite, temporal creatures, and yet we have an idea of an infinite and eternal God. How then, Descartes asked, can we create concepts of properties, which we neither discover in our experience, nor in ourselves? From such reasoning, he concluded that mathematical ideas and the idea of God must be of a special category, called 'innate', which must be implanted in us by some agency other than ourselves and other than the events of our lives.

Developing the concept of a Perfect Being. Descartes concluded that this idea can only be caused by something that had at least the same perfections as the idea itself exhibited. The idea is that of 'a substance that is infinite, eternal, immutable, independent, all-knowing, all-powerful, and by which I myself and everything else, if anything else does exist, have been created'. I do not have properties like these to make use of in inventing an idea, and in my experience I never see anything with such perfection. Therefore, the idea of a Perfect Being must come from something that is at least as perfect as the idea. Hence, Descartes reasoned, there must be a God, who has created me, and who has implanted in me the idea of a Perfect Being.

Further Certainties. Having now established two truths, 'I think, therefore I am,' and 'God exists,' Descartes searched for still further certainties. 'It seems to me that I have now found a road that will lead us from contemplating the true God (in whom all the wonders of science and wisdom are contained), to knowledge of the other objects of the world.' The first stage along this road is to realize that if God is a Perfect Being, then He is incapable of deceiving human beings. Fraud and deception, Descartes insisted, are imperfections, and hence cannot be characteristics of a perfect being.

This discovery—on the basis of the clear and distinct idea of God —that the Perfect Being cannot be a deceiver, guarantees to Descartes that God is not, and cannot be, the evil demon he had envisaged earlier. If God is not that, then a great deal of the information that had earlier been considered suspect, can now be considered reliable. All that is needed is to find out what God, the Non-Deceiver, wants and makes us to believe is true. Since God cannot deceive us, we can place complete faith in the knowledge He gives us.

From an analysis of our rational faculties, Descartes found that the only **judgments we are forced to make** are those regarding clear and distinct ideas. We are compelled to assent to any clear and distinct ideas and to believe that whatever is clear and distinct is true. Since the all-powerful God forces this upon us, we cannot be mistaken when we believe that something that we clearly and distinctly conceive is true, because God cannot be a deceiver. On the other hand, we can withhold our judgment with regard to matters that are unclear and indistinct. God does not force us to come to any conclusions in this area; if we do, it is *our* responsibility, not His. Therefore, with respect to such ideas, we have no guarantee that what we believe is true. **The faculty of judgment functions reliably in relation to the clear and distinct innate ideas that God has implanted in us.** But since we are imperfect creatures, we insist on using our faculties beyond this range, and judge matters about which we have no assurance. Therefore, we make mistakes when we misuse our faculties. But, we cannot make mistakes when we use them as God intends and forces us to do.

Some examples may help here. According to Descartes, God has given us clear and distinct mathematical ideas. When we examine our ideas of '2' and '3' and '5' we find that it is clear and distinct that $2 + 3 = 5$. Since God has given us the ideas and the judging faculty, and has forced this belief upon us, and since He cannot be a deceiver, then '$2 + 3 = 5$' must be true. But when we see a group of colour patches that look like some people walking, it is not clear and distinct that these are people, that this may not be part of a dream—hence we are not forced to judge that what we see is 'some people'. If we judge in this case, it is at our own risk, since we have no Divine guarantee.

. . . I have found the source of falsity and error. And certainly there cannot be any other than that which I have explained, since as long as I restrain my will within the limits of my knowledge that it makes no judgment on any matters except those which are clearly and distinctly conceived by the understanding, I can never be deceived. Every clear and distinct conception is certainly something, and therefore cannot come from nothing, but must necessarily come from God—God, I say, who is supremely perfect, and cannot be the cause of any error. Thus, we must conclude that such a conception or judgment is true.

The Argument for Objective Reality. Of what, then, can we be certain? We can be certain of our own existence, of God's and of God's guarantee that whatever is clearly and distinctly conceived is true. On this basis, Descartes claimed, we can be positive that the entire realm of mathematical knowledge is true, since it deals only with clear and distinct innate ideas. This knowledge is true whether I am awake or asleep, since it is clear and distinct in either case, and God would not deceive me. But this mathematical knowledge only gives me truths about concepts in my mind. Is it possible that I can also be certain that there is a world outside me, and that certain things are true about it?

By an elaborate argument which we shall not examine, Descartes sought to establish the reliability of our natural belief that there is a world outside our minds, and that our experience consists of ideas which come from this world. The basic reason offered is that since the belief in an external world is a natural one, God would be deceiving us unless it were true. Since God cannot be a deceiver, there must be an external physical world. The properties that we can safely attribute to it are those which we find in our clear and distinct ideas of bodies—namely, that they are extended, that geometrical and arithmetical truths apply to them, and so on.

Although Descartes began with the most extreme doubts about knowledge and belief, he concluded with an extensive theory about the degree of certain knowledge we can possess, claiming that we can be absolutely certain of our own existence, of God's, of God's not deceiving us, and hence of all clear and distinct knowledge, including all mathematical knowledge which can also be applied to physical objects as well as to mental ones. On the basis of clear and distinct innate ideas, we can possess a wealth of certain knowledge. However, regarding matters that are not clear and distinct, such as our sense experience, we can never have complete certainty. We can know the laws of physical bodies in so far as they are mathematical relationships, but we cannot know with any certainty the indistinct or unclear features of the world (e.g., its colours, sounds, smells), which may be, for all we can tell, illusions or dreams. The world of innate ideas, the clear and distinct ideas that God implanted in us, provide all the certainty we can have, but it is *absolute* certainty. The method of doubt, the testing of our information by questioning it, enables us to distinguish what is certain from what is not. When we are done, Descartes claimed, we have a vast amount of certain knowledge about our clear and distinct ideas, some of which can be applied to the external world, giving us the basis for certain knowledge of nature. If we avoid judgments based on unclear and indistinct ideas, we will never make any mistakes.

Rationalist Theories of Knowledge. Theories of knowledge like those of Plato and Descartes are called 'rationalistic' because they assert that by employing certain procedures of **reason alone** we can discover knowledge in the strongest sense, knowledge that can under no circumstances possibly be false. Usually such rationalistic theories (and both of the theories presented here do so) maintain that we cannot find any absolutely certain knowledge in sense experience, but have to seek for it only in the **realm of the mind.** Both Plato and Descartes claim that true knowledge is already within us in the form of innate ideas which we do not acquire, but are born with. It is further maintained by rationalists that what we know as certain by various rationalistic procedures *is* the real world. The world that cannot be known with certainty is generally judged to be an illusory or unreal or unimportant world.

Criticism of 'Rationalist' Philosophy. The claims of the rationalists to have discovered such certain truths have met with objections. Opponents have challenged philosophers like Plato and Descartes, denying that we ever actually possess such certainty or that there are any 'Platonic Ideas' or 'innate', 'clear' and 'distinct' ideas. (In fact, a seventeenth-century French sceptic wrote some large books offering hundreds of reasons why the statement 'I think, therefore I am' may not be at all certain.)

Sceptical Criticism. Sceptical opponents of the rationalists suggested that what philosophers like Plato and Descartes were offering as certain knowledge, was really nothing more than their personal fantasy. The vast range of opinions that rationalistic philosophers presented as indubitable truths have made many people extremely suspicious. The alleged certain knowledge might well be mere beliefs taken much too seriously by those who held them. The worlds of 'Platonic Ideas' or of Descartes' 'innate ideas' are neither visible nor tangible. The evidence for the existence of such worlds has not struck all philosophers with the force and conviction that it had for Plato and Descartes. Hence, many thinkers of a sceptical turn of mind have rejected rationalist claims of complete certainty.

This opposition to the doctrine of certain knowledge is grounded in the development of human knowledge, and the revolutions in thought that have occurred throughout history. When we examine critically the matters that were regarded as assured truths in Plato's day, and compare them with our modern knowledge, it is difficult to understand how the science of dialectic can lead to certain truths already existing in the mind. The advance of scientific knowledge and the changes in scientific theory over the centuries have made many thinkers reluctant to consider anything an absolutely certain and permanent truth.

Rationalists like Plato and Descartes might claim that the development of scientific theory does not really discredit their theories since science deals only with the visible world, which can never, according to them, be known with absolute certainty. The certain knowledge of the rationalists deals with a different realm entirely—the real world of 'pure ideas'—and this world never changes, nor does our knowledge of it change. When one has grasped a truth about this 'real world', it is true for all time.

But the opponents argue that, first of all, there has been a conflict of opinion among the rationalists as to what is true about the real world. The history of philosophy from Plato to Descartes does not inspire confidence in the claims of any particular rationalist—almost every truth that has been asserted with complete assurance by one philosopher has been disputed by another who, with just as much assurance, has advanced contrary claims. Almost every truth concerning the real world that has been held by a rationalist to be self-evident, has proved to be open to some question or doubt. When one examines the alleged 'self-evident', 'absolutely certain' truths of such rationalists as

Aristotle, St. Augustine, Descartes, and others, one sees that these propositions are actually very much open to question.

Even in an area of human knowledge that various rationalists have used as a model—mathematics—there is some basis for disputing claims of absolute truth. The history of mathematics indicates that developments and changes have taken place in our mathematical knowledge, and that some theorems that were regarded as true have had to be modified or discarded. Even today mathematicians disagree as to which branches of the subject, and which theorems, are really certain. No doubt there has been less diversity of opinion here than in any other area of human inquiry, and hence mathematics has always served as the model for the complete assurance rationalist philosophers have sought. But the fact that disputes and revisions are possible, tends to support the doubters, and in any case, as we saw in Chapter I (page 6), not all knowledge is analogous to mathematical knowledge.

Non-Euclidean Geometries. In particular, an important modern development has made most theoreticians of mathematics doubtful of rationalist claims. In the early nineteenth century it was discovered that various alternative systems of geometry could be developed in which different theorems would be true. If one replaced the axiom of Euclidean geometry which stated that one, and only one, line could be drawn parallel to another line through a given point, with another axiom which stated that either *no* line could be drawn parallel to another line through a given point, or that an *unlimited* number of lines could be drawn parallel to a given line through a given point, then perfectly consistent systems of geometry could be constructed. But these alternative systems of geometry, the so-called **Non-Euclidean geometries,** contain theorems which are not true in Euclidean geometry. If one asks, which of these geometries contains the truths about the real world?—there does not seem to be a satisfactory answer. Each of the geometries is as logical, as consistent as the others. The theorems in each seem as true as those in the others. To call one set of theorems absolutely true, and the others not true, appears to be completely arbitrary and indefensible. Thus, the development of alternative systems of geometry has cast grave doubts on the claim that mathematics contains a unique set of absolutely certain truths about the real world.

Certainty and Probability. Besides the conflict of theories and the developments in science and mathematics, one of the major reasons for doubting the claims that human beings can possess 'certain' knowledge has been the question of **whether we ever need or use absolutely certain knowledge.** The information that we employ for ordinary purposes, the critics point out, is not indubitable. We manage to live our lives without truths which under no possible conditions could be false. With the aid of scientific information about the visible world, which may some day prove false or inadequate, we resolve the questions which confront us. Plato and Descartes pointed out the dangers of basing our actions upon information which may not be completely reliable; nevertheless, the opponents claim, for all ordinary purposes, all that we seem to possess and employ is *probable* knowledge. If there really is 'certain' knowledge, it does not appear to be required for the ordinary purpose of life, nor does it even seem to be sought by people in the quest for answers to their questions.

EMPIRICAL PHILOSOPHY

Owing to doubts about the rationalist theory of knowledge, many philosophers have searched for a theory of knowledge which would be consistent with ordinary human behaviour. Instead of seeking absolutely true knowledge about an alleged real world, they have tried to discover where we do *in fact* get our information from, and what degree of reliability it *actually* possesses. Rather than rejecting the data we acquire through our senses in favour of some completely certain knowledge about a non-visible realm, **these philosophers have begun with our sense experience as the source and basis of what we know, and have tried to construct an account of knowledge in terms of sense experience.** This type of theory, which attempts to explain knowledge in terms of sense experience, is called **empiricism.**

The Social Context of Empiricism. The empirical approach to the problem of knowledge has usually developed in countries where the dominant interests have been practical and worldly ones. Thus, empiricism has been the prevailing theory of knowledge in England and, to some extent and in various forms, in the United States, but has played a relatively minor role in the intellectual history of other countries. The modern theory of empiricism grew out of the philosophical struggles in seventeenth-century England, at a time when that country was rapidly developing, commercially and industrially. Men were just beginning to realize the possibilities that lay in controlling and utilizing the physical world. The great English scientists such as Robert Boyle, Robert Hooke, and Isaac Newton were developing the basis of our modern scientific and technological world.

In such an atmosphere, many philosophers came to regard the age-old quest for absolute knowledge as fruitless; information offered by the leading British scientists seemed to be useful and important. Over and over again, one finds the scientists of the time proclaiming that their aim is not to discover the real, indubitable truths of the universe, but **only to develop probable hypotheses about the world around us.** With the tremendous advances that resulted from this new knowledge, some philosophers felt that one had to abandon the search of the rationalists, and work out a theory of knowledge more in keeping with the **actual achievements of the scientists.**

So, in seventeenth-century England, one finds a few brave thinkers striking out along new lines, to discover a theory of knowledge in keeping with the new knowledge discovered by the practising scientists of the time. These philosophers in quest of a different point of view were, by and large, not professional philosophers, but men of affairs who were not concerned with the classical problems which baffled philosophers, or over which philosophers had disputed over the centuries. Starting with SIR FRANCIS BACON (1561–1626) who was Lord Chancellor under King James I, the leading lights of the 'new philosophy' in England were, almost without exception, men removed from the ivory towers of the academic world, men who gained their fame in the world of practical affairs.

JOHN LOCKE

Bacon was the first important proponent of the empirical approach in seventeenth-century England. Later in the century, JOHN LOCKE (1632-1704), a medical doctor by profession, tried to work out an explanation of our knowledge in terms of sense experience in his *Essay Concerning Human Understanding*. In this work Locke argued that our knowledge comes to us through our senses and that we have no innate ideas. Systematically he attempted to show how various concepts or ideas come from or are built up from different kinds of experience, starting from the simple sense awareness of one quality, such as yellow, to the most elaborate compounds of qualities, such as a city.

By examining the nature and origin of our knowledge in these terms, Locke believed that he could greatly aid mankind in realizing what sorts of thing they could actually know about, and what sort of assurance they could have.

If, by this inquiry into the nature of the understanding, I can discover the powers thereof, how far they reach, to what things they are in any degree proportionate, and where they fail us; I suppose it may be of use to prevail with the busy mind of man to be more cautious in meddling with things exceeding its comprehension; to stop when it is at the utmost extent of its tether; and to sit down in a quiet ignorance of those things, which upon examination, are found to be beyond the reach of our capacities.

Denial of Innate Ideas. When we examine our information, Locke insisted, we discover first that we possess no innate knowledge. There are no principles or ideas that we have any reason to believe we have prior to, or independent of, our sense experience. The examples which previous rationalists had offered of truths that were implanted in the mind, Locke claimed, are not actually known by all human beings. Neither children nor idiots are aware of these alleged innate truths. To say that these truths are in their minds, even though they do not know them, is nonsense. 'To say a notion is imprinted on the mind, and yet at the same time to say that the mind is in ignorance of it, and never yet took notice of it, is to make this impression nothing.'

The 'White Paper'. Instead, Locke maintained, if everyone will look at his own observations and experience, he will realize that originally his mind was just a 'white paper, void of all characters, without any ideas'. All the many things that anybody knows about or thinks about come from experience. All of our information is based upon our experiences, either through our senses, or by reflecting on what goes on in our minds. Thus, according to Locke, there are just two sources of our knowledge: one is sensation, and the other is reflection.

Let any one examine his own thoughts, and thoroughly search into his understanding; and then let him tell me, whether all the original ideas he has there are any other than of the objects of his senses, or of the operations of his mind, considered as objects of his reflection; and how great a mass of knowledge soever he imagines to be lodged there, he will, upon taking a strict view, see that he has not any idea in his mind, but what one of these two have imprinted, though perhaps with infinite variety compounded and enlarged by the understanding.

Simple Ideas. In order to justify his empirical claims, Locke patiently tried to show how all our information derives either from experiences of reflection or of sensation. The most basic elements of our knowledge are what Locke called **simple ideas. These are ideas that are not compounded of any other elements.** As examples of such simple ideas, Locke offered the experience of the taste of sugar, the smell of a rose, the whiteness of a lily, or the coldness of a piece of ice. These simple ideas are presented to us only in sensation and reflection. The mind has the power, we are told, to store up, to repeat, and to combine these basic ideas, once it has experienced them.

Certainty. In the course of his lengthy *Essay Concerning Human Understanding*, Locke tried valiantly to show how the various parts of our knowledge come from different experiences of sensation or reflection. A basic difficulty that he ran into, which has plagued empirical philosophers ever since, was that of showing which of our ideas are real, that is, which parts of our information 'have a conformity with the real being and existence of things'. We have a great many ideas in our minds which we do not believe relate to anything that actually exists in the world, such as our ideas of mermaids, unicorns, and the like. How do we tell just from the examination of our ideas which ones of them ought to be considered as real, and which are only the result of our imagination, or of the mind's ability to combine various experiences it has had in the past? The answer Locke gives to this question enables him to work out a theory about the character and reliability of knowledge

Primary and Secondary Qualities. Locke divided the sensations that we have into two groups—**the ideas of primary qualities, and the ideas of secondary qualities.** The primary qualities are those items in our experience which must belong to the objects that we are experiencing, whereas the secondary qualities 'in truth are nothing in the objects themselves, but powers to produce various sensations in us by their primary qualities'. For example, according to Locke's account, size and shape are primary qualities, while the colour that we see in objects is not. The colour is the result of certain conditions, or as he called them, 'powers' in the objects, which act upon our minds so that we see colours, when the actual objects that we are experiencing do not, in fact, have any colour in them. The distinction that Locke was trying to draw is that between the **scientific description** of an object, what properties scientists report an object has, and our **ordinary experience** of the same object.

The particular bulk, number, figure, and motion of the parts of fire, or snow, are really in them, whether any one's senses perceive them or no; and therefore they may be called real qualities, because they really exist in those bodies; but light, heat, whiteness, or coldness, are no more really in them than sickness or pain is in manna. Take away the sensation of them; let not the eyes see light or colours, nor the ears hear sounds; let the palate not taste, nor the nose smell; and all colours, tastes, odours, and sounds, as they are such particular ideas, vanish and cease, and are reduced to their causes, *i.e.* bulk, figure, and motion of parts.

If, then, there are certain qualities, called primary ones, which we experience and which belong to objects, how do we get our ideas of objects? Locke claimed that when we observe that several **simple ideas constantly appear together, and always seem to be conjoined, we presume that these ideas belong to one thing.** We are unable to conceive of these simple ideas existing without belonging to, or being attached to, some one thing. Thus, we suppose that there must be a substance, or a substratum, something which either holds all the qualities together, or which gives rise to them. When we experience the qualities together that we ordinarily call 'gold' (the colour, the hardness, and other qualities), Locke claimed that we also suppose that there is a 'substance' or 'substratum' to which these qualities belong, or from which they come, something that underlies all these qualities and holds them together. We can give no clear or precise notion of what these substances are, except in terms of the qualities that belong to them. If one is pressed to give an exact description of a substance, all one can say, Locke pointed out, is that one does not know what it is, but one still finds that one must suppose that there is something that the various elements of our experience belong to. To make clear what the type of difficulty is that occurs when one tries to describe a substance, Locke compared it to the case of 'the Indian before mentioned, who, saying that the world was supported by a great elephant, was asked what the elephant rested on? to which his answer was, a great tortoise. But being again pressed to know what gave support to the broad-backed tortoise, replied, something, he knew not what.' On this rather vague and hazy basis, we attribute various elements of our experience to different substances, either as that to which they belong, in the case of primary qualities, or that by which they are caused, in the case of secondary qualities.

Kinds of Knowledge. But how much knowledge can we have by means of sensation and reflection, and how reliable will it be? The fourth book of Locke's *Essay* is devoted to trying to work out an answer to these questions. All of our knowledge deals with various ideas that we have acquired through experience in the course of our lives. Knowledge is the result of the examination of ideas to see if they agree or disagree in some respect. The first sort of knowledge is achieved by the inspection of two or more ideas to see if they are **identical or different.** Thus, for example, one could compare the ideas of 'white' and black', and see immediately that they are different.

The second sort of knowledge about ideas deals with the co-existence of two or more ideas, that is, the discovery that **two or more ideas belong together or go together.** This usually amounts to finding out that these ideas are parts of, or are caused by, the same substance. A third kind of knowledge about our ideas is the discovery that two or more ideas are **related together in some manner.** The fourth and last type of knowledge is the discovery of whether or not any of our ideas are **experiences of something that exists outside of our minds, that is, if they are ideas of some real existences.**

> Within these four sorts of agreement or disagreement is, I suppose, contained all the knowledge we have, or are capable of: for all the enquiries that we can make concerning any of our ideas, all that we know or can affirm concerning them, is, that it is, or is not, the same with some other; that it does, or does not, always coexist with some other idea in the same subject; that it has this or that relation to some other idea; or that it has a real existence without [i.e., outside of—A. V. K.] the mind.

Intuitive Knowledge. If these are all the different kinds of knowledge that we can have, according to Locke, how much knowledge can we have of each type, and how certain will it be? The greatest degree of assurance that we can have is when our knowledge is intuitive, that is, when simply by looking at two or more ideas, we see immediately that something is true about them. 'This part of knowledge is irresistible, and like bright sunshine, forces itself immediately to be perceived, as soon as ever the mind turns its view that way; and leaves no room for hesitation, doubt or examination, but the mind is presently filled with the clear light of it.' This type of complete certainty, Locke claimed, we can have about truths like 'white is not black', 'a circle is not a triangle', and '$3 = 2 + 1$', which intuitively we see are true.

Demonstration. Unfortunately not all of the agreements and disagreements between ideas can be known in this intuitively certain manner. Sometimes when we merely consider certain ideas together, we are unable to tell if they do or do not have something in common, and must, instead, first connect the ideas we are comparing with some others before we can come to any knowledge. This process Locke called **demonstration.** When we go through several steps in order to reach a conclusion about the agreement or disagreement of one idea with another, we do not immediately see or recognize a truth. Instead we discover the truth only indirectly. But, Locke insisted, the type of assurance we acquire through reasoning is just a string of intuitions. Each step in a proof is seen immediately by the mind to be certain, and so, if each part of a demonstration is certain, the conclusion will also be. However, it is often the case that in carrying out the chain of steps we leave something out, or do not notice that there is no intuitive certainty between some of the steps. Because of these sorts of error, Locke pointed out, we cannot rely on demonstrative knowledge with the same degree of assurance that we have in simple intuitions.

'Sensative' Knowledge. In a strict sense, Locke was willing to admit, only intuitions and demonstrations could give us knowledge we could be sure of. But, in addition to these two, there is another degree of assurance, which though not as certain, is still relied on by nearly everyone, and hence, ought to be included as a degree of knowledge also. This is what Locke called 'sensative' knowledge, **which assures us of the actual existence of particular things.** In spite of all the doubts raised by Descartes and the sceptics, we are still pretty sure that some of our experiences are of things that exist outside of our minds, while others are not.

But whether there be anything more than barely that idea in our minds, whether we can thence certainly infer the existence of any thing without us, which corresponds to the idea, is that whereof some men think there may be a question made; because men may have such ideas in their minds, when no such thing exists, no such object affects their senses. But yet here, I think, we are provided with an evidence, that puts us past doubting: for I ask any one, whether he be not invincibly conscious to himself of a different perception when he looks on the sun by day, and thinks on it by night; when he actually tastes wormwood, or smells a rose, or only thinks on that savour or odour? We as plainly find the difference there is between any idea revived in our minds by our own memory, and actually coming into our minds by our senses, as we do between any two distinct ideas.

Even though it may possibly be the case that nothing really exists outside of our minds, or that we may be dreaming all the time, or some other strange possibility, it is nonetheless true, Locke insisted, that there is a common-sense assurance that we all have by which we know about the existence of things outside of our mind. This type of assurance, though much weaker than that of intuition or demonstration, is our sensative knowledge. It may be false, but it is sufficient for our ordinary purposes.

With these three degrees of assurance or certainty, how much are we actually capable of knowing? First of all, we can only know about those matters of which we can have ideas. But, even regarding just the ideas that we can and do have, Locke observed, our knowledge is quite limited. We can 'intuit' or 'demonstrate' very little about the various ways in which ideas may agree or disagree. By means of sensative knowledge, we can only be sure of the existence outside of us of some of the ideas immediately present to the mind.

We can be sure, Locke claimed, intuitively whether any two ideas are identical or different. With regard to the coexistence of ideas, our knowledge is, however, sharply limited. Our only way of judging which ideas belong together is by the conjunctions that occur in our experience. From these we cannot tell which of our ideas have to take place together. Thus our knowledge about coexistence is limited to what we have already experienced. This is especially the case, Locke pointed out, in relation to the coexistence of primary and secondary qualities, because 'there is no discoverable connection between any secondary quality and those primary qualities which it depends on'.

Only through experience can we tell which objects will appear yellow to us, will taste sweet, and so on.

We are able to find out a great deal about the relation between different ideas, mostly in terms of mathematical ideas. Here, large bodies of knowledge have been developed. Locke believed that in addition to the mathematical disciplines, we can acquire a great deal of information about ethics and politics by examining the relations between ideas—for example, of the relations between the ideas of 'government', 'justice', 'liberty', and the like.

The Limitations of Knowledge. In what is probably the most important area of knowledge, we are most severely limited. When we examine what we can know about the real existence of things, Locke was willing to admit only one case that we can be intuitively certain of, namely, our own existence. In addition, we can have demonstrative knowledge of God's existence. For anything else, we can only have sensative knowledge, which extends only to the objects that are present to our senses. For those items for which we do not have even sensative knowledge, we can never be sure whether they have real existence. All we can do is accept the limitations to our knowledge, and rest content in our ignorance.

Since our knowledge of coexistence and real existence is limited, Locke concluded that a science, in the sense of absolutely necessary and true information, is not possible for either the physical world or the spiritual world, if all of our information is restricted to empirical elements which we have acquired from sensation or reflection. We can never discover, except from experience, what qualities occur together. But, from our experience, we never know enough to find out why these qualities have to occur together. We can never be absolutely sure that some things have to happen, and that others cannot happen. Therefore, any sciences that man can develop about the world must always fall short of complete certainty, and must be based only on his limited experience of the relationship between qualities previously experienced. Complete understanding of the natural world will, unfortunately, always be beyond the limits of our knowledge.

Thus, in Locke's empirical theory, knowledge is limited to the respects in which various ideas of ours agree or disagree. Perhaps, if we can only rely upon experience, it may actually be the case that we cannot know *anything* about what goes on outside of the ideas in our minds. As Locke put the possibility:

> I doubt not but my reader by this time may be apt to think, that I have been all this while only building a castle in the air; and be ready to say to me, 'to what purpose all this stir? Knowledge say you, is only the perception of the agreement or disagreement of our own ideas: but who knows what those ideas may be? Is there any thing so extravagant as the imaginations of men's brains? Where is the head that has no chimeras in it? Or, if there be a sober and wise man, what difference will there be, by your rules, between his knowledge and that of the most extravagant fancy in the world? They both have their ideas, and perceive their agreement and dis-

agreement one with another. If there be any difference between them, the advantage will be on the warm-headed man's side, as having the more ideas, and the more lively.'

External Reality. In order to prevent his empirical theory of knowledge from ending in the above-suggested conclusion (i.e., that what we call knowledge is just one man's opinion based on what goes on in his own mind), Locke attempted towards the end of his *Essay* to show that even with our limited information gained from experience, we have some basis for claiming that we know something about what goes on outside of our minds. His argument is that our knowledge of our own ideas is more than just our own imagination, and there is a conformity between our ideas and the real nature of things. How do we tell when our ideas really represent something outside of our minds? Locke's answer is first that we can be sure that all simple ideas represent something real. The mind, he insisted, is incapable of inventing simple ideas, since they cannot be formed from any other ideas that we already possess. 'From whence it follows, that simple ideas are no fictions of our fancies, but the natural and regular productions of things without us, really operating upon us.' If we cannot invent the simple ideas, then they must be the effect of something outside us. In the case of secondary qualities, we can be sure, Locke claimed, that these ideas are the results of some powers that external things have. In the case of primary qualities, these are not just ideas of ours, but also properties of objects as well. With respect to mathematical and moral studies, in which all of our knowledge consists of either intuitive or demonstrative truths, Locke claimed that this knowledge was about real objects if there happen to be actual triangles and squares, or property and justice, in the external world. From this, Locke concluded that 'Wherever we perceive the agreement or disagreement of any of our ideas, there is certain knowledge: and wherever we are sure those ideas agree with the reality of things, there is certain real knowledge.'

John Locke tried to work out a theory of knowledge which would show how all of our information comes from our experiences. If our knowledge is based on our sensations and reflections, Locke attempted to show that there were certain conditions under which we could be sure of what we know, and even sure that what we know applies to something outside of ourselves.

Conclusions and Criticism. In the course of working out his empirical theory of knowledge, and trying to show how knowledge derives from our sense experience, Locke revealed certain characteristics and difficulties of the empirical approach. In the first place, if all of our knowledge comes from experience, then a good deal of the knowledge that philosophers such as Plato and Descartes claimed that we had, or could have, would have to be considered as illusory or fictitious. The knowledge that depended upon Platonic Ideas or innate ideas, would have to be declared invalid, since such ideas do not appear in, or develop from, our sense experience. In general, an empirical theory of knowledge, Locke's work pointed out, would yield only limited results, in that those claims to knowledge which could not be justified in terms of our experiences would have to be discarded. All the beautiful pictures of what the world is 'really' like, which previous philosophers had presented, would have to be rejected as imaginative day-dreams or nonsense, if they could not be derived from experience. On the other hand, if Locke is right and they are imaginative day-dreams, then, of course, we should reject them.

Secondly, Locke's attempt to develop his theory of knowledge indicated that the empirical approach might engender certain difficulties. If all of our information is based upon the ideas that we acquire from experience, and our knowledge is about the agreement and disagreement of our ideas, how could we ever tell if our knowledge is actually about something outside of us? Locke claimed that we had to suppose that there is something called substance, or substratum, that our ideas, or at least some of them, belong to. By an examination of the nature of our ideas, he insisted, we could distinguish those that do in fact represent some actual features of this substance or substratum, and hence, discover some actual knowledge about the real world. But some of Locke's opponents pointed out that his 'way of ideas' made such knowledge-claims difficult to support, since all we had to go on were the ideas in our mind. The supposition that there is anything outside of us to which we can attribute ideas seemed to have no justification, if one adhered strictly to the empirical thesis that all of our knowledge comes from experience. The claim that by inspection of the ideas—and the agreements and disagreements among them —we can discover truths about the real world also seemed questionable. All our ideas appeared to be on the same level: they are all in our mind. Then, the opponents asked, how can we tell which to take seriously, which to use as a basis for knowledge about the world and which to discard as personal fancy or imagination? The attempt to work out these implications of the empirical theory of knowledge appeared in the works of two eighteenth-century philosophers, Bishop Berkeley and David Hume.

BISHOP GEORGE BERKELEY

GEORGE BERKELEY (1685-1753) was born and educated in Ireland. While he was a Fellow of Trinity College, Dublin, in his early twenties, young Berkeley worked out his philosophical theories, and wrote his two most important works, *A Treatise Concerning the Principles of Understanding*, 1710, and *Three Dialogues between Hylas and Philonous*, 1713. After failing to create much interest in his theories, he spent several years in such minor jobs as secretary and tutor. Then he became interested in founding a college in the New World, in Bermuda. In 1729, he went to America, living in Rhode Island for a couple of years. Although he never succeeded in his plan, he exerted significant influence on the development of institutions of higher education in America, especially at Yale, to which he gave money and a library, and at Columbia, whose first president was a disciple of Berkeley's. A few years after his return to England, Berkeley was appointed Bishop of Cloyne in Ireland and stayed there most of the rest of his life. One of his most intense interests in later life was trying to convince people of the virtues of tar water as a cure for many of the ills of mankind.

Berkeley's Philosophic System. The philosophical theory that Berkeley offered was intended, he wrote, 'to demonstrate the reality and perfection of human knowledge, the incorporeal nature of the soul, and the immediate providence of a Deity: in opposition to sceptics and atheists'. Part of the cause of these pernicious views, that is, scepticism and atheism, Berkeley charged, was due to the theories of John Locke and of many other philosophers before him. Locke and others had claimed that some of the ideas that we have are not reliable, while others give us true knowledge of real things. As soon as any doubts have been cast on the reliability of our sense information, 'Then', Berkeley wrote, 'we are insensibly drawn into uncouth paradoxes, difficulties, and inconsistencies, which multiply and grow upon us as we advance in speculation; till at length, having wandered through many intricate mazes, we find ourselves just where we were or, which is worse, sit down in a forlorn scepticism.' What makes all the trouble, Berkeley insisted, is that philosophers refuse to believe what everyone else does, and persist in distinguishing the real nature of things, from the experience of their senses. Even Locke, in separating primary and secondary qualities, and claiming that only the primary qualities really are qualities of actual substances, has developed a theory in which real things are different from the items of our sense experience. This sort of distinction leads to 'scepticism and paradoxes', and leaves philosophers spending their lives 'in doubting of those things which other men evidently know, and believing those things which they laugh at and despise'. The dangerous effect of this is 'that when men of less leisure see them who are supposed to have spent their whole time in the pursuits of knowledge profess an entire ignorance of all things, or advancing such notions as are repugnant to plain and commonly received principles, they will be tempted to entertain suspicions concerning the most important truths, which they had hitherto held sacred and unquestionable'.

Thus, Berkeley's thesis is that the theories of philosophers like Locke lead to paradoxes and doubts, which in turn produce a general scepticism. When the ordinary man sees what sort of odd theories the so-called wise philosophers advance, and sees that philosophers deny the most basic things that ordinary people believe, this will make him doubtful too. And, finally, when philosophers have engendered this sort of scepticism, this will lead to doubts even about religious truths. Hence, atheism will be the ultimate outcome.

Three Dialogues. In order to advance his claims by the most striking means, Berkeley wrote the *Three Dialogues*, in which a discussion takes place between Philonous, who represents Berkeley's views, and Hylas (which means 'matter'), representing the opposition. The first dialogue begins with Hylas saying that he has heard that Philonous is an extreme sceptic in that he holds that there is no such thing as material substance in the world. Philonous says that he certainly holds that opinion, but that it is neither sceptical nor opposed to ordinary common sense, and that he will show that it is the philosophers who believe that there is something called material substance, or matter, who are really the sceptics.

(A sceptic, we are told, is 'one who doubted of everything . . . or who denies the reality and truth of things'. Hylas, then, accuses his friend Philonous of denying the real existence of sensible things, or of pretending to know nothing about them. A 'sensible thing' is defined as a thing immediately perceived by the senses—that is, something seen, or heard, or felt directly in our immediate sense experience. Now Berkeley is ready to state his case.)

Does Matter Exist? What do we perceive immediately by our senses? Only colours and shapes, sounds, tastes, odours, tangible qualities, and the like. Then what constitutes the reality of sensible things besides their being perceived? Hylas, the believer in some sort of material substance, insists that the real existence of sensible things is independent of their being experienced. They exist 'distinct from, and without any relation to, their being perceived'. Then, Philonous suggests, consider the case of heat. On Hylas' theory, heat must exist outside of the mind, as something independent of our experience. But when we experience extreme heat, what we actually feel is a great pain, and no one believes that material substance contains pains. Hylas protests, and says that one has to distinguish between the pain that is in the mind, and the heat which is in the material object. Just try, Philonous suggests, putting your hand near a fire, and see if you feel two things, heat *and* pain, or only one thing, a pain. Hylas yields and is willing to admit that our sensible experience of extreme heat, a pain, exists only in the mind, and not in the object. Philonous immediately shows him that the same reasoning applies to all the various degrees of heat which are felt as either pleasant sensations of warmth, or as pain, and that Hylas certainly does not believe that there is either pleasure or pain in material objects. Further, Philonous points out, if one hand is warm, and the other cold, and they are put into a bowl of water at room temperature, the water will feel cold to one hand, and hot to the other. Hylas would not want to claim that both qualities, heat and cold, are in the same object, the water, at the same time. Hylas finally concedes 'that heat and cold are only sensations existing in our minds'.

Taste. But what about other qualities that we experience? Philonous shows Hylas that the same point can be applied to taste. Sweet and bitter tastes are experienced as different kinds of pleasure or pain. No one believes that sugar contains various pleasures, so that pleasant experience must be in the mind, rather than in the sugar. At this point Hylas suddenly thinks of a response to this sort of reasoning, much like a theory of Locke's, namely, that these qualities as perceived by us, are pleasures and pains, but as they exist in external objects they are something different. Philonous regards this new line of defence with complete scorn. We are talking about sensible things, that is, things which we immediately perceive by our senses.

Whatever other qualities, therefore, you speak of, as distinct from these, I know nothing of them, neither do they at all belong to the point in dispute. You may, indeed, pretend to have discovered certain qualities which you do not perceive, and assert those insensible qualities exist in fire and sugar. But what use can be made of this to your present purpose, I am at a loss to conceive. Tell me then once more, do you acknowledge that heat and cold, sweetness and bitterness (meaning those qualities which are perceived by the senses) do not exist without [i.e., outside of— R. H. P.] the mind?

Poor Hylas is crushed and yields.

Other Sensations. Then the same point is raised in connection with odours, and Hylas admits that they are just pleasant or painful sensations, and vary with different observers. Therefore, they are only in the mind. But when Philonous continues this line of reasoning into the subject of sounds, Hylas balks. Sounds, the noises that we hear, Hylas is willing to admit, are only sensations that we have. But, at the same time, he insists, there are sound waves which exist in the exterior physical world, apart from us. But, Philonous points out, this means that real sound, the sound waves, are never heard. Only noises are heard. The sensible thing that we perceive is noise. The sound wave we do not hear. So once again Hylas must admit that the sensible thing, the noise, exists in the mind; the 'real' thing, the sound wave, is not a sensible thing, and hence not relevant to their discussion. (The reader may be familiar with another version of this point, namely, 'Is there any sound when a tree falls in a forest and no one is there?' What Berkeley is pointing out, is that if we mean by sound, *experienced* noise, then the answer is 'no', if no one hears it.)

After this they go on to discuss colours, with the same results. The colours that we experience differ depending upon lighting conditions, our own state, the types of optical device that we employ, and other factors. No one would want to claim that the object had all the different colours that we see. Hylas tries to answer this by introducing the theory of light waves. The colours that we see may be in our minds, but there are real colours outside of us, in the sense of light waves. Philonous again points out that Hylas is admitting that the sensible colours that we perceive exist only in our minds, not outside of us in some material object.

To avoid the conclusion that Berkeley is aiming at, **that the objects that we perceive are only ideas in our mind, and do not exist outside of, and independent of the mind,** Hylas comes forth with Locke's theory of primary and secondary qualities. The secondary qualities—such as colours, smells, tastes—exist only in the mind. But the primary qualities—e.g., extension, motion, gravity—really exist in bodies. Therefore, some of our sense information is only of ideas in our minds, but some refers to the *actual* qualities of external, material objects.

Berkeley's Criticism of Locke. Berkeley then tries to show that if one is a *consistent* empiricist, one will not be able to maintain this

theory of Locke's. If one admits that some of our sense experience consists of ideas which exist only in the mind, then one will have no basis
for making an exception of the primary qualities. Exactly the same
reasoning that convinces one that the secondary qualities are in the
mind, applies to the primary qualities as well. Our experience of size,
shape, motion, and so on, varies depending upon where we are, how
we feel, and other factors. Thus, the primary qualities appear to be just
ideas in our minds, just as colours and sounds were, and no special
reason can be given as to why we should regard our ideas of extension
and motion as being real qualities in material bodies, if we admit that
other qualities are only parts of our experience and exist in us.

To put his case another way, Berkeley points out that **all our experience consists of sensations.** Sensations belong only to sentient [i.e.,
capable of feeling] beings, not to inanimate objects. Therefore, we
cannot attribute to material objects, which are not thinking beings,
sensations, which as far as we know, only thinking beings can have.
Material objects do not have pleasures or pains, or sensations in
general. If we admit that the sensible things we know are only sensations, then we cannot claim that they are unthinking, unfeeling
material things.

But after all this, Hylas, like anyone else confronted with Berkeley's
reasoning, is unwilling to give up.

> I acknowledge, Philonous, that upon a fair observation of what
> passes in my mind, I can discover nothing else, but that I am a
> thinking being, affected with variety of sensations; neither is it
> possible to conceive, how a sensation should exist in an unperceiv-
> ing substance. But then, on the other hand, when I look on sensible
> things in a different view, considering them as so many modes and
> qualities, I find it necessary to suppose a material *substratum*,
> without which they cannot be conceived to exist.

Thus, like John Locke before him, Hylas still finds it necessary to
suppose that our sensations belong to something outside of us, something that we call matter.

Philonous responds by saying that we do not learn of this material
substratum by our senses, which only tell us about sensible things,
sensations, not something that exists apart from sense experience.
Also, if we try to conceive of what this matter is like, we can only
think of it in terms of our sensations, not as something unlike them,
which exists apart from all experience. Finally, to make his point,
Philonous challenges Hylas, 'If you can conceive it possible for any
mixture or combination of qualities, or any sensible object whatever,
to exist without the mind, then I will grant it actually to be so.'

Matter and Mind. Hylas thinks this is simple. 'What more easy than
to conceive a tree or a house existing by itself, independent of, and un-
perceived by, any mind whatsoever? I do, at this present time, conceive them existing after that manner.' Philonous replies that this tree
or house is being conceived by Hylas, and is in *his* mind. Nothing
can be thought of, or experienced, except by some mind that thinks
of it, or experiences it. Therefore, one cannot even imagine or conceive

of what it would be like for something to exist outside of, or independent of, the mind. As soon as one imagines this, it is an idea in a mind.

Hylas still is unwilling to surrender. He admits by now that whatever is immediately perceived is an idea, and that ideas cannot exist outside of a mind. But why can't there also be something called 'real things', or 'external objects', that exist independently of the mind, and are known or represented by our ideas? Why can't this be like looking at a picture of Julius Caesar (an idea) that represents Julius Caesar (a real, external object)?

But how did we ever find out about these alleged real objects? By our senses? No. Our sense information consists entirely of ideas, and so could not tell us about something that is not an idea. If one is an empiricist, and believes that all of our knowledge comes from the senses, then how can he accept this claim that we can know about something that is not part of sense experience? The example of the picture of Julius Caesar does not help, Berkeley argued, since we learned about both people and pictures from sense experience, but we do not learn about real objects from any of our sensations, if all of our sensations are ideas.

If our ideas are said to represent these supposed real objects, then, Berkeley argued, this is a weird claim. The ideas are fleeting, changing, ephemeral, and the real objects are supposed to have a fixed and real nature. Ideas can be perceived, but the real objects cannot be. Thus, the ideas cannot be like the objects they are supposed to represent. 'Can a real thing, in itself invisible, be like a colour; or a real thing which is not audible, be like a sound? In a word, can anything be like a sensation or idea, but another sensation or idea?'

Philonous claims that he has shown that this notion of a real, material object makes no sense. This enables us to see that Hylas' views lead to scepticism. Hylas had originally asserted that the reality of sensible things consisted in their existence outside the mind. But Hylas has now been forced to deny that sensible things, our experiences, exist outside the mind. Hence, he has been forced to deny that they are real. By his own definition of 'sceptic', he has been shown to be a sceptic.

'To Be Is To Be Perceived.' By this stage in the argument, Hylas has been reduced to complete doubt. His belief that there were real, external material objects has been destroyed. Now he is convinced that there are no real objects, and that everything is just a dream. But Berkeley is at great pains to point out that this sad result is due to holding some of the views that Locke had formulated. As long as Hylas believes that there must be some real, material substratum that exists outside the mind, then he is forced to admit that none of our sense experience can belong to this matter. As long as he believes in the theory of primary and secondary qualities, he is led to the conclusion that all of our experience consists of secondary qualities that exist only in the mind. One of the reasons that Hylas has been forced to complete scepticism is that he, like Locke, was not completely an empiricist. He insisted on believing that there must be independent material objects that our sensations belong to. Now that he has been shown that there cannot be such objects, he suddenly feels that there cannot be *anything* in the universe, and that *everything* that he perceives must be illusory, since it cannot consist of objects existing outside of the mind.

What Berkeley has shown, up to this point, is that if one seriously accepts the empirical theory of knowledge, all that we can know is what we experience. What we experience are not independently existing material objects, but rather a series of ideas. All that we can know about these ideas is what we perceive. Hence, we cannot tell from what we see, if they exist apart from minds which perceive them. In fact, as he has pointed out, we cannot even conceive or imagine, in terms of our experience, what it would be like for our sensations to exist apart from being thought of. Thus, in Berkeley's famous phrase, **the existence of things consists in their being perceived,** or as he put it in Latin, '*esse est percipi*' (literally, 'to be is to be perceived').

Berkeley's Positive Theory. Does this mean that if we rely only on the information we gain from our sense experience we can never be sure that things exist other than as ideas? Does this mean that we cannot be sure that the chairs and tables in the room exist except when we perceive them? At this point in the discussion, Berkeley revealed that he had a radically different theory from that of Hylas, and hence does not conclude in the complete scepticism to which Hylas has been reduced. Speaking through Philonous, Berkeley declared:

> I deny that I agreed with you in those notions that led to scepticism. You indeed said that the reality of sensible things consisted in an *absolute existence* out of the minds of spirits, or distinct from their being perceived. And pursuant to this notion of reality, you are obliged to deny sensible things any real existence: that is, according to your own definition, you profess yourself a sceptic. But I neither said nor thought the reality of sensible things was to be defined after that manner. To me it is evident, for the reasons you allow of, that sensible things cannot exist otherwise than in a mind or spirit. Whence I conclude, not that they have no real existence, but that, seeing they depend not on my thought, and have an existence distinct from being perceived by me, *there must be some other mind wherein they exist.* As sure, therefore, as the sensible world really exists, so sure is there an infinite omnipresent spirit, who contains and supports it.

Immaterialism. This explanation that Berkeley presented is a theory called **immaterialism.** All that we can perceive is an idea. Ideas can belong only to minds, and cannot have an existence independent of minds. Since the ideas that I am aware of do not depend upon my wishes, these ideas must have some kind of existence apart from my mind. But ideas can only belong to some mind. If I am not responsible for the ideas I perceive, and cannot invent and control all my ideas at will, then there must be some other mind that possesses, controls and maintains the ideas. And so, Berkeley claimed, there must be some Universal Mind, or God, in whose thoughts the ideas are located. Thus, the things that I perceive exist distinct from me in the mind of God, and do not leap in and out of existence as and when I experience them. My house is always perceived by God. Hence, although the house is only an idea, it continues to exist whether I perceive it or not, since God always perceives it.

This thesis of Berkeley's has been summed up in a famous limerick by Ronald Knox:

> There was a young man who said, 'God,
> I find it exceedingly odd
> That this tree that I see
> Should continue to be
> When there's no one about in the Quad.'
> Reply.
> 'Dear Sir:
> Your astonishment's odd:
> *I* am always about in the Quad.
> And that's why the tree
> Will continue to be
> Since observed by
> > Yours faithfully,
> > GOD.'

Berkeley's Claims. Berkeley claimed that his strange theory, besides being a consistent empiricist philosophy, was also the only theory of knowledge that was in agreement with ordinary common-sense beliefs. Other theories led to scepticism, and to paradoxes, and ended up denying what everybody knew and was sure of. His view, on the contrary, combined the best elements of philosophical reasoning and common sense. Philosophers, like Locke and Descartes, had concluded that '*the things immediately perceived are ideas which exist only in the mind*'. On the other hand, ordinary people believe that '*those things they immediately perceive are the real things*'. Berkeley insisted that his theory, and only his theory, was in agreement with both the philosophers and ordinary folk, and did not lead to any of the sceptical or paradoxical conclusions that he had shown were involved in the theories of knowledge offered by previous thinkers.

Theories of knowledge had always distinguished things from ideas, and had tried to learn how we discover any knowledge about things from our information about ideas. All that we are immediately aware of are ideas. If things are different from ideas, then how do we relate knowledge about ideas, to something outside of our ideas? Berkeley, by reasoning astutely from the empirical claim that all of our knowledge comes from our experiences, which are ideas in the mind, showed that if things are different from ideas, we can never know anything about them. This reduced Hylas to his 'forlorn scepticism'.

In order to avoid this sad conclusion, that we can never know anything at all about what real things are like, Berkeley offered his theory of immaterialism. First of all, he insisted, things are only the ideas we have of them. It is the philosophers who have invented this strange unknown item, called 'an independently existing material object'. Everybody believes that what he perceives (an idea) is a real thing.

H

He thinks there is a tree in his garden because he sees it, touches it. It is his experience, his ideas, which give him his information about things. The real things of the world are only the ideas that we have. But then, Berkeley claimed, the world is not only the sequence of the ideas in *my* mind, but is a real continuously existing series of things, because the ideas that I perceive are also perceived by God. When I am not looking at the tree, it is still an idea in the mind of God, and hence it is still perceived. The information that I gain through my senses is accurate information about the ideas in God's mind, and consists of true knowledge about real things. In terms of the various ideas that I have, I can develop sciences about the order and relation of ideas in God's mind.

Berkeley's Theory of Notions. However, as Berkeley saw, he had to hold that we have knowledge which did not come from our sense experience. Our knowledge about God was not derived from sense experience. Rather, Berkeley insisted, in addition to the ideas in our mind, there are also other items called **'notions'. The basic notion is our awareness of ourselves.** We do not see ourselves as we perceive chairs and tables, as a series of sensory qualities, colours, shapes, and the like. What we are aware of, Berkeley claimed, is that we are active agents who think, will, act. This conception, or awareness, of the active spirit called 'myself' or 'me' gives us our primary notion. We also develop a notion of God, as the omnipresent spirit, who thinks and perceives all the ideas. It is through notions that we learn about the structure of the world. This accounts for all of our ordinary information, and explains how we get our knowledge about the world of experience, or things, and why it is true.

In spite of Berkeley's high hopes that he had succeeded in solving all the difficulties that had arisen in earlier theories of knowledge, and had developed a theory that would be compatible with ordinary common sense, his contemporaries regarded his theories as fantastic. The immaterialistic conception of the universe was regarded with suspicion, and Berkeley's philosophy—if one rejected his world of spirits, with God always perceiving everything—seemed to terminate in the weird claim that everything is nothing but an idea in the mind, with no real existence outside the mind. It is said, for example, that once when Berkeley visited Dean Swift, he was left to stand on the doorstep, on the grounds that if his philosophical views were correct he could enter through the closed door. There are other stories of similar reactions to his views. Some thinkers, who took Berkeley's arguments seriously, were willing to admit that he had made out a good case, and had offered a series of proofs which might 'admit of no answer', but at the same time, they saw that Berkeley's reasoning also 'produced no conviction'.

DAVID HUME

But one of the philosophers who came shortly after Berkeley, pursued his reasoning to an even more disastrous and shocking conclusion, and thereby exposed some of the limitations of all empiricist theories of knowledge. This was the Scottish sceptic, DAVID HUME (1711-76) who is probably the most influential philosopher of modern times. Hume grew up in Ninewells, near Edinburgh, and briefly attended the University of Edinburgh, leaving there at the age of fifteen. After a series of ill-starred attempts to enter various careers, he went to France to write a great philosophic work. By the time he was twenty-six he had finished his *A Treatise of Human Nature*, which he thought would radically change the course of philosophy. Instead, when it appeared in 1739, it 'fell dead-born from the presses', as Hume lamented, and elicited no great interest from any of his contemporaries. His later *Enquiry Concerning Human Understanding* attempted to present his views in more popular form, but still failed to get Hume the recognition he sought. Finally his political writings and his popular *History of England* brought him fame, and made him one of the best known writers in the English language in the latter half of the eighteenth century. When he served as secretary to the British Embassy in Paris in the 1760's he was hailed by the French intellectuals as the most important writer of the British Isles. Hume's irreligious views made him a hero to the French sceptics and 'Enlightenment' leaders. Back in England, he served briefly as under-secretary of state, and became a leading advocate of freedom for the American colonies. Hume's unorthodox views in religion and politics gained him great notoriety, so that by the time he retired he was generally known as 'the gentle sceptic' and the 'great infidel'.

Hume's Theory of Knowledge. Hume's philosophy appears to have grown out of two strands. One, a deep interest in scepticism, and an extreme doubt that philosophers were capable of discovering the truth about any matter whatsoever. Secondly, a conviction that what was needed in order to uncover what knowledge, if any, we were capable of, was an inquiry into what he called 'the science of man'. This science would examine the processes by which we think and try to find out how people form their views, and come to believe what they do about the nature of events.

Psychology. Hume's greatest philosophical work, his *Treatise of Human Nature*, claims at the outset to be the application to the mental world of the scientific method that Isaac Newton had so successfully employed in solving physical problems. What is to be examined is the mental nature of human beings, their psychology, in order to see the actual processes by which our alleged knowledge develops. All the sciences that we have, like physics, and disciplines like mathematics have been discovered by human beings; and so, Hume suggested, by understanding what human beings are like, we may find out something important about the nature of the knowledge that human beings possess. From the outset, Hume conceded that he probably would never be able 'to discover the ultimate original qualities of human nature', but by examining our experiences, we may be able to find some general hypotheses about human nature that could be of the greatest value. This is what had earlier been done in developing a science about the physical world, and could have even more significant results in the mental world.

We must therefore glean up our experiments in this science from a cautious observation of human life, and take them as they appear in the common course of the world, by men's behaviour in company, in affairs, and in their pleasures. Where experiments of this kind are judiciously collected and compared, we may hope to establish on them a science which will not be inferior in certainty, and will be much superior in utility to any other of human comprehension.

Impressions and Ideas. Hume begins by pointing out that everything that we are aware of can be classified under two headings, **impressions and ideas.** The difference between these two is the **'degree of force and liveliness,** with which they strike upon the mind'. The impressions are more forceful and lively than the ideas. Also, there are **simple** impressions and ideas, and **complex** ones. The difference is that the simple ones 'admit of no distinction or separation'. Thus, the perception of the quality, blue, is simple, whereas the perception of a blue *picture* is complex, and can be separated into parts. When we examine our impressions and ideas, Hume claimed, we find a great resemblance between them. However, some of our complex ideas, we find, never appear as impressions, as for example, our complex idea of a mermaid. But, on careful inspection of our ideas and impressions, we find that in every case our simple ideas are just like our simple impressions, and that the impression always occurred first. Thus, our first acquaintance with a simple quality, like orange, first occurred as a forceful and lively impression, and later occurred as an identical idea. As Hume pointed out, this law that simple impressions always precede the simple ideas which resemble them in our experience amounts to a **denial that there are any innate ideas, and also to the claim that all of our ideas come from experience.**

Memory and Imagination. Further, we find, with regard to our ideas, that we have two different faculties, one called **memory,** in which we have present in the mind a series of ideas in a fixed order or sequence. The other faculty is called **imagination** by which we can arrange our ideas in any order we like. But, in spite of this freedom of the imagination, we find that our ideas come in patterns. When we think of an idea, we have a tendency to think also of a resembling idea, or of an idea that was contiguous to it in time or space, or of an idea that is causally related to it. These patterns are the **associations of ideas.** We find that one of the principles of human nature is that there 'is a kind of Attraction [i.e., a tendency for ideas to become linked with one another—A. V. K.], which in the mental world will be found to have as extraordinary effects as in the natural, and to show itself in as many and as various forms'.

Hume's Analysis of Causation. The importance of this claim about the association of ideas is brought out when Hume investigates what constitutes our knowledge, and especially our information about what events are causally related to each other. Knowledge, according to Hume, consists of information that can be gained from the inspection of two or more ideas. If we look at two or more ideas, we can tell immediately whether they resemble each other, whether they are different, whether one is darker than another, whether one is larger than another. **This type of knowledge by immediate inspection of two or more ideas, Hume insisted, was intuitive and certain.** It could not be false, since it merely depended on bringing two or more ideas to mind in our imagination, and then examining them. On the basis of this sort of knowledge, coupled with a series of demonstrations, we can develop an indubitable branch of knowledge like arithmetic.

But when we ask, how do we discover that two or more ideas are *causally* related together, we discover something very peculiar. This sort of information, which constitutes perhaps the largest part of our information about what is going on does *not* merely depend upon looking at two or more ideas. If we examine a situation in which we frequently say, 'This event causes that event' (for instance, the experience of seeing a rock striking against a window pane), do we actually perceive, as a feature of the impression, a part called 'the cause'? There is no quality, such as green, which we find in every experience that we call 'a causal sequence'. Then, Hume suggested, perhaps the causal connection between events is a relation between the elements in an impression, or between successive impressions. But when we examine a situation like that of the rock striking the window, we find that the elements, window and rock, are contiguous, that is, the rock at some moment is next to the window, and also we find that there are some motions of the rock prior to the shattering of the glass. But, besides the **contiguity** and **succession** of the events, is there anything else? Well, we feel that there must be more, some element or property by which the cause *produces* the effect. But all that we see, Hume pointed out, is only the contiguity of two things, and the succession of events. This point is well illustrated by a story of two children who were travelling on a train with their mother. The mother gave each of them a banana. As the first child bit into the banana, the train rushed into a tunnel. 'Don't eat that banana!' he cried out in panic to his brother, 'It makes you go blind.' The contiguity and the succession were there. Why, then, do we not accept the causality? This is Hume's point.

Shall we then rest contented with these two relations of contiguity and succession, as affording a complete idea of causation? By no means. An object may be contiguous and prior to another, without being considered as its cause. There is a Necessary Connection to be taken into consideration; and that relation is of much greater importance than any of the other two above-mentioned.

This crucial element in our reasoning about causally related events is not immediately evident. It does not seem to be one of the parts, or relations, that we discover in our impressions. But, if the empirical theory of knowledge is accepted, our idea of necessary connection must derive from some impression, or some feature of our impressions. Since the source of this basic idea is not located simply by examining and dissecting impressions, Hume felt that he might find the answer to his question by first finding out the answers to the two following problems: (*a*) 'For what reason we pronounce it *necessary*, that every thing whose existence has a beginning, should also have a cause?' And (*b*) 'Why we conclude, that such particular causes must *necessarily* have such particular effects; and what is the nature of that *inference* we draw from the one to the other, and of the belief we repose in it?'

The Problem of Cause. The mere asking of the first question is a bit startling. Everyone had taken for granted that every event has a cause, and that everything that exists has a cause for its existence. But, Hume asked, why do we believe this? What evidence do we have for this causal principle? It is not intuitively obvious. When we look at the various impressions and ideas in our minds, we do not see as a feature of the impressions or ideas that they must have a cause. There is no connection between the ideas that we have of a new existent—i.e., something that has just begun to exist—and the idea of a cause. This can be shown by the fact that since all ideas that are distinct can be separated by the imagination, anyone is capable of thinking of the idea of a new object without also thinking of its cause. Hence, the two ideas are not linked together.

Then, why do we think that every object that begins to exist must have a cause? Hume examined the various arguments that such philosophers as John Locke had offered to prove this causal assertion. Their proofs, Hume found, are inconclusive, because somewhere in the proof they assume the very claim they are trying to establish. For instance, in Hume's version of Locke's argument, the proof is that if things were produced without any cause, then they would have *nothing* for a cause. But *nothing* is not something, and therefore cannot act as a producing agent. But, as Hume pointed out, this argument proceeds only by supposing that every object must have a cause, and then showing *nothing* cannot be a cause. And what has to be proven is the supposition that everything has to have a cause.

After examining the types of argument presented by various philosophers, and showing that they are invalid, Hume concluded, 'Since it is not from knowledge or any scientific reasoning, that we derive the opinion of the necessity of a cause to every new production, that opinion must necessarily arise from observation and experience.' The next question, then, should naturally be, 'How does experience give rise to such a principle?' In order to answer this question, Hume found it was first necessary to solve his other problem—Why do we think that particular causes must necessarily have particular effects, and why do we form an inference from one to the other?

Elements of Causal Analysis. Our causal reasoning seems to involve three sorts of element. One is a **present impression**, which we believe is connected with another item, some **idea** we have of a related event. The third element is the **connection or inference** and this is what Hume was searching for. When a detective discovers a body—the present impression—he immediately reasons to the idea, some *cause* of death. If the body contains a bullet, the detective immediately infers that there must have been a gun from which the bullet came. It is this reasoning process, from impression to idea, that Hume was trying to analyse. The body does not appear with a sign on it announcing that it is the result of a gun having been fired. The detective, like anyone else, could have thought of an unlimited number of ideas instead of a gun. Then, Hume asked, why is it that although we do not see the cause, we think immediately of an idea which we think was necessary to produce the experience that we do have? Merely from an examination of the particular impression, no specific ideas have to be called to mind. The imagination is capable of thinking about any idea that one has. One could just as well think of the taste of a pear, instead of a gun. But one doesn't. The sort of inference the detective makes is like that any of us make. When we see one event, although it does not force us to think of any particular idea, we do in fact tend to think of something that we call the 'cause' or the 'effect' of the impressions we are having. When we hear a certain sound, we think of a piano being played, even though the impression, the sound that we hear, does not contain the visual element of the piano and the player.

Then, how and why do we make this sort of inference? Hume asked. Not by reasoning, because just from the impression, no necessary conclusion follows. Any other idea could be *thought* of. Then, it must be due to something in our experience.

> We remember to have had frequent instances of the existence of one species of objects; and also remember, that the individuals of another species of objects have always attended them, and have existed in a regular order of contiguity and succession with regard to them. Thus we remember, to have seen that species of object we call 'flame', and to have felt that species of sensation we call 'heat'. We likewise call to mind their constant conjunction in all past instances. Without any further ceremony, we call the one *cause* and the other *effect*, and infer the existence of the one from that of the other.

Constant Conjunction. Then, what happens, according to Hume, is that in experience we are aware of two items occurring together, that is, constantly conjoined. When this has happened often enough in the past, we come to consider them as causally related, and when we experience just one of these items, we immediately infer that the other one must also exist. But why, to explore the problem further, should past experience have this effect upon us? If it were by means of a rational procedure, it would require that a principle like that of the uniformity of nature must be true, that is 'that instances, of which we have had no experience, must resemble those, of which we have had experience, and that the course of nature continues always uniformly the same'. Thus, in order to prove from our past experience that when we hear a certain sound someone is now playing the piano, we would have to presume that the same sort of experience we had in the past must be taking place in the present, and that the constant conjunctions that we discovered in the past continue in the present.

But is there anything that we can ever discover from our experience that gives us any guarantee that the principle of the uniformity of nature is true? No, Hume insisted, because no matter how uniform our experience has been in the past, it is always possible that the future will be different. We can examine our experience from now until doomsday and we will never be able to show that future events must be similar to previous ones, or that the apparent uniformity of nature up to any point in our experience is adequate evidence that nature will continue to be uniform in our future experience.

Uncertainty. Here Hume discovered something most peculiar. The principle of the uniformity of nature is involved in nearly all of our inferences as to what is going on in the world beyond what we immediately perceive. Almost all our interpretations of the impressions we have—the sounds, the colours, the smells—are based upon assuming that matters which were constantly conjoined in past experience, are still conjoined in the present, and will be in the future. But, if we are asked for evidence for this all important principle, we find that we have none. We cannot demonstrate it, since it is always possible that when we wake up tomorrow the universe will be radically different from what it has been until now. It is always possible that the constant conjunctions of items in our experience will be altered in the future, and that salt will taste sweet, that water will burn, and so on. No amount of observation and study of experience will help establish this principle, because all that we will learn thereby is that nature has been uniform, we still cannot be sure that it will *continue* to be so. Thus, to make Hume's point more forcefully, even the best-tested scientific laws, such as the law of gravity, depend upon the principle of the uniformity of nature. We can never be sure, no matter how many objects have been tested to see if they gravitate towards the earth, that the law will be true in the future.

Human Nature. If the principle of the uniformity of nature is so basic to our information about the world, and if we can neither prove it, nor offer sufficient evidence for it, then why do we believe it? Hume's answer is that the belief is due to a psychological custom or habit that people have, so that after they have experienced the constant conjunction of two impressions often enough, and one of the conjuncts occurs again in their experience, they are immediately led to think of the other as an idea in their imagination. But we think of the idea usually associated with the impression in a special manner. We could, since our imagination is free, think of *any* idea. But only the associated idea is thought of with 'force and vivacity', or is believed in. Thus, when I hear a certain sound, I could if I wished, conjure up any idea I wished, say that of the taste of a pear. But naturally, Hume pointed out, I think of this idea of someone playing the piano, and I think of the idea with 'force and vivacity.' I believe that someone is actually playing the piano, whereas I do not believe that a pear is being tasted. The belief that occurs in one case and not the other is only the result of the different ways the two ideas are conceived. Only the associated idea (that is, associated in past experience) is thought of **forcefully.** Any other idea would merely be thought of.

What is it that makes us conceive some ideas forcefully and vivaciously? In order to explain this phenomenon, there must be some basic habit or custom of human nature so that whenever any impression is presented to us, the mind is not only led to think of the idea or ideas associated with this impression, but is also led to think of the idea with some of the force and vivacity of the impression. Somehow the strength of the impression is carried over to the idea, whenever the idea is one that has usually been constantly conjoined with the impression in the past. Thus, our reasoning about what goes on in the world beyond what we immediately see, is not due to any rational procedures, but instead, is due to some basic quirks of human nature which make us believe that 'instances of which we have no experience, must necessarily resemble those of which we have'. We do not reason that this has to be the case, but rather find that we are so constituted that we automatically believe certain ideas, or conceive of them more forcefully than others. Thus:

'Tis not solely in poetry and music, we must follow our taste and sentiment, but likewise in philosophy. When I am convinced of any principle, 'tis only an idea, which strikes more strongly upon me. When I give the preference to one set of arguments above another, I do nothing but decide from my feeling concerning the superiority of their influence. Objects have no discoverable connection together; nor is it from any other principle but custom operating upon the imagination, that we can draw any inference from the appearance of one to the existence of another.

If our reasoning beyond our immediate impressions, and our conclusion that particular causes have particular effects, is the result of this habit or custom by which certain ideas are automatically brought to mind, and certain strong feelings attach to them, which constitute our belief, then what is our idea of necessity which leads us to say that certain objects are necessarily connected? It is not one of the features of our impressions, since we do not perceive any necessity or power which makes events occur, we only perceive the succession of events. But when we have seen several similar instances of successions of impressions, we then begin to consider the events as necessarily connected. Thus, the idea of necessary connection seems to be involved with something that occurs with the **repetition of resembling events.**

But what happens when the same sequence of impressions occurs repeatedly? If the sequences are similar, Hume pointed out, then we perceive approximately the same thing each time. If we do not perceive the necessary connection between events in one case, we will not perceive it any more from a hundred, since, if the cases are resembling, then the same qualities must be present each time. We do not see anything new after watching the same process over and over again, that we did not see the first time. But what happens is that we have a different mental attitude than we did before, and it is this different mental attitude which constitutes our belief that events are necessarily connected.

For after we have observed the resemblance in a sufficient number of instances, we immediately feel a determination of the mind to pass from one object to its usual attendant, and to conceive it in a stronger light upon account of that relation. This determination is the only effect of the resemblance; and therefore must be the same with power or efficacy, whose idea is derived from the resemblance. The several instances of resembling conjunctions lead us into the notion of power and necessity. These instances are in themselves totally distinct from each other, and have no union but in the mind, which observes them, and collects their ideas. Necessity, then, is the effect of this observation, and is nothing but an internal impression of the mind, or a determination to carry our thoughts from one object to another.

Denial of Cause. Thus, 'necessity' is something that exists in the human mind, and not as a quality or feature of objects, as far as we can ever tell. The necessity that we believe exists, that a glass window must break when struck with a hammer, is only, Hume insisted, a determination of the mind to think of one idea when experiencing a certain impression, and to think of that idea most forcefully, owing to its constant conjunction with the present impression. If we examined our impressions of the hammer and of the glass, we would not find any part or feature of either impression that was the necessity of the glass breaking. The necessary connection between these two events, the hammer and the broken glass, lies in the way the mind thinks about them, and not in the events themselves. Hume asserted that we have a propensity to join our internal experiences to the external ones that occur at the same time. Thus, although the necessity occurs only as a mental determination upon experiencing certain impressions, we have a tendency to locate this mental event in the observed events, and to think of it as occurring there with the events, even though it is actually taking place in our minds.

As Hume well realized, this analysis of our idea of necessary connection, and the nature of our causal reasoning, might sound strange and incredible. 'I doubt not but my sentiments will be treated by many as extravagant and ridiculous. What! the efficacy of causes lie in the determination of the mind!' But, odd as this analysis may seem at first reading, Hume insisted, it is the only way of making sense of the reasoning that we carry on about our sense experience. If we honestly examine what we perceive, we do not experience any necessary connections between the various items of our sensory world. We find no reason why one event must follow another. But we do discover that we have a mental determination to think of certain ideas which have in the past been constantly conjoined to the present impressions, and to think of them in a forceful and lively manner. Hence, the only actual connection that we ever discover between events is a **psychological** one, a way in which we think, and not a physical one, an actual link between one event and another. Thus, all that we mean by the notion of cause is 'An object precedent and contiguous to another, and so united with it in the imagination, that the idea of the one determines the mind to form the idea of the other, and the impression of the one to form a more lively idea of the other.'

Application of Hume's Theory to Science. As startling as Hume's claim may be, he maintained that this was perfectly **in keeping with the actual achievements of scientific investigation.** What scientists are finding out are the constant conjunctions of events that occur in human experience, and the expectations that people have as to what will happen next, in view of how they think about these events. Thus, the scientific 'fact' that alcohol boils at 80° Centigrade under normal atmospheric conditions, means, according to Hume, that it has been observed many times that a certain impression, called alcohol boiling, has been constantly conjoined with another impression, of a thermometer reading of 80° Centigrade. No one actually sees the temperature cause the alcohol to boil. But, because these two impressions have been conjoined over and over again in the past, we have a determination to think of one as soon as we either see or recall the other, and to expect that they will be conjoined again in the future. We can neither prove that they are necessarily connected, nor that the conjunctions observed in the past will continue into the future. But owing to our mental determinations and habits, the observed constant conjunctions of events are taken as guides for future expectations and predictions. Our scientific information does not tell us about any necessary relationships in Nature, but rather about some regular sequences that have been observed to occur over and over again in the past. On the basis of this information about observed regularities, we expect and predict that similar regularities will occur under similar circumstances in the future. The expectations and predictions are based, not upon finding some hidden connections in Nature, but only upon certain **psychological habits of human nature,** that lead us to think of certain ideas in a more lively and forceful manner after having experienced their constant conjunction in the past.

One might protest that this account of what scientific discoveries are about may fit some of the more elementary laws that have been observed, but that present-day sciences are much more complicated than mere compilations of various sets of regularities observed in human experience. Contemporary followers of Hume, however, many of them quite prominent scientific theorists, maintain that in spite of manifold involvements of sciences like physics and chemistry, they essentially conform to Hume's claim. The systematic organization of these sciences consists only in discovering the most general regularities in human experience, from which others can be derived. Even such sciences as atomic and nuclear physics can be conceived of as the discovery of certain basic regularities between events, and the systematic organization of these regularities into a body of knowledge, on the basis of which predictions can be made, presuming that our mental determination to believe that the future will resemble the past proves to be the case.

Hume's Complete Scepticism. David Hume, starting out from an examination of our sense experience and how we organize it, concluded with **complete scepticism about the possibility of human beings knowing anything about the universe.** All that we are aware of is a series of impressions with no necessary relations to each other. From these we derive our ideas, which we associate together not on the basis of any actual properties of the impressions, but because of our mental customs or habits. When we search for some object outside of us to which our impressions belong, we find no impression of something called a body, or a material object. When we search inside ourselves for something which contains these impressions and ideas, something called a self, we find no such item in our experience.

The Nature of Experience. If all of our information about the world is restricted to what we actually experience, then we must recognize that what we experience is only a sequence of impressions, unrelated to each other, and, as far as we can tell, not attached to, or belonging to, either external objects or an internal object called the self, or mind. Even the spirits that Berkeley had claimed were 'experiencers' who possess the experiences, cannot be known through experience. The only basis that we have for ordering or interpreting the sequence of unrelated experiences is our mental habits or customs. There is one habit that leads us to ordering our experiences causally, to relating the constantly conjoined sequences. We have other habits, Hume claimed, that lead us to believe that there are external bodies, that lead us to believe that there is some sort of continuous thing inside us that holds our experiences together, called a self; and that lead us to believe that there is probably some sort of intelligent ordering to our experience. These habits or customs give a kind of order and coherence to the sequence of impressions and ideas in our minds. Some habits yield one kind of order; others, another. Sometimes these habits even give us conflicting orders to our experience, and lead us to believe something on the basis of one habit which we disbelieve on the basis of another.

'Normal' and 'Abnormal'. With such a picture of human nature, what is meant by being 'reasonable' is operating on the basis of the set of mental habits which we call 'normal'. The man who believes that fire will burn, that $2 + 2 = 4$, that the sun will rise tomorrow, that there are external objects which exist even when not experienced, and that there is some sort of internal continuity to his experience, called 'himself', has the 'normal' set of beliefs, and is considered a reasonable human being. Someone else, operating with different mental habits and customs, who thereby has a different set of beliefs, is 'abnormal' and 'unreasonable'. But which of the two has true knowledge? Which of the two believes something that actually corresponds to what is going on in the world?

The Compulsion to Believe. As Hume pointed out, we can never answer these questions. Any beliefs that we have only show what mental quirks we operate by. There is no justification for believing one thing rather than another, except that we find that we have a strong feeling or tendency to do so. When we try to find a reason for, or evidence for, believing something, we discover that we can find none, and can only report that our minds work in the curious manner that we think that the belief is true. The further we explore the bases for belief, the more we find out about the irrational and unjustifiable foundation of our mental behaviour. But, at the same time, we discover that no matter how little basis we may have for our beliefs, we also cannot avoid believing. No matter how sceptical we may become about the merits of, or the foundations for, what human beings believe, at the same time our human nature prevents us from giving up these beliefs. We may not be able to tell if they are true, and may even have some good reason to suspect that at least some of our beliefs are false. But all the same, we are compelled to believe certain things, and to act and talk and live on the basis of that belief.

Thus, in theory, Hume became a complete sceptic, when he concluded that the information about the world which we derive from our experience is based only on a peculiar set of mental habits or customs to conceive of certain ideas in a forceful and lively manner. But Hume, like everyone else, found that when he stepped out of his philosophical study, he was compelled to be a believer in the uniformity of nature, in the existence of external objects, in the continuous existence of himself, and so on. Even his belief in his own philosophy he found to be indefensible by reason; but it was at the same time a theory about human nature which he could not avoid accepting, when it struck most forcefully upon him. Thus he advocated his views as the feelings he had on those occasions. He concluded the first book of his *Treatise of Human Nature* by saying:

> If the reader finds himself in the same easy disposition, let him follow me in my future speculations. If not, let him follow his inclination, and wait the returns of application and good humour. The conduct of a man, who studies philosophy in this careless manner, is more truly sceptical than that of one, who feeling in himself an inclination to it, is yet so overwhelmed with doubts and scruples, as totally to reject it. A true sceptic will be diffident of his philosophical doubts, as well as of his philosophical conviction; and will never refuse any innocent satisfaction which offers itself, upon account of either of them.
>
> Nor is it only proper we should in general indulge our inclination in the most elaborate philosophical researches, notwithstanding our sceptical principles, but also that we should yield to that propensity, which inclines us to be positive and certain in *particular points*, according to the light, in which we survey them in any *particular instant*. 'Tis easier to forbear all examination and enquiry, than to check ourselves in so natural a propensity, and guard against that assurance, which always arises from an exact and full survey of an object. On such an occasion we are apt not only to forget our scepticism, but even our modesty too; and to make use of such terms as these, *'tis evident, 'tis certain, 'tis undeniable*; which a due deference to the public ought, perhaps, to prevent.

A Matter of Mood. Thus, for Hume, even the philosophy one believes in is a matter of taste and of habits and customs. With his habits and customs, even though he knew that he could not justify them, these are the beliefs he held at various times. If others have the same feelings, all well and good; if not, there is nothing that one can do, except to point out that other people operate according to different principles and habits and propensities. For Hume himself, in those moments when the doubts about the reliability of human beliefs were paramount, he was a sceptic. At other moments, he was a normal believer, like anybody else, when the force and vivacity of certain ideas were foremost in his mind. Hume's 'gentle scepticism' consisted in doubting everything when he felt he must, and believing all sorts of things, including his own theory about the nature of human beliefs, when he had to.

SUMMARY OF THE EMPIRICAL THEORY OF KNOWLEDGE

Beginning with John Locke, those philosophers who developed theories of knowledge maintaining that all knowledge comes from sense experience were led gradually to Hume's conclusion. If our only source of information about the world is the impressions that we gain through our senses, then a great deal of what we think that we know turns out to be illusion. What we gain through our senses are qualities such as colours, sounds, shapes. As Berkeley showed, there is nothing in our sense experience which shows us that these qualities belong to any so-called material, or external, objects. All that we see are the qualities themselves. As Hume showed, our experience does not contain any necessary relations or connections between the various items of our sense experience. Any connections that we impose upon our experiences are due, not to what we see, but to our mental habits or propensities.

The Empiricist Critique of Rationalism. The empiricists, beginning with a grave doubt about how much the rationalist philosophers claimed we could know, concluded with a theory which proposed grave doubts as to whether we could really know anything, in the strict sense, at all. In turning away from magnificent realms of perfect knowledge (e.g., those which Plato and Descartes had conceived) and looking instead at the more familiar world of ordinary experience for information as to what actually took place, the empiricists found that only a very limited amount of information was available through this source, and our assurance about it would always be far less than perfect.

But at the same time, the empiricists could always insist that, limited as their picture of human knowledge might be, it at least could not be accused of being fanciful. Plato's world of Ideas could not be pointed to, or demonstrated, in the ordinary world of affairs. But the ingredients and elements which the empiricists perceived were the actual features of everyone's experience. One might not be sure what it was an experience of, or whether its properties would persist into the future, but at least the items were open to everybody's inspection.

Our information about our experience may never be more than merely probable, but, the empiricist claims, this probable information has been, and probably will always be, more important and useful to mankind than all of the alleged certainties of the rationalists. For all their claims of absolute certitude, the rationalists have not been able to agree as to what it is that is so certain. Many of their claims have had to be retracted. But, the empiricists maintain, the more tentative claims made upon the limited basis of human sense experience and human fallibilities, are more open to correction and development, and to the test of further experience. As evidence for the empiricist's viewpoint, he can point to the fact that the area of the most obvious improvement in human understanding over the last few centuries, has not been in our grasp of the so-called 'real' world of Plato or Descartes, but in the empirical sciences. Fully realizing the limitations of such understanding, in terms of Hume's analysis of our empirical knowledge, one can still point out that even if such information is uncertain, dependent on our senses and psychological habits, it is still the information that has most affected human life. Those who have developed the extremely complex picture of the physical world from the nuclear particles of the atom, to the grand picture of the solar and stellar universes, from the protein molecule to the latest medical and psychological theories about the behaviour of human beings, have, by and large, not been seeking for absolutely certain knowledge about the real world, but for uniformities and regularities in the world of appearances. No matter how little faith various rationalist philosophers may have had in the merits of sense information, one cannot avoid being impressed, possibly even over-impressed, with the achievements of empirical research in the last three hundred years.

SUMMARY

We began this discussion by raising the question of what human beings could know with certainty. In spite of our ordinary assurance, we found that to some degree nearly everything we claim to know is open to doubt. For this reason, philosophers have tried to develop a theory of knowledge to account for the source, basis, and certainty of our knowledge. Some philosophers—the rationalists—have tried to find a completely certain foundation for our knowledge, in terms of certain procedures of human reasoning. They sought for knowledge in the strongest possible sense, i.e., information which under no circumstances could be false. Usually, the rationalists found that such knowledge could not be discovered in sense experience, but only in some mental realm.

As a reaction against such rationalist theories, another approach to the problem of knowledge was developed, that of the empiricists. Beginning with John Locke, empiricists hoped to discover a basis for our knowledge in sense experience. But from Locke to Berkeley to Hume, they found that our sense experience yielded far less information about the world than we might have hoped for. Hume indicated that a thorough examination of what we in fact know from sense experience would lead to a most depressing scepticism about the possibility of any genuine knowledge. If we can believe Hume, it is only the curious psychological make-up of human beings that leads to our views as to what occurs around us. What we consider our knowledge is only a manner of organizing the experience that is thrust upon us.

The devastating results of the English philosophical tradition in the eighteenth century, especially the work of Berkeley and Hume, have inspired philosophers either to develop a more perfect form of an empirical theory of knowledge—as John Stuart Mill tried to do in the nineteenth century and as modern positivists have tried to do in this century—or to find some way of modifying, or circumventing, the conclusions of Berkeley and Hume in order to work out some compromise theory of knowledge, admitting the claims of the empiricists, yet trying to salvage some of the elements of the rationalistic theory of knowledge. Beginning with the great German philosopher, Immanuel Kant (who said that Hume awoke him from his dogmatic slumbers), thinkers have attempted in many ways to construct a theory of knowledge which would guarantee the certainty of some of what we know, while at the same time accepting the force of Hume's scepticism.

By and large, philosophers have found that when they try to account for the assurance that ordinary mortals have in what they know, their task is extremely difficult. The attempt to construct an adequate theory of knowledge raises some of the most difficult problems that human beings have had to cope with. Whether anyone has succeeded in settling all these problems is still a matter in dispute. Possibly the trouble, as Bertrand Russell once suggested, is that no one has succeeded in developing a theory which is **both credible and consistent.** Some of the more believable theories appear to contain grave inconsistencies, and some of the most logical theories appear to be unbelievable.

SUGGESTED FURTHER READING

Classical Authors:

Berkeley, George, *Three Dialogues between Hylas and Philonous*. (Berkeley's best presentation of his argument, in dialogue fashion, discussing all the possible objections that he could think of.)

Descartes, René, *A Discourse on Method*. (The method of Cartesian doubt.)

Descartes, René, *Meditations on First Philosophy*. (The best presentation of Descartes' theory of knowledge.)

Hume, David, *An Enquiry Concerning Human Understanding*. (Hume's more popular statement of his views.)

Hume, David, *A Treatise of Human Nature*. (The most complete statement of Hume's theory.)

Kant, Immanuel, *Critique of Pure Reason*. (Kant's attempt to show that empiricism can lead to a more positive theory of knowledge.)

Locke, John, *An Essay Concerning Human Understanding*. (Locke's famous statement of his empirical theory of knowledge.)

Plato, *Meno*. (A short dialogue setting forth the problem of knowledge.)

Plato, *The Republic*. (The most extended discussion of the Platonic theory of knowledge.)

Modern Authors:

Ayer, A. J., *Language, Truth and Logic*. (A presentation of the contemporary positivist view on the theory of knowledge.)

Montague, William P., *The Ways of Knowing*. Allen & Unwin: London, 1925. (A survey of various problems about knowledge, and solutions that have been offered.)

Moore, G. E., *Philosophical Studies*. Routledge & Kegan Paul: London, 1922. (A series of essays by one of the most important thinkers dealing with the problem of knowledge; contains some criticisms of some of the classical theories.)

Russell, Bertrand, *A History of Western Philosophy*, 2nd ed. Allen & Unwin: London, 1968. (Especially good in its criticisms of various theories of knowledge.)

Russell, Bertrand, *Human Knowledge, Its Scope and Limits*. Allen & Unwin: London, 1948. (A fairly recent statement of a modified version of empiricism.)

Russell, Bertrand, *The Problems of Philosophy*. Oxford University Press: London, 1967, paperback. (An excellent introduction to the problems involved in the theory of knowledge.)

CHAPTER VI

LOGIC

The Definition of 'Logic'. As we have tried to demonstrate through-out this book, reflection is the very stuff of which philosophy is made. A man who behaves mechanically or habitually in everyday life is not a philosopher; he does not philosophize until he begins to reflect or speculate about himself, about his place in the scheme of things, about his experiences and his relations to others. For almost every type of such reflection there is a corresponding branch of philosophy. For example, when one thinks about the nature of his conduct, he is engaged in ethical speculation; when one reflects on the nature of the universe, he is involved in metaphysics. **Logic may be defined as that branch of philosophy which reflects upon the nature of thinking itself.** It attempts to answer such questions as: What is correct reasoning? What distinguishes a good argument from a bad one? Are there any methods to detect fallacies in reasoning, and if so what are they? It can be seen from these remarks that **logic is perhaps the most fundamental branch of philosophy. All branches of philosophy employ thinking; whether this thinking is correct or not will depend upon whether it is in accord with the laws of logic;** hence the need for a thorough grounding in logic.

In defining logic as the branch of philosophy which deals with the nature of thinking, certain important qualifications must be made. We have *not* intended to imply that logic is a branch of psychology, or that logic deals with *all* types of thinking. **Logic differs from psychology in that it does not deal with all types of thinking such as learning, remembering, day-dreaming, supposing and so forth, but only with that type of thinking called 'reasoning'.** Furthermore, while the psychologist is concerned with the mental processes of the thinker, the logician's interest is in the reasoning itself; he is concerned not with why people think in certain ways but with the formulation of rules that will enable us to test whether any particular piece of reasoning is coherent and consistent, i.e., whether it is **logical.**

In order to illustrate how reasoning differs from other types of thinking, such as remembering, or day-dreaming, it will be useful here to discuss an actual example.

Suppose I have agreed to meet a friend one hour hence at a place which is three miles away. Upon reflection I wonder whether I can be at the designated place in time for our appointment. I have only two means of getting there, since I do not own a car: either I must walk or I must take a bus. Now, as a result of previous military service, I know that I can walk at a maximum average speed of two and a half miles per hour. But since my destination is three miles away, and since

224

I must be there in exactly one hour, I cannot reach it in time by walking. Therefore, if I am to reach it on time, I will have to do it by bus. The next bus will pass my present location in fifteen minutes, and then will take another thirty minutes to travel to the place where I am to meet my friend. Thus I conclude that I can keep my appointment by taking the bus.

Let us consider this example in closer detail in order to show why it is an instance of reasoning. To begin with, we have a certain problem: can I arrive at the place of my appointment within an hour, given the means of transportation which are available? I first raise the question of whether I can keep the appointment on time by walking. I decide I cannot, and the reasons why I cannot are: the distance is three miles; I must be there in an hour; and I can only walk at a speed of two and a half miles per hour. In giving these reasons, I am supplying evidence for my conclusion that I cannot arrive there on time by walking. On the other hand, in supplying the following reasons: A bus will pass in fifteen minutes; it will take thirty minutes to arrive at the appointed place; and the appointment is scheduled for an hour hence—I am providing evidence for the conclusion that I can keep the appointment by taking the bus.

What is characteristic of reasoning, as may be inferred from the word itself, is that we produce reasons as evidence for a certain conclusion we wish to establish. As the above example makes clear, reasoning is closely connected with inferring. The reasons we provide allow us to infer a certain conclusion. If true, they serve the function of providing evidence for the truth of the conclusion. Now logic is the discipline which attempts to distinguish bad reasoning from good reasoning, or (what is equivalent) good inferences from bad ones. It attempts to formulate rules which can tell us whether the reasons we have given are 'good' reasons for inferring the conclusion we wish to establish. Logic might be defined, without too great distortion, as the science of 'good reasons'.

It should be noted that the reasons we give in support of a conclusion are always expressed in language. Because this is so, logic has sometimes been characterized as a discipline which deals with the relations between sentences, or *propositions*, as the logician prefers to call them, since he is not concerned with interrogative or exclamatory sentences, but only with those that make assertions. Inference is considered to be a process which allows us to establish the truth of a certain proposition, called the conclusion of an argument, from the truth of other propositions which constitute the evidence for the conclusion. On this interpretation, one might define logic as the branch of philosophy which attempts to determine when a given proposition or a group of propositions permits us correctly to infer some other proposition.

Deductive and Inductive Logic. Philosophers have traditionally divided logic into two branches. These are called 'deductive logic' and 'inductive logic' respectively. Both branches are concerned with the rules for correct reasoning, or correct 'argumentation' as philosophers frequently say. Deductive logic deals with reasoning which attempts to establish **conclusive inferences**. To say that an inference is 'conclusive' means that if the reasons given are true, then it will be impossible for the inference based upon these reasons to be false. Such reasoning is called 'valid' reasoning or 'valid' inference. Deductive logic is thus concerned with the rules for determining when an argument is valid.

Not all reasoning in daily life attempts to provide conclusive evidence for the truth of a given conclusion. Sometimes, by the very nature of the case, conclusive evidence cannot be produced. But very often for practical purposes we do not need conclusive evidence. We merely want the evidence to show that the conclusion we have arrived at is **well founded,** that it is more **probable** than some other conclusion we might have reached. It is easy to imagine situations in which it is important to make a decision even where conclusive information is not available. For instance, if we are the judge in a murder trial, we may wish to know whether a conclusion we have arrived at is **reliably inferred from whatever evidence we have on hand.** Inductive logic deals with cases such as these; it is not concerned with the rules for correct reasoning in the sense of 'valid' or conclusive reasoning, but rather **it is concerned with the soundness of those inferences for which the evidence is not conclusive.** In particular, while deductive logic is concerned with inferences from the general to the particular (i.e., from assertions about the whole of a class of things to assertions about some of them), inductive logic is concerned with inferences from the particular to the general, and the inference of a general proposition from particular assertions can never be conclusive. Perhaps an example or two will help make the distinction somewhat clearer.

Suppose one wishes to establish the truth of the sentence, 'All Englishmen are mortal.' He can do this in two different ways: either by deductive reasoning or by inductive reasoning. Let us illustrate the former technique first. One may assert, as reasons in support of the above sentence, that the following statements are true: (a) 'All Englishmen are human beings,' and (b) 'All human beings are mortal.' Now if both of these sentences are true, then it will be impossible for the sentence, 'All Englishmen are mortal' to be false. In short, the truth of the sentences (a) and (b) provides conclusive evidence for the truth of the sentence, 'All Englishmen are mortal.' Here we have an inference from an assertion about **all** human beings to an assertion about **some** human beings, i.e., Englishmen, and this, therefore, is an example of the use of **deductive reasoning.**

On the other hand, one may not believe that the sentence, 'All human beings are mortal', is true. After all, one could know this with certainty only after every human being had died—a difficult matter if one includes himself among the class of humans. So, in order to establish the truth of 'All Englishmen are mortal,' he may wish to adopt a different procedure. He may wish to use as evidence propositions which he knows to be true and to argue from the particular to the general. He may say (a) 'Every Englishman born before 1830 has died.' (b) Englishmen are still dying.' The truth of (a) and (b) makes it probable that 'All Englishmen are mortal' is true; but unlike the reasons provided in the deductive argument above, the truth of these reasons does not make it *certain* that all Englishmen are mortal. It is still possible that (*a*) and (*b*) may both be true, and yet that someone alive today or who may be born in the future, will be immortal. Hence, even though our reasoning is sound, and even though we have correctly inferred our conclusion from the evidence we have, it is possible (although highly improbable) that the conclusion may be found to be false at some future time. **Inductive logic is thus not concerned with valid inferences, but with inferences which are probable, given as evidence the truth of certain propositions, upon which they are based.**

Inductive logic has one of its most important uses in connection with science. The scientist employs deductive methods, and even intuitive guesses, in order to investigate the world, but it is inductive logic which is his most important tool. Some writers have in fact spoken of 'scientific method' and 'inductive logic' as if they were synonyms—a mistake, but one which is not far from the truth. Let us describe some of the major steps in scientific activity in order to show why inductive logic is essential to scientific inquiry.

The most rudimentary stage of scientific investigation consists of the description of individual happenings and occurrences. For example, Galileo described the rate at which a particular body accelerated when he dropped it. He then dropped other bodies and in each case measured their rate of acceleration. If we were to reconstruct his activity, we might say that he arrived at a number of true individual statements describing the rate at which particular bodies accelerated. He noticed, for instance, that body A when dropped accelerated at a rate of 32 feet per second per second; body B fell with the same acceleration, so did body C, and so forth. Now from the truth of such individual or particular propositions (i.e., propositions describing particular events) he inferred a general truth of nature, sometimes called a **'law of nature'**. He inferred that *all* bodies when dropped will fall with an acceleration of 32 feet per second per second. From the standpoint of inductive logic, we might say that the individual propositions provided him with sound reasons for inferring the general conclusion that all bodies fall at a certain rate of increase of speed.

Put most generally, we may say that **inductive logic is a theory about what reasons provide evidence for a given conclusion's truth when the reasons in question are not conclusive ones.** In practice, inductive logic thus coincides with what has been called **'probability theory'**. Inductive logic is concerned with the **relation between the evidence and a conclusion drawn from the evidence.** The main question which such a discipline is concerned with is that which asks 'When does the evidence make the truth of the conclusion more probable than not?'—or more exactly, 'What is the probability that the conclusion is true, given the evidence in question?'

Because of the highly intricate nature of probability theory and of statistical analysis (which is based upon probability theory), in this section we shall confine our discussion of logic to **deductive logic.** It should be stressed before so doing, however, that logic in recent years has been one of the most actively pursued studies in the whole area of philosophy, and therefore, even our discussion of deductive logic alone must be severely limited.

DEDUCTIVE LOGIC: THE SYLLOGISM

In this section, we cannot study all types of deductive reasoning. In order to introduce the reader to the study of deductive logic, we shall therefore restrict our discussion to one of the most famous types of deductive reasoning: **the syllogism.** Roughly, **a syllogism may be defined as an argument which contains two premises and a conclusion—** but we hasten to add that this is not an exact definition. Since the exact definition can only be understood after some technical terms have been defined, we shall postpone giving such a definition. Let us now consider some of these technical terms in order to begin a discussion of the theory of the syllogism.

THE TERMINOLOGY OF LOGIC

Every syllogism must be composed of three propositions—no more and no less. The proposition which one is trying to prove or establish is called the **conclusion** of the argument, while the other two propositions provide reasons for asserting that the conclusion is true. These propositions are called the **premises** of the argument. Consider the following examples of a syllogism:

(i) All dogs are vertebrates.
(ii) All vertebrates are animals.
(iii) All dogs are animals.

Propositions (i) and (ii) are the **premises** of this syllogistic argument, while proposition (iii) is its **conclusion.** It should be noticed that the reasons in this case are **conclusive,** i.e., since they are true, it will be impossible for the conclusion to be false. In such a case, we say that the premises **imply** the conclusion, or equivalently, that the conclusion **follows from** the premises. What has been called 'the theory of the syllogism' is the system of rules which enables us to tell when syllogistic arguments are such that their premises imply the conclusion, and when they are not. In short, by telling us which arguments are valid and which are not, the theory of the syllogism provides us with a technique for distinguishing good from bad reasoning.

It should also be noticed that each of the propositions which make up a syllogism contains four parts. For example, proposition (i) is composed of four words, 'all', 'dogs', 'are' and 'vertebrates'. Proposition (ii) is similarly composed of four parts, the words 'all', 'vertebrates', 'are' and 'animals'. And likewise for proposition (iii). Every syllogism must be composed of propositions having these four elements; they determine what is called the 'standard form' of a syllogistic sentence. This form must be the following: The proposition must begin with what is called a **quantifier.** The word 'all' plays the role of a quantifier in each of the propositions in the syllogism we have examined above. Secondly, the proposition must contain a word which is its **subject**. This is called **'the subject term'**. The word 'dogs' is the subject term of proposition (i). Thirdly, the proposition must contain a **'predicate term'**; in this case the word 'vertebrate' is the **predicate**. And finally, it must contain a word which **connects or relates subject to predicate**, and this word is called the **'copula'**. The word 'are' performs this role in our simple syllogism above. In short, **a syllogism must contain exactly three propositions, all of which are in standard form—i.e., they must have a quantifier, a subject term, a predicate term, and a copula.**

A word of explanation about the use of these technical terms may assist the reader. **The subject term refers to that thing or entity about which we assert something. The predicate term designates that which is asserted of the subject. The copula will always be some form of the verb 'to be'**—usually it will be either 'are' or 'is'. **The function of the quantifier is to indicate the extent to which we refer to the members denoted by the subject term.** The usual words which are employed are 'all', 'some', 'none', 'no', or 'nothing'.

Throughout this section, in order to assist the reader, we shall provide exercises which will serve as a check on his understanding of the subject matter. The answers to the exercises will be found at the end of this chapter. See pages 258-62.

Exercise I

Identify the subject term, predicate term, copula and quantifiers (if any):

1 Some mad dogs are happily married.
2 All bats are members of the class of rodents.
3 James is wicked.
4 Horses are man's best friend.
5 Some tables are not mahogany.
6 Nothing green is in the room.

AFFIRMATIVE AND NEGATIVE PROPOSITIONS

In part depending upon the purpose for which they are used, and in part depending upon their grammatical structure, the sentences of the English language may be divided into various classes. Let us begin with a classification of these sentences which depends upon their grammatical form. We can thus distinguish (*a*) **declarative or indicative sentences,** (*b*) **interrogative sentences,** (*c*) **imperative sentences** and (*d*) **optative sentences,** from one another. If we turn to the uses of these sentences we can distinguish (*a*) **assertions,** (*b*) **questions,** (*c*) **commands** and (*d*) **wishes** from each other. Since it would take us too far astray to attempt to define the above uses of language precisely, or to attempt to delineate the grammatical structure of such sentences exactly, we shall here characterize them roughly. The point of these remarks is that, as we have already mentioned, **logic deals only with declarative sentences, i.e., with those types of sentence which are used for the purpose of making assertions.**

The reason why logic does not deal with all of the types of sentence above is that **only declarative sentences, which are used to make assertions about the world, can be either true or false.** An interrogative sentence is used to ask a question. If I say 'Is the door open?', I am not making any claim about the door. I am not asserting or stating that it is open. As a result, what I say cannot be either true or false. For a sentence to be either true or false it must make some claim about the world. It must assert that something is the case. For instance, if I say 'There are 12 cars in the garage', I am making a claim about the number of cars in the garage. My sentence is thus either true or false. It is true if and only if there are 12 cars in the garage; otherwise it is false (i.e., either if there are less than or more than 12 cars in the garage). Similarly, an imperative sentence is generally used for the purpose of issuing a command. If I say 'Right Face!' this utterance is neither true nor false. I am not making an assertion such as 'He always obeys my commands', but rather I am issuing a command. A command may either be followed or not followed; but whether it is followed or not, we do not say that a command is true or false, since it makes no declaration about the entities in the world. An optative sentence is a sentence used for the purpose of expressing a wish. If I say 'Oh, would I were King!' I am again not making a statement such as 'I am King'. I am merely expressing the hope that I might become King, and this is different from asserting that I am or that I will be King.

Logic thus deals only with declarative sentences, i.e., sentences used for the purpose of making some claim or assertion about the world. This is why the logician prefers to use the term **'proposition'**, to distinguish such sentences from those he is not concerned with. In the case of arguments of a syllogistic type, such declarative sentences or propositions must always be of the subject–predicate form. They must always be such that the predicate asserts something of the subject. Thus if I say 'The table is brown', I am asserting that the colour 'brown' belongs to the thing called 'the table'. Or again, if I say 'All cats are mammals', I am asserting that the property of being mammalian belongs to each and every cat.

The reason why logic deals only with declarative sentences is clear if one reflects upon the remarks we made earlier about the nature of logic. We pointed out that logic deals with correct reasoning. Correctness of reasoning is closely connected with truth and falsity, although it is not to be identified with them. The connection is this: **when one reasons correctly, if the premises of his argument are true, it will be impossible for the conclusion to be false.** Since other types of sentence are not capable of being either true or false, it would be impossible to define correct reasoning in relation to the truth of such sentences; and this is why logic restricts itself to those sentences which are used to make assertions.

Declarative or assertive sentences or propositions may be further divided into those in which the predicate **affirms** something of the subject, and those in which the predicate **denies** something of the subject. We call the former 'affirmative' and the latter 'negative'. An example of an affirmative proposition is: 'All lions are ferocious'. The presence of a word like 'no' or 'none' or 'not' or 'nothing' indicates that the proposition is negative, as in 'No teachers are wealthy', or 'Some teachers are not wealthy', and so on.

When we describe a proposition as 'affirmative' or 'negative' we are speaking of the **'quality'** of the proposition. We shall see in the next section that quality must be distinguished from the 'quantity' of a proposition.

Sometimes it is difficult to determine whether a proposition is affirmative or negative. The two propositions 'Some Moslems are non-drinkers', and 'Some Moslems are not drinkers', are equivalent in meaning; they both say that part of the class of Moslems is excluded from the class of those who drink. But the former is affirmative. It asserts that some Moslems belong to the class of non-drinkers; while the latter is negative: it denies that some Moslems belong to the class of drinkers. In the first case the word 'non' modifies the predicate; in the second case, the word 'not' modifies the copula. Thus, from the fact that an adjective or noun is modified by such a word as 'non' we cannot always infer that the proposition in question is negative. What determines a proposition to be negative is whether the word 'not' or 'no' modifies the copula. When it does, it is negative. Thus, such a proposition as 'No dogs are feline' is negative because it denies that feline qualities can be asserted of dogs.

Exercise II

Determine whether the following propositions are affirmative or negative.

1 James is very unhappy.
2 Lions are not untrustworthy.
3 She was not disinclined to come.
4 None but the lonely heart is filled with sadness.
5 Nothing tried, nothing gained.
6 He has been unwell for months now.
7 Some philosophers are intuitive.
8 No non-addicts can understand the problem.
9 All non-S are non-P.
10 All except women may attend.

UNIVERSAL, PARTICULAR AND SINGULAR PROPOSITIONS

We have just pointed out that declarative sentences may be classified as either negative or affirmative. Such a classification is referred to by logicians as one of **'quality'**. But there is another important classification of such sentences—into those which are **'universal'**, or **'particular'** or **'singular'**. This distinction is termed one of **'quantity'**.

Whether a proposition is universal, particular or singular depends upon whether we are speaking about *all* of the entities referred to by the subject term, about *some* of them only, or about a *single* individual. If I say 'All film stars are wealthy', I am uttering a sentence whose subject term refers to each and every film star. This is why we say such a sentence is 'universal' in scope. On the other hand, if I qualify my remarks by saying that 'Some film stars are wealthy', I am not necessarily referring to each and every film star. I am referring to a certain set or group of them—this is why we term such a proposition as 'particular'. On the other hand, if I say 'Bing Crosby is wealthy', I am referring to one and only one person, and thus my judgment is said to be 'singular'.

In the theory of the syllogism, for purposes which we shall explain immediately, **singular propositions are always interpreted as 'universal' ones.** This achieves considerable theoretical simplification, since it reduces the number of classifications of sentences according to their 'quantity' to two: those which are universal and those which are particular. Singular propositions are regarded as universal ones for two reasons. First, because in such a proposition as 'Bing Crosby is wealthy', we are referring to *all* of Mr. Crosby, not merely to a part of him. This being characteristic of universal propositions as well, it is natural to designate singular propositions as 'universal'. Secondly, singular propositions are regarded as universal for another reason. Syllogistic logic deals with the relations between classes of things. When I say that 'All men are mortal', the terms 'men' and 'mortal' refer to classes of entities—the class of men and the class of mortals. On the class interpretation of the proposition, I am asserting that the class of men is included within the class of mortals. I am thus specifying a relation between the two classes, the relation of 'being included within'. On the other hand, when I say 'Jack is an American', I am ordinarily suggesting that Jack is a citizen of the United States, or more accurately, a member of a certain group. The relation of being a member of a class is different from the relation of one class being included within another. Syllogistic logic would become much more complicated if it had to distinguish between such relations. In order, therefore, to deal with singular propositions, this sort of logical system interprets singular propositions as universal ones. Such a proposition as 'Jack is an American', can be interpreted as saying that a class containing only one member, namely Jack, is included within the class of Americans.

When the subject class has no quantifier as in 'Tenors love spaghetti', we are uncertain sometimes whether the proposition is to be interpreted as being universal or particular. **The rule in such cases is that 'all' is intended, unless 'some' is clearly indicated.** Hence, 'Tenors love spaghetti' is to be interpreted as 'All tenors love spaghetti'. On the other hand, such a proposition as 'Men have climbed Mt. Everest', is to be interpreted to mean 'Some men have climbed Mt. Everest', rather than 'All men have climbed Mt. Everest'.

Exercise III

Determine whether the following propositions are universal or particular:

1 Fish are mammals.

2 Some dragons are fierce.
3 This table is brown.
4 That system is useless.
5 They are crazy.
6 Hard-working students are successful.
7 Albert Einstein was a genius.
8 Those tins seem heavy.
9 That bottle of aspirin is not full.
10 No human beings are infallible.
11 Some cats are not wise.
12 Men have climbed Mt. Everest.
13 All Germans are not cruel.
14 All golfers are wealthy.
15 Some babies are small.

THE FOUR STANDARD PROPOSITIONS OF LOGIC

According to the logical system we are now considering, **every declarative sentence will be either universal or particular, and either affirmative or negative.** All syllogistic reasoning or argumentation will thus involve the use of these types of proposition. If we combine them in various ways, we can see that **there are four and only four possible types of proposition dealt with by logic.** It is assumed by logicians that much of the discourse in a natural language, such as English, can be translated into one or another of the four propositions of syllogistic logic. It is thus assumed that the type of logic we are considering is capable of dealing with numerous cases of reasoning which one might encounter in his everyday activities. The four types of proposition are:

(*a*) Those which are **universal and affirmative.**
(*b*) Those which are **universal and negative.**
(*c*) Those which are **particular and affirmative.**
(*d*) Those which are **particular and negative.**

(It will be recalled that singular propositions are interpreted as universal ones in this schema.)

Traditionally, logicians have given names to each type of proposition for purposes of convenience in discussing them. The names are the vowels, 'A', 'E', 'I' and 'O'. Thus, **universal-affirmative propositions are called 'A' propositions** (the name being derived from the initial letter of the Latin word *affirmo*, meaning 'I assert'); **universal-negative propositions are termed 'E' propositions** (from the initial vowel in *nego*, 'I deny'); **particular-affirmative propositions are designated by the letter 'I'** from the second vowel of *affirmo*; while **particular-negative propositions are denoted by the letter 'O'** from the last vowel in *nego*. **The affirmative forms are A and I; the negative forms are E and O; the universal forms are A and E; the particular are I and O.**

Exercise IV

Determine whether the following propositions are to be designated as A, E, I, O, and also determine their quantity and quality, i.e., whether they are universal and affirmative, etc.

1　No Germans are kind.
2　All doctors are interested in medicine.
3　Some lawyers are golfers.
4　Joe Louis is no longer heavyweight champion.
5　Lord Byron was a champion of freedom.
6　Some conductors are non-luminous.
7　All football players are excluded from the class of authors.
8　Some football players are not authors.
9　That paper was well read.
10　Each and every lion is ferocious.

THE DISTRIBUTION OF TERMS

As we shall show later, it is possible to develop a set of rules which enable the student, in a very simple way, to determine whether a syllogistic argument is valid or invalid. One of the basic notions involved in the statement of such rules is the notion of 'distribution'. It is very important, therefore, to understand the following section if the student wishes to be able to apply correctly the rules we shall develop later.

Distribution is a very simple idea. We say that **a term is distributed when the term refers to all the members of the class denoted by the term.** For example, if I say 'All Englishmen are insane', the term 'Englishmen' is distributed because I have referred to *all* Englishmen. On the other hand, if I say 'Some Englishmen are wise', the term 'Englishmen' is not distributed since I am referring only to part of the class of Englishmen. Let us now see how all the A, E, I, O propositions distribute their terms. Since each of these propositions contains two terms, a subject term and a predicate term, we shall have to determine for each type of proposition whether both, one or neither of its terms is distributed.

Distribution of the terms in the 'A' proposition. In an 'A' proposition (i.e. a universal-affirmative proposition such as 'All lions are carnivorous'), the subject term is obviously distributed since we are referring to *all* lions. But the predicate term is not distributed. We are not referring to all carnivorous things when we say that 'All lions are carnivorous'. We are merely saying that the class of lions is included in the class of carnivorous things; but we are not speaking about *all* carnivorous things and hence the predicate term is not distributed. This can be seen if we were to reverse the subject and predicate terms in a true 'A' proposition. If I say 'All lions are carnivorous', the proposition is true; but, on the other hand, if I say 'All carnivorous things are lions', the proposition is false. This shows us that we were not referring to all carnivores in the proposition 'All lions are carnivorous'. For this reason, as we have said, the predicate term is not distributed.

Distribution of terms in the 'E' proposition. Both the subject and predicate terms are distributed in the 'E' proposition (a universal-negative proposition, e.g., 'No dwarfs are blonde'). Here we are saying that the class of dwarfs is entirely excluded from the class of blondes. We are thus referring to all dwarfs and to all blondes and are saying that both classes are disjoint.

Distribution of terms in the 'I' proposition. Both the subject and predicate are undistributed in the 'I' proposition (i.e., a particular-affirmative proposition: 'Some birds are black'). Here we are asserting that the class of birds and the class of black things have a common member. But we are not speaking about *all* birds and about *all* black things, but only about some in each class. Hence both subject and predicate are undistributed.

Distribution of terms in the 'O' proposition. In the 'O' proposition (i.e., a particular-negative proposition: 'Some paths are not steep'), we find the subject term to be undistributed and the predicate term to be distributed. It is easy to see that the subject term is undistributed, since it refers merely to part of a class; but why is the predicate term distributed? This is because we are saying that some paths are excluded from the entire class of steep things. In short, we are speaking about the whole class of steep things and thus the predicate term is distributed.

We may summarize our results as follows:

Both universal propositions distribute their subject terms, but the A proposition does not distribute its predicate; although the E proposition does. Both particular propositions do not distribute their subject terms, and the I does not distribute its predicate, although the O does. The following diagram may help to make this somewhat easier to understand:

DISTRIBUTION OF TERMS IN A, E, I, O PROPOSITIONS

Type of Proposition	Subject Term	Predicate Term
A	Distrib.	Undist.
E	Distrib.	Distrib.
I	Undist.	Undist.
O	Undist.	Distrib.

Exercise V

Indicate which terms are distributed and which are undistributed in the following examples:

1 All Japanese are good swimmers.
2 No conductors are overpaid.
3 Some swans are not black.
4 Some swans are beautiful.
5 Twiggy is a model.

6 All Yorkshiremen are non-farmers.
7 Some Yorkshiremen are not farmers.

MIDDLE, MAJOR AND MINOR TERMS

In order to comprehend the rules for determining when a syllogism is valid, one must understand three pieces of logical terminology: (*a*) the distinction between affirmative and negative propositions, (*b*) the meaning of the term 'distribution' and (*c*) what is meant by the 'middle term', 'major term' and 'minor term' of an argument. We have already, in the preceding sections, discussed (*a*) and (*b*). We shall therefore now proceed to explain (*c*)—i.e., what is meant by **'middle term'**, **'minor term'**, and **'major term'**. After that we shall be in a position to lay down the rules for assessing the validity or invalidity of a syllogistic argument.

As we explained near the beginning of this chapter, a syllogism can roughly be characterized as an argument containing two premises and a conclusion. We are now prepared to make this characterization more exact, and in so doing, we shall also be explaining what such terms as 'minor term', 'major term' and 'middle term' mean. Since a syllogism contains two premises and a conclusion, it is composed of three propositions of the subject-predicate form. It thus contains six terms, i.e., three subject terms, three predicate terms. Consider the following syllogism as an example:

All idiots are happy.
All football players are idiots.
Therefore, All football players are happy.

It will be noticed that there are three *different* terms among the six terms which occur in the three propositions making up the argument. Each of the three different terms (i.e., 'Idiots', 'happy', 'football players') occurs twice. **Now by the 'middle term' we mean the term which appears in both premises. The middle term does not appear in the conclusion since each term is used twice and only twice.** In the foregoing example the word 'idiots' is the middle term, since it occurs in both premises. **By the 'major term' we mean the term which occurs as the predicate of the conclusion.** The major term is also found in the first premise of our sample argument. In the example above, the word 'happy' is the major term. **The phrase 'major term' is applied to the predicate of the conclusion since it is the term designating the class with the largest extension.** In the argument above we are saying that the class of football players is included in the class of idiots; the class of idiots is included in the class of happy people; hence the class of football players is included in the class of happy people. The word 'happy' thus refers to the largest class, and this is why the predicate of the conclusion is called the 'major term'. **The subject of the conclusion, on the other hand, is called the 'minor term'.** The minor term also occurs, it will be noticed, once in the premises, as well as being the subject of the conclusion. In the example we have selected, the term 'football players' is the minor term.

As a further matter of terminology, we should mention that the **major premise is that premise which contains the major term,** while the **minor premise contains the minor term.** Each premise, of course, contains the **middle term.**

It is frequently convenient for purposes of exposition to let certain letters stand for the corresponding terms. Traditionally, logicians have designated the letter 'M' to stand for the middle term, 'S' for the minor term and 'P' for the major term. Our argument could thus be symbolized, using the above letters as follows:

> All idiots are happy.
> (All   M   are   P)
> All football players are idiots.
> (All   S   are   M)
> Therefore, All football players are happy.
> (All   S   are   P)

The form of the argument put symbolically is:

> All M are P
> All S are M
> _____
> Therefore, All S are P

This can be further abbreviated by employing the vowels which we have seen are used to signify the quantity and quality of a proposition. In this case, all are universal-affirmative propositions, 'A' propositions, so that our syllogism can be expressed:

> M a P
> S a M
> ∴ S a P

Exercise VI

Identify the middle, major and minor terms of the following syllogisms. Also, designate the premises as major and minor:

1 All men are fallible.
  I am a man.
  Therefore, I am fallible.
2 Some politicians are ignoble.
  No one who is ignoble is wise.
  Some politicians are not wise.
3 All singers are temperamental.
  No lorry drivers are temperamental.
  No singers are lorry drivers.
4 All S is M.
  No M is P.
  No S is P.
5 S i M
  P i M
  S i P

RULES FOR DETERMINING VALIDITY
AND INVALIDITY

We are now ready to state and discuss the rules for determining when a syllogistic argument is valid or invalid. It will be understood, of course, that no argument can be both invalid and valid. If it is valid then it cannot be invalid, and conversely. The rules we are about to lay down are such that if one cannot prove by them that an argument is invalid, then he can assume that the argument is valid. In short, **if a syllogistic argument does not violate any of the five rules we are about to give, it is a valid syllogism. If it violates any of the rules, then it is invalid.**

These rules can be divided into two sets: those which refer to the **quantity** of a proposition (i.e., **rules of distribution**) and those which refer to the **quality** of a proposition (i.e., whether it is **affirmative or negative**).

Rules of Quantity:
RULE 1. The middle term must be distributed at least once.
RULE 2. If a term is not distributed in the premises, it must not be distributed in the conclusion.

Rules of Quality:
RULE 3. No conclusion can follow from two negative premises.
RULE 4. If either premise is negative, the conclusion must be negative.
RULE 5. A negative conclusion cannot follow from two affirmative premises.

Before discussing each of the above rules, it is important to mention to the reader that **the above rules apply only to syllogistic arguments.** Therefore, before applying the rules to an argument one must first check to make sure that the argument is of the syllogistic form or can be expressed in syllogistic form (i.e., it must have two premises and a conclusion, three and only three terms, each of which is employed twice in the argument, and finally the middle term must appear in both premises). If an argument satisfies the above conditions, then one can apply the five rules we have stated in order to determine whether such reasoning is valid or invalid.

We turn now to a detailed discussion of the rules.

RULE 1. **The middle term must be distributed at least once.**
The following syllogism violates the rule:

All men are human beings.
All women are human beings.
Therefore, all women are men.

The middle term in the above argument is 'human beings'. Since it is the predicate term in both premises, and since both premises are A propositions, neither premise distributes its predicate. Thus, the middle term is undistributed. The error or fallacy in the argument is this: even though it is true that all men are human beings and that all women are human beings, it does not follow that they cannot both belong to the same class, i.e., human beings, and yet be different from each other, since at no stage does the syllogism assert that either men or women constitute **the whole class** of human beings. In short, **the two premises are not connected by the middle term.** This fallacy is called **'the fallacy of the undistributed middle'.**

At this point, it is necessary to mention explicitly a distinction we hinted at earlier. It is very important to distinguish between the **validity of an argument,** and the **truth or falsity of the premises and conclusion of the argument.** It is possible for the premises of an argument to be true (as in the above example) and yet for the argument to be invalid. Or again, all the premises of an argument may be false, and yet the argument may be valid. Validity depends upon *how* one reasons. To say that reasoning is valid is not to say that the premises one employs are true. **It is to say that IF they are true, and if one's reasoning is valid, it will be impossible for the conclusion to be false.** The following examples will illustrate the distinction between validity and truth:

    If   1 is greater than 2, and
    If   2 is greater than 3,
    Then 1 is greater than 3.

It will be noted that both premises and the conclusion are false; yet the argument is valid; for *if* the premises were true, it would be impossible for the conclusion to be false, as can be seen from the following example:

    If   3 is greater than 2, and
    If   2 is greater than 1,
    Then 3 is greater than 1.

On the other hand, it is important for the reader also to realize that simply because an argument has true premises and even a true conclusion, it may not embody valid reasoning.

We cite here an example of an argument violating rule 1 in which both premises and the conclusion are true. But since the argument does not distribute its middle term, it is invalid:

    All Yorkshiremen are mortal,
    All Englishmen are mortal,
    Therefore, all Yorkshiremen are Englishmen.

RULE 2. **If a term is not distributed in the premises, it must not be distributed in the conclusion.**

The following syllogism violates this rule:

    All cats are mammals,
    No dogs are cats,
    Therefore, no dogs are mammals.

I

The fallacy involved in the violation of this rule is sometimes called 'illicit process', or 'illicit distribution'. It should be noted that the term 'mammals' is distributed in the conclusion, but not in the major premise. This is because the major premise is an A proposition and does not distribute its predicate; but the conclusion is an E proposition which does. **The error of 'illicit process' is one in which the conclusion attempts to give us more information than is contained in the premises.** The premises do not tell us about *all* mammals; but the conclusion does. The argument would be valid if and only if we could infer that *all* mammals are cats; but this statement goes beyond our information which is merely that all cats are mammals.

RULE 3. **No conclusion can follow from two negative premises.**

The following syllogism violates this rule:

> No dogs are cold-blooded,
> No cold-blooded things are capable of barking,
> Therefore, no dogs are capable of barking.

When we have two negative premises, we fail to establish any connection between the terms of the argument. For example, in order to show that no dogs are capable of barking, we have to show that dogs belong to the class of cold-blooded things; but this would be to assert an affirmative premise, i.e., All dogs are cold-blooded—which contradicts the information given us in the premises. Hence, no conclusion follows.

RULE 4. **If either premise is negative, the conclusion must be negative.**

The following syllogism violates this rule:

> All head-hunters are primitives,
> Some Londoners are not primitives,
> Therefore, some Londoners are head-hunters.

It should be noted that the above argument satisfies all the other rules we have discussed. The middle term is distributed, no term is distributed in the conclusion which is not distributed in the premises, and at least one premise is affirmative. Nevertheless, the argument is invalid, since the premises are true and the conclusion is false. The fallacy consists in inferring that because some Londoners are excluded from a certain group, some must belong to the group. This does not follow, since even though we only assert that some are excluded from a group, all may be.

RULE 5. **A negative conclusion cannot follow from two affirmative premises.**

The following syllogism violates this rule:

> All men are mortals,
> All mortals are fallible,
> Therefore, some fallible things are not men.

Again this syllogism satisfies the previous rules. It distributes the middle term 'mortals', and it does not contain a distributed term in the conclusion which is undistributed in the premises. Likewise, it violates neither of the two rules of quality we have just discussed. **But again it commits a fallacy, since we go beyond the information given us when we infer that some fallible things are not men.** We know, on the basis of the two premises, that all men are fallible. But we cannot conclusively infer *either* that there are some fallible things which are not men, or that there are not some fallible things which are not men.

Exercise VII

Determine whether the following syllogisms are valid or invalid. If invalid, state the fallacy they commit.

1 All accountants are tennis players,
   All youngsters are tennis players,
   All accountants are youngsters.
2 All men are substances,
   All animals are substances,
   All men are animals.
3 All poets have creative imagination,
   No poets are good business men,
   No good business men have creative imagination.
4 Some modern poetry is interesting,
   Everything interesting has value,
   Nothing which has value is worthless,
   Some modern poetry is not worthless.
5 All Buddhists are vegetarians,
   George Bernard Shaw is a vegetarian,
   George Bernard Shaw is a Buddhist.
6 Some Moslems are non-drinkers,
   All Arabs are Moslems,
   Some Arabs are non-drinkers.
7 All footballers are well paid,
   Some teachers of philosophy are not footballers,
   Some teachers of philosophy are not well paid.
8 Some bus riders are alcoholics,
   Some train riders are not alcoholics,
   Some bus riders are train riders.
9 No Germans are democrats,
   Some democrats are not fascists,
   Some Germans are not fascists.
10 Some teeth are not white,
   All white things are beautiful,
   Some beautiful things are not teeth.

TRANSLATING ORDINARY SENTENCES INTO LOGICAL SENTENCES

We have presented the formal theory of the syllogism. In terms of the five rules given, every syllogistic argument can be shown to be either valid or invalid. It is easy to apply these rules once discourse has been put into the standard A, E, I, O propositions of logic, but there is difficulty in applying the rules directly to examples of reasoning in everyday life. Generally, such reasoning does not take place in propositions having neat logical forms of the sort we have discussed. Logicians are thus faced with the problem of translating ordinary English into the standard, and somewhat artificial, propositions of logic—since it is only when sentences are in such standard form that arguments containing them can be determined to be valid or invalid by the methods we have outlined above.

In this section, therefore, we shall give some rules for translating irregular sentences of ordinary discourse into the standard A, E, I, O propositions of formal logic.

RULE A: **Clearly identify the subject and predicate of the English sentence.**

Consider the following: 'Seldom have sailors had such acclaim'. The subject here is not 'seldom' but 'sailors'. The sentence should be transformed to read: 'Sailors have seldom had such acclaim', or if we introduce the appropriate part of the verb 'to be' as copula, 'Sailors are persons who have seldom had such acclaim'. Another example is: 'All take great risks who put their eggs into one basket'. This again should be rendered so that the subject and predicate are clearly identifiable. When we do this, the sentence will read:

> 'All persons who put their eggs in one basket are persons who take great risks'.

RULE B: **Supply the Missing Quantifier.**

When no quantifier is present, supply the missing quantifier. Unless it is clear from the context that 'some' is intended, the rule is that 'all' is meant. Thus, in a proposition such as 'Psychotics are dangerous', one should add the word 'all'. This will put the proposition into standard logical form, e.g., 'All psychotics are dangerous'. In such a proposition as 'Americans are great sprinters', however, 'some' is intended, not 'all'. The revised proposition should read 'Some Americans are great sprinters', unless, of course, we mean by it 'All **American sprinters** are great sprinters'.

Further examples of such revisions follow:

(a) 'Dogs bark', should be rendered as 'All dogs bark'.
(b) 'Cats are carnivorous', should be rendered as 'All cats are carnivorous'.
(c) 'Germans suffer from Buerger's Disease', should be translated as 'Some Germans suffer from Buerger's Disease'.

RULE C: **Add the Missing Complement.**

Since the terms of logic designate classes, it is sometimes necessary to add what is called a '**complement**' to an adjective or to a describing phrase to show that they refer to classes. For example, if I say 'Some lions are docile', since we cannot point to 'a docile', strictly speaking we must say 'docile creatures', or 'docile animals'. Consider the following examples:

(a) 'Communists are losing ground', should be rendered as 'Communists are persons who are losing ground'.

(b) 'The foolhardy are losers in the end'. This should be rendered as 'All foolhardy persons are losers in the end'.

RULE D: **Supply the Missing Copula.**

In propositions such as 'Dogs bark', or 'Some ancients believed in devils', the copula (i.e., the word 'are' or 'is') is missing. These propositions should be rendered as 'All dogs *are* barking animals', and 'Some ancient peoples *are* people who believed in devils'.

RULE E: **Exclusive Sentences.**

Some sentences begin with words such as 'only' or 'none but'. For example, if I say 'Only men are priests', or 'None but non-smokers need apply', these sentences are not in standard form. It is important in such cases that we reflect upon the meanings of these sentences before putting them into standard logical form. For example, 'Only men are priests', surely does not mean that 'All men are priests'. Rather it means that 'All priests are men'. The rule therefore with regard to such sentences is: drop the word 'only' or 'none but', and add 'all' as a quantifier; then reverse the order of subject and predicate. Thus, in order to transform such sentences into standard form, two steps are required: (a) **Drop the words 'only' or 'none but' and replace them by 'all'.** (b) **Interchange subject and predicate terms.**

EXAMPLE: 'None but adults are admitted', is equivalent in meaning to 'All those persons admitted are adults'.

RULE F: **Negative Sentences.**

To begin with, such words as 'nothing', 'none' or 'no one' are to be treated by replacing them with the quantifier, 'no'. Thus, such a sentence as 'None of the damned is happy', is to be rendered as a standard proposition as follows: 'No person who is damned is a happy person'. Or again, such a sentence as 'Nothing human frightens me', will require the following steps in order to transform it into a standard proposition:

1 The quantifier becomes 'no'.
2 Subject is 'human being'.
3 Add the copula.
4 Complement the predicate.

The result of these operations is a proposition in standard form: 'No human beings are things which frighten me'.

Secondly, it should be noted that English propositions of the form 'All . . . are not', are frequently ambiguous. It is not clear sometimes whether they should be interpreted as an O proposition or as an E proposition. **The rule is that we should interpret them in every case as an O proposition, unless an E is clearly intended.** Thus if I say 'All

Germans are not Nazis', I do not mean that 'No Germans are Nazis', but rather 'Some Germans are not Nazis', which is, of course, an O proposition.

RULE G: **Exceptive Sentences.**

Sentences which contain the word 'except' cannot be exactly translated into any *one* of the A, E, I, O propositions. For instance, if I say: 'Everyone except women may attend', I mean something which is expressed by the following two propositions:

(1) All who are not women may attend (and)
(2) No women may attend.

The first proposition is an A proposition, and the second is an E proposition. Since a syllogism can contain only three propositions, if we were to allow *both* propositions as being the translation of the exceptive sentence, arguments in syllogistic form would no longer be syllogisms since they would contain more than three propositions. Hence the rule is that either the A proposition or the E proposition may be used, but not both. Any argument which contains an exceptive sentence and which is valid will remain valid if the exceptive sentence is interpreted either as an A proposition or as an E proposition.

RULE H: **Sentences containing 'Anyone', 'Anything', 'Whoever', 'The', 'If ... then', 'Whatever'.**

Consider the following sentences:

1 Anyone who comes must participate.
2 Anything which comes must participate.
3 Whoever comes must participate.
4 Whatever comes must participate.
5 Everyone who comes must participate.
6 If anyone comes he must participate.
7 The person who comes must participate.

Sentences containing the above terms can all be translated into A propositions, e.g., 'All who come must participate', or 'All persons who come must participate', and so on.

RULE I: **Sentences containing 'Someone', 'Something', 'There is', or 'There are'.**

Consider the following:

1 Someone opened the door.
2 Something opened the door.
3 There are things which opened the door.
4 There is something which opened the door.

All such sentences are to be translated into I propositions, e.g., 'Some persons are persons who opened the door'.

The reader should study the above rules carefully, since by following them he will be able to translate sentences of ordinary English into propositions of standard logical form. Once this is accomplished, it is simple to determine whether arguments containing such propositions are valid or invalid. The above list of rules, it should be mentioned, is not complete; and thus the reader who examines a body of discourse taken from literature or the daily newspaper, will frequently have to exercise his ingenuity in order to transform irregular sentences into the standard propositions of logic.

Exercise VIII

Put the following into standard logical form.

1 Ships are beautiful.
2 Joan is a blonde.
3 The whale is a mammal.
4 Whoever is a child is silly.
5 Snakes coil.
6 None but golfers appreciate Hogan.
7 Only indicative sentences make assertions.
8 Nothing ventured, nothing gained.
9 All but the brave die many deaths.
10 All swans are not white.

EQUIVALENT SENTENCES

There is one further logical technique which we must consider before concluding the formal theory of the syllogism. This is a technique which, like the foregoing discussion, enables us to put reasoning which is not in syllogistic form, into such a form that its validity can be assessed. The purpose of the technique is to transform certain propositions into other propositions which are equivalent in meaning, but which may have a different logical form—**with the advantage that an argument which may not be in strict syllogistic form can be transformed into a syllogism** by the use of these techniques. Perhaps this can be explained more clearly by an example. Consider the following:

> No unwise people are trustworthy,
> All wise people are unaggressive,
> No trustworthy people are aggressive.

This argument clearly seems to be valid, but we cannot test it by the rules we have formulated above, since it contains more than three terms. In fact, it seems to contain five terms, 'unwise people', 'trustworthy people', 'wise people', 'unaggressive people', and 'aggressive people'. But the second premise means the same thing as 'All aggressive people are unwise'. Consequently if we substitute this latter proposition for the original proposition we get the following argument:

> No unwise people are trustworthy,
> All aggressive people are unwise,
> No trustworthy people are aggressive.

The argument now contains three and only three terms, and hence is a syllogism. We can now test it with our five rules, and can thus ascertain that the argument is valid.

The techniques which allow us to transform a given proposition into an equivalent one are called **Obversion, Conversion** and **Contraposition.** Let us turn to an examination of these techniques now, beginning with Obversion.

OBVERSION

In obverting a given proposition we do two things:

(*a*) We change the **quality** (but not the quantity) of the proposition. That is, **if it is negative, we make it affirmative; and if affirmative, we make it negative.**

(*b*) We then **negate the predicate.**

> EXAMPLE: 'No Marines are unreliable'.
> First we change the quality. Thus the proposition becomes:
> 'All Marines are unreliable'.
> Then we negate the predicate:
> 'All Marines are not unreliable'.

The proposition 'All Marines are not unreliable' is equivalent to 'All Marines are reliable', (two negatives make a positive) and thus our final proposition 'All Marines are reliable', is equivalent to our original one, 'No Marines are unreliable'.

It is possible to obvert every A, E, I, O proposition. There follows a diagram with the original proposition and its obverse:

Type of Sentence	Original	Obverse
A	All men are mortal.	No men are non-mortal.
E	No men are mortal.	All men are immortal.
I	Some men are mortal.	Some men are not immortal.
O	Some men are not mortal.	Some men are immortal.

Care must be exercised in obverting propositions in ordinary speech, since one may use an English term which does not negate the predicate. Some of the English prefixes such as 'im' or 'un' or 'in' do not always express simple negation. Furthermore, words such as 'small' and 'poor' are not the negations of 'large' and 'rich'. In such cases, in order to negate the predicate, the prefix **'non'** is ordinarily employed by logicians. Thus, the negation of 'wealthy' is not 'poor' but 'non-wealthy'.

In obverting, there must be no change in the **quantity** of the sentence, but only in its **quality.** Thus, **a universal sentence remains universal, a particular remains particular.**

CONVERSION

When we convert we merely **interchange subject and predicate.** Thus, the proposition 'No cats are dogs', is equivalent to the proposition, 'No dogs are cats'. Unlike obversion, **not every standard** proposition of logic has an equivalent converse. In fact, **only the E proposition and the I proposition can be converted.** Thus, 'No horses are mice', is equivalent to 'No mice are horses'. Likewise, the I proposition 'Some horses are animals', is equivalent to 'Some animals are horses'.

The O proposition cannot be converted. From 'Some men are not priests', we cannot infer 'Some priests are not men'.

The A cannot be converted simply. From such a proposition as 'All horses are animals', we cannot infer 'All animals are horses'. However, it is possible **partially to convert** the A. Logicians call this **'Conversion by Limitation'. When we convert a true A proposition, we can transform it into a true I proposition.** Thus, 'All horses are animals', when partially converted gives us 'Some animals are horses'. Partial conversion, however, does not result in a statement which is exactly equivalent in meaning to the original, since the quantity of the original statement is changed.

The following is a table of permissible conversions:

Type of Sentence	Original	Converse
E	No men are mortal.	No mortals are men.
I	Some men are mortal.	Some mortals are men.
A	All men are mortal.	Some mortals are men. (Partial converse)

The O, it must be remembered, cannot be converted.

CONTRAPOSITION

Contraposition is the third method of altering propositions into their equivalents. To obtain the **contrapositive** of a proposition three operations must be performed: **first we obvert, then convert, then obvert once again.** The contrapositive of a given proposition has, for this reason, sometimes been defined as **the obverse of a converted obverse.** Let us illustrate this by an example:

	Original sentence:	All dogs are animals.
Step 1, Obvert:		No dogs are non-animals.
Step 2, Convert:		No non-animals are dogs.
Step 3, Obvert:		All non-animals are non-dogs.

Contraposition, like conversion, cannot be applied to all four standard propositions of logic. The A and O propositions have contrapositives. The I has no contrapositive. The E has a partial contrapositive. Since contraposition is generally applied only to A propositions, we shall not discuss this form further here.

The above discussion completes our informal disquisition upon methods of translating irregular propositions into regular ones, and of translating certain propositions into equivalent ones. Given the above machinery, as well as the formal theory of the syllogism explained earlier, it should now be possible for the reader to transform large parts of English discourse into arguments of a syllogistic form, and then to test their validity.

Exercise IX

A. Obvert the following:

1 Some Londoners are braggarts.
2 No trains are buses.
3 Some magazines are not articulate.
4 Only dwarfs are kind.
5 All fairies are immortal.
6 All except John will be admitted.
7 Whoever is intelligent is appreciated.

B. Convert the following:

1 Some cats are white.
2 No lions are tame.
3 Some Russians are not Communists.
4 All non-conductors are non-metallic.
5 All cars are expensive.
6 Some golfers are champions.
7 Some cars are not expensive.
8 Nothing ventured, nothing gained.

C. Contrapose the following:

1 All superstitions are ridiculous.
2 All prejudices are unwarranted.
3 Some horses are not unintelligent.
4 Some horses are not intelligent.
5 Only the considerate deserve the fair.

FALLACIES

In the preceding pages we discussed the rules for determining when reasoning of the kind called 'syllogistic reasoning' is valid or invalid. The five rules we formulated are tests which determine whether an argument is valid; and they are likewise tests which determine whether an argument in syllogistic form is invalid. **When an argument which has the form of a syllogism seems valid, but is not, we say that it is 'fallacious'.** Such errors as 'undistributed middle', or 'illicit process', are examples of fallacies.

However, the word 'fallacy' has a much broader signification than merely the violation of one or another of the five rules above. **A fallacy is any sort of mistake in reasoning or inference; it is a term used to denote anything that causes an argument to go wrong.** The number of types of fallacy, in this sense of the term, is so great that no complete list has ever been drawn up. For this reason, it is difficult to specify in general why an argument is fallacious. It may be fallacious for all sorts of different reasons. The usual way of treating fallacies, therefore, is to discuss specific fallacies in order to show how they employ incorrect reasoning. We shall follow this procedure here, but at the same time we shall attempt to classify some of the more common types of fallacy.

Fallacies of Ambiguity. Ambiguity is one of the major sources of fallacious reasoning. We say **a term is ambiguous if it has more than one meaning**. Thus, if I say 'He has a good grip', it is not clear whether I mean 'He has a strong handshake' or 'He has a good suitcase'. The word 'grip' is thus ambiguous since it may be interpreted in at least two different ways. Ambiguity, it should be mentioned, is not always a source of confusion or of invalid reasoning. Words may have more than one meaning, but it may be clear which meaning is intended from the context in which they are used. **It is only when we cannot tell which meaning is intended that confusion may** result. Consider a common noun such as 'brother'. It may be used in a number of different ways without leading to confusion. For instance, examine the following utterances:

John is the brother of Jane.
All men are brothers under the skin.
Bill and Max are fraternity brothers.
'Oh brother!'

Although the word 'brother' is being employed differently in each of the above cases, no confusion results; but consider what happens when the sense of 'brother' in the first sentence is confused with the sense of 'brother' in the second. We may be led into a fallacious argument of the following sort:

All men are brothers in a common fraternity.
All brothers in a common fraternity are college students.
All men are college students.

The fallacy here is one of ambiguity. When we say that 'all men are brothers in a common fraternity', we mean that there are no fundamental differences among men with regard to their being human beings, and with regard to their having certain universal human rights (e.g., freedom of speech, religion, etc.). But when we say 'all brothers in a common fraternity are college students', we mean that each and every member of a college fraternity is a college student. The resulting argument is invalid because the same word is used in two different senses. (The word 'fraternity' is also ambiguous in the argument.) The fallacy which occurs when an inference is invalid because a single word may be used in two different senses is called **'equivocation'**.

A second type of fallacy involving ambiguity occurs when the whole sentence, as contrasted with single words, is ambiguous. Each and every word in the sentence may not be ambiguous, yet the whole sentence will be because of its grammatical structure. Such a fallacy is called an **'amphiboly'**.

There is a legend that the oracle at Delphi, in Ancient Greece, was never wrong. One reason for its infallibility was that it made its predictions in an amphibolous way—they could be taken in at least two different senses; hence if either event happened, the oracle's prediction could be confirmed as correct. During the conflict between the Greeks and Persians, a Greek commander is supposed to have asked the oracle who would emerge as the eventual victor. The oracle replied, 'Apollo says that the Greeks the Persians shall subdue.' Here it is not clear whether the Greeks are to be the victors or the Persians. Again when Cyrus the Great contemplated war against a certain King, the oracle answered his request about who would conquer by saying, 'The King yet lives that Cyrus shall depose.'

It should be noted that amphibolies occur because of the construction of a sentence. The ambiguity in such cases is not due to the fact that individual words are taken in two senses, but that **we do not understand the meaning of the whole sentence.**

Two common types of amphiboly are due to (*a*) **dangling participles,** and (*b*) the **inexact use of negation signs in ordinary English.**

In committing the grammatical error called 'dangling participle' one fails to attach a noun to a participial phrase which precedes it. For example, I would have committed this error, if I had written the previous sentence as follows: 'In committing the grammatical error called "dangling participle", a phrase is left unattached.' Here it looks as if it is a phrase which has committed the error, rather than a person using the phrase who has committed the error. Since a phrase is not the sort of thing which can commit errors, the ambiguity here is not seriously misleading, but it is grammatically incorrect and in other contexts this kind of misleading sentence structure can make it impossible to be clear about the meaning of the sentence. Sometimes amphibolies which are due to a dangling participle can be very amusing. A certain newspaper once described a boat-race as follows: 'The *Newport Beach* was far ahead of the others when she crossed the finish line. Her nose up in the air, salt-water pouring across her bows, Mrs. Williams guided her skilfully past the cheering crowd.'

The use of 'not' in ordinary English is another source of confusion. Sentences which begin 'All . . . are not . . .' can be interpreted in two different ways, as an E proposition or as an O proposition. Since we have discussed this point earlier, we shall not comment upon it here again, except to mention that one must be on guard against an improper interpretation of negative sentences beginning with 'all'.

Contextual Fallacies. Some very common types of fallacy do not depend upon grammatical misuses of language, or upon formal mistakes in reasoning. They depend upon the context in which an utterance is made. The context may tend to suggest that the utterance has a certain significance, but in fact it may not have such significance at all. Hence, the utterance will be misleading to one who hears or reads it. Such fallacies we call 'contextual fallacies'. Let us consider some of these now.

One of the most common is the **fallacy of 'significance'.** Suppose I say 'Twenty-eight per cent of the people in Birmingham have cavities in their teeth!' Before one can know whether this is a 'significant' remark or not, one would have to compare Birmingham with cities of a similar size in order to see whether it has a high or low proportion of people suffering from dental defects. Advertising claims very often commit the fallacy of significance. It is not uncommon to see such a slogan as '62 per cent of those doctors who smoke, smoke Raspies!' This is misleading since it does not say how many doctors do *not* smoke, nor does it say that they smoke *only* Raspies. It may well be that most doctors who smoke, smoke some other brand more frequently than Raspies, although they may try them, too, when they wish to change brands.

Another common contextual fallacy depends upon the **incorrect emphasis of the words in a sentence.** Thus, an insurance firm may make such a claim:

PROTECTION GUARANTEED AGAINST EVERYTHING

except death, injury, disease

By printing the first sentence in large type they suggest that they are giving full protection, but by printing the exceptions in very small type, they are taking back most of their claims. Again, advertising firms often employ this fallacy—the **'fallacy of emphasis'**—to full advantage in order to sell their product.

The **fallacy of 'Quoting Out of Context'** is another common fallacy which depends upon the context. A critic in reviewing a novel may write:

'I would enjoy this book if and only if it were the only book in the world, or if I were on a desert island and had nothing else to read.'

But the publisher, in order to sell the book, might lift certain of the critic's remarks from the whole sentence, and the review would then look as follows:

'I would enjoy this book . . . if I were on a desert island . . .'

By careful manipulation of the context, the publisher thus gives the reader the impression that the review was favourable, when the contrary is the case.

Fallacy of Argumentum ad Hominem. One of the most difficult fallacies to expose, as well as being one of the most common, is what is called 'argumentum ad hominem'. These words refer to an argument that is directed **against a man, rather than against what a man says, in order to show that what he says cannot be true.** Politics affords us many examples of *argumenta ad hominem*. Suppose a Socialist Member of Parliament should argue: 'It is extremely important that we limit atomic bomb tests, since it is possible that their long-range effects will poison the atmosphere.' A Conservative might retort by saying: 'Oh, well, you can't believe what he says, since he is a Socialist, and you know that they are always trying to control military expenditure.' The Conservative has directed his argument against the *man*; he has tried to refute what the Socialist has said by pointing out that the speaker is a member of the opposing party. But such a refutation is based on a fallacy, since the proper way to refute such an argument would consist in marshalling facts to show that what the speaker said is false; namely, that atomic tests are not likely to poison the atmosphere, and so forth.

What makes the *argumentum ad hominem* so persuasive, and so difficult to refute, can be shown by the following example. Suppose a witness, in a trial, is testifying that he saw a crime committed by the defendant. Suppose further, that in cross-examination it is proved that the witness has testified in other cases, and that in some of them, his testimony was false (assume, for purposes of the example, that he has even been convicted of perjury). Our temptation, as a juror, would be to disregard what the witness has said on the ground that he is an unreliable source of information. But to disregard his testimony entirely is to commit the fallacy of *argumentum ad hominem*. What he says may be true; if possible it should be tested against other evidence we have in the case. The important thing is to recognize that we should consider what is said apart from who says it. **A statement cannot be shown to be false merely because the individual who makes it can be shown to be a person of defective character.**

The Fallacy of Arguing from Authority. Argument from authority is another common type of fallacy. It has the following form. Smith says that a certain statement is true. If questioned, he answers, 'Because X, who is an authority, says so.' But the fallacy is this: **One cannot prove the truth or falsity of a given statement merely because someone, even an authority, says so. It is not the prestige of an authority which makes a statement true or false, but rather the citing of evidence either to confirm or refute the statement.** Thus, if I say, 'Ben Hogan is a greater golfer than Sam Snead', and someone challenges this remark, I would be committing a fallacy to say, 'Because Walter Hagen, who is an authority, says so'. One could prove the proposition only by citing the tournaments won by Hogan and Snead, by comparing their records in other respects, and so forth. The fact that an authority has made a statement cannot be *itself* regarded as evidence; what constitutes evidence are the *facts* which the authority produces—and these are quite different from a mere verbal pronouncement. We might be prepared, however, sometimes to take on trust the pronouncement of an expert on some matter within his expertise, but there can never be any good reason for accepting his assertions in other fields. I might not go far wrong if I accepted Walter Hagen's word on a golfing matter; I am likely to go very wrong if I place as much credence on his views of politics.

Arguments which Appeal to Sentiments. There are a number of arguments which commit the following fallacy. **These arguments attempt to establish that a given statement is true or false by reporting how people feel about it.** Thus, if I say, 'The world is flat', and you challenge my remark, I might attempt to beat down your challenge by saying, 'But everybody believes that'. Such an answer would be to commit a fallacy, since one cannot prove whether the world is flat or not by citing the beliefs of the majority of people—but rather, by citing evidence from geography, astronomy and so forth. There are numerous cases, the above example being a famous one, where the majority have held beliefs which are false.

The appeal to pity, or to emotion, which is a variant of the above argument, is sometimes called **'The Argumentum ad Misericordiam'**. An attorney who implies that the defendant could not have committed the crime because he has a wife and six children is employing the *argumentum ad misericordiam*. His family responsibilities are irrelevant with regard to his guilt, although they may be relevant with regard to determining his punishment.

Argumentum ad Ignorantiam. A common type of argument, which commits a fallacy, is called the **'argument from ignorance'. This argument contends that some statement must be true because there is no evidence to disprove it.** The argument from ignorance is plausible because it apes a legitimate type of argument. One might hold (legitimately) that a certain view is true because we have considerable evidence, all of which shows that the view is true, and none of which shows that it is false. Thus, one might hold that, under specified conditions, the statement 'Water boils at 212 degrees Fahrenheit' is true because every time we have tried to boil water it has boiled at 212 degrees, under these specified conditions—and, moreover, there have been *no* contrary instances. But the argument from ignorance, which looks like this argument, holds that a certain statement is true *simply* because there is no evidence against it. But this is fallacious, since **it is not enough to show that a view is true simply because there is no contrary evidence; we must also show that there is positive evidence in favour of it.** Otherwise, we could prove that dragons, elves, sea-serpents and unicorns exist, since there is no contrary evidence against them. Religious disputes often employ the argument from ignorance. People will assert that 'God exists' is true since there is no evidence that He does not. But if this is the manner of proof, it is inconclusive, for the reasons we have stated above.

Petitio Principii. The Fallacy of Begging the Question. This fallacy occurs when either the same statement is used both as a premise and a conclusion in an argument, or when one of the premises could not be known to be true unless the conclusion were first assumed to be true. This fallacy is sometimes described as **'assuming what you are trying to prove', or 'circular argumentation'.** The closer the premises of a circular argument are to the conclusion, the easier the fallacy is to detect; but sometimes when premises and conclusions are widely separated by a long chain of argumentation, it may be difficult to discover that the whole argument is circular. An example of the fallacy of begging the question is the following:

A says: 'Mohammed is divinely inspired.'
B says: 'How do you know?'
A: 'Because the Koran says he is.'
B: 'But how do you know the Koran is reliable?'
A: 'Because it was written by Mohammed who is divine.'

The Fallacy of Composition. In the fallacy of composition what is assumed to be true of a part is asserted to be true of the whole. This fallacy is made plausible because it looks like a sound inductive argument. Let us exhibit the difference between the fallacy of composition and a sound inductive inference by the following two examples:

(*a*) John O'Brien is an Irishman and belligerent; therefore, Ireland is belligerent.

(*b*) John O'Brien is an Irishman and belligerent; therefore, Irishmen are belligerent.

(*a*) commits the fallacy of composition, because it says that what is true of a member of a country is true of the whole country. This is simply mistaken. From the fact that X is wealthy, we cannot conclude that the country in which he resides is wealthy (e.g., Franco is wealthy, therefore, Spain is wealthy). On the other hand (*b*) is a sound inductive inference. Whether the conclusion is true or false, of course, will depend upon how many Irishmen besides John O'Brien can be found to be belligerent; but the inference is itself sound.

The Fallacy of Division. The fallacy of division commits the opposite mistake from that made by the fallacy of composition. **It holds that what is true of a whole must be true of all its parts.** Thus if I say, 'The United States is a wealthy country; therefore, Joe Smith is wealthy', I am committing the fallacy of division. It does not follow that because the whole country is wealthy each and every citizen of it will be wealthy. Tourists, who are frequently charged exorbitant rates in foreign countries, may protest against such charges on the grounds that the fallacy of division is being committed (although this protest will probably be unsuccessful). From the fact that one comes from a wealthy nation, it does not follow that one is wealthy.

The fallacy of division is plausible and easy to commit because it looks like one type of valid argument, called **Argument by Specification.** If we say, 'All Americans are wealthy, Joe Smith is an American', we can validly infer that Joe Smith is wealthy. This is because the statement 'All Americans are wealthy', attributes wealth to each and every American. And if it is true, and if Joe Smith is an American, then it will be true that he is wealthy. But what is true of the whole country (i.e., that the United States is wealthy) is not true of each and every one of its members.

The Fallacy of Ignoratio Elenchi. This fallacy, also called **'irrelevant conclusion'**, is an argument in which one starts out to prove that something is the case, but instead proves something else. For instance, if I attempt to prove that the English League has better footballers than the Scottish League, but instead establish that the English League is wealthier than the Scottish League, I have committed the fallacy of irrelevant conclusion. For even if it is true that the English League is wealthier than the Scottish League, it still does not follow that wealthier leagues have better footballers than poorer ones. What happens in an *ignoratio elenchi* is that the disputant thinks he is proving *p* (the English League has better players) when in reality he is proving *r* (that the English League is wealthier). Thus, he arrives at a conclusion which is irrelevant to the conclusion he was trying to prove.

The Fallacy of Non Sequitur. Almost every fallacy involves, in some respect, a *non sequitur*. The phrase *'non sequitur'* means the same as **'does not follow'.** Thus, the fallacy of *ignoratio elenchi*, which we discussed above, involves a type of *non sequitur*. From the fact that the English League is wealthier than the Scottish League it does not follow that English League footballers are better than Scottish League players. This would have to be shown by marshalling sets of statistics concerning the relative performances of the players in both leagues. Sometimes the phrase *'non sequitur'* has a formal meaning. In this case we say that **the conclusion of an argument does not follow from the premises when it is possible for the premises to be true and the conclusion to be false.** But generally, *'non sequitur'* is used in a broader sense; for example, **where a conclusion may be true, but irrelevant, we will say that a 'non sequitur' has been committed.** This fallacy is also sometimes called **'argumentative leap'**.

Statistical Fallacies. It is commonly asserted that 'you can make statistics prove anything'. This is so, to be sure, if one misuses the statistical method. There is a famous story which exhibits a misuse of statistics. Two philosophers decided to find out why they kept becoming intoxicated; and they decided to apply the statistical or scientific method to discover the cause. They proceeded to their favourite tavern, where they had dinner and during the process consumed several drinks composed of Scotch whisky and water. They became intoxicated and had to be taken home. The next night they repeated the process. They had exactly the same food, but this time, as a beverage, they drank Irish whisky and water. Again they became intoxicated and had to be carried from the premises. The third night they repeated the same steps, varying only the drink. This time they drank rye whisky and water, again becoming drunk. They concluded, in accordance with the statistical method, that since water was the only constant factor in all their drinks it must be water which was making them intoxicated!

One must handle the findings of statistics with extreme caution unless one knows the methods that were applied, the controls over the data that were exercised, and so forth. These are highly intricate and technical matters, which demand careful supervision to maintain proper controls over all possible variables. Thus, such a statement as 'Schnooko, the great washday detergent, washes 91 times cleaner than any other soap', must be disregarded, unless one knows what sort of tests were applied, how one defines 'cleaner than' and so forth.

With the above remarks, we shall conclude our discussion of types of fallacy. We reiterate that the list is not complete, indeed it may be impossible to provide such a list; but in any case, we have tried to select some of the commoner types of mistake in reasoning. A reader who seriously studies the above mistakes in reasoning, and who applies what he has learned to everyday speech, is not apt frequently to be misled.

Exercise X

Identify the fallacies committed in the following:

1 Water the plant when thoroughly potted.
2 He: 'Dance?'
  She: 'Love to!'
  He: 'Marvellous, that's better than dancing!'

3 Jones was not intoxicated today.

4 Your contention that alcohol is injurious is without merit since you drink.

5 It has been argued that the Crusades were a noble endeavour, since men of high purpose founded them and whole peoples supported them.

6 'Educated people do not believe in ghosts,' he said. 'Ah,' I replied, 'some college people do.' 'Oh, but they are not educated just because they went to college,' he answered, 'for if they were they would not believe in ghosts.'

7 'There can be no doubt that atomic bombs can poison the atmosphere. Einstein himself has said so.'

8 But Doctor, surely your advice to me to stop smoking cannot be serious, since I happen to know that you smoke.

9 Socrates is a man; man is a species; therefore Socrates is a species.

10 Every attempt to prove that men are not immortal has failed. No evidence can be found which shows that men's souls do not exist after death; hence, immortality must be true.

LOGIC AND SEMANTICS

Our account of the nature of logic would be incomplete without a brief reference to the relation between logic and semantics. We should preface such an account by pointing out that the word **'semantics'** is currently used in a number of different senses. As it is used by professional linguists, it refers to the historical study of the changes in the meaning of words. Philosophers use the word differently from linguists; as they employ it, it has a wider and a narrower sense. **In its wider sense, 'semantics' refers to the science of the study of language. In its narrower sense, it refers to that branch of the study of language which deals with 'meaning'.**

As opposed to dealing with the expressive or directive uses of language, semantics is primarily interested in **the use of language in order to communicate.** Semantics has two branches: **a positive** and **a negative** one. The positive branch attempts to give an account of the nature of communication by providing us with **a theory of meaning or significance.** The negative account attempts **to dissolve barriers to proper communication** (the discussion of fallacies which we have just completed falls within the province of semantics).

Let us see briefly how the positive theory works (i.e., how semanticists speak about 'meaning'). According to one of the common contemporary semantical theories, linguistic expressions (e.g., words, phrases or sentences) *mean* in two different ways. This can be illustrated by considering a word like 'brother'. If someone were to ask us 'What do you mean by the word "brother"?' we could answer this question in two different ways: either we could point to someone who was a brother, or we could define the term verbally. We could say in the latter case, 'By the word "brother", I mean anyone who is a male and a sibling.' In the latter case, we employ words to do the job which pointing does in the former case. Logicians employ a technical vocabulary to distinguish between giving the meaning of an expression in the former case and giving the meaning in the latter. Where we point, we are giving the **extensional** meaning of the word; we are indicating the thing or event which the word refers to. In the latter case, where we produce a verbal definition, we are giving the **intensional** meaning. The notions of extension and intension (also called '**denotation**' and '**connotation**' respectively) are among the basic concepts in semantical meaning analysis: for one explains the meaning of a term by giving either its denotation or its connotation.

Syntax. Syntax is the branch of the science of language which deals with the relations between words. Here we are no longer concerned about the relation of a word to its user or interpreter, or even about what the word or phrase or sentence refers to or means (as in semantics). Instead, **we deal in syntax with the grammatical structure of the arrangement of the elements of language.**

Logic, it should be clear by now, is a type of language. It is not a language, of course, of the same kind as English or French, which are languages that have developed *naturally*. It is instead a **well-formed or artificial language, but a language it is since it employs signs or symbols.** These signs or symbols have certain properties. Depending upon the properties which we are interested in when we study logic, **logic falls either into syntax or into semantics.** Let us illustrate each of these points. We have in the foregoing discussed the syllogism. The syllogism is an argument containing terms which refer to classes of things. **The relation between a term and its referend (i.e., the relation of 'referring', or 'naming' or 'designating') is a semantical relation.**

On the other hand, **the relation of 'inclusion' which we have also studied in logic, is a syntactical relation rather than a semantical one.** We can abstract from any semantic considerations when we speak about such a relation as 'inclusion'. We can state that **an argument will be valid regardless of what the terms in the argument refer to, provided that the terms are arranged in a certain order.** Thus, an argument having the following form (regardless of what descriptive meaning we give to its constituent terms) will be valid:

$$\frac{\text{All M is P}}{\text{All S is M}}$$
$$\text{All S is P}$$

On the other hand, merely by analysing the syntactical arrangement of the terms in the following argument, we can state that it is invalid:

$$\frac{\text{All P is M}}{\text{All S is M}}$$
$$\text{All S is P}$$

We may summarize our long discussion of the nature of logic by pointing out that logic falls both within semantics and within syntax, depending upon what sort of logical relations we are emphasizing at the time. If we are dealing with 'referring', we are concerned with semantics; if we are dealing with 'logical form', we are in the branch of the study of language called 'syntax'.

SUMMARY

In this chapter, we have tried to present a brief account of the nature of logic. It should be understood that we have done little more than introduce the reader to the barest essentials of logic. **The system of inference which we have studied is called the 'syllogism'.** This is one common type of argument. Logic in its more advanced branches deals with many different types of inference, as well as with syllogistic inference.

In the foregoing, we have tried to define 'logic', and to show how logic differs from psychology. In doing this, we have called attention to the difference between reasoning and other types of thinking, such as supposing, remembering, guessing, doubting, believing and so forth. We then distinguished between deductive logic and inductive logic. In deductive logic, we argue from general to particular statements so that the reasons adduced as evidence for the truth of the conclusion of an argument are conclusive, whereas in inductive logic, where we are attempting to argue from the particular to the general, they merely make the conclusion more probable. We then considered the syllogism as one type of deductive inference, and then discussed various types of fallacy.

The result of the above discussion has been to prepare the reader for further study of logic, and to give him a substantial amount of equipment for distinguishing good from bad reasoning. One who studies the above material carefully will not only find that it has numerous applications to discourse in everyday life, but moreover, that by continuing to apply logic to such discourse he will become clearer and sounder in his own reasoning.

SUGGESTED FURTHER READING

Elementary Texts:

Black, Max, *Critical Thinking*. 2nd edn. Prentice-Hall: London, 1952. (This is a very simple, yet sound text on logic.)

Copi, Irving, *Introduction to Logic*. 2nd edn. Collier-Macmillan: London, 1961. (A recent, excellent introduction to the elements of traditional and modern logic.)

Stebbing, L. S., *A Modern Elementary Logic*. Methuen: London, 1961. (An introduction to formal logic, specially designed for private study and containing many exercises with answers.)

Thouless, R. H., *Straight and Crooked Thinking*. 2nd edn. English Universities Press: London, 1959. (A discussion of many of the ways in which argument can go wrong.)

More Advanced Texts:

Copi, Irving, *Symbolic Logic*. 2nd edn. Collier-Macmillan: London, 1965.

Stebbing, L. S., *A Modern Introduction to Logic*. Methuen: London, 1930.

ANSWERS TO EXERCISES

Exercise I. (Identify the subject term, predicate term, copula and quantifiers, if any.)

The following letters will stand for the corresponding term: 'S' for subject term; 'P' for predicate; 'C' for copula; 'Q' for quantifier.

```
   Q       S      C       P
1 Some   mad dogs  are  happily married.

   Q  S   C              P
2 All bats  are members of the class of rodents.

     S     C     P
3 James   is   wicked.

     S     C        P
4 Horses  are   man's best friend.

   Q      S      C         P
5 Some  tables  are not   mahogany.

   Q      S    C      P
6 Nothing green  is  in the room.
```

Exercise II. (Determine the following to be affirmative or negative.)

1 James is very unhappy. (affirmative)
2 Lions are not untrustworthy. (negative)
3 She was not disinclined to come. (negative)
4 None but the lonely heart is filled with sadness. (affirmative)
5 Nothing tried, nothing gained. (negative)
6 He has been unwell for months now. (affirmative)
7 Some philosophers are intuitive. (affirmative)
8 No non-addicts can understand the problem. (negative)
9 All non-S are non-P. (affirmative)
10 All except women may attend. (affirmative)

Exercise III. (Determine whether the following are universal or particular.)

1 Fish are mammals. (universal)
2 Some dragons are fierce. (particular)
3 This table is brown. (universal)
4 That system is useless. (universal)
5 They are crazy. (universal)
6 Hard-working students are successful. (universal)
7 Albert Einstein was a genius. (universal)
8 Those tins seem heavy. (universal)
9 That bottle of aspirin is not full. (universal)
10 No human beings are infallible. (universal)
11 Some cats are not wise. (particular)
12 Men have climbed Mt. Everest. (particular)

13 All Germans are not cruel. (particular)
14 All golfers are wealthy. (universal)
15 Some babies are small. (particular)

Exercise IV. (Determine whether the following propositions are to be designated as A, E, I, or O, and determine their quantity and quality.)

1 No Germans are kind. (E, Universal-Neg.)
2 All doctors are interested in medicine. (A, Universal-Affirm.)
3 Some lawyers are golfers. (I, Particular-Affirm.)
4 Joe Louis is no longer heavyweight champion. (E, Universal-Neg.)
5 Byron was a champion of freedom. (A, Universal-Affirm.)
6 Some conductors are non-luminous. (I, Particular-Affirm.)
7 All football players are excluded from the class of authors. (E, Universal-Neg.)
8 Some football players are not authors. (O, Particular-Neg.)
9 That paper was well read. (A, Universal-Affirm.)
10 Each and every lion is ferocious. (A, Universal-Affirm.)

Exercise V. (Indicate which terms are distributed and which are undistributed.) 'D' will stand for 'distributed', and 'U' for 'undistributed'.

D		**U**
1 All Japanese	are	good swimmers.
D		**D**
2 No conductors	are	overpaid.
U		**D**
3 Some swans	are not	black.
U		**U**
4 Some swans	are	beautiful.
D		**U**
5 Twiggy	is	a model.
D		**U**
6 All Yorkshiremen	are	non-farmers.
U		**D**
7 Some Yorkshiremen	are not	farmers.

Exercise VI. (Identify the major, middle and minor terms of the following syllogisms, and also designate the major and minor premises.) 'M' will stand for middle, 'Ma' for major, and 'Mi' for minor.

    M   Ma
1 All men are fallible. (Major premise)

Mi   M
I am a man. (Minor premise)

      Mi   Ma
Therefore, I am fallible.

      Mi   M
2 Some politicians are ignoble. (Minor premise)

      M   Ma
No one who is ignoble is wise. (Major premise)

      Mi   Ma
Some politicians are not wise.

    Mi   M
3 All singers are temperamental. (Minor premise)

    Ma   M
No lorry drivers are temperamental. (Major premise)

    Mi   Ma
No singers are lorry drivers.

  Mi M
4 All S is M (Minor premise)

    M   Ma
No M is P (Major premise)

    Mi Ma
No S is P

Mi M
5 S i M (Minor premise)

Ma M
P i M (Major premise)

Mi Ma
S i P

Exercise VII. (Determine whether the syllogisms in this exercise are valid or invalid. If invalid, state the fallacy they commit.)

1 Invalid. Undistributed middle.
2 Invalid. Undistributed middle.
3 Invalid. Illicit process (Rule 2 violated).
4 This example has more than three terms, hence it is not a syllogism.
5 Invalid. Undistributed middle.
6 Invalid. Undistributed middle.
7 Invalid. Illicit process (Rule 2 violated).
8 Invalid. Affirmative conclusion derived from a negative premise.
9 Invalid. No conclusion can be drawn from two negative premises.
10 Invalid. Illicit process (Rule 2 violated).

Exercise VIII.

  1 All ships are beautiful things.
  2 Joan is a blonde woman.
  3 All whales are mammals.
  4 All children are silly creatures.
  5 All snakes are coiling things.
  6 All persons who appreciate Hogan are golfers.
  7 All sentences which make assertions are indicative sentences.
  8 No non-ventured things are gained things.
  9 Nothing which is brave is a thing which dies many deaths,
or

    All things which are not brave are things which die many deaths.
10 Some swans are not white.

Exercise IX.

  A. The following are the results of obverting the corresponding sentences in Exercise IX.

    1 Some Londoners are not non-braggarts.
    2 All trains are non-buses.
    3 Some magazines are non-articulate.
    4 No kind persons are non-dwarfs.
    5 No fairies are mortal.
    6 No one who is not John is a non-admitted person.
    7 No one who is intelligent is a non-appreciated person.

  B. The following are converted propositions.

    1 Some white things are cats.
    2 No tame creatures are lions.
    3 (The O cannot be converted.)
    4 Some non-metallic objects are non-conductors. (Partial conversion.)
    5 Some expensive things are cars. (Partial conversion.)
    6 Some champions are golfers.
    7 (The O cannot be converted.)
    8 Nothing gained, nothing ventured.

  C. The following are contraposed propositions.

    1 All non-ridiculous things are non-superstitions.
    2 All warranted things are non-prejudices.
    3 Some intelligent things are not non-horses. (i.e., some intelligent things are horses.)
    4 Some non-intelligent things are not non-horses. (i.e., some unintelligent things are horses.)
    5 All non-considerate persons are non-deservers of the fair.

Exercise X. (Identify the fallacies.)

  1 Amphiboly.
  2 Emphasis.

3 Significance or Amphiboly.
4 *Ad Hominem.*
5 Appeal to Sentiment.
6 Begging the Question.
7 Appeal to Authority.
8 *Ad Hominem.*
9 Equivocation.
10 *Ad Ignorantiam.*

CHAPTER VII

CONTEMPORARY PHILOSOPHY

In this final section, we shall examine some of the major movements in modern philosophy. In selecting **Pragmatism,** the various forms of **Philosophical Analysis,** and **Existentialism,** we are not, of course, exhausting the possibilities. Many forms of traditional philosophy continue to hold the interest of twentieth-century philosophers, and still command many adherents.

However, primary consideration is owing to those developments which have had a decisive effect upon modern philosophical activities. **Pragmatism,** a movement of American origin, has deeply influenced intellectual life in America, and is becoming increasingly influential in Britain; **Philosophical Analysis,** originated in England and Vienna, and has had a great impact on thought first in Britain, and more recently in the United States; **Existentialism,** which has its roots in various nineteenth-century ideas, has recently become prominent in Continental European thought, especially in France and Germany, and has more recently received considerable attention in the English-speaking world.

PRAGMATISM

In the late nineteenth century a method of philosophizing called 'Pragmatism' developed in America as a revolt against what some thinkers (e.g., WILLIAM JAMES, CHARLES SANDERS PEIRCE, and JOHN DEWEY) felt to be a sterile philosophical tradition in the American colleges, and the useless metaphysical tradition then flourishing in Europe. The pragmatists felt that their method and theory could be of tremendous utility in solving intellectual problems and in forwarding man's progress.

Background of Pragmatism. The America in which this movement developed was just beginning to awaken in the post-Civil War period to its cultural potentialities. For a long time, American philosophical activity—such as it was—merely reflected European influences. Early in the nineteenth century, the very astute observer of the American scene, ALEXANDRE DE TOCQUEVILLE, remarked that in no country in the civilized world was philosophy taken less seriously than in the United States. Philosophy probably seemed too abstruse and too remote from the immediate concerns of a young, vigorous nation.

The views of the seventeenth-century New England Calvinists, for example, were a continuation of English philosophical discussion, and the objective was the application of these views to the current problems of their new society. Even the man who was perhaps the most original metaphysician in American history, the great New England preacher, JONATHAN EDWARDS, was greatly influenced by such European contemporaries as JOHN LOCKE, the CAMBRIDGE PLATONISTS, and possibly NICHOLAS MALEBRANCHE. In the eighteenth century American philosophy felt the impact of the French Enlightenment philosophers and in the early nineteenth century it felt that of the German romantics. By the end of the eighteenth century, 'academic' philosophy had become a sterile and rigid version of the ideas of the Scottish Common Sense Realists, whose purpose was to refute the 'dangerous' scepticism of DAVID HUME.

In the mid-nineteenth century there were gathering indications of a philosophic revival which would repudiate the exhausted academic and European traditions. German immigrants (refugees from the failure of their revolution of 1848), disciples of Hegel who were impressed with the implications of new scientific theories, especially with the theory of evolution, provided the essential impetus for the revival. Known as the St. Louis Hegelians, they founded the first philosophical journal in the United States, the *Journal of Speculative Philosophy*, which presented translations of contemporary European philosophers, and provided an outlet and audience for American philosophers who were venturing on fresh approaches.

William James. Amid this intellectual ferment, the man who was to contribute fundamentally to the new philosophical movement, **Pragmatism,** developed his system. WILLIAM JAMES (1842–1910), brother of the great novelist, HENRY JAMES, was the son of HENRY JAMES, SR., who was himself a philosopher and a man of immense learning. Trained as a doctor, he taught at the Harvard Medical School, but later turned his attention to psychology, in which field he became one of the most important theorists of his day. From his studies of the psychology of man's intellectual and religious life, James turned to philosophy, becoming professor of philosophy at Harvard, and the foremost advocate of pragmatism.

What is Pragmatism? Pragmatism is, first of all, a method for solving or evaluating intellectual problems, and a theory about the kinds of knowledge we are capable of acquiring. William James shared in the American distrust of purely theoretical or intellectual activity, and asked bluntly, what is the point of theorizing? What difference does it make? Why is it important to deal with the intellectual problems that theorists bother about?

'Cash-Value.' Before determining if any given philosophical claim is true, James first thought it necessary to determine the **'cash-value'** of the claim—that is, what function it had and what difference it would make if it were true. According to the pragmatic theory, our intellectual activity, our philosophizing, has as its purpose the attempt to resolve difficulties that arise in the course of our attempts to deal with experience. The cash-value of our ideas is to be found in the use to which ideas can be put. With regard to any theory we can ask, what difference would it make if I believed it, and what consequences would follow from my activities if I act on the theory. If a theory has no cash-value, this means that it would not make the slightest difference whether one believed it true or false and it would not at all affect one's actions.

Theories as 'Instruments'. According to James, we think only in order to solve our problems, so that our theories are **instruments** that we employ in order to solve problems in our experience, and the theories, therefore, ought to be judged in terms of their success at performing this function. If one is walking in the woods and loses one's way, then, according to the pragmatic view, one way of dealing with this situation is through theoretical activity. Taking into account such data as the sun's position, the direction in which one has been walking and one's previous knowledge of the terrain, one can develop a theory about how to extricate oneself from this predicament. The cash-value of the theory can be evaluated in terms of the possible differences it would make if it were true or false. The theory will be judged according to whether it serves as a successful way of dealing with the problem.

In contrast to such instances in which theories have obviously foreseeable consequences for experience, many classical philosophical theories have little or no cash-value. What difference would it make if one believed that the universe was really only one vast mind, or if one believed such a theory false? The immediate problems that one is faced with would remain exactly the same, and one would get no clues as to how to resolve them. At best, a metaphysical belief, such as the one just mentioned, might make one happy or sad, but beyond that would have almost no cash-value. There would be no foreseeable consequences to evaluating the merits of such a metaphysical theory about the ultimate nature of the universe.

From judging that the function of theory is to deal with experience, **the pragmatists conclude that a theory is true if it works.** If we ask, what do we mean by saying that a given theory or belief is true, the pragmatists answer that it has been verified if it has been found to deal successfully with experience. Conversely, the falsity of certain ideas is determined by showing that attempts to verify them fail, or that they do not 'work' in our experience.

Pragmatism and Science. This criterion of evaluation of the truth of theories, the pragmatists claim, is essentially that of science. When a scientist tests a theory, he designs an experiment which tests whether the theory works under specified conditions. Thus, in the test of the Salk polio vaccine, the method employed was to see whether the vaccine worked as a preventative for the disease. The success of the experiments was the basis for the claim that the theory was true.

Pragmatism and Traditional Philosophy. Pragmatists such as William James opposed the traditional philosophical view that the truth of ideas is a property independent of human experience. Philosophers such as Plato had held that a theory was true absolutely, whether anyone knew it or not. The pragmatists contend, in opposition to such a theory of truth, that the only reason people have for calling one view true, and another false, is that the one works in human experience and the other does not, not that it does or does not conform to some absolute standards independent of all human experience. Our only basis for judging the alleged absolute truths of Plato, Descartes, or any other great philosophical rationalist is by evaluating them in relation to their effect on concrete aspects of life. **James maintained the only reason we**

have for asserting that anything is true is that it works. Any claims about the independent, objective, absolute nature of truth are meaningless, as far as we can ever determine from our experience and judgments.

Pragmatic Truth. One consequence of the pragmatic theory of truth is, then, that truth is something that happens to an idea, rather than being a fixed property of an idea which we are trying to uncover. Before one discovers whether an idea, a theory, or belief, works, it is neither true nor false. Through the process of testing the view in terms of its consequences and its compatibility with other beliefs, the idea becomes true or false, or more true or less true. Thus, prior to the discovery of America, the view that 'There is a large land mass located between Europe and Asia,' was neither true nor false. However, as a consequence of the discoveries of Columbus and other early explorers, this theory became true. When this view became true, its denial became false.

In the course of time, various ideas have different developments. As they are employed in relation to the problems and difficulties that confront mankind as means for dealing with these difficulties and problems, the ideas become true in so far as they work, and false in so far as they do not. Thus, an idea might work for a while, and hence become true. Later it might cease to yield satisfactory results, or no longer be verified by further experience, and so, then, become false. Various now-discarded scientific theories have had such a career. The phlogiston theory of chemistry worked fairly well for a while, but after certain experiments in the eighteenth century it no longer yielded satisfactory results, and so it was discarded.

Truth, then, is not something static and unchangeable: instead, it grows and develops with time. At various times in human history, certain theories and ideas may be satisfactory for the problems then current. However, with further experience and difficulties, that which is true expands and grows to meet the newer conditions. Presumably, at no time will we ever reach a completion or culmination of this process. There has been, and will be, a continuous process of developing new ideas to meet new situations. The attempts of human beings to cope with their universe will lead to unending inquiries, which in turn will lead to newer theories, which in turn will become either true or false, or truer and falser. At each stage in the development without end, what we will call truth will be that which enables us to deal satisfactorily with the problems that are then current.

Pragmatism and Ethics. There is also, according to James, an intimate connection between the pragmatic conception of truth and the notion of goodness. Since truth is that which works, or yields satisfactory results in terms of our experience, what is true, in these terms, turns out to be what is profitable for us to believe, or what is good. So put, a type of ethical theory can be developed from pragmatic theory. The pragmatist's method of determining what is good or bad, or right or wrong, is the same as that for determining if an idea is true or false. Thus, given a problem in human behaviour, we can ask 'Would performing certain actions be right in order to solve a given problem?' The answer to the question is to be judged in terms of whether the actions yield satisfactory results in the resolution of difficulty. If one ponders whether the right way to solve one's financial problems is to rob a bank, the test is the pragmatic one. Here, presumably, a careful evaluation of the possible consequences of bank-robbing would lead one to the conclusion that such a theory does not work, because of all the possible unsatisfactory consequences to oneself, like imprisonment, and the unsatisfactory consequences to others. Therefore, one would conclude, that the bank-robbing solution to one's difficulties is 'wrong'. On the other hand, one might just as readily conclude that this solution is 'right'. Clearly, then, pragmatism cannot offer any absolute moral principles. We must always act on the hypothesis which works, and this must involve a purely subjective evaluation.

The Pluralistic Universe. Corresponding to his theory of truth and goodness, James developed a conception of the universe. To begin with, experience is not an object that we examine; instead there is just a 'humming-buzzing confusion' out of which we differentiate various aspects that we call 'ourselves', 'physical objects', etc. These differentiations are made with reference to problems or difficulties that arise in experience and are carved out of experience as ways of dealing with the problems. The organization and selection of the items that make up our universe relate to our need to deal satisfactorily with various obstacles to successful action. **There is no fixed world to be uncovered through experience, but rather a continuous quest for workable solutions to difficulties.** No single concept of the universe is to be regarded as the final and complete answer. Instead, the continuing development of our knowledge of the world represents the meaningful idea that we have of the natural world. As new ways of organizing and selecting aspects of our experience are tried, new features of the universe emerge. Both our knowledge and the world are regarded as having an **evolutionary quality of growth and development to meet new situations and new needs.**

This novel conception of the universe was in direct opposition to the more rigid and all-encompassing metaphysical schemes of earlier philosophers. The materialists, the idealists, and others offered a picture of the universe in which certain determinate features pervade it for all time. In contrast to this, the pragmatists envisage a **pluralistic universe, one with many features and possibilities** which cannot be examined and unravelled all at once. Instead the universe has to be studied tentatively, as it emerges and develops. As the process of nature unfolds, our understanding of it will also, in the same progressive and developing manner.

Instrumentalism. In the twentieth century, the form of the pragmatist view which has been most prevalent was constructed by JOHN DEWEY, a view sometimes called **instrumentalism.** Dewey, who was perhaps the most influential American thinker in recent times, developed a theory of knowledge essentially in terms of the biological and psychological role that the knowing-process plays in human affairs, and then tried to employ this conception as a guide in directing the application of human intellectual activities to contemporary social problems.

Dewey's Concept of Experience and Thinking. According to Dewey, what constitutes our brute experience is the **interaction between a**

biological organism and its environment. Experience is not an object known, but rather **an action performed.** In the course of the organism's activities, it encounters situations in which it can no longer act. **Thinking arises as a means of dealing with these disturbing situations, by working out hypotheses, or guides to future actions.** The merits of these intellectual acts are determined by a practical criterion, by whether the organism can now function satisfactorily again. **Thought, especially scientific thought, is instrumental in problem-solving.** The occurrence of problems sets off a chain reaction of mental activity directed towards discovering a functional solution to the difficulties that confront the organism.

Much of earlier philosophizing, Dewey claimed, is actually a hindrance to the task of problem-solving. In separating theorizing from practical concerns, and searching for absolute solutions to philosophical questions, philosophers have got away almost completely from the human needs which give rise to thought, and have also tried rigidly to impose certain preconceived schemes upon human thought, and have refused to allow any new beliefs and new solutions in human affairs. What is needed nowadays, Dewey insisted, is a reconstruction of philosophy in terms of the problems that now confront us. In this role, philosophy will no longer be an abstruse subject, of little or no value in the immediate concerns of the day, but will, instead, be the overall directive force in developing new instrumental techniques for assisting the human organism in its struggles with its environment, and in building a better world in which some of the problems now confronting us will gradually be resolved.

Some Applications of Pragmatism. In terms of the more practical point of view of much of American culture, one can easily conceive of the appeal of pragmatism in America. Some of its success has been in the application of its philosophy to certain social problems. By and large, the earlier pragmatism of William James was directed towards resolving certain individual questions of belief, whereas the later instrumentalism of John Dewey was concerned more with broader social questions confronting America in its rapid development in this century.

James on Religious Belief. Possibly owing to his personal heritage, James devoted much effort to examining religious beliefs in pragmatic terms. Unlike the theologians who insist upon the truth of certain religious beliefs, and the scientifically-inclined persons who insist upon judging religious views by the latest scientific findings, James was concerned to examine the 'cash-value' of belief. Why do people accept certain beliefs and not others, and what difference does it make to them in their lives?

In his studies on *The Varieties of Religious Experience* and *The Will to Believe* James claimed that there were some people, 'tough-minded people', who were temperamentally inclined not to believe anything except on scientific evidence. They were more concerned not to risk holding possibly false beliefs than to hold beliefs which, if they turned out to be true, might be very pleasant, but for which not much evidence was available. On the other hand, there is another group, the 'tender-minded', who want to believe, and who want to believe things about the world which make them happy. Which group is right? A pragmatic analysis, James suggested, revealed that it was actually a question of which attitude worked best. If one could regard the problem of belief undogmatically, that is, without worrying about whether a given belief is actually true or not, one can see that for some people, a certain set of beliefs works, that is, a certain set of beliefs, when accepted, provides a more satisfactory life. In so far as these beliefs work as guides to life, or as satisfactory attitudes, then, pragmatically speaking, these are true beliefs for certain people. Thus, James felt, his pragmatic analysis could remove questions of moral and religious belief from the realms of theological controversy or scientific scrutiny.

Dewey and 'Progressive' Education. John Dewey regarded his type of pragmatism as having far-reaching applications in our society. One such employment of his theory was in the realm of education. Previous educational techniques, Dewey felt, were aimed primarily at inculcating a mass of factual information into students, without giving them any means of utilizing it. They were crammed with the experience of the past rather than prepared to meet the problems of the future. Instead, he proposed that the educational system should try to develop methods for **problem-solving.** If the student learned how to solve problems, presumably he would be better fitted for living in our everchanging world with its manifold perplexities and ever-new problems.

Out of this application of Dewey's theory grew the progressive education movement. Rather than being trained in various disciplines, the child would be trained by being confronted with various situations in which he would have to develop methods for overcoming the difficulties that beset him. He would learn how to make satisfactory 'adjustments' to his environment, and thus develop various means which would aid him in solving the larger problems of the social world in which he would have to live.

This type of education would train people for living in a democratic society, and it would strengthen the development of this type of social and political organization. A democratic society is one that is better able to confront new situations, and try new solutions, since it does not have any rigid or preconceived ideology. It is essentially a system of social organization that is open to exploration of new means for meeting difficulties. It is designed to evolve, to meet change and to adapt to new developments. The student trained in problem-solving will be able to be an active citizen of such a society, utilizing his techniques for dealing with unresolved problems in co-operation with the larger social group in their common search for satisfactory ways of dealing with the practical difficulties which hinder the best functioning of society.

Some Criticisms of Pragmatism. In spite of the evident appeal of the pragmatic point of view for Americans, and its apparent success in becoming perhaps the dominant philosophy in America, some philosophers have objected to this theory. They have attacked the basic pragmatic conception of what constitutes true knowledge, and asked if we can really evaluate ideas in terms of whether they work. At what point, they demand, can one tell if an idea has worked? In considering the example offered earlier of the man who believed that the way to solve his financial difficulties was by bank-robbing, we saw that it would be easy to conclude that this solution was 'right', and one cannot deny that there have been occasions on which it has worked. In attempting to deal with this anomaly, the pragmatists insist that one should take into account not only immediate consequences, but also the long-run effects. In response the critics point out that one could never be sure whether an idea worked, since its long-run consequences can go on forever. At certain times the idea might work successfully, then fail, and then again be successful. One would have to wait indefinitely in order to be able to evaluate the consequences of any belief, and to determine whether it worked. Furthermore, it is not possible to make an evaluation, to say whether something works or not, unless one has some criteria to appeal to. Such criteria the pragmatist expressly denies us. What is meant by 'what works'? Are we to be concerned with what works for us as individuals, for our society, for humanity, or what? We need some moral framework, some idea of what is good and bad, desirable and undesirable, some notion of aims and objectives, in order to know what it might mean to say that something works or does not. But the pragmatist wants us to settle our moral disputes also in the same way, by an appeal to 'cash-value'; he sees 'good' itself as synonymous with 'what works'; and thus he denies the validity of all other criteria and makes it impossible for us to decide what works.

In addition, some of the critics hold, in assessing the working of ideas in terms of the satisfaction certain beliefs afford people, all sorts of personal idiosyncrasies and preferences will become the standards for judging truth and falsehood. Some people may enjoy believing that the moon is made of green cheese, but does that make it true? The critics contend that the pragmatists are confusing the human problems and feelings that are often involved in our attitudes toward various ideas, with the merits of the ideas themselves, and are making human 'adjustment' the ultimate goal of all investigations, instead of seeking objectively true knowledge.

The pragmatists, in response to these objections, insist that there is no way of investigating the truth or falsehood of theories and beliefs except in terms of how they affect human beings, and that their critics are introducing abstruse and artificial standards which have nothing to do with the real problems of human experience.

SUGGESTED FURTHER READING

Dewey, John, *Reconstruction in Philosophy*. Muller: London, 1956. (One of Dewey's important statements of his philosophy.)

James, William, *Essays in Pragmatism*. (A collection of some of James' most famous papers.)

James, William, *Pragmatism. A New Name for Some Old Ways of Thinking*. Longmans: London, 1943. (One of James' best statements of his views.)

Nagel, Ernest, *Sovereign Reason*. Collier-Macmillan: London, 1954. (A recent statement of the pragmatic theory by one of its leading spokesmen.)

K

Russell, Bertrand, *A History of Western Philosophy*. 2nd edn. Allen & Unwin: London, 1968. (The chapter on Dewey is a rather severe criticism of pragmatism.)

Schneider, Herbert W., *A History of American Philosophy*. Oxford University Press: London, 1946. (An excellent picture of the development of American thought, especially the pragmatic movement.)

Wiener, Philip P., *Evolution and the Founders of Pragmatism*. Oxford University Press: London, 1949. (An important study of the origins of American pragmatism.)

PHILOSOPHICAL ANALYSIS

What Is Philosophy? Although people in the Western World have philosophized for more than 2500 years, the exact nature of philosophy is still a matter of dispute. Philosophy began originally as a curious mixture of scientific, theological, magical and ethical 'explanation' of the common and uncommon features of the world. The early Greek thinkers, such as THALES, HERACLITUS, ANAXAGORAS, PYTHAGORAS, and others, thought of philosophy as we now think of contemporary science. They assumed that through philosophical reflection the nature of the world would be revealed to them. Thales, for example, invented an ingenious hypothesis about the fundamental composition of the universe. He believed that all objects are variations of one basic ingredient—water. For water, he argued, if heated becomes steam, and thus all entities which are gaseous, such as the atmosphere, can be described as rarefied water; water in its natural state is a liquid, and all things which flow must be made up of it; and finally, if water is cooled sufficiently it becomes a solid, ice. It seemed plausible, therefore, that all solids must be condensed forms of water. Thales, with a minimum amount of factual information, was able by reflection to devise an ingenious hypothesis to account for such diverse things as the gaseous, liquid and solid characteristics of the earth.

Subsequent philosophers, pursuing substantially the same method (i.e., reflection) devised even more striking theories. DEMOCRITUS, for example, worked out a crude version of the atomic theory some 2000 years before careful investigation could produce any empirical confirmation of it. As man's curiosity about nature grew, and as his knowledge of it increased, his explanations became both more sophisticated and more satisfactory. In time, the study of nature became an activity which broke away from philosophy, and a new discipline was developed called 'science'. But this, it should be pointed out, is a comparatively recent development. Even as late as the nineteenth century, university courses in physics, for instance, were described as 'natural philosophy'. Now science itself has been fragmented into a host of sub-disciplines; each science, so to speak, has selected some aspect of nature for intensive study—physics, for example, deals with the nature of inanimate objects; botany with plants, astronomy with celestial phenomena, and so on. Nevertheless, all these scientific activities, as different as they are from one another, each utilize a common method: a method which is too complex to be described accurately here, but which not only employs reflection about the world, but more importantly which also involves the patient observation of and experimentation with it. The main presupposition of scientific activity is that it is only through such observation of, and experimentation with, the objects in the world (as well as reflection about them, of course) that we can acquire accurate information about the characteristics of these objects. To put it briefly, **knowledge of the world can be acquired only through the use of scientific method.**

The Problem of Knowledge. Now this method differs importantly from philosophical activity. The philosopher does not perform experiments; he does not patiently observe the behaviour of natural objects, either animate or inanimate (except perhaps his students). And yet philosophy purports to give us knowledge about the world. What kind of knowledge does philosophical activity result in? Is philosophy like science except that it deals with a different subject matter—that is, is it like physics, or botany or astronomy, but treating of different kinds of things (e.g., universals, concepts, theories)? Or is philosophy different from science? Does it give us a kind of knowledge, but one which is different from scientific knowledge of the world? Or is it possible that philosophical activity does not result in knowledge at all? But if not, then how can philosophy be justified? To put it simply—what then is philosophy and what does it tell us about the world?

Recent Developments. In the past forty years, at least three influential philosophical movements have developed, each with a different answer to the above questions. They are called, respectively, **Logical Atomism, Logical Positivism** (or **Logical Empiricism**) and **Ordinary Language Philosophy.** We shall discuss them together here since all of them maintain that **the main (and perhaps the sole) function of philosophy is analysis.** We shall not, at this stage, attempt to define 'analysis', since they disagree radically both about the nature of analysis (i.e., what one does when one engages in analysis), and also about what kind of information analysis gives us about the world. But on one point they stand firmly together: **analysis is concerned with the use and function of language. Thus they all agree that philosophical problems are at least in part linguistic problems, and accordingly that in so far as these problems can be solved, it is through some sort of clarification of language.** Let us now turn to Logical Atomism which, historically, is the earliest of these movements.

LOGICAL ATOMISM: THE PHILOSOPHY OF BERTRAND RUSSELL AND THE EARLY LUDWIG WITTGENSTEIN

It is extraordinarily difficult to state the philosophy of Logical Atomism in a simple and brief way for the average (non-specialist) person. This is because in order to understand it such a person must know the essentials of a new discipline, invented only in this century by BERTRAND RUSSELL and ALFRED NORTH WHITEHEAD called **Mathematical or Symbolic Logic.** In a sense which does not too greatly distort the facts, **Logical Atomism may briefly be described as the philosophy of mathematical logic, or perhaps more accurately, of Principia**

Mathematica, the great work on mathematical logic by Russell and Whitehead. Let us try, here, to explain in a simple way the main ideas of *Principia*.

The New Logic. It had been assumed, even as late as the nineteenth century, that Aristotle had said the last word on logic. Kant, for instance, had asserted that logic as developed by Aristotle was, of all philosophical disciplines, a finished and complete subject, even down to its details. This view was shown to be wholly mistaken by Russell and Whitehead. Around the turn of the twentieth century, and after more than ten years of work, **they developed a new type of logic which was much broader in scope than Aristotelian logic; indeed, it contained classical logic as a very minor part.** This new logic resembled a mathematical calculus, such as Euclid's Elements, except, again, that it was of much greater generality: it did not mention lines, points and planes, but talked merely about the relations of symbols to each other. (This is why it has been named Symbolic Logic.) The main difference between Aristotelian logic and the new logic can be put as follows: **Aristotelian logic was essentially a logic of classes, whereas Russell's logic was a logic of propositions.** By a class we mean an entity denoted by a term such as 'man', or 'brother', or 'mortal', etc. The basic propositions of Aristotelian logic such as 'All men are mortal', or 'Some men are mortal', state the relations of classes of things to each other. For example, the proposition 'All men are mortal', states that the class of men is included in the class of mortal things, while the proposition 'Some men are mortal', states that some of the class of men are included in the class of mortal things. Russell's logic, on the other hand, talked about the relation of propositions to each other (e.g., 'If it is raining, then the streets are wet'). The sentences 'It is raining', and 'the streets are wet', both express propositions, which stand in a certain relation to each other—a relation which Russell called **implication.** Russell was able to show that in terms of this logic, the relation between classes of things could also be explicated; hence his logical system not only included Aristotle's treatment of logic, but at the same time went beyond it.

Principia Mathematica was of great importance for philosophy for at least two reasons: (*a*) **It proved that mathematics, which had been thought to be a distinct discipline, is in fact a part of logic.** Russell showed this by deducing from purely logical notions a set of postulates laid down by the great Italian mathematician, PEANO; and from these postulates it was known that arithmetic could be derived. (*b*) **Russell showed, further, that everyday or 'natural' languages, such as English, have a basic structure similar to that of Principia Mathematica.** Although natural languages resemble *Principia* in this respect, they are defective for purposes of philosophical analysis, since they are less precise. **It was accordingly believed that mathematical logic would provide philosophy with a tool of razor sharpness for clarifying the meaning of English sentences.** This in turn gave rise to the hope that philosophical disputes at last could be treated definitively with the use of a new logical machinery. Since we are interested in the influence of *Principia* upon philosophy, rather than in its treatment of the foundations of mathematics, we shall restrict our discussion to that aspect of it.

The Nature of Sentences. What, then, is meant by the 'basic structure' of English sentences? This can be explained as follows: Russell distinguished between what he called **'atomic propositions'**, and **'molecular propositions'. An atomic proposition is a proposition which has no parts which are themselves propositions.** Thus, 'John is human', is an atomic proposition, since its parts are individual words, not propositions. On the other hand, a proposition like 'John and Mary are going to the cinema', is a molecular proposition. Upon analysis, it can be seen to be a **complex proposition containing two parts, each of which is itself a proposition**, i.e., (*a*) 'John is going to the cinema', and (*b*) 'Mary is going to the cinema'. A molecular proposition is built up out of atomic propositions by the use of what Russell called **connecting words,** such as 'and', 'or', and 'if . . . then'. In part, symbolic logic can be regarded as the study of such words, since the rules for the employment of these words allow us to build up complex propositions out of more simple ones. Through the logical machinery of *Principia*, Russell laid down a set of rules which, if followed, would allow one to build molecular propositions out of atomic ones. **He was thus able to analyse any molecular proposition into a set of atomic propositions, plus the logical connectives.** Thus the meaning of a molecular proposition could, so to speak, be unravelled by breaking it down into its constituent atomic propositions. The question now remained—how do we analyse the meaning of an atomic proposition?

Russell's answer was that an **atomic proposition is always of the subject-predicate form.** For example, 'John is mortal', can be analysed into a subject term, which is a proper noun or proper name, 'John', and into a predicate term, such as 'is mortal'. The subject term in such a case always refers to an individual thing—in this case the person, John—and the predicate term to a characteristic or 'property' which the subject term possesses, in this case the characteristic of being mortal.

At this point, the philosophical implications of Russell's system become apparent. When an atomic proposition is true, the subject term denotes an individual thing or object, and the predicate term refers to some characteristic of this thing or object. And in showing that atomic propositions refer to such objects and characteristics, *Principia* gives us information about the real world. **It informs us that the world is made up of 'facts', and that all such facts are atomic in nature, i.e., every fact can be described by an atomic proposition.** There are no molecular facts in nature, since every molecular proposition can be translated into, or reduced to, a set of atomic propositions, plus the logical connectives, such as 'and', 'or', 'if . . . then', and so forth. These connectives, of course, themselves refer to nothing in the world; they are linguistic devices which enable us to combine atomic propositions in various ways; their use is thus, as Russell put it, 'syntactic' only. It should also be stressed that there are no 'general' facts in the world either. There is no fact corresponding to the general proposition 'All men are mortal', since this proposition again reduces to a set of atomic propositions such as 'John is mortal', 'James is mortal', and so forth for every individual human who is mortal. **The ultimate constituents of the world are thus 'facts', and a fact is made up of an individual thing with its individual characteristics.**

Through the study, then, of mathematical logic we are able to discover the essential structure of the world, i.e., we are able to discover that the world is made up of atomic facts. The answer of Logical Atomism to the set of questions we posed about philosophy can now be stated: **the function of philosophy is to inform us about the world.** In particular, it is to inform us that the structure of the world is mirrored by the structure of the basic propositions of *Principia*.

The Theory of Descriptions. But this was not the sole use to which *Principia Mathematica* could be put for philosophical purposes. Further, and perhaps as importantly, its machinery could be used to solve problems which had puzzled thinkers for centuries—problems which had important **ontological** consequences. We can illustrate this by a discussion of what Russell called 'The Theory of Descriptions'.

The point of the theory of descriptions is to show that philosophers, through the faulty analysis of language, have been misled by specious arguments into believing that the sorts of things which ordinary men regard as fictitious or non-existent, in some sense actually do exist. The problem which these philosophers found perplexing is an ancient one; it occurs even in Plato. It can be stated as follows: We seem to be able to make significant and indeed sometimes even true, statements about 'objects' such as Medusa, Hamlet, the mythical country of Atlantis, and so forth. When we say, for example, that 'Hamlet murdered Polonius', this proposition seems to be true; and yet, upon reflection, we realize that there never was any such thing as Hamlet. But how can the proposition be true unless it is about something existent? Or again, when we say 'Medusa does not exist', are we not saying, 'There exists something, Medusa, which does not exist'. But this is an obvious contradiction. Is it then impossible for one to deny the existence of anything without contradicting oneself? There is something obviously wrong here, and through the machinery of *Principia Mathematica*, Russell set out to eliminate the difficulty.

Russell put the puzzle in this way. He asked: How is it possible for a sentence such as 'The present King of France is wise', to be significant even though there is no King of France. Now the answer given to this question by a group of philosophers who preceded Russell notably ALEXANDER MEINONG, was that such entities as 'The present King of France', or 'Medusa', or 'Hamlet' are real things. True, they do not exist in the actual world, but at least they do exist; they exist in some shadowy realm. Meinong described them as 'subsisting' instead of 'existing'—but his point is that in some sense they *are*. 'Medusa', 'Hamlet', 'the present King of France', etc. are genuine constituents of the world, but they do not exist in the same sense as Harold Wilson and Edward Heath. Meinong and those influenced by him were led into this curious way of thinking (sometimes called **Philosophical Idealism**) by an argument which might be stated as follows:

(*a*) The phrase 'The present King of France' is the subject of the sentence 'The present King of France is wise'.

(*b*) Since the sentence 'The present King of France is wise', is *significant*, it must be about something—i.e., it must be about the present King of France.

(*c*) But unless the present King of France existed, the sentence would not be about anything and hence could not be meaningful at all.

(*d*) Since 'the present King of France is wise', is meaningful or significant, it therefore must be about some entity—the present King of France, hence such an entity must exist (or 'subsist').

Symbolic Logic. Russell now showed, through the techniques developed in his Symbolic Logic, that this argument rests upon a fallacy. In order to understand his criticism, and accordingly to understand the Theory of Descriptions which is part of the criticism, it is necessary to make a distinction between what Russell called the **grammatical form** of a sentence, and its **logical form.** A sentence may be of the subject-predicate form from a standpoint of English grammar, and yet when translated into the language of *Principia Mathematica*, may be of a different form, logically speaking. Thus, consider the sentence 'God exists'. In such a sentence, the word 'God' is grammatically the subject of the sentence and 'exists' is the predicate. If we were to rephrase this sentence, and put it into its proper logical form, i.e., if we were to make clear the proposition it asserts, the word 'God' would no longer be the logical subject, but instead would be the logical predicate; and the word 'exists' would no longer be the logical predicate, but would have a different function. It would be what Russell called a '**logical quantifier',** that is, it would have the same function as such an indefinite pronoun as 'someone' or 'something'. Such words are used to refer ambiguously to an indeterminate class of things, and because they refer *indefinitely*, are words expressing generality. Thus when put into its proper logical form the sentence 'God exists', says: 'Something, and only one thing, is omnipotent, omniscient and benevolent'. In short, when we analyse the meaning of the sentence 'God exists', we see that it means that a certain indefinite something has a certain set of properties (being omnipotent, omniscient and benevolent). **The sentence is thus, logically speaking, not of the subject-predicate form but is a general proposition, a proposition of an entirely different structure from that of an atomic proposition.**

Now the same thing is true of the sentence 'The present King of France is wise'. Its grammatical structure leads us to believe that the phrase 'The present King of France' is logically the subject term, and 'is wise' is logically the predicate term, and that such a sentence therefore is an atomic proposition, denoting a fact of the world. But such a sentence is not *logically* of the subject-predicate form. When it is analysed according to the techniques developed in *Principia Mathematica* it analyses into the following propositions:

(1) Something is current monarch of France.
(2) Not more than one thing is current monarch of France.
(3) Whatever is current monarch of France is wise.

It should be noticed that each of these three propositions which together comprise the meaning of 'The present King of France is wise', is a *general* proposition, not an atomic proposition. This can be seen since **no proper names** occur in them, but instead such *general* words as 'something', 'whatever', etc. The phrase 'The present King of France' which occurred in the sentence 'the present King of France is wise', is thus, from a logical point of view, not the subject of the proposition at all, for upon analysis it is eliminated from the analysing propositions. Instead we have propositions containing **no proper names at all, but only indefinite pronouns and predicates.** Thus, the phrase, 'the present King of France' is not logically a proper name, although from a grammatical standpoint it has the same function as a proper name. Meinong would have been right, Russell argued, in inferring that if such a phrase *were* a proper name it would refer to something, and thus right in inferring that the present King of France 'subsists'. But analysis into logical terminology shows us that the grammatical form of the sentence is misleading with respect to giving us the *actual form* of the proposition; for when so analysed, it turns into a set of general propositions. Now general propositions do not refer to anything *directly in the actual world* since only atomic propositions can designate facts. Meinong's fallacy was to conclude that the phrase 'the present King of France' was a proper name because it functioned as the grammatical subject of a sentence. In showing that 'the present King of France is wise' is logically a *general* proposition, not an atomic proposition, Russell was in effect showing that such a phrase does not directly denote any object in the world. **Only the subjects of atomic propositions are capable of direct denotation or reference.**

Russell called such expressions as 'the present King of France' **definite descriptive phrases. They are 'definite' because they connote that one and only one individual satisfies the description—this is the function of the word 'the'.** Russell's point about descriptions not being logically proper names can be put in yet a different way. He elsewhere described them as **'incomplete symbols'**, rather than as 'proper names'. Such phrases are 'incomplete' because they have no meaning by themselves. They function much as brackets do in a sentence, which also have no meaning by themselves. However, definite descriptive phrases can take on meaning in the context of a whole sentence which contains them. Thus, if one were to ask: 'What does the phrase "the present King of France" mean?' then, according to Russell, a proper reply would be, 'It means nothing at all—by *itself*.' This is because only proper names *mean* independently of a whole sentence, they *mean* the object they are used to refer to (for instance the name 'Julius Caesar' means the object Julius Caesar). Now since the phrase 'the present King of France' can be shown by analysing it (as above) into the language of *Principia* not to be a proper name, it has no meaning of its own—i.e., it does not by itself directly refer to anything in the world. However, sentences containing such a phrase may have meaning. Thus, the sentence 'The present King of France is wise', means the same as 'One and only one thing is the current monarch of France, and this thing is wise'. In this way, through the notion of an 'incomplete symbol' Russell was able to solve Meinong's perplexity about how it is possible for a sentence like 'The present King of France is wise', to be significant even though the phrase 'The present King of France', does not directly denote anything.

Logical Atomism. The assumptions upon which the Theory of Descriptions rests are those of Logical Atomism. **It is assumed by Russell that Principia Mathematica gives us the sketch of a perfect language; it is perfect because it mirrors the structure of the actual world.** When we translate a sentence of ordinary English into this perfect logical language, its meaning becomes clear. **If it turns out, upon such translation, not to be of the subject-predicate form, then there is nothing that its grammatical subject will directly refer to, since in the perfect language every subject term will denote an actual object in the world, and every predicate term will denote an actual characteristic of that object.**

Logical Atomism received its most careful and complete statement in a cryptic work written by a philosophical genius named LUDWIG WITTGENSTEIN, who was a pupil of Russell's. Wittgenstein in a book called *The Tractatus Logico-Philosophicus*, published in 1922, developed a version of Logical Atomism which is now called the Picture Theory. According to Wittgenstein, the ideal language (*Principia*) pictured or mirrored the world, just as a map mirrors it. If we wish to discover whether town A is North of town B in Scotland, we can do so by referring to a map, since a map in a sense pictures the terrain. It pictures it because there is identity of structure between the points on the map and the points on the ground. A perfect language is like a map. It pictures the structure of reality. For every proper name in the language there is a corresponding entity, and for every predicate a corresponding property. The ideal language thus gives us the structure of facts, since facts are composed of objects and their properties.

We may summarize the main tenets of Logical Atomism as follows: **Philosophy is a genuine activity,** just as science is. Unlike science, though, philosophy does not discover new facts for us. The knowledge we acquire through the study of philosophy is not knowledge of new facts. Instead, philosophy tells us about the structure of the world, how its basic ingredients are constructed. Roughly speaking, it tells us that the world is composed of a set of atomic facts, i.e., objects and their properties.

The Proper Function Of Philosophy Is Analysis. Analysis consists in rewriting sentences of natural languages in such a way that these sentences will exhibit their proper logical form. When they are put into their logical form, their meaning will become clear, and philosophical perplexity will be eliminated.

As can be seen from the above remarks, **the philosophy of Logical Atomism is a metaphysical system in the traditional sense. It contends that philosophy is an activity which gives us knowledge of the world; not the same kind of knowledge which science gives us, to be sure, but knowledge nonetheless.**

The philosophy of Logical Atomism flourished, especially in England, in the 1920's and 1930's; but it has declined steadily in popularity since then. One of the main reasons for its eclipse was the rise of **Logical Positivism, another philosophy which was influenced by the** development of mathematical logic. But this doctrine utilized mathematical logic to show that metaphysics was nonsense, and since Logical Atomism was clearly a form of traditional metaphysics, it was rejected by thinkers who accepted the newer view.

LOGICAL POSITIVISM: SCHLICK, CARNAP, A. J. AYER

Logical Positivism is often though to have been initiated by a remark of Wittgenstein in the *Tractatus* to the effect that philosophy is not a theory, but an activity. Logical Positivism was the philosophical movement initiated by a group of thinkers who lived in Vienna in the 1920's. (This group later became famous under the name of the 'Vienna Circle'.) Among its members were MORITZ SCHLICK, professor at the University of Vienna, HANS HAHN, FRIEDRICH WAISMANN, HERBERT FEIGL, OTTO NEURATH and RUDOLF CARNAP. These men held informal seminars and, in particular, closely studied the writings of Wittgenstein. They elaborated upon the view that philosophy is not a theory but an activity. They held that philosophy does not produce propositions which are true or false; it merely clarifies the meaning of statements, showing some to be scientific, some to be mathematical and some (including most so-called philosophical statements) to be nonsensical. Their views, put in brief, were that every significant statement either is a statement of formal logic (in the broad sense of *Principia Mathematica*, and thus including mathematical statements) or is a statement of science (again the phrase 'scientific statement' was broadly interpreted to include singular sentences such as 'This is white', as well as statements of physical laws). All other types of statement were, strictly speaking, nonsensical. If they had any meaning whatsoever, it was described as 'poetical', or 'emotive', or 'pictorial', or 'motivational', but it was not cognitive. The statements of theology such as 'God exists in a heavenly place' fell into this category as did such traditional philosophical statements as 'We can never directly observe physical objects', 'I can never know that you have a mind', 'No men are free, but everyone is determined by his past', and so forth. It was not held, it must be made clear, that such statements were *false*; they were literally without sense, just as the statement 'T'was brillig and the slithy toves', is without sense. Philosophy pursued in the traditional manner was thus deprecated; philosophy had a legitimate function, to be sure, but it was not a function which resulted in propositions. Rather it was an activity which led to the clarification of the meaning of questions in order to show how these could be answered by the appropriate disciplines. Professor Herbert Feigl's witty remark about the nature of philosophy, practised in the traditional way, beautifully epitomizes the outlook of this school of philosophers. 'Philosophy,' he remarked, 'is the disease of which it should be the cure.' Let us trace the steps which led to this position.

The Verification Principle. In order to understand the powerful attack which Logical Positivism made upon traditional philosophical systems, including Logical Atomism, it is necessary to analyse two of its basic tenets: first, a distinction which was adhered to between what are called **'analytic'** and **'synthetic'** propositions, and secondly, **the criterion for determining when a proposition was cognitively meaningful,** sometimes called 'The Verification Principle'. Let us explain first the distinction drawn between analytic and synthetic propositions.

Consider first the following two propositions:

> (*a*) All husbands have heads.
> (*b*) All husbands are married.

Now both of these propositions are similar in being true; yet they differ in the way they are true. Proposition (*a*) happens to be true of every husband. We never see a husband without a head. But, and this is the important point, it would be possible to imagine a husband who had no head. Imagine a man born without a head, who lived, who was fed through tubes, who married. This man would be exactly like other men, except he would lack a head. But, because he would have married someone, he would be a husband. On the other hand, proposition (*b*) is not merely true as a matter of fact; but it is *impossible* to imagine or conceive of any circumstances whatever in which somebody could be a husband and yet not be married. It does not merely happen to be the case that all husbands are married; it follows from the very meaning of the word 'husband' that anyone who is a husband *necessarily* is married. We can thus see that if anyone were in doubt about the truth of these propositions he would establish them in quite different ways. In order to prove the first proposition true, he would actually have to observe every single husband. This would require, as we say, empirical investigation; some sort of actual survey of existing husbands. But one does not have to conduct any investigation to prove that the proposition 'All husbands are married' is true. He merely has to understand the meaning of the words which make up the proposition. Once he understands these words, he can see that it is part of the *meaning* of the word 'husband' that all husbands are married—for 'husband' means the same as 'married male'. Thus the proposition can be seen to be true without any sort of empirical investigation at all.

Propositions which require some sort of empirical investigation for their confirmation are termed 'synthetic' while those whose truth follows from their meaning are called 'analytic'. It is the contention of logical positivism that every significant proposition must be either analytic or synthetic, but none can be both. Broadly speaking, all analytic propositions belong to formal logic—they are true in virtue of their formal structure, while all synthetic propositions are like the propositions of science—they require empirical investigation before their truth can be established. To put it differently, analytic propositions are so called because, since their predicate is contained in the definition of the subject term, all that the proposition is doing is to assert something of the subject that is obtained *by analysis* of the subject term (e.g., 'All husbands—i.e., married males—are married). Hence we verify such propositions by examining the words they contain. Synthetic propositions, on the other hand, are so called because they are the result of **joining together, i.e., making** *a synthesis* **of, two logically unrelated things** (e.g., 'This desk is brown'). Hence they can only be verified by observation and empirical investigation of whether in fact this relation is true.

One further consequence of this distinction must be mentioned. Analytic propositions, it was held, do not refer to the world in the way in which synthetic propositions do. From the truth of an analytic proposition, we cannot infer that the items mentioned by the terms in the proposition exist. Thus, from the analytic truth that 'All giants are giants' we cannot infer that there are any giants. On the other hand, if such a proposition as 'This desk is brown' is true, we can infer that the world contains at least one desk. The logical positivists described the difference between the two types of proposition by saying that analytic propositions are **'trivial'**, whereas synthetic propositions are **'informative'**. The former are trivial in the sense that although they appear to be talking about items in the world, upon analysis it can be seen that they make no claim about the world; this was put by saying that **they are true merely in virtue of their logical form, or by definition** (i.e., the definition of a 'husband' is that a husband is a married male) or by saying that they are **assertions about words.** On the other hand, **a synthetic proposition is 'informative' in the sense that it purports to make some claim about reality, and when true, in fact does make such a claim.**

Now it is easy, through the mathematical and logical techniques developed by Russell and Whitehead, to tell whether a proposition is analytic or not. But how can we tell when a synthetic proposition, or one which purports to be about the world, is significant?

Is such a proposition as 'God exists in a heavenly place' significant? It purports to be about the world—but is it?

In order to answer this question, the positivists developed a test for the significance of synthetic propositions: the famous Verifiability Criterion of Meaning. Any proposition which passed this test was held to be significant in a factual sense. If it failed to pass the test, it must either be analytic (and hence not about the world) or non-significant, i.e., nonsensical. All propositions which therefore aim to express genuine knowledge about the world must pass the test of being empirically verifiable before they can be admitted to be significant. What then is the Verifiability Criterion?

This criterion has been formulated in various ways by different philosophers. Schlick in a famous paper called 'Realism and Positivism' formulates the principle in at least five different ways. One of its most famous statements is to be found in a book by A. J. Ayer, published in 1936, called *Language, Truth and Logic.* According to Ayer **a sentence will be factually (i.e., not analytically) significant to a given person if and only if he knows how to verify the proposition which it purports to express; that is, if he knows what observations would lead him under certain conditions to accept the proposition as being true, or reject it as being false.**

The important word in the above formulation is the word **'observation'.** The point of the principle is that it must be possible to describe what sorts of observation would have to be made in order to determine whether a proposition is true or false. **If some observation can be described which would be relevant in determining the truth or falsity of a proposition then the proposition will be significant; if not, it will be meaningless.** Schlick produced a striking example to illustrate the use of this principle. Suppose somebody asserted 'The universe is shrinking uniformly'. Suppose further that by 'uniformly' he means that everything will remain exactly proportional to everything else; all our measuring sticks would shrink at the same rate; all people would grow smaller proportionately; and thus there would be no discernible or measurable difference between things after the universe had shrunk and things before it had. Would it then make sense to say that the universe had shrunk? Obviously not, since no possible observation could prove that it had shrunk. Since the word 'universe' denotes everything which exists, no one—even in principle—could get outside of it; thus no one could measure any such shrinkage; and thus to assert such a set of words is to assert something nonsensical.

Philosophical theories, according to Schlick, make just such assertions. To say 'We never directly perceive physical objects' is either to utter a triviality or to make a remark which is, if significant, false. But if a philosopher holds that it is neither trivially analytic or false, then, according to Schlick, since it could not be verified, it would be nonsensical, since no possible observation could be described which would determine it to be either true or false.

In explaining the Verifiability Criterion a further distinction must be made. It is necessary to distinguish between propositions which are veri*fied* and those which are verifi*able*, or to put it in other words, between *practical* verifiability and verifiability *in principle*. Consider the following proposition: 'There are men on the planet Mars'. Now this proposition has never been verified by anyone; yet it is a proposition which is verifiable. We can describe the steps we must take in order to verify it. We must first find some means of getting to Mars and then look to see if there are men on it. If there are, then the proposition will be true; if not, it will be false. The proposition in any case is significant, since we have described the conditions under which it would be known to be either true or false. Even though we cannot at the present time actually verify the proposition, since we do not now have the available means for travelling to Mars, nonetheless it is in principle verifiable, and hence is significant.

Now consider by way of contrast such a proposition as 'God exists in a heavenly place'. What conditions would reveal this proposition to be true? What steps could we possibly take in order to show it to be verifiable, even in principle? There is no relevant observation we could make which would show the proposition either to be true or false (to argue that if we died, we could then determine which it was, is simply another way of stating that no observation, in the present sense of that word, would be relevant). Since no conceivable way of verifying the proposition, even in principle, exists, this sentence expresses no proposition—it is not a **cognitively significant** utterance.

Implications. What are the consequences for traditional philosophy if we accept the tenets of logical positivism? The main effect of accepting such a doctrine will be that in so far as philosophy purports to tell us something about reality, and in so far as it claims that the propositions purporting to tell us something about reality are neither empirically verifiable nor analytic, we can reject such claims as being without sense. Thus, consider the following example of philosophical prose from a book by a contemporary existentialist, HEIDEGGER, *What is Metaphysics?* Heidegger writes:

> Why are we concerned about this nothing? The nothing is rejected by science and sacrificed as the unreal. Science wants to have nothing to do with the nothing. What is the nothing? Does the nothing exist only because the not, i.e., negation, exists? Or do negation and the not exist only because the nothing exists? We maintain: the nothing is the simple negation of the totality of being. Anxiety reveals the nothing. The nothing itself nots.

Rudolf Carnap in an examination of the above discourse shows that its propositions are not capable of confirmation, since it is not possible to formulate an observation proposition by which the propositions can be tested. He thus rejects them as nonsensical, and the above piece of writing, he believes, is typical of traditional philosophy. **Traditional philosophy purports to tell us something about the world, but because its utterances are in general empirically unverifiable, they are either trivially analytic or meaningless.**

Does this then mean that philosophy has no legitimate function whatever? The positivist thinks that philosophy does have a legitimate function—what we have called **analysis.** But by 'analysis' he does not mean analysis in Russell's sense, i.e., **the translation of statements in ordinary language into statements which accurately exhibit their logical form.** Rather, **the function of analysis is to take any problem, to show which questions in it are capable of being answered by mathematical or logical reasoning, and which questions are capable of being answered by some sort of empirical investigation.** It is not the function of philosophers, as such, to *answer* these questions: it is merely their function **to clarify the meaning of the questions so that one will know what sorts of question they are, and how to proceed to answer them.** Philosophical problems of the traditional sort, as we have tried to show elsewhere in this book, are extraordinarily complex. They are a composite of a whole host of queries, puzzles, questions—some of which are answerable only by empirical investigation, some of which require mathematical or logical techniques for their solution. Some questions are the products of emotion and bias; some are simply senseless, for one reason or another. Philosophical analysis is thus conceived as a process which is *preliminary* to any sort of answer to a question. One must first **analyse the question in order to discover what it means**—indeed as Professor DAVID RYNIN in his excellent statement of the Verifiability Criterion puts it—**to discover what a question means is identical with discovering how one would go about answering it.** The analyst himself suggests no answers—and hence when he philosophizes properly no propositions are forthcoming. Philosophy thus makes no claims about the world—it merely attempts to unravel those perplexities of everyday life and science which bother people, and which people cannot sensibly answer without first discovering what sort of an answer would be relevant. In so far, then, as philosophy solves puzzles and clears heads, its function is therapeutic. Those who advocate the use of philosophy for such purposes have often been described as **'therapeutic positivists'.**

ORDINARY LANGUAGE PHILOSOPHY: THE LATER WITTGENSTEIN, RYLE

The third important contemporary movement in analytical philo- sophy has sometimes been styled **'the Ordinary-Language School'** of philosophy. Although many philosophers who philosophize in this manner would deny that they form a school, there is sufficient similar- ity in their methods (and their univocality in denying that they do form a 'school') to justify the application of a common designation. This, if it is indeed a movement, is a very recent one. It began in the late 1930's in Cambridge University, where Wittgenstein, one of the original proponents of Logical Atomism, had abandoned that doc- trine. It now flourishes both at Cambridge and Oxford Universities, as well as in Canada, Australia and the United States—but it is mainly restricted to these countries and is comparatively unknown upon the Continent where philosophy of a more traditional sort prevails.

Wittgenstein. In the 1930's Wittgenstein came to realize that the search for a perfect language which accurately mirrored the world could not be realized. We cannot here reliably state in detail his reasons for abandoning Logical Atomism since he published little during this period. His doctrines come down to us from students who attended his lectures, and who took voluminous notes which were, for years, surreptitiously distributed under such mysterious names as 'The Brown Book' or 'The Blue Book'. Wittgenstein's influence upon con- temporary philosophy has been tremendous, but it is an influence which was mainly exercised upon those with whom he was in direct contact, rather than through his writings. Since his death in 1952, how- ever, some of these manuscripts have been published (see *Philosophical Investigations*, ed. by G. E. M. Anscombe).

In any case, in this period, it is clear that Wittgenstein came to realize that the way to clarify philosophical problems did not lie in translating them into a formal language; but rather, since he came to believe that philosophical perplexity arises from certain rather subtle misuses of everyday language, the way to eliminate philosophical per- plexity was to exhibit the correct use of the key terms which make up philosophical discourse, and thus to show how a philosopher's use of these terms can be misleading.

Wittgenstein thus began to chart the actual features of everyday discourse through a method now called **'the method of language games'.** He did this by showing in detail how language was actually used in its ordinary employment by ordinary speakers of it, and how subtle extensions of the ordinary use of such terms could lead to philosophical difficulties. Instead, therefore, of trying to discover the meaning of certain terms through analysis in the Russell sense, the function of the philosopher was to indicate the significance of these terms by showing how they are in fact used. Wittgenstein is responsible for a famous utterance which characterizes the activity of ordinary language philosophers: 'Don't ask for the meaning,' he said, 'ask for the use.'

Gilbert Ryle. A recent and masterful use of this technique is to be found in a book by GILBERT RYLE called *The Concept of Mind*. Ryle shows that many ordinary people, and many philosophers, have a certain theory about the nature of the mind which is riddled with difficulties, and which is on the whole untenable. This theory arises from misunderstanding the logic of certain key terms used to describe mental phenomena, e.g., 'knowing', 'believing', 'inferring', etc. Ryle calls this theory 'The Ghost in the Machine'. This refers to the view that there exists within the body a certain mysterious entity called 'the mind'. This mind is invisible (and hence like a ghost); but it feels, it thinks, it deliberates, it believes, it knows. The operations of the mind are supposedly just like external operations such as walking, jumping, etc., except that these are bodily operations and are not hidden or secret. Ryle shows that this view of the mind rests upon the assumption that certain words such as 'know' directly designate these internal episodes or operations. This incorrect assumption can be remedied by the correct use of these terms. He points out that the mind's operations are just as visible and just as evident as such operations as jumping, skipping, etc. This is because many of the operations of the mind are 'dispositions'. Take solubility as an example. To say that sugar is soluble is to say that if we put sugar in water it would dissolve. Solubility is a disposition which sugar possesses—i.e., the disposition or tendency to dissolve when put in water. Now knowing, or believing, etc., are dispositions in exactly this sense. For to say that a man 'knows' something is to say, in effect, that under certain conditions (say a test) he is able to give a performance of a certain kind. Thus knowing is not a secret operation of a hidden entity but the observable exercise of a capacity and thus the view that the mind is some internal, mysterious ghost-like substance is false.

Implications. The effect of the practice of Wittgenstein and Ryle upon contemporary philosophy has been, on the whole, positive. Unlike the positivists who felt that philosophy's sole function was to clarify the various questions involved in a problem so that they could more profitably be answered by some other discipline, the ordinary language philosophers believe that philosophy can itself solve certain problems; and that in a sense, its activities give knowledge about the world. This is knowledge of the use of certain concepts in everyday life —concepts such as 'believe', 'know', 'infer', 'doubt', and so forth. By charting the 'logical geography' of such concepts, as Ryle puts it, we become clearer about the nature of the mind, for instance. And similar analyses have been made of other crucial, common notions such as 'responsibility', 'promising', and so forth.

Because of the comparatively recent development of this mode of philosophizing, it is dangerous as yet to generalize about its methods and achievements. For this reason, we shall curtail our survey of contemporary analytic philosophy at this point. However, it is not too early to hazard the guess that these new approaches to philosophy may be among the most fruitful in its history.

SUGGESTED FURTHER READING

Ayer, A. J., *Language, Truth and Logic*. Gollancz: London, 1946. (The classical statement of logical positivism.)

Ayer, A. J., *et al.*, *The Revolution in Philosophy*. Macmillan: London, 1956. (A series of lectures by leading and contemporary philosophers on all aspects of Philosophical Analysis.)

Flew, A., *Logic and Language*, 1st and 2nd series. Blackwell: Oxford, 1951–53. (A good collection of articles.)

Hare, R. M., *The Language of Morals*. Oxford University Press: London, 1952. Paperback edition, 1964. (An attempt to apply the techniques of linguistic analysis to the problems of morals.)

Ryle, Gilbert, *The Concept of Mind*. Hutchinson: London, 1967. (The application of linguistic and logical analysis to the mind–body problem.)

Ryle, Gilbert, *Dilemmas*. Cambridge University Press: London, 1954. (A slightly modified version of the Tanner Lectures of 1953; Ryle attempts to sort out a number of dilemmas by clarifying the logic of the language in which they are expressed.)

Toulmin, S. E., *The Place of Reason in Ethics*. Cambridge University Press: London, 1968. (An attempt to use recent advances in our understanding of logic and the nature of reasoning to discover if moral principles can be founded on reason.)

Warnock, G. J., *English Philosophy since 1900*. Oxford University Press: London, 1958. (A good summary of the major developments of this century.)

Wittgenstein, Ludwig, *Philosophical Investigations*. Blackwell: Oxford, 1965. (The posthumous publication of some of the manuscripts outlining the doctrines of this great philosopher.)

EXISTENTIALISM

The last form of contemporary philosophy we shall consider is the view called Existentialism. This is the name given to a number of very different philosophies and should not be seen as implying that these philosophies have more than a very tenuous connection with each other. They have little more in common than that they are all 'philosophies of life'; they all try to answer in different ways the questions that men are inclined to ask about human existence; they are all, therefore, opposed to 'rational' philosophy, and they see philosophy as having a more positive role to play than any of the modern analytical movements are willing to ascribe to it. This kind of view has been extremely popular in France and Germany since the Second World War, and is becoming influential in the English-speaking world. In order to understand this philosophical theory, it is best to go back to its origins in the nineteenth century, and then examine certain of the most general features of contemporary existentialist thought.

SÖREN KIERKEGAARD

The underlying theory of this movement goes back to a brilliant Danish philosopher and theologian, SÖREN KIERKEGAARD, and his war against rational philosophy and theology. Kierkegaard was born in 1813, lived most of his life in Copenhagen, and wrote a series of strange books until his death in 1855. By and large, these writings and the career of their author made a very slight impression on his times. In Copenhagen, Kierkegaard was regarded as a peculiar crank, as a nuisance to the Danish Church. Outside of his homeland he was hardly known at all. However, near the beginning of this century, his works were translated into German, French, English and other languages, and now, a century after his death, his influence is deep and widespread. The histories of philosophy written fifty years ago hardly mention him, but current philosophical journals and publications contain more and more studies of his work each year. So, although Kierkegaard has been dead over a century, he is really a contemporary thinker.

The Works. One of the puzzling features of his works is that they are attributed to a series of authors with names like Johannes Climacus, Johannes de Silentio, Anti-Climacus, and the like, and only occasionally to himself. The works vary from almost fictional writings such as *Either/Or*, to philosophical studies such as the *Philosophical Fragments* and *Fear and Trembling*, to religious rhapsodies such as his *Edifying Discourses*, to bitter satirical diatribes such as the *Attack upon Christendom*. However, as Kierkegaard argued in one of his works, there is a method in all this apparent madness, a problem and a message which the author felt could only be conveyed in this peculiar fashion through the points of view represented by the various pseudonyms.

The Central Question. Fundamentally, in its most simplified form, the problem that Kierkegaard raised in his works was, 'What is the point of man's life?' 'What sense can he make out of human existence?' 'What is the purpose of human events?' Kierkegaard attempted in his literary works to reveal an image of human life as anguished and absurd, harrowing and meaningless. In his philosophical writings, he developed arguments on the basis of this view of human existence. His religious writings and his satires attempted in other ways to make the reader acutely conscious of these questions.

'Johannes Climacus.' For our purposes, the clearest presentation of Kierkegaard's view is set forth in the *Philosophical Fragments*; his proposed solution also appears there. This work is alleged to have been written by one Johannes Climacus. This name was probably chosen because there had been such an author at least a thousand years earlier who wrote a work called *The Ladder to Paradise*. On the title-page of Kierkegaard's book, the supposed author, Climacus, posed the problems of the book in three questions: Is an historical point of departure possible for an eternal consciousness? How can such a point of departure have any other than a mere historical interest? Is it possible to base an eternal happiness upon historical knowledge? What

Climacus wished to point out is that the solution to man's problems lies in somehow being able to find a link between man's historical or temporal life and some sort of eternal knowledge. As the argument of the book is intended to make out, the answer to each of the questions must be both completely negative and also completely affirmative.

The Socratic Paradox. In order to develop his paradoxical theory, Kierkegaard begins the *Philosophical Fragments* with a classic philosophical puzzle posed by Plato. In the dialogue, the 'Meno', Socrates had asked, can we learn that which we do not know? He argued that if we really do not know it, then we would not be able to recognize this knowledge when we learn it. If I do not now know what 7,689 times 4,547 is, how can I distinguish the right answer from the wrong answer when I see it? If I can tell the right answer from the wrong one, then, Socrates insisted, in some sense I must already have known the right answer (see page 177). On the basis of such an argument, Socrates came to the conclusion that learning is impossible—that is, it is not possible to acquire true knowledge that one does not already have. Either one learns what one already knows, in which case one does not *learn*, or one has no way of learning anything, since one has no way of recognizing the truth of what one is trying to learn. The significance of all this, for Socrates and Plato, was that one did not actually learn anything new, but must have all possible knowledge within oneself, and that what we call learning is really nothing but recollecting true knowledge that we already have within us. The stimulus of certain occasions, such as conversations with Socrates, only has the effect of jarring our memories, so that we become aware of something we already know.

Kierkegaard's Solution. Kierkegaard accepted the problem raised by Plato as genuine, but suggested that a different solution could be offered in place of the Platonic theory of recollection. Let us suppose that the learner does not have all knowledge within him. Then prior to acquiring knowledge, the learner has no means of recognizing truth when he encounters it. But if one does learn anything, then, according to Kierkegaard's hypothesis, something extremely strange must occur. Something must happen at the moment of learning that makes the learner different from what he was before, that makes him capable of recognizing a truth which he previously could not do. Prior to this change in the nature of the learner, he must have been in complete ignorance, incapable of telling truths from falsehoods, knowing no truths. Then, suddenly, a moment of enlightenment must have taken place, which has removed the previous ignorance, and made it possible for him to distinguish truth from falsehood. In other words, Kierkegaard's hypothesis, instead of explaining knowledge as recollection, explains knowledge as miraculous, as due to some inexplicable transformation that takes place in the learner at some decisive moment in his existence.

Once the moment of enlightenment has taken place, what one knows is absolutely certain for the learner; it is eternal knowledge for him. In view of the learner's inability to bring about his own enlightenment, since he was completely ignorant before it occurred, and in view of his own inability to comprehend what has happened to him, or how it has taken place, Kierkegaard suggests calling whatever is the cause of one's enlightenment—God. Such a God, whatever He or It may be, must enter into the series of historical events that constitute man's life in order to produce this radical and complete transformation in the learner.

The Decisive Moment. One further element to the Kierkegaardian hypothesis must be introduced. Kierkegaard claims that his explanation differs from that of Socrates in one crucial detail. For Socrates, the moment of recollection is not really important, since the learner had all the knowledge within himself all the time. But, in Kierkegaard's theory, the moment of enlightenment is decisive for the learner in two respects: he is completely changed from total ignorance to possessing eternal knowledge; and the moment is decisive as part of *his* life. What this latter claim means is that although the transformation is miraculous from the human point of view, it must still be significant for the individual as the dramatic culmination of something which occurs in his own life.

To make the moment of enlightenment decisive from man's point of view, man must desire this transformation, but because of his ignorance must desire it without knowing what it would involve and what it would be like. In order to illustrate this, Kierkegaard offers a possible interpretation of his theory in terms of a story. Suppose a mighty king (God) wants to marry a humble maiden (the human learner) but can marry her only if she loves him for himself, and not because of his wealth and power. If he shows her his power and his wealth, she may marry him for the wrong reasons—she will merely be overpowered by his grandeur. If he forces her to marry him, again she will not do it because of love of the king. The only way the king can achieve his end—gaining her because she wants him for himself—is to conceal all those elements that might lead her to make her choice for the wrong reasons. Similarly, if the learner can see the *benefits* of enlightenment, he will be enticed. If God causes the enlightenment without any desire for it on the part of the learner, it will have no significance for him. So, Kierkegaard claimed, if the moment is to be significant for a human being, it must involve his prior desire for enlightenment, without his either being forced to desire it, or being enticed into desiring it because of its possible advantages.

Scepticism and Faith. Put in less picturesque terms, the theory Kierkegaard set forth is that human beings of and by themselves are incapable of knowing anything that is certain, and that only through some sort of miraculous event in their lives can they ever acquire such knowledge. But this miracle of knowing can only be significant or decisive for a human being if he desires its occurrence without being able to form any judgment about the advantages or disadvantages of the transformation. A good deal of Kierkegaard's philosophical writing is devoted to developing a type of complete scepticism, to showing that human beings by themselves can know nothing. After developing that scepticism he maintained that the solution to man's total ignorance lies first in recognizing our tragic plight and then, blindly, irrationally, seeking a way out of that wretched predicament through faith alone, faith that there can be a form of contact between man and God in man's historical existence.

The only information we have in our benighted state of ignorance is either factual, historical information about our experience, or logically derived information about concepts. But whether any of this is necessarily true about anything in this world, we can never tell. In our unenlightened state we are completely unable to tell if God exists. In fact, our ignorance is such, that His non-existence is more compatible with our information than His existence.

Uncertainty. Our sense experience and historical information are always changing. We cannot tell whether any of our sense information is necessarily true. We lack means for establishing the necessary truth of any knowledge we acquire by experience. In order to be absolutely certain we would have to be able to show that it is impossible that it could be false. But the very fact that our sense experience deals with changing things, with things that come into being, change and disappear, shows that anything we believe that we know could be false. There is nothing about the changing world that has to be the way it is since it keeps altering its qualities. Hence, as regards anything historical, anything that takes place in time, we can only notice the temporary arrangement of qualities, but can never be sure that experienced objects *must* have certain properties, and cannot be otherwise. (The point Kierkegaard is making is much like Hume's claim that we can never have necessary knowledge about matters of fact (see pages 209–20).)

With regard to the apparently certain knowledge that we have in mathematics and other such disciplines, here all that we know, according to Kierkegaard's analysis, is that *if* we define certain concepts in certain ways, *then* certain consequences follow. This tells us about the logical relationships of concepts, but tells us nothing at all about whether any items in our experience have these properties. Geometry may allow us to formulate certain theorems about 'points', 'lines', and 'planes', but it does not allow us to tell whether there are objects in our experience to which these theorems apply. Even if there are no 'points', 'lines' or 'planes' in our world, Euclidean geometry is still valid. But the geometry of objects in our experience is a matter of sense investigations, which can never yield any completely certain or necessary conclusion.

Kierkegaard's scepticism is summed up in his claim that a logical system of knowledge is possible, that is, a body of knowledge is possible in which the conclusions can be justified as necessarily true since they are logical consequences of the initial concepts and definitions. **On the other hand, an existential system, a body of necessary knowledge dealing with experience, is not possible, because we are incapable of discovering any necessary truths about historical or changing events.** As the logical positivists have contended, all our information consists either of logically true propositions which have no factual content, or of factual propositions which cannot be shown to be true by logical procedures.

The Problem of God. In view of these extreme limitations on the possibility of human knowledge, we have no way of proving the existence of God as an object which operates in our historical world. If we define God as many theologians do, as an eternal, unchanging Being, it may be possible, if the definition is carefully contrived, to show that a proposition of the form 'God necessarily exists' follows from the definition. But this procedure has no bearing on whether there is such a Being in the world of our experience (see page 158). It merely shows the logical relationship that exists between concept and conclusion. If we try to discover from our experience whether God exists, we are confronted with a different kind of difficulty. Everything we experience is temporal and changing, and hence not God, since God is eternal and unchanging. Some of the items that we experience may be the effects of God's activities, but this we could only tell if we already knew that there is a God.

With respect to the theologian's concept of God as an eternal and unchanging Being, we can see that it would be logically impossible for God to be part of the historical world. By definition, no historical or temporal properties apply to God. If one believed that God existed in time, that God was able to act in human historical situations, one would be believing something that is logically absurd.

The Human Predicament. It is now possible to present the full flavour of Kierkegaard's theory, and then its more general formulation in contemporary existentialism. As human beings in our state of total ignorance, all that we can do is realize the necessity of complete scepticism, our inability to know anything about the world that is true or necessary. However, if we reflect on our plight, we realize also that we are trapped in an awful condition. We have no real knowledge, and yet we have a need for such knowledge to be certain of what we ought to do, what we ought to believe, and so on. The quest for knowledge, in the strongest possible sense, is unavoidable, if we are concerned to find the meaning of human existence. But, in view of our ignorance, we have no means for discovering a solution. This can only occur if the miracle of enlightenment occurs, and we cannot even tell if there is an Enlightener in the universe.

The 'Risk' of Faith. Since there are no guides for us, no way of determining what we ought to do, or how we can become enlightened, all that we can do is either to remain in our darkness as sceptics forever, or take 'the leap into absurdity', accept a belief, blindly and irrationally, that there is some agent called 'God' who can and does act in time, and who will, if we desire it, effect our enlightenment. How does one know what to believe in? One cannot. All one can do is believe. Man's solution lies solely in the decision to believe, to have faith. One can never be sure before the event that it is the right decision, or if as a result of the decision, one's life may become meaningful, and the quest for knowledge be at an end. One may also have made the wrong decision, opted for the wrong belief. The risk is enormous, and there is no way of establishing a basis for belief.

Christian Belief. The faith that Kierkegaard advocated was an interpretation of Christianity in terms of his theory. Assuming his hypothesis about how knowledge occurs, he believed that the miracle of enlightenment took place through the Incarnation of Jesus, through God's appearing in human history and saving those who believe. The crucial stumbling-block for Kierkegaard's version of Christianity is involved in finding out what to believe, what form the Incarnation took. God, like the king in Kierkegaard's story, has created a situation in which He is unrecognizable, so that human beings will believe in Him through faith alone. Those who were alive in Palestine in the first century A.D. were no better off than we in determining what to believe. The contemporary of Jesus saw only a human being and was aware that God cannot be a human being. At any time, the problem of being a believer is the same. There is *no* evidence. All that one can do is believe by faith alone. The evidence of Scripture is not convincing unless one already believes that the New Testament reveals the life of God. This one can never find out from the Book. If one points out that it is a contradiction in terms for God to have had a history, Kierkegaard answers with Tertullian's assertion 'I believe that which is absurd'. If one points out how implausible and ridiculous it is to believe that Jesus of Nazareth was God, Kierkegaard replies, quoting an earlier German irrationalist, 'Lies, fables and romances must needs be probable, but not the foundation of our faith.'

'**Absurdity.**' This idea of pure belief as the solution to man's problems is developed in Kierkegaard's brilliant portrayal of his hero, the Biblical Abraham, in *Fear and Trembling*. The knight of faith is somebody who believes and acts 'in virtue of the absurd'. The test of faith is whether one's beliefs can be held in the face of overwhelming evidence to the contrary, in the face of complete irrationality. Abraham—in consenting to sacrifice Isaac on God's command and God's promise that if Abraham sacrificed his only child he would then become the Father of the Faithful—was performing an action that was brutal and meaningless according to human standards. Its sole justification was that it was an act of faith.

In view of the irrationalism of the solution Kierkegaard is offering, he saw that it would be a violation of his theory to claim that he could teach the truth. People could only find this in blind faith. For this reason he claimed that his writings represented *indirect discourse*. All that he could do was raise certain questions, pose certain problems, but each person would have to find the solution in his own way. The point, apparently, in the use of various pseudonyms for his works was that each, in his own way, could raise certain questions, suggest certain answers. But the reader, himself, would have to find his own solution. Truth exists solely in the subjective, personal certainty of the believer.

CONTEMPORARY EXISTENTIALISM

Contemporary existentialism represents mainly a broadening and generalizing of Kierkegaard's themes, in so far as it takes up the questions he was concerned with. The answers it offers, however, are rather different. Rather than advocating Kierkegaard's Christianity as the resolution of the human predicament, some contemporary existentialists have grave doubts that there is any God to help us. Having taken seriously Nietzsche's message that God is dead, thinkers like JEAN-PAUL SARTRE have insisted that Kierkegaard's portrayal of man's plight properly describes our situation, but reject the claim that the solution lies solely and completely in the act of belief, in the decision to accept faith.

The Existentialist View. We are 'trapped in existence', living in a completely meaningless world. No principles that we use for ordering or comprehending events have any basis. But we cannot escape having to deal with 'existence', having to make sense out of it. All that we can tell is that this world which we are confronted with is utterly arbitrary. When we realize the unintelligibility of the world, our inability to withdraw from contact with it, and our need for finding some principle of order or intelligibility, we are then ready for the existentialist message. One first has to be overpowered by the 'nausea of existence', has to acknowledge that the pattern of our lives is due to totally arbitrary ways of living and that any others would do as well.

At this point, we are confronted with our **'dreadful freedom'**, **recognizing that we are completely free to choose our world-view, our way of living in the world. However, there is no way in which we can find guides for our choice, no way we can avoid making a choice, and no way of escaping from the consequences of the choices—our basic decisions.**

'Nausea.' Sartre's famous novel, *Nausea*, portrays most forcefully this condition of man's plight. The hero has been moving through life on the basis of an unquestioned acceptance of a certain outlook. But his dissatisfaction with events forces him to ask whether this is the proper outlook. The quest for some justification for his way of life brings about its disintegration into pure nausea, as the arbitrary framework into which he has previously organized his world disappears. All that he is left with is the complete confusion of his inescapable existence, and the realization that it has no meaningful order. When he becomes aware that only by his decision can he find a means of organizing experience and a way of life, he is overwhelmed with the magnitude of the predicament that confronts him. He cannot avoid being a free agent. He cannot act unless he exercises his freedom and chooses some arbitrary outlook in order to make sense out of his world. Possibly most frightening of all, he is permanently burdened with all the consequences of his decision for which he, and he alone, is responsible. Even the saving grace of Kierkegaard's irrationalism is impossible, that there might be a right faith to choose, and once having chosen it, the responsibility for what follows would be God's not man's.

A Humanist Philosophy. The existentialist concern is not so much to understand the philosophical questions that interest the analytic philosophers (although in part this too is involved in their theory), as in answering the question, **How is man to live in this irrational, meaningless world?** Some of the existentialists feel that the answer lies in religious faith, in the manner of Kierkegaard. Others, like Sartre, being atheists, **search for more humanistic beliefs**, ways of dealing with one's experience so as to make life meaningful without appeal to any God. In general, the existentialists regard other philosophers either as wasting their time in defending intellectual systems that are indefensible, or as refusing to face the real problems that confront mankind, and instead occupying themselves with unimportant concerns about language and logic, which cannot supply a solution to man's predicament.

On the other hand, many philosophers regard the existentialists as having abdicated the philosopher's quest, as having turned their backs on a rational examination of man's world. According to some, the existentialists are more poets of a harrowing variety than serious thinkers.

Regardless of who is right, or whether the existentialists are the ones who are fulfilling the philosopher's role, one can appreciate why they have so deeply influenced the contemporary intellectual life of Western Europe, and are gradually making inroads into the philosophical scene in England and America. The catastrophic collapse of Europe, the horrible experience of the Nazi dictatorship and occupation of France, have left people with a sense that their views and values are meaningless. The world in which they, and we, have to live no longer seems susceptible to rational examination. Instead, only arbitrary beliefs seem able to give us a key to how to live in the face of an unintelligible universe.

CONCLUSION

In this section we have attempted briefly to survey some contemporary philosophical trends. These indicate some of the means by which philosophers in our time have conducted the quest for comprehension, for some general statement of the significance of our experience, and for ways of dealing with some basic questions. All of these current views are of great significance for all branches of philosophy, since they concern themselves with the nature of philosophical activity and the kind of question it is appropriate for the philosopher to ask. From our brief discussion of them, the reader will be able to see the kinds of view they lead their exponents to in the spheres of ethics, religion, politics, metaphysics and epistemology. He should now be able, therefore, to round off for himself our earlier discussions of these branches of philosophy by applying some of the techniques of contemporary philosophy to the questions that have concerned philosophers in these fields. He will thus discover for himself what is meant by the 'revolution in philosophy' that many claim has taken place in this century. He will also be starting out on his own philosophical inquiries and the purpose of this book will have been fulfilled.

SUGGESTED FURTHER READING

Blackham, H. J., *Six Existentialist Thinkers*. Routledge & Kegan Paul: London, 1952. (Kierkegaard, Nietzsche, Jaspers, Marcel, Heidegger and Sartre.)

Collins, James, *The Mind of Kierkegaard*. Regnery: Chicago, 1955. (A detailed examination of Kierkegaard's thought.)

Kierkegaard, Sören, *Philosophical Fragments*. Princeton University Press: New Jersey, 1962. (A short, but most important exposition of Kierkegaard's fundamental philosophical argument.)

Murdoch, Iris, *Sartre*. Fontana Books: London, 1967. (A discussion of Sartre's philosophy by a contemporary novelist and philosopher.)

Sartre, Jean-Paul, *Being and Nothingness*. Methuen: London, 1957. (Sartre's major philosophical treatise, presenting the basic theory of the French existentialists.)

Sartre, Jean-Paul, *Existentialism and Humanism*. Methuen: London, 1948. (A popular and elementary presentation, in brief form, of Sartre's point of view.)

Sartre, Jean-Paul, *Nausea*. Penguin Books: London, 1965. (One of the best existentialist novels of the present age.)

Warnock, M., *Ethics since 1900*. Oxford University Press: London, 1966. (Contains a good chapter on Sartre.)

INDEX

INDEX OF PROPER NAMES

301